Knowledge-Based Programming for Music Research

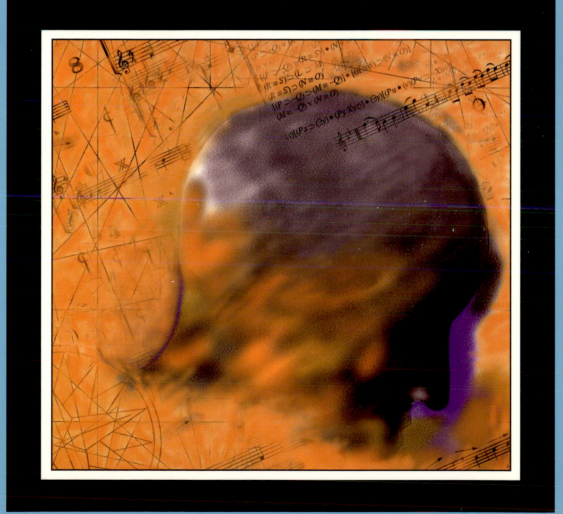

JOHN SCHAFFER AND DERON MCGEE

KNOWLEDGE-BASED PROGRAMMING
FOR MUSIC RESEARCH

THE COMPUTER MUSIC AND DIGITAL AUDIO SERIES
John Strawn, Founding Editor
Christopher Yavelow, Series Editor

DIGITAL AUDIO SIGNAL PROCESSING
Edited by John Strawn

COMPOSERS AND THE COMPUTER
Edited by Curtis Roads

DIGITAL AUDIO ENGINEERING
Edited by John Strawn

COMPUTER APPLICATIONS IN MUSIC: A BIBLIOGRAPHY
Deta S. Davis

THE COMPACT DISC HANDBOOK
Ken C. Pohlmann

COMPUTERS AND MUSICAL STYLE
David Cope

MIDI: A COMPREHENSIVE INTRODUCTION
Joseph Rothstein
William Eldridge, *Volume Editor*

SYNTHESIZER PERFORMANCE AND REAL-TIME TECHNIQUES
Jeff Pressing
Chris Meyer, *Volume Editor*

MUSIC PROCESSING
Edited by Goffredo Haus

COMPUTER APPLICATIONS IN MUSIC:
A BIBLIOGRAPHY, SUPPLEMENT I
Deta S. Davis
Garrett Bowles, Volume Editor

GENERAL MIDI
Stanley Jungleib

EXPERIMENTS IN MUSICAL INTELLIGENCE
David Cope
Text edited by John Strawn
CD-ROM edited by Christopher Yavelow

KNOWLEDGE-BASED PROGRAMMING FOR MUSIC RESEARCH
John Schaffer and Deron McGee
Text edited by John Strawn

■

Volume 13   •   THE COMPUTER MUSIC AND DIGITAL AUDIO SERIES

KNOWLEDGE-BASED PROGRAMMING

FOR MUSIC RESEARCH

John William Schaffer

Deron McGee

A-R Editions, Inc.

Madison, Wisconsin

Library of Congress Cataloging-in-Publication Data

Schaffer, John W.
    Knowledge-based programming for music research / John William
Schaffer, Deron McGee.
            p.   cm. — (The computer music and digital audio series ; v.
13)
    Includes bibliographical references and index.
    ISBN 0-89579-378-4
    1. Music—Data processing.   2. Music—Computer programs.
3. Expert systems (Computer science)   4. Artificial intelligence—Data processing.   I. McGee, Deron.   II. Title.   III. Series.
ML74.S33   1997
781'.0285'63363—dc21   97-25717
                                                            CIP
                                                            MN

A-R Editions, Inc., Madison, Wisconsin 53717–1903
    © 1997 by A-R Editions, Inc.
    All rights reserved.
    Printed in the United States of America.

    10 9 8 7 6 5 4 3 2 1

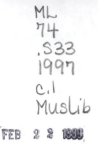

Contents

Preface

Knowledge-based computational models, frequently referred to as *expert systems* or *production systems,* have had a significant impact on the development of computer-aided research tools based on artificial intelligence (AI). Most notably, these advances have taken place in the various hard sciences; however, scholars in the humanities, social sciences, and fine arts are quickly beginning to seek the potential benefits this technology offers. We create knowledge-based systems around the notion that a humanlike response can be drawn from a computer *if* we endow that computer with domain-specific knowledge in the form of factual information and relational rules associating that information *and if* we design it to provide us access to that knowledge through human-emulating evaluation mechanisms. Put another way, a knowledge-based system is a computer program that employs knowledge and inference procedures to aid us in the solution of problems that often require the added expertise of a human authority in the field. The requisite information, together with the inference procedures necessary to perform at such a level, can be thought of as representing one of the better practitioners in the field.

Knowledge-based systems are proving to be worthy successors to the more traditional computer-aided tools used in studies of the past three decades—even though they no longer represent the cutting edge of the AI community's quest to discover the true workings of the human mind. Nonetheless, such models have been criticized for their apparent inability to infer information or draw logical conclusions from a domain of programmed information in which the response is greater than the sum of its parts. It is precisely, however, the inherent ability of knowledge-based systems to encode specific domains of information in their totality and to do so in such a manner as to facilitate flexible, powerful levels of interaction that enable us, as human researchers, to develop extremely powerful analytical tools and simulations capable of interacting with us in flexible "hypothesize-test" cycles. For example, researchers may interact with the computer by having a knowledge-based system test the rationality of complex theorems, interpret the resultant information with the often subjective help of the human researcher, and then, if necessary, manipulate and retest. This process is particularly relevant to our field of music theory because purely human modeling and testing of analytical paradigms suffers from both the refractory nature of many musical compositions and the subjectiveness of human interpretation as well as from the general inability of the analyst to apply these models consistently and objectively across a large amount of musical material. By melding the objective analytical prowess of effectively designed knowledge-based systems with the subjective strengths of the human analyst, we hold the potential to achieve just such a profitable working relation.

Our purpose for this book is to detail those aspects of AI research specifically related to the theory, design, and implementation of knowledge-based systems and to explore in detail the development and implementation of such systems for music research. In particular, we attempt to address four important areas: (1) the basic concepts of knowledge-based programming, including a succinct but sufficient tutorial/overview of Prolog (PROgramming in LOGic), one of the most frequently employed AI computer languages for this type of development; (2) introductory through advanced concepts and strategies necessary for programming such systems; (3) the exploration and development of a universal data representational model for music analysis and inquiry; and (4) several comprehensive examples that detail numerous facets of designing and working with knowledge-based systems. Specifically, we include a model for developing advanced theorem testing and manipulation that is based on the recent work of Eugene Narmour as well as a comprehensive harmonic progression rule structure for use in an intelligent tutoring system.

Music theories can contain both objective and subjective elements. They may define principles or elemental structures—such as pitches, intervals, registral directions, and durations—for which there are objective means of identification and classification. These elemental definitions, however, often combine to generate precepts describing more complex objects, such as harmonies and counterpoints, that are also objective constructs in the sense that they are definitively defined; yet they are somewhat subjective in that the theories they are part of do not always define explicitly how they are to be applied. By using knowledge-based programming techniques, we can encode the rules of a particular theory as a working knowledge base. We can also define logical ways to apply those rules to given musical examples as part of an inference engine and, thus, strive to generate plausible analytical results. Applying the nuances of the inference engine as a strategic control for searching the knowledge base for problem solutions (in this case, a musical analysis) can provide us with an isomorphic model of a specific analytical process. By combining these components (the knowledge base and inference engine) into computer programs, we are able both to create knowledge-based simulations of music theories and to design significantly more powerful tutoring systems.

The process of constructing such programs provides us with a powerful tool for investigating and, subsequently, critiquing our musical discourse. This process includes extracting rules or relations and incorporating them into the knowledge base of a system. The extraction and codification process requires that we engage and scrutinize the underlying theoretical premises to a degree not necessarily required, although preferable, when manually applying those same assumptions. The process also includes our extracting and defining explicitly the manner in which the rules are applied to create an effective model; our computer simulation, therefore, is a model of some real process. In other words, the activities of our programs have the potential to parallel actual human analytical processes, at least the rational ones, to an extent greater than is possible with other forms of models. We can often benefit greatly from these processes because, even in simple, well-specified theories, it is possible to "watch" the analytical process unfold. Therefore, the computer should be able to generate plausible analytical results on the basis of the knowledge base and inference engine designed from the theory. If such analyses are not generated by the program, reasons for this must be explored and corrected, resulting in our modifying the model and, subsequently, the theory.

We aim this book at a number of different groups, all of whom are assumed to have a basic understanding of computers and computer programming. Perhaps the most important group is represented by music scholars and pedagogues desiring to attain a working grasp of knowledge-based systems and how to apply them to their own research; specifically, we aim at those who wish to learn how to program and use knowledge-based systems in their own work yet have neither the additional time nor the resources to pursue these avenues in any formal way. By presenting a text that distills several years of unguided work and effort into six months or so of creative endeavor, we believe that a significant number of programming researchers can use this text to take the next step in the self-development of their computational skills.

An added virtue is that this text can be used successfully as a textbook for graduate-level courses on advanced computer music programming. Although our work is not necessarily intended as an introduction to basic computer music usage, there is no reason it could not also be used quite successfully as a text for adventurous beginners or advanced programmers. Chapters 2, 3, and 5, as well as much of the material that appears throughout this book, have been used quite successfully in the introductory and advanced semesters of a graduate seminar entitled "Computer Programming for Music Research" given at the University of Wisconsin, Madison. In fact, much of this course is designed around the core materials in these chapters.

In addition to an audience of music researchers seeking outside knowledge of AI techniques, we feel that this book can serve the nonprofessional musician as well. Specifically, chapters 5 through 7 are ideally suited to those persons who have computer knowledge and a strong desire to undertake music-related projects but who lack sufficient understanding of many of the problems associated with the design and manipulation of musical data. One of the fundamental principles underlying this book is the presentation and exploration of a powerful and flexible list-based data model for the analytic encoding of musical scores. This book supplies our intended audience with enough relevant information to undertake music-related projects while ameliorating the burdens imposed by a limited understanding of the musical domain. We also believe that this book appeals to the general intellectual community, that is, those readers who simply desire an overview of the marriage between music research and the application of knowledge-based systems—although this is not the book's primary focus.

In closing, we wish to thank all those persons who have helped in the conception, formulation, and completion of this book. In particular, we wish to thank those unnamed graduate students at the University of Wisconsin–Madison who had a subtle yet important role in helping to define the multifaceted nature of this text. Last, but by no means least, we wish to thank our families for their unending support and patience. Without them, we would never have completed this task. It is to our families that we dedicate this book.

John William Schaffer　　　　　　　Deron McGee
University of Wisconsin–Madison　　　*University of Kansas*

ONE

Introduction

Musicians dramatically expanded the application of computer technology for research and instruction with the advent of the first commercially available microcomputers in the late 1970s. Early applications were largely dictated by individuals' access to computer hardware: the capabilities of the machines in terms of processing speed, internal memory, and external storage and the availability of appropriate programming languages. Although this newfound accessibility alleviated many of the problems associated with large mainframe and minicomputer systems, many constraints remained, such as slow processing speeds and memory limitations. For example, only a few general purpose programming languages, such as BASIC and Pascal, were available on early microcomputer platforms, and, because these languages rely primarily on numerical representational schemes, many conceptual abstractions had to be overcome to facilitate meaningful musical applications. Some musical projects were highly amenable to such representation, such as generating analyses using set theoretic operations, whereas others, such as creating analyses using implication-realization models, were not.

Programmers using languages such as BASIC, C, or Pascal frequently rely on the sequentially based "divide and conquer" approach to programming, in which a problem is repeatedly divided into smaller problems until an explicit step-by-step method, or *algorithm*, for attaining a solution is found. Alexander Brinkman (1990) defines algorithm as "a detailed, unambiguous set of instructions for accomplishing a particular task" (p. 917). Algorithms might be defined to count occurrences of surface-level phenomena, such as chords or chord progressions, or to compute statistics on the basis of the results of such analyses. Designing algorithms to account for more intangible aspects of musical styles, such as experience, perception, and higher-level organization, proves considerably more difficult. Fortunately, there are models to assist in dealing with these sorts of problems.

Developments in the field of AI provide such tools, specifically ones designed for investigating how people acquire, store, and employ knowledge. One line of development facilitates the concept of *knowledge-based programming*: creating programs that attempt to apply human knowledge and problem-solving heuristics for dealing with various nonlinear sorts of problems. In such systems, knowledge is usually stored in the form of *rules* and *relationships* used by the computer program to deduce solutions to a problem logically, thereby modeling, or at least mimicking, human reasoning. Knowledge-based programs are not new, but a lack of sophisticated AI programming languages designed to work in microcomputer implementations limited their use in music research until recently.

The programming language Prolog is built around a *declarative* model, as opposed to more traditional *procedural* languages (such as Pascal and BASIC) that require programmers to state explicitly each detail of a program and the specific order in which the instructions are to be executed, thereby forcing the programmer to concentrate on *how* the program solves problems. Prolog programs are primarily concerned with describing and defining relationships between objects. In other words, they are concerned more with *what* is the nature of a particular problem and *what* are the various relationships of the relevant components than with the procedural details of how that output is obtained. Prolog uses the relationships defined by the programmer to search for solutions to questions posed to the system while working out many of the procedural details on its own. In addition, Prolog primarily processes and manipulates *symbols*, a significant step beyond the numerical methods used by most traditional general purpose languages. Symbols may be anything from characters, words, or sentences to representations of graphic images, an asset that enables the programmer to define properties and relationships among various symbols and to construct significant inferences between them. This ability makes Prolog a valuable tool for much AI research, particularly projects involving natural language processing, the development of expert systems, intelligent tutorial systems, intelligent user interfaces, and other types of knowledge-based systems.

■ BACKGROUND

Before we can attempt to learn how to write our own declarative programs or even grasp the nuances of AI languages such as Prolog, we need a clear understanding of the nature of AI research and, more specifically, knowledge-based systems. To attempt a foray into the field without an awareness of its history—both its successes and its failures—would prove no more fruitful than trying to undertake a musical analysis without understanding any music theory—possible, perhaps, at a very rudimentary level but certainly a painful and unproductive way to proceed! The remainder of this chapter, then, is devoted to such an examination. We look briefly at the history of the field, highlighting some of the more significant events, and end by taking a peek at some of the more promising music-related knowledge-based applications.

Artificial Intelligence: Historical Views

Relatively few people are aware of the precise nature and potential use of knowledge-based systems, in part because AI scientists themselves are still attempting to understand and define just what constitutes intelligence. Only when this task is accomplished can we attempt an adequate definition. For the present, perhaps it is best for us to examine several definitions. One of the more interesting viewpoints on AI is presented by John Haugeland (1985):

> Artificial Intelligence [is] the exciting new effort to make computers think. The fundamental goal of this research is not merely to mimic intelligence or produce some fake. Not at all. "AI" wants only the genuine article: machines with minds, in the full and literal sense. This is not science fiction, but real science, based on a theoretical conception as deep as it is daring: namely, we are, at root, computers ourselves. (p. 2)

Although Haugeland's concept is certainly colorful, it represents only one aspect of the more multifaceted views taken by most scientists regarding the actual role of AI research. Yoshiaki Shirai and Junichi Tsujii (1984) present us with a more traditional perspective:

> Broadly considered, artificial intelligence can be viewed from two standpoints. The first is the scientific standpoint aiming at understanding the mechanisms of human intelligence, the computer being used to provide simulation to verify theories about intelligence. The second standpoint is the engineering one, whose object is to endow a computer with the intellectual capabilities of people. Most researchers adapt the second standpoint, aim-

ing to make the capabilities of computers approach those of human intelligence without trying to imitate exactly the information processing steps of human beings. (p. 1)

Although Shirai and Tsujii do not actually define AI, they do have something interesting to say, particularly in regard to the frequent lack of defined sequential solutions for solving many real-world problems. In their brief but laudatory discussion of the computer's ability to manipulate large quantities of data with relative ease, they temper their enthusiasm by stating that

the ability of computers to see an object and recognize it, or to hear, for example, the Japanese language and understand it, does not yet approach that of a human infant. The object of research into artificial intelligence is to elucidate how such mental work which does not have a determined solution sequence can be performed. (1984, p. 1)

Although considerable progress has been made as a result of AI research in the past decade, we hasten to add that this statement is still valid and accurate today.

One of the simplest yet most telling definitions of AI is given by Elaine Rich and Kevin Knight (1991): "*Artificial Intelligence* . . . is the study of how to make computers do things which, at the moment, people do better" (p. 3). The implication of this statement is significant, namely, that AI tends to deal with that realm of problem solving directly related to human thought processes—something that can often be vague, ambiguous, inefficient, and, most important, occasionally incorrect. (Attempting to program human thought processes brings with it the risk of programming human failings—a normal and, unfortunately, integral part of the process.) Computers are unintelligent devices that require very specific, absolute, and totally comprehensive sequences of rules and directions to accomplish specified tasks. As humans, on the other hand, we tend to rely on less quantifiable methods, such as intuition based on previously similar yet different circumstances or partial recognitions that can trigger more complete and knowledgeable responses.

On a more abstract level, AI is often described as a system of symbol manipulations, or in other words, a way in which we deal with the relationships of symbolic representations (e.g. names and labels), as opposed to the manipulation of actual finite representations (e.g. mathematics and algorithms). Newell and Simon (1976) get to the core of defining what AI research represents through their "physical symbol system hypothesis," which they describe as follows:

A physical symbol system consists of a set of entities, called symbols, which are physical patterns that can occur as components of another type of entity called an expression (or symbol structure). Thus a symbolic structure is composed of a number of instances (or tokens) of symbols related in some physical way (such as one token being next to another). At any instant of time the system will contain a collection of these symbol structures. Besides these structures, the system also contains a collection of processes that operate on expressions to produce other expressions: processes of creation, modification, reproduction and destruction. A physical symbol system is a machine that produces through time an evolving collection of symbol structures. Such a system exists in a world of objects wider than just these symbolic expressions themselves. . . . A physical symbol system has the necessary and sufficient means for general intelligent action. (p. 116)

Randall Davis and Douglas Lenat (1982) say basically the same thing but in a manner slightly more accessible:

Artificial intelligence research is that part of computer science that investigates symbolic, non-algorithmic reasoning processes, and the representation of symbolic knowledge for use in machine inference. Its most fundamental views are as follows: that intelligence can be explained as symbol-manipulating activity; that as Newell and Simon pointed out in their famous ACM Turing Award lecture (1976), such activity is realizable in a physical symbol system (in particular, by digital computers as universal symbol-manipulating devices); that the various aspects of human intelligence can be modeled by such physical symbol systems; and, as a working hypothesis, as a long-range goal, that there can be discovered a theory of intelligence general and powerful enough to encompass the phenomena of both human and machine intelligence. (p. xv)

Although the definitions of AI we have presented thus far can be applied to all symbolic reasoning, the specific methods required for implementing intelligent applications have limited current AI research to a somewhat modest subclass of specific domains. Rich and Knight (1991, pp. 3–6) include the following list of AI problems in their discussion: (1) game playing; (2) theorem proving; (3) general problem solving; (4) perception, including vision and speech; (5) natural language understanding; and (6) "expert" problem solving (i.e., expert systems), including medical diagnosis, chemical analysis, and engineering design.

Artificial Intelligence: A Brief History

The term artificial intelligence has seen widespread use since 1961—when Marvin Minsky published his famous paper "Steps Towards Artificial Intelligence"—although we can more accurately say that the origins of our current understanding of the field began in 1956. This was the year that a group of ten computer scientists, meeting at Dartmouth College, held the first conference on AI. At this meeting, predictions were advanced that within twenty-five years computers would be doing all the work for us while we relegated our energies to thought and relaxation (Gevarter 1984, p. 8). Unfortunately, these predictions proved to be miserably inaccurate.

The first major achievement in the fledgling field did not really come until 1957 with the development by Newell, Shaw, and Simon of a program called the General Problem Solver (GPS) (Sell 1985, p. 2). Although GPS represented an important contribution, it was unable to solve certain problems, simply because it was based on two mistaken assumptions. First, because the program was designed around general problem-solving algorithms, its authors assumed that they could readily expand it to deduce the appropriate solution algorithm for any given problem and therefore make the program universally "smart," an aspect of human intelligence that still eludes us today. Second, the authors also assumed that *general* problem-solving methods could be made powerful enough to handle a diverse range of problems.

We now consider it a mistaken assumption that intelligence is based primarily on smart deductive reasoning techniques, which in turn implies that any person with enough logic prowess could readily devise a computer algorithm able to duplicate even the best human intelligence. As an added drawback, the computing time required to solve problems utilizing smart algorithms tends to grow exponentially with the increased complexity of the problems. By the early 1960s, scientists were beginning to believe that even rudimentary human intelligence problems required so much computing time and power that research almost came to a complete halt. In fact, one very well known program called ELIZA (written by Weizenbaum at MIT in 1966), which has captivated many people with its apparent ability to psychoanalyze, was really designed as an effort to show how ridiculous it was to actually expect a computer to have "true natural language understanding in a machine" (Gevarter 1984, p. 8). By the mid-1980s, it had become one the more popular AI programs among novices.

The year 1964 signaled the beginning of a new understanding. Joshua Lederberg, a professor of genetics at Stanford University, began work on a program designed to aid in the enumeration of all possible atomic structures. He called his program DENDRAL (DENDRitic ALgorithm). In the process of developing the necessary algorithms, he slowly began to realize that one of the solutions to earlier failures (e.g. the General Problem Solver) was to base his program on domain-dependent methods (utilizing knowledge in one area), rather than domain-independent methods (processes generic to all areas) previously employed. This shift of emphasis from power-based to knowledge-based methods was to serve as the foundation for most future AI research and, more specifically, knowledge-based systems.

The rude awakening brought on many computer scientists by this shift of emphasis, as well as through programs such as DENDRAL, offers us several important lessons. First, the trial-and-error algorithms used for solving early problems were generally very prone to combinatorial explosion. This mathematical concept is frequently used in AI literature to refer to the exponential increase in search time required to solve a problem as the level of required search depth increases. For example, if a chess program has 50 potential moves to investigate and is programmed to look ahead only 2 more moves in advance, then the total number of moves the program has to test is 125,000 moves ($50 \times 50 \times 50$). (An increase of only one more level would bring that number to 6,250,000!) Because such purely empirical data-driven methods were often subject to unsystematic wandering, it was quickly realized that some sort of *heuristic* search method that combined the best of these two strategies (in other words, intensive level searches based on a thoroughly substantive domain-specific knowledge base) would be required to solve more complex AI problems within an acceptable time frame. The term heuristic, often defined as the process of learning through self-discovery, implies both intelligence and learning. In general, a heuristic search is one that uses informed deductions to control and confine a problem-solving algorithm. A heuristic search process may also use self-learning to help deduce a solution, just as a detective might use given clues and intelligent reasoning to solve a case. In other words, "Knowledge without search has limited utility as has search without knowledge" (Berliner 1984, p. 116).

Second, because little contextual knowledge was utilized in most problem-solving algorithms, heuristically controlled searches were very difficult. Again, domain-specific strategies helped to solve this problem by limiting the frame of expertise to a confined domain, thus enabling the execution of better control decisions based on a complete body of knowledge. Additionally, because logic-based (as opposed to knowledge-based) search algorithms are very poor at handling broader intelligence concepts, such as intuition or "best guesses," the development of methods for representing domain-specific knowledge relationships were developed to help fill that gap.

The 1970s saw a refreshing revival of AI research as well as the development of the basic tools necessary for successful AI applications. The primary impetus for all this was the realization among most AI scientists that the key to successful problem solving lay in the utilization of domain-specific knowledge applied with a heuristically driven control mechanism as opposed to a purely deductive analytic search algorithm or purely empirical data-driven search (Mitchell 1984, p. 81). During this period, new techniques and languages for building AI programs were developed. Programs utilizing these new techniques began to proliferate and prove themselves capable of achieving their stated goals. One measure of success came from the willingness of computer scientists to branch out experimentally into other fields of research where their methods could be applied with the help of noncomputer specialists. Some of the various developments of the 1970s include programs such as SHRDLU (Massachusetts Institute of Technology), HEARSAY II (Carnegie Mellon), and HARPY—all capable of understanding natural language with at least a 90% accuracy level. The SR1 Vision Model served as the basis for many of today's most sophisticated vision-oriented control systems, and MYCIN was a highly successful medical diagnostic tool (Gevarter 1984, pp. 11–12).

It would be incorrect for us to imply that all AI research uses only domain-specific knowledge-based methods. Research now shows that humans tend to think in various combinations of three different methods (Sell 1985, pp. 4–5). First, many mundane and rudimentary tasks are handled through algorithmic methods—in other words, doing things that require finite series of discrete steps, such as simple arithmetic. The second method, *generate-and-test*, relies primarily on trial-and-error strategies. Just as with computers, however, human logic processing is subject to the same problem of combinatorial explosion. Finally, we frequently tend to greatly simplify the generate-and-test approach (thus avoiding combinatorial explosion) by relying on expert knowledge to limit and control the bounds of our problems. The application of this last model has, by and large, proved to be the most successful in the development of knowledge-based systems.

Knowledge-Based Systems and Expert Systems

Expert system technology represents one of the more useful and practical developments in the field of AI today. Although clear and succinct definitions are few and hard to come by, we find that several credible attempts have been made. A very simple yet insightful viewpoint is given by Igor Aleksander (1984), who proposes that

the focal point of artificial intelligence has been the realization that an intelligent response by human standards implies the storage in computers of human knowledge. . . . If the knowledge of an expert can be encapsulated in a program, and the program stored [in a computer], then this knowledge can be made available to non-experts. (p. 117)

The educational implications of this description clearly point to the notion that expert systems ought to be used for the purpose of disseminating the knowledge of experts (teachers) to those without such knowledge or expertise (students). In other words, knowledge-based systems can offer students more access to expertise than could ever be practical in today's more traditional educational environment.

A much more detailed yet equally comprehensible definition is given by E. A. Feigenbaum (Gevarter 1984):

> An "expert system" is an intelligent computer program that uses knowledge and inference procedures to solve problems that are difficult enough to require significant human expertise for their solution. The knowledge necessary to perform at such a level, plus the inference procedures used, can be thought of as a model of the best practitioners of the field.
>
> The knowledge of an expert system consists of facts and heuristics. The "facts" constitute a body of information that is widely shared, publicly available, and generally agreed upon by experts in a field. The "heuristics" are mostly private, little-discussed rules of good judgment (rules of plausible reasoning, rules of good guessing) that characterize expert-level decision making in the field. The performance level of an expert system is primarily a function of the size and quality of the knowledge base that it possesses. (p. 71)

What is not stated by Feigenbaum is that one goal of expert system research is to discover and codify these supposedly private heuristics associated with expert reasoning, thus freeing them from their secretive environment and, it is hoped, making them accessible to other people.

Another characteristic implied by Feigenbaum's definition is that expert systems should have the ability to generate solutions to problems by progressing through a sequence of specific steps, even though those steps are not necessarily described explicitly in the program. An AI program typically specifies a series of facts and relationships among facts (rules) concerning a subject or topic. The program is queried about a subject and searches through the defined relationships looking for an acceptable solution to the problem. The program does not need to describe the specific steps required to find a solution. Rather, it contains strategies, or heuristics, that suggest how the program might find a sequence of steps to generate a solution. The actual sequence of steps taken by the program is frequently based on the particular question(s) we ask of the system, the relationships defined in the program, and the heuristics employed. Artificial intelligence programs may arrive at a solution through a variety of processes or sequences of steps in a manner resembling our own thinking processes. These programs can also trace the steps employed to arrive at a specific answer, thereby revealing which facts and rules were used, the respective order in which they were examined, and, in a sense, the "logic" used to reach the solution.

Another implication of this definition developed by Widman, Loparo, and Nielson (1989) is the ability of AI programs to negotiate "ill-structured" problems. A problem is considered ill-structured if an algorithm cannot be created to describe it *or* if the data required to find a solution to a problem are incomplete. Because AI programs use encoded knowledge (facts and rules) to solve problems, they can often infer solutions or arrive at partial solutions on the basis of the knowledge available, that is, without a complete representation of the knowledge domain. In contrast, procedural programs have difficulties with ill-structured problems because of their algorithmic foundation. If an algorithm can be designed to solve a problem, all the data required by that algorithm must also be available. If the data are not complete in a procedural program, the computer cannot reach a solution (even a partial one) because the computations cannot be executed without all the relevant data.

Sell (1985) tries to define expert systems not so much by what they do or by how they do what they do as by *why* they are built to do what they do. He begins by stating that

> Artificial Intelligence has two different products: models of human cognition and intelligent artefacts [sic]. Expert systems belong to the latter. They were created not so much to model how experts set about solving problems and, hence, to understand better the workings of an expert's mind, but for the practical purpose of reaping the benefits from the expert thought embedded in a computer system. Of course, the two areas interact with beneficial side-effects. Building expert systems is in a sense creating a model of expert thought, and this allows us to cast better models of cognition. And better models of cognition, obtained perhaps from a different field, allow us to build better expert systems. (p. 14)

After pointing out that, indeed, it is human knowledge and not cognitive processes that constitute the primary basis for expert systems, he expands his definition by detailing the typical knowledge realm of such entities:

> Of the two main methods of problem solving used by intelligent artefacts, namely general or domain-independent and special or domain-

specific, expert systems come into the second, domain-specific category. A large class of these domain-specific methods relies on knowledge culled from human experts; they are known as knowledge-based systems or even intelligent knowledge-based systems (abbreviated KBS or IKBS). Expert systems form a subclass of knowledge based systems, a subclass that focuses on a single area, which restricts itself to a single domain of expertise. (p. 14)

Sell alludes to the fact that knowledge is so essential to an expert system that if a system is not knowledge based it cannot be an expert system. Unfortunately, encoding human knowledge into a computer-usable format is often very difficult and problematic. First, the volume of knowledge required for what might initially appear to be a simple task is usually extraordinary large and complex. Second, the often subjective and incomplete nature of so much of our knowledge can make it difficult for us to capture it in a computer program, and, because our conceptualizations of that knowledge are continually changing, the way we represent it in our programs must allow for easy modification. Third, knowledge is not always amenable to reduction into simple numeric relations or algorithms, which makes programming knowledge-based applications especially problematic. Yet, Sell's definition is essential, for without working models, as well as methods for manipulating them, expert systems cannot be successfully developed. Regarding these ideas, he states that

> in order to avoid philosophical difficulties about just what is knowledge, practitioners treat as knowledge any rules, facts, truths, reasons, and heuristics gleaned from experts that have been found useful in the domain of solving problems. . . . Furthermore, expert system [knowledge] domains are areas of expertise, in contrast to common sense; expert systems typically possess very little common sense . . . the power of an expert system lies precisely in these [knowledge representation] rules. In order to do its job, an expert system needs to perform relatively few numerical calculations but a lot of symbolic processing. Symbolic processing implies that facts, observations, and hypotheses are represented by symbols and are manipulated as symbols. In other words, the expert system does not know in any sense what these symbols mean or stand for. Nevertheless, by these rules of transformation it is able to convert its input to some conclusion. (1985, pp. 14–15)

What Sell is referring to is the *process of transformation*, in other words, the ability of humans to describe real-life objects and concepts with symbols. These symbols, in and of themselves, are meaningless, but it is our human intelligence that enables us to transform our knowledge into a representational world described by symbols and symbolic relationships. An expert system can manipulate these symbols according to the rules that we have defined for them without requiring an understanding of their meaning. If our human logic is accurate (and properly defined), the end result of the computer's symbolic manipulations should leave the symbol world in a state that allows for humans to transform them back into meaningful real-world understandings. For example, we can say that if John (B) is a blood descendant of William (A), and Allison (C) is a blood descendant of John (B), then Allison (C) is also a blood descendant of William (A). Once we associate the given letter symbols (A–C) with each of these persons, symbolic relationships that are purely abstract yet logical can just as readily be employed to represent the same relationship. In other words, the relationship "if A implies B, and B implies C, then A implies C" is really no different than the real-life description given above.

Computer-based symbols typically take the form of strings of characters and often spell meaningful words. These words become *tokens* for the real-world objects they represent. Programming languages such as Lisp and Prolog emerged specifically to facilitate such symbolic programming. By contrast, traditional computer programming languages such as Pascal, C, and FORTRAN use numbers for their basic computational unit. These languages are known for their numeric processing capabilities and their algorithmic structure, which require programmers to define explicitly every aspect of their programs. Traditional programming languages also require the reduction of real-world knowledge to numeric representations that are often less intuitive than symbolic representations. (Although numbers can take on symbolic meaning as well, the computer treats them simply as values, thus negating much of the elegance and flexibility of our nonnumeric symbolic representations.)

Figure 1.1 shows two different computer representations of the pitch E-flat, octave 4. The encryption on the left is a binomial representation (4032) developed by Alexander Brinkman (1986b) for a generalized musical data structure in Pascal. The right-most digit of the binomial representation (2) represents the letter class of the pitch, where 0 = C, 1 = D, . . . 6 = B. The tens and hundreds digits combine (03) to represent the specific pitch class, where 0 = C, 1 = C-sharp or D-flat, 2 = D . . . 11 = B. The thousands digit (4) represents the octave, where 0 = C0 – B0, 1 = C1 – B1 . . . 9 = C9 – B9. The representation on the right is a Prolog symbol identifying the same pitch. The symbolic (Prolog) representation and the numeric (Pascal) representation are equally accurate in terms of representing the pitch. The symbolic representation, however, more closely conforms with

Figure 1.1   Simple data representations.

Pascal	Prolog
4032	e-flat 4

our conceptualization of the pitch because we are trained from an early stage to identify pitches with letter names. Because so much of our knowledge is acquired through and represented with natural languages—such as English, French, or German—and the written aspect of languages consists of symbols, it follows that symbols (in a computer programming context) frequently represent knowledge in a manner more consistent with our individual conceptualizations. Symbols help eliminate the additional level of abstraction required by numeric representations when compared with natural-language representations of the same information.

Donald A. Waterman (1986) offers us a definition that is geared more to the layperson's point of view. At the same time, he conveys succinctly several important concepts:

> Expert systems are sophisticated computer programs that manipulate knowledge to solve problems efficiently and effectively in a narrow problem area. Like real human experts, these systems use symbolic logic and heuristics—rules of thumb—to find solutions. And like real experts, they make mistakes but have the capacity to learn from their errors. However, this artificial expertise has some advantages over human expertise: It is permanent, consistent, easy to transfer and document, and cheaper. In sum, by linking the power of computers to the richness of human experience, expert systems enhance the value of expert knowledge by making it readily and widely accessible. (p. xvii)

Specifically, Waterman touches on four important qualities that help make knowledge-based systems a desirable goal. First, a good system can help preserve, or make permanent, expertise. Because of the mortality of human experts and thus the volatility of their skills and knowledge, this ability can prove to be highly desirable not only for the purpose of perpetuation but also for the ability to submit the knowledge to careful study and scrutiny over a long period of time. This first trait leads naturally to Waterman's second point, namely, that an expert system can allow for easy documentation and transportation of expert knowledge. In other words, once the expert knowledge is codified, it becomes a simple process to enable its use in numerous different guises. Waterman's third point is that, because of the absolute nature of a codified knowledge base, we can expect consistent results and therefore can readily make provisions for finding concrete methods by which to amend, expand, or test the database. Consistency is important because human interpretation of our knowledge can often be quite fickle. For example, a person's perception of different events may vary greatly depending on the amount of sleep the observer had the night before. In other words, how they interpret their *human* knowledge base and expertise may not always be consistent and reliable! A computer-based expert system, on the other hand, suffers no such inconsistencies. Waterman's fourth consideration (mundane yet very important) is cost. Although the initial outlay for a properly designed expert system may be high, it can often work without a vacation and has the potential to embody the knowledge and expertise of many human experts.

The issue of inconsistent and erroneous knowledge is very important. It has been stated that, just as humans have the potential to make mistakes because of imperfect knowledge representation, so do expert systems on the basis of human knowledge. John McDermitt (1981), a computer scientist working with the Digital Equipment Corporation on a program designed to reconfigure a computer's architecture intelligently, sounds the warning as well as anyone:

> I have hammered on the theme that a knowledge-based program must pass through a relatively lengthy apprenticeship stage and that even after it has become an expert, it will, like all experts, occasionally make mistakes. The first part of this message got through, but I suspect that the second has not. My concern, then, is whether, as this characteristic of expert systems is recognized, Digital (or any large corporation) will be emotionally prepared to give a significant amount of responsibility to programs that are known to be fallible. (pp. 29–30)

Obviously, this statement has strong ramifications and should not be overlooked. Because expert systems can only be as perfect as the knowledge they represent, imperfect expert systems represent a fact that can be changed only when we can learn to develop a perfect understanding of human knowledge. Perhaps, as both Sell and Patrick Winston alluded to previously, the continued development of expert systems can help us attain this goal.

■ Knowledge Representation Methods

Through the use of symbols, AI programs incorporate specific knowledge (facts and rules) about part of the real-world domain in which they operate. The results of the past thirty years of research into AI have given us several ways to handle the challenges of incorporating our knowledge into computer programs. These models include a number of knowledge representation techniques that enable pro-

Figure 1.2   A property list representation.

Root-position dominant-seventh chord:

Four different pitches

One pitch is the *root*
One pitch is the *third*
One pitch is the *fifth*
One pitch is the *seventh*

The *third* is a major third above the *root*

The *fifth* is a perfect fifth above the *root*

The *seventh* is a minor seventh above the *root*

grammers to reflect more accurately the knowledge communicated to them by "experts." We spend the remainder of this section discussing briefly some of the more prevalent schemes, specifically, property lists, production rules, frames, and semantic networks.

Property Lists

A property list is a structure that identifies the characteristics of a specified object. The items in the list belong specifically to the individual object and are not shared or inherited by other objects in the system. Figure 1.2 presents a property list describing one instance of a root-position dominant (major-minor) seventh chord. Actually, several different property lists may be necessary to account for multiple contexts and definitions of a chord, such as a dominant-seventh chord with a doubled root and omitted fifth. The knowledge represented in a property list can be quickly modified, and changes in the definition of an individual object do not affect other discrete objects in the knowledge base. These characteristics facilitate updating the knowledge base in light of the dynamic nature of knowledge. Property lists provide a good method for representing *syntactic* (factual) information but are not effective for describing relationships among such facts.

Production Rules

Production rules are collections of symbols that represent knowledge using logical associations—specifically *predicate logic*. Production

Figure 1.3   A production-rule representation.

a. is_a_dominant_in(g_major, c_major)

b. IF Chord #1 is a dominant
   AND Chord #2 is a tonic
   AND both chords are in root position
   AND Chord #1 contains the tonic pitch in the soprano
   THEN we have a perfect authentic cadence

rules are employed extensively in knowledge-based systems since they are easy to encode, are quickly modified, and remain independent from one another, thus allowing changes in one rule without affecting other discrete structures. Figure 1.3a uses a production rule to define that a G-major triad is the dominant chord in the key of C major. A production rule in which a specific action or known entity occurs, given a specified set of criteria, takes the form of an "IF-THEN" statement: IF the criteria are satisfied, THEN a specific condition exists. Figure 1.3b expresses a perfect authentic cadence in the form of a production rule. Production rules furnish a means for efficiently modifying the knowledge represented in an AI program and provide a format for expressing relationships among "factual" components of that knowledge.

Frames

A frame is a data structure that consists of the name of an object, a list of categories (or slots) that describe that object, and a range of descriptions that may be inserted in each slot. Figure 1.4 presents a frame describing a trio sonata. Slots in this representation are present for the composer, a keyboard, the solo instrument, and the number of movements. The selection of parameters is arbitrary; that is, frames can have as many slots as necessary to describe the object adequately for the purposes of the program. This trio sonata frame could also include slots for the title or the date the composition was written, but essentially the frame should contain whatever level of detail we require. At any given time, some of the slots may be filled while others may remain empty, waiting to be filled by information on the basis of preexisting boundaries represented by the values in parentheses in figure 1.4. The information in a frame can be easily modified, making it an appropriate structure for handling the dynamic nature of knowledge. Frames are well suited for representing syntactic information and provide an acceptable means for

Figure 1.4   A frame-based representation.

FRAME: Trio Sonata

    composer: (Corelli, Scarlatti, Bach, Mozart, Beethoven, etc.)

    instrument 1: (keyboard)

    instrument 2: (violin, cello, flute, oboe, trumpet, etc.)

    movements (1, 2, 3, 4, 5, etc.)

    etc.

representing incomplete information. However, they are not designed to define relationships among the syntactic components they represent, thereby limiting their value in constructing knowledge-based systems.

Semantic Networks

A semantic network is a collection of expressions that can be represented in a graph structure where facts are shown symbolically and relationships between the facts expressed as lines (Nilsson 1980, p. 370). Figure 1.5 shows a semantic network relating specific information about Beethoven and some of his works.

The two relations designated in this network are `is_a` and `wrote`. The relation `wrote` is applied to specific pieces of music that Beethoven composed, and `is_a` represents a relation of type. For example, Beethoven `is_a` composer and Op. 125 `is_a` symphony. The properties of a semantic network allow items connected in that network to inherit or infer those properties throughout the network. For example, there is not a direct connection indicating that Beethoven composed or wrote songs, however, because the network shows that Beethoven wrote Op. 48, which `is_a` song. Therefore, we can infer that Beethoven `wrote` songs. The inheritance properties of semantic networks can be very powerful because they allow the programmer to make certain specific connections and rely on the structure to propagate that information throughout the system. Unfortunately, when we modify the knowledge in this type of representation, a minor change in one part of the network affects everything connected to it as well, a characteristic that may be beneficial but is often a nuisance when "debugging" and modifying programs. Semantic networks do provide an expedient and efficient means for changing the knowledge base in light of new knowledge, and they have

Figure 1.5   A semantic network representation.

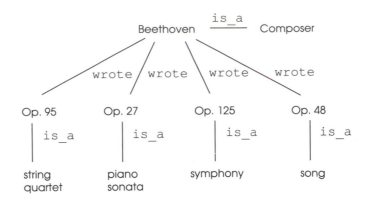

the inherent ability to express relationships among the factual components of the system. These properties make semantic networks a powerful knowledge representation method and one that has won favor in knowledge-based programming.

■ **Symbolic**
Representations
Only two of the rather large number of methods (from which these four examples are drawn) have proven significant in expert system design: semantic networks and production rules. Within each of these knowledge representation schemes are several different methods for computing logic. *Propositional logic* is based on simple true-or-false statements using standard logic operators such as AND, OR, NOT, IMPLICATION, and EQUIVALENCE. Propositional logic is somewhat limited in that it can only deduce true or false answers. The second scheme, based on *predicate logic*, overcomes this limitation by allowing the logician to make assertions about objects within a statement and allows for the use of variable substitutions within clauses. For example, with the statement FATHER(BILL , SUSAN), propositional logic can give us only a true or false answer depending on whether Bill was or was not the father of Susan. On the other hand, predicate logic allows for the substitution of names with variables. The same clause written in predicate logic as FATHER(X , SUSAN) no longer requires a true or false answer. Instead, the clause is satisfied by finding the correct substitute value for the variable X. Thus, the solution to the clause is not true or false but BILL. Because most expert systems and intelligent tutoring systems use symbolic knowledge representations, predicate logic, with its

inherent ability to manipulate symbols, is frequently considered the representation of choice.

■ **Knowledge-Based Systems and Music**

Until recently, few musicians have had the necessary hardware and software conveniently available to pursue knowledge-based projects, nor had they the requisite computer programming experience necessary to pursue these types of projects. Both of these limitations are no longer significant because many musicians today have basic computer skills and access to the sophisticated hardware and programming. The relatively modest number of knowledge-based systems developed for musical uses reflects a variety of applications including compositional, performance, pedagogical, and theoretical projects. There have been a few *intelligent tutoring systems* devised that coach students through such diverse tasks as writing "correct" sixteenth-century counterpoint (Newcomb 1985), generating tonal harmonic progressions (Schaffer 1991), and assisting in the acquisition of keyboard skills (Dannenberg et al. 1990). Other programs have been designed to assist composers in generating musical materials or otherwise assist compositional processes (Camurri 1990; Cope 1991). Still other programs have employed knowledge bases to assist in the coordination of electronic instruments during "real-time" performance situations (Baird 1990; De Poli, Irone, and Vidolin 1990). Most of the knowledge-based systems developed in music were developed within the realm of music theory and were designed to investigate theoretical positions or claims, assist in the formation of theoretical hypotheses, provide analytical tools, generate analyses, and generate musical harmonizations. The remainder of this chapter is devoted to presenting a brief overview of several significant theoretical projects developed with the aid of knowledge-based techniques.

Winograd

Some time ago, Terry Winograd (1968) presented us with one of the earliest knowledge-based systems for musical analysis. After developing a systemic grammar for tonal harmonies, he implemented his grammar in the form of a computer program using the symbolic language Lisp. The goal of the program was to generate plausible harmonic analyses of the music submitted to the system. The program took as input the notes representing the harmonies for each beat, which required some pre-analysis by the programmer. This approach to encoding the music lacked generality but avoided many of the problems associated with segmentation and, most important, focused the program on examining the effectiveness of the grammar. Winograd's program searched through the encoded music twice. During the first pass, the program determined the syntactic components of the music—in other words, labeled the harmonies—then searched through the music a second time to determine the function of the chords.

Winold/Bein/Maxwell

Winograd's program was limited in scope, as it dealt primarily with harmonies and relatively simple textures. However, it did appear capable of some rather sophisticated analyses within this context. The system, although never fully developed, had a significant impact on the program BANALYZE, developed by Allen Winold and Jonathan Bein at Indiana University (see Winold and Bein 1983). BANALYZE employs a rule base to create harmonic analyses of Bach chorales. The goal of the project was to gain insight into Bach's harmonic language by subjecting the analytical results to statistical analysis (Schaffer 1988, p. 22). H. John Maxwell (1984) also employed a rule-based program that expanded on the work of Winold and Bein. His program analyzed the harmonic structure of Bach but expanded the stylistic boundaries of the program in an effort to analyze Bach suites. Maxwell also made an effort to design the rule base explicitly to make the program more adaptable to further development.

Ebcioglu

CHORALE is a rule-based expert system that was designed during the mid-1980s by Kemal Ebcioglu (1988) at IBM research laboratories. The goal of the project was to create a system able to take melodies from Bach chorales and generate not only acceptable harmonizations but musically pleasing results in the style of Bach. The program takes a chorale melody as input, then begins a series of "generate-and-test" steps based on the rules in the knowledge base and inference engine. The knowledge base of CHORALE encodes three types of information. First, it contains production rules for generating possible solutions. Second, the knowledge base includes constraints for rejecting possible solutions (generated by the production rules) that are certain to fail. Finally, there are heuristics (domain-specific strategies) for guiding the search toward a desirable solution the first time. The system is very large and complex, running on an IBM 3081-3090 computer, and typically takes three to thirty minutes to generate an acceptable harmonization, but some examples have taken several hours. Due to the size of the program, it does not appear to be applicable to microcomputer installations, so its portability is reduced. The system does provide musical harmonizations but by no means is it a replacement for Bach. Ebcioglu (1988) states that "its competence approaches that of a talented student of music who has studied the Bach chorales" (p. 49). His system does not claim to model the human cognitive process accurately, but it does attempt to parallel the process to such an extent that musical results are generated by simulating the compositional process within a limited context. Despite its limitations, CHORALE represent an important application of AI technology to music theory and composition.

Smoliar

Stephen Smoliar (1980) created a Lisp-based program that aids analysts in generating Schenkerian analytical sketches. (For those readers unfamiliar with Schenker's work, we refer you to Schenker 1979, Forte & Gilbert 1982, and Neumeyer & Tepping 1992.) Smoliar begins by manually creating a series of symbol lists representing all the structural levels of a composition from the background through to the foreground. He then creates a database of transformations (derived from Schenker) that function to transform each structural level into the next higher level. The program performs such transformations as octave transpositions, in which it inserts passing tones and auxiliary (neighbor) notes. The program does not automatically create an analysis, rather it is a tool for analysts to use when creating Schenkerian sketches. The analyst can observe the results of the transformations and learn about the interactions of such operations because the computer displays the structure that results from each series of transformations. In addition to its primary role as an analytical tool, Smoliar's system also has pedagogical implications. Students can learn about the various transformations employed in Schenkerian analysis by actually manipulating the musical levels and creating new structures through various experimental operations. Unfortunately, the system suffers from an unfriendly user interface, and the output is difficult to understand for those unfamiliar with the conventions of Lisp. Access to the system is also restricted because it is implemented on a large time-share computer system. Its availability and use could be significantly increased if the program were implemented on one of the microcomputer platforms currently available. The significant advances in the size, speed, and storage capacity of microcomputers (as well as the availability of sophisticated symbolic languages like Lisp and Prolog) would certainly facilitate implementing such a translation.

Roeder

John Roeder (1988) presents a computer program that automatically segments nontonal compositions according to Forte's (1973) primary segmentation rules. He presents this as a declarative analytical system and describes the operations in terms of first-order predicate logic. Throughout the article, he presents logical arguments using a syntax appropriate for the Prolog programming language. Roeder's system requires knowledge of four properties for each event: "its pitch, the instrument that plays it, its attack time, and its duration" (p. 25). Once a piece has been encoded, a series of rules segment it according to events occurring in the same instrument, temporally adjacent pitches, and events with the same duration. Once the piece has been segmented, the resulting segments can be analyzed by submitting them to typical set theory manipulations. Roeder's purpose in writing this program is to create a system that "models the structure of analytical understanding better than do existing procedural programs" (p. 21). The relationships also pose an interesting way to "view" the segmentation process as defined because the user can observe how the system applies the rules in the knowledge base and, in a sense, watch the analytical process in time. Further, Roeder's knowledge base can be easily modified and extended to introduce alternative segmentation criteria. This work, although operating within a quite limited context, represents an excellent model for further research using knowledge-based systems.

Camilleri/Carreras/Duranti

Camilleri, Carreras, and Duranti (1990) also describe a knowledge-based system that was designed primarily for modeling current theories concerning rhythmic and metric segmentation. They are also concerned with the ability to encode alternative analytical assertions in an effort to refine, modify, and extend current theories while examining the synthesis of multiple analytical approaches. They began with the rule structures of Lerdahl and Jackendoff (1983) (rhythm and meter) as well as those of Cooper and Meyer (1960) while integrating ideas from other fields such as semiotics and music perception. The primary goal of the project was twofold: to create a flexible analytical environment and to create a vehicle for testing the content of the theories involved. In operation, the text of a composition is submitted to their production rules for analysis on the first level. Once this level has been completed, the results are recursively subjected to the rules (up to a maximum of six levels).

The output is useful not only for observing and understanding the music under consideration but also for how it shows which specific rules are being applied and used. However, this aspect of the program is not discussed.

Nord

Timothy Nord (1992) designed and implemented a knowledge-based program that simulates certain grouping aspects of Lerdahl and Jackendoff's (1983) generative theory of music. The program takes a musical excerpt, subjects it to a limited amount of pre-analysis, encodes it in a machine-readable form, and analyzes it using a knowledge base containing representations of Lerdahl and Jackendoff's preference rules. In addition to generating an analysis, the program provides complete decision-making information (why certain choices were made rather than others), representing an explanation of the logic invoked to create the analysis. The program provides an operational model of the theory and the analytical process. Access to the program is relatively easy because it is written in a microcomputer-based Prolog implementation on an Apple Macintosh™ microcomputer.

■ CONCLUSION

Many of the earliest knowledge-based projects were primarily concerned with determining the feasibility of such systems. Could they be implemented using the prevailing technology, and would they have a use in music research? At some point, researchers in this area began to believe the answer on both counts was a resounding yes, albeit with a number of reservations. With this realization came a new level of complication and sophistication, as seen in the bulk of the work done in the 1980s. In the 1990s, we are finally beginning to see the use of knowledge-based systems for investigating theoretical premises and claims through complex modeling techniques. These projects are beginning to model and simulate the application of music theories in an attempt to test the theoretical claims. In chapter 6, in fact, we present a knowledge-based simulation of a current music theory and illustrate how the information derived through the process of developing the simulation provides a foundation for criticizing and reformulating portions of the theory.

Knowledge-based systems still cannot do what humans do. After all, they are not human, nor will they ever be! Essentially, these systems are doing precisely what knowledge-based systems do best: they function as powerful tools that work in harmony with, not against or in lieu of, the human researchers using them. Research in AI continues to strive toward the laudatory goal of exploring and comprehending the human mind. What is left in its wake, however, is a technology that is finding increasingly practical use. Whether we view these systems as "intelligent" assistants or simply as powerful and flexible analytical aids, it is in this spirit that the remainder of this book is written.

TWO

A Prolog Overview

■ BACKGROUND

The purpose of this chapter is to serve as an overview of the Prolog language to aid readers of this book in understanding knowledge-based computational models and strategies. Although not intended to teach the language in all its nuances and complexities, this chapter does aim to explain Prolog in enough detail to be of value in understanding the code presented in the remaining chapters. For further details on the specifics of the Prolog language, we strongly recommend the book *Programming in Prolog* by Clocksin and Mellish (1987) as the definitive source.

In the most abstract sense, Prolog is a programming language built around the concept of asserting truth—not truth in the purely empirical sense but simply truth defined as logic assertions. Prolog represents the earliest successful attempt to use logic as a foundation for a programming language. The language was developed in the early 1970s jointly by Robert Kowalski and Maarten van Emden at Edinburgh and Alain Colmerauer at Marseilles. Although there exist many different implementations, or *flavors,* of Prolog, throughout this book we will use an extended version of the most common and perhaps most universally employed variant: the *Edinburgh* syntax (Clocksin and Mellish). Every attempt will be made, however, to employ the standard syntax whenever possible.

Prolog is often referred to as a *declarative* language, in which relationships are stated and associations inferred, as opposed to more traditional *procedural* languages, which require programmers

Figure 2.1   Partial truth table.

X	Y	$\neg X$	$\neg Y$	$X \wedge Y$	$X \vee Y$	$X = Y$	$\neg((X \wedge Y) = Y)$
T	T	F	F	T	T	T	F
T	F	F	T	F	T	F	F
F	T	T	F	F	T	F	T
F	F	T	T	F	F	T	F

not ($\neg$)   and ($\wedge$)   or ($\vee$)   equality ($=$)

to state explicitly each detail of the program and the order in which the instructions are to proceed. In theory, because Prolog works out many procedural details on its own, a programmer does not have to spend needless time with these issues but instead is able to concentrate on defining the logic behind the problem to be solved. Emphasis and focus should, whenever possible, be on the declarative aspects of the problem under consideration. In practice, however, the programmer must know something about the procedural workings of Prolog. Unfortunately, the explicit and highly structured organizational schemata of many procedural languages, particularly strongly *typed* ones such as Pascal, ensure that they are frequently the first language taught to beginners, and these continue to be used by a large number of productive programmers. Even though these languages are more than sufficient for many programming tasks, they often begin to show the weakness of their heritage when defining and manipulating complex logic relationships.

Many of these traditional languages rely on *propositional logic* for defining truth. Propositional logic is based on symbolic propositions (*symbols*) or statements about relationships that can be either true or false. For example, the statement "Beethoven wrote sonatas" represents a symbolic proposition representing a truth about Beethoven's compositional output. Sentences, or *well-formed formulas,* are created by connecting more than one symbol with the atomic logic operators AND, OR, NOT, IMPLIES, and EQUALS. In larger sentences, parentheses are often added to group symbols into subexpressions, thus controlling the logic of the symbolic interrelations. All well-formed formulas rely on truth tables to express their logic, and the various mappings represent a possible world of interpretation. Figure 2.1 exhibits a partial truth table for two symbols, X and Y.

By itself, propositional logic is of dubious value because the problems inherent in a limited logical universe restricted to truth and falsity represent a serious hindrance. Prolog, however, employs a significantly more powerful syntax based on *predicate logic,* a scheme that deals with the limitations of propositional logic by allowing the logician both to make assertions about objects within a statement and to use dynamic variable substitutions (*bindings*). For example, the same propositional statement "Beethoven wrote piano sonatas" drawn from figure 1.5 in the previous chapter really only states whether Beethoven's *œuvre* contains such pieces. In Prolog, this simple statement about Beethoven can be *asserted* in the form of a relational predicate, `wrote(beethoven,piano_sonatas)`, stating a logical association between two elements (*atoms*), in this case `beethoven` and `piano_sonatas`. Through the power of selective binding, we can enable two variables such as `X` and `Y` to take on the values of the atomic symbols. The previous assertion about the composer no longer has to return an answer restricted to true or false. Instead, the clause can be satisfied by finding the value *bound* to either or both of the variables. Thus, if we ask the question `wrote(beethoven,X)`, our query returns not the values `true` or `false` but instead `X=piano_sonatas`. By asserting multiple variants of the predicate `wrote()`, including different genera and composers, Prolog can find all the possible bindings for `X` that are paired with the atomic symbol `beethoven`. Similarly, `wrote(X,Y)` would return a complete list of all defined composers and their works asserted in the language. Because most expert systems and intelligent tutoring systems use some form of symbolic knowledge representation, predicate logic, with its inherent ability to manipulate symbols as well as truth tables, is an ideal representational scheme.

It is precisely this ability of Prolog to process and manipulate symbols that makes it such a powerful language and that stands it in direct contrast to many other languages that focus more on numerical manipulations and simple propositional relations between *typed* data models. Prolog symbols, in contrast, are *untyped* (i.e., they do not have to be limited to prespecified data types) and may include anything from words, numbers, or sentences to representations of graphic images and complex relationships of other symbols. The abstract nature of this representational model is an asset that enables the programmer to define relationships among various symbols and to construct inferences among them in which the programmer alone applies meaning. This ability has made Prolog a valuable tool in AI research, particularly in research involving natural language processing, expert systems, intelligent tutorial systems, intelligent user interfaces, and other types of knowledge-based systems built primarily around rule-based interactions. In fact, this is why we have chosen Prolog for this study.

■ BASIC OVERVIEW OF THE PROLOG STRUCTURE

A Prolog interpreter incorporates three basic components: (1) an internal database of facts, rules, and relationships; (2) a built-in pattern-matching mechanism; and (3) a mechanism for backtracking and reassessing previously viewed relationships in search of one or more problem solutions. Prolog programs essentially consist of a database that is filled with facts and relationships defined by the programmer and that, once created, can be consulted as a means of extracting some of that knowledge. In one sense, working in a Prolog environment is analogous to working with a relational database program. Just as a relational database consists of one or more discrete data records linked together in a manner facilitating data retrieval, a Prolog program consists of one or more facts related through rules and accessed through the Prolog query mechanism. More precisely, a Prolog query, just like a database inquiry, searches the data to determine a solution or solutions to the question on the basis of the information already present and the relationships drawn between them. We examine each component in greater detail below.

Internal Database   The internal Prolog database consists of programmer-defined *predicate* relations. Individual *clauses* of these predicates take the form of *facts, queries,* and *rules.* Throughout this chapter, we follow the convention that text in a different font (in this case, `Courier`) indicates either items that may be entered into the Prolog system or responses returned from the Prolog system. In addition, most Prolog systems provide two types of windows or screens: the *edit* window and the *query* window. The edit window allows the programmer to create, edit, and save the files that constitute Prolog programs. The query window is used to ask various questions of a database once it has been entered into the Prolog system. All questions are typed following the standard Prolog question-mark prompt (`?-`). You should consult your own system for any possible variations.

■ **Facts**   Facts are Prolog assertions of what is already defined to be true by the person programming the database. The fact that in the key of G major a D-major chord is the dominant, for example, could be represented in Prolog as

```
key_member(gmaj,dmaj,dominant).
```

For this relationship, we choose `key_member()` as the *predicate* name and the symbols `gmaj`, `dmaj`, and `dominant` as the *arguments*. The symbolic name of a predicate relationship is called its *functor,* whereas the number of arguments a relationship contains is called the *arity* of the relation. In this example, the arity is three, although a predicate relationship may contain any number of arguments, including other predicate functors. A factual *clause* represents a single *instance* defining the property or relation of an object. Facts are treated as being unconditionally true within the Prolog system and are therefore self-standing; in other words, Prolog does not need to look for further confirming facts or relationships to assert the truthfulness of the relation. We have chosen to define the predicate of this fact as

```
key_member(Key,Chord,Function).
```

We could have just as easily defined the fact in the form

```
key_member(Chord,Function,Key).
```

The order is important only in that it must be used consistently. Once a predicate has been declared, all clauses of that predicate should follow the same conventions; otherwise, queries will obviously return incorrect information.

Our Prolog predicate can be expanded to include chords and their functions in several keys by adding more clauses to the database, resulting in the Prolog program shown in figure 2.2.

When a series of facts have been collected and entered into the internal database, Prolog can be asked questions, or *queried,* about these facts. We might, for example, ask the database, "Does a G-major chord function as a dominant in the key of C major?" This query can be posed to the Prolog system as

```
?- key_member(cmaj,gmaj,dominant).
```

Because the fact `key_member(cmaj,gmaj,dominant)` is present in our database, Prolog will respond

```
yes
```

Figure 2.2   Keys, chords, and functions.

```
key_member(cmaj,cmaj,tonic).
key_member(cmaj,cmin,tonic).
key_member(cmaj,gmaj,dominant).
key_member(cmaj,fmaj,subdominant).
key_member(cmaj,fmin,subdominant).
key_member(cmin,cmin,tonic).
key_member(cmin,cmaj,tonic).
key_member(cmin,gmaj,dominant).
key_member(cmin,fmin,subdominant).
key_member(cmin,fmaj,subdominant).
key_member(gmaj,gmaj,tonic).
key_member(gmaj,dmaj,dominant).
key_member(gmaj,cmaj,subdominant).
key_member(fmaj,fmaj,tonic).
key_member(fmaj,cmaj,dominant).
key_member(fmaj,bbmaj,subdominant).
key_member(dmaj,dmaj,tonic).
key_member(dmaj,amaj,dominant).
key_member(dmaj,gmaj,subdominant).
```

Another query could be presented that asks the question, "Does a G-major chord in the key of D major function as a mediant?" In Prolog this is represented as

```
?- key_member(dmaj,gmaj,mediant).
```

Because this fact is not present in our database, Prolog will respond

```
no
```

Prolog draws the conclusion that a G-major chord does not function as the mediant in the key of D major, not because it understands tonal chord functions and found this one to be incorrect but simply because the fact could not be found in the database. Prolog attempts to match the information in the query with the information in the database. If the query has a corresponding match in the database, then the *goal* (a goal is the result of a query, and the two terms will be used interchangeably) succeeds, and the systems responds with

```
yes
```

If it does not, the goal fails, and Prolog quits the search. As can be seen from this example, truth is defined by what appears in the database, not necessarily by truth as we think of it in a philosophical sense. We could very easily add the following factual clause to our program:

```
key_member(cmaj,cmaj,mediant).
```

In a musical sense, this statement is false, but if we add it to our database, Prolog will treat it as a fact and will interpret it as unconditionally true.

The ability of Prolog to match *terms* (a term is a generic name for any individual occurrence of a Prolog clause, constant, or variable) represents one of the most important concepts for understanding how the language operates. Two terms are said to match if they are identical, that is, if they have the same functor, arity, and arguments or if the variables in both terms can be bound (*instantiated*) such that the terms become identical.

We can observe the first of these conditions, for example, if we query the system with the following statement:

```
?- x = y.
```

Prolog will respond with

```
yes
```

because x is identical to x. However, if we type

```
?- x = y.
```

Prolog will respond with

```
no
```

because x does not match y. In Prolog, the equals sign (=) is used to compare two terms. The use of this symbol does not imply mathematical equality, only that the terms match. Prolog is very particular about how it matches the functor, arity, and arguments of a predicate. If any item is not identical, Prolog will not consider it a match. For example, the following are examples of terms that do not match:

```
key_member(cmaj,cmaj,tonic) =
    key_member(cmaj,cmaj).
key_member(cmaj,cmaj,tonic) =
    key(cmaj,cmaj,tonic).
key_member(cmaj,cmaj,tonic) =
    key_member(cmaj,cmin,tonic).
```

In the first example, the two terms have different arities, in the second they have different functors, and in the third the second argument of the relations do not match. If we query the system with each of these, Prolog will respond to all three with

```
no
```

We may pose more challenging and useful queries of our database. For example, the question "What key or keys have a D-major chord as a dominant?" can be represented as

```
?- key_member(X,dmaj,dominant).
```

Prolog will not respond with a simple yes or no; rather, it attempts to determine a value of X that makes the above statement true. Prolog responds with

```
X = gmaj
```

X functions as a *variable* in this case and returns the value gmaj when the functor key_member() and the arguments dmaj and dominant are found in the database. In reality, Prolog has only two data types: *constants* (symbols) and *variables*. All the following represent valid variable identifiers in Prolog:

```
X    Var_time    Key_of_C    Accidental
```

Specifically, Prolog syntax requires that all symbol names begin with a lowercase alphanumeric character and variable names with either an uppercase or an underlined character.

Prolog variables can exist in one of two exclusive states of being: *unbound* or *bound*. When a variable is first encountered in a Prolog clause, it exists in an unbound state, receiving a value only through *instantiation* ("taking ownership") of a Prolog symbol. Once a variable has been instantiated to a constant, it is said to be *bound* to that value. Any further comparisons or matching operations will use the bound value of the variable, and no further instantiation of it can occur except through backtracking (i.e., when the program retries a previous clause in the process of seeking a solution). Once a variable is bound to a value, it must remain unchanged.

In the previous example, X is initially unbound. Prolog attempts to match first the functor key_member() and then the constant arguments, in this case dmaj and dominant. When Prolog finds a match for these arguments, X is then bound to the value in the corresponding position of the argument list, in this case the first position. The query succeeds when X is bound to gmaj.

Prolog will also consider two terms a match if an unbound variable can be bound to a term in such a way that the two terms *become* identical. For example, if we pose the following question to the Prolog system,

```
?- X = y
```

it will respond with

```
X = y
```

In this instance, X is a variable, and all variables are initially unbound, which means they are in a sense empty and waiting to be bound to some value. When the Prolog system receives the statement above, X immediately becomes bound to the value y. (This is similar to an assignment statement in Pascal that X now holds the value y.) Prolog then compares the two terms, which now internally represent y = y and therefore match. Prolog responds by returning the value of X, which now happens to match the initial value given on the right-hand side of the equal sign. It is important for us to be aware that any Prolog variable can bind to only one value and cannot exist outside the clause in which it first appears. There are no global variables like those in Pascal. All values must be passed into or out of clauses as part of the arity of the predicate to maintain viability in other clauses.

We can continue to query the database. For example, the question "What are the keys that have a G-major chord as a dominant?" can be posed to the Prolog system as

```
?- key_member(X,gmaj,dominant).
```

This time, there is more than one answer to the question. Prolog initially responds with one solution:

```
X = cmaj
```

We may now request another solution (in most Prolog implementations by typing a semicolon, which stands for the logical OR operation), and Prolog will find

```
X = cmin
```

We may continue repeating the process until Prolog finds all the solutions or until we explicitly stop the search (often by typing a return <CR>).

Anonymous variables, represented as the underscore character (_), enable us to ignore unwanted or irrelevant information. It is often the case that a predicate may contain more information than we need at any particular moment. Instead of cluttering our programs with a vast array of variables that will not be used, we can insert an anonymous variable as a sort of "placeholder" within the relation and simply ignore the information in that particular position. In searching for a solution, anonymous variables always succeed. For example, if we want to know which keys contain a G-major chord regardless of its function within the key, we could pose this question in Prolog:

```
?- key_member(Key,gmaj,_).
```

Prolog will respond to this query with

```
Key = cmaj
```

Because we are not interested in the function of the chord, we use the anonymous variable. Although none of the information found in that position of the predicate has any adverse effect on the outcome of the query, neither will that information actually become bound to the anonymous variable. The specific information is effectively ignored.

Queries: Searching and Backtracking

Prolog searches its database for solutions in a systematic manner, beginning with the first predicate clause that it finds. In the example just cited, we can see by quickly scanning down the facts in our database that there are several answers to this query and that the Prolog system will find all of them if we ask it to do so. When receiving the query

```
?- key_member(Key,gmaj,_).
```

Prolog attempts to match the functor and arity with the first clause of `key_member()` in the database. Prolog, in effect, creates the following statement in an attempt to match the query with the first clause of the predicate relationship `key_member()`:

```
key_member(Key,gmaj,_) =
    key_member(cmaj,cmaj,tonic).
```

Once Prolog has found a functor with the correct arity, it attempts to match the arguments in the relations. The first argument is the unbound variable `Key`, which becomes bound to `cmaj` and consequently succeeds. The third position contains the anonymous variable and therefore automatically matches as well. However, the symbol `gmaj` does not match the symbol `cmaj` in the second argument position, which causes the entire goal to fail.

When a goal fails, Prolog automatically continues looking for another occurrence of `key_member()`. This process is referred to as *backtracking* ("retrying"). Prolog automatically moves backward in the code one level (i.e., it looks for a different solution for the current predicate or returns to whatever predicate was executed immediately prior to executing the current one) and begins searching for another solution. If the initial attempt offers no new solutions, the program will continue to backtrack until one of two conditions is met: (1) it identifies a different possible solution that will enable it to begin moving forward again or (2) it backtracks all the way to the end of the query without finding a solution and fails the attempt. In this case, Prolog looks at the second clause of `key_member()`. Now Prolog essentially creates the following statement:

```
key_member(Key,gmaj,_) =
    key_member(cmaj,gmaj,dominant).
```

This time the second argument (`gmaj`) matches, the anonymous variable automatically matches in the third position, and the variable Key is bound to cmaj. Because Prolog succeeds in finding a solution, it responds with

```
Key = cmaj
```

If we want Prolog to continue searching for additional solutions, we can trigger the backtracking mechanism into acting as if the query has failed by typing a semicolon (logical OR) after the solution. Prolog maintains its current position in the database at all times so that it can begin looking for the next possible match without duplicating the previous one. In this instance, when asked to retry the query, Prolog will begin with the third clause in the database (it has already tried the first two), which fails, as does the fourth one. When Prolog reaches the fifth entry, it succeeds and responds with

```
Key = cmin
```

If we ask Prolog to continue searching for additional answers after each solution, backtracking will eventually exhaust all the possibilities, and Prolog will finally fail the query and respond with

```
no
```

indicating that no other possible solutions can be found.

All our queries to this point have contained only one goal. There may be more than one answer to the questions as shown above, but in each instance there has been only one goal. Prolog also allows for compound queries requiring the satisfaction of multiple goals. For example, the question "What key can we modulate to from C major that uses a G-major chord as a pivot chord?" can be solved by locating all the keys other than C major that contain a G-major chord. This task can be posed to Prolog as

```
?- key_member(Key,gmaj,_), Key \= cmaj.
```

This example represents a compound query consisting of two parts connected by a comma, or logical AND. Prolog uses the symbol `\=`

to denote "not equal." These two parts represent subgoals of a compound query in which each part must succeed for the query to succeed. The first part

```
key_member(Key,gmaj,_)
```

asks Prolog to find those keys that contain a G-major triad. Once the system satisfies this goal, it proceeds to the second goal, comparing Key to cmaj.

Prolog attempts to answer the first part of the question with the first clause containing a second argument of gmaj. When it finds this member in the database—in this case, in the third clause—it binds Key to cmaj. Then Prolog attempts to satisfy the next question by comparing Key to cmaj and finding that they are the same, therefore failing that subgoal. Prolog automatically backtracks and begins searching the database for other possible solutions to key_member(). The first solution that meets the criteria is returned by Prolog:

```
Key = cmin
```

By typing a semicolon and pressing the return (<CR>) key, Prolog presents another solution:

```
Key = gmaj
```

By typing another semicolon, Prolog presents the final solution:

```
Key = dmaj
```

Notice that we used the anonymous variable in the third argument position. We could just as easily gain insight into the function of the G-major chord in the new key(s) by replacing the anonymous variable with a bindable variable such as Function. The results of the three queries would then be

```
Key = cmin
Function = dominant;

Key = gmaj
Function = tonic;

Key = dmaj
Function = subdominant;

no
```

This same question could be posited in a more general manner by eliminating the reference to gmaj, which would allow us to find all pivot chords for all keys. We can state the query, "What pivot chords exist between any two different keys?" as

```
Key_member(Key1,Chord,_),key_member(Key2,
    Chord,_),Key1 \= Key2.
```

Obviously, this query holds the potential to generate an excessive amount of information. Strategies for restraining the search might include substituting symbols for one or both of the variables Key1 and Key2. We can then ask questions such as "Which keys can modulate to C minor through a pivot chord?":

```
key_member(Key1,Chord,_),key_member(cmin,
    Chord,_),Key1 \= cmin.
```

Or, "which keys have pivot chords serving as a dominant in the new key?":

```
key_member(Key1,Chord,_),key_member(Key2,Chord,
    dominant), Key1 \= Key2.
```

Notice that in all these examples the variable used in the position of the second argument is the same in both subgoals. When Prolog attempts to solve the first part of the query, it binds a value to the free (unbound) variable `Chord`. This value remains immutable for the rest of the query (except during backtracking) and therefore works like a symbol (constant) in the second part of the query. In this case, whatever chord is found in the first part of the query must match with any possible solution for the second part. Prolog supports the three logical operators AND, represented by a comma (`,`), OR by a semicolon (`;`), and NOT by the predefined operator not.

■ **Rules**   Facts are an important facet of a Prolog program, but they are limited in that they can really convey only limited amounts of information. We have seen how combining facts into query subgoals can produce a significantly greater amount of information, yet the more complex the relationship, the more difficult it becomes to query the system each time a question is posed. Fortunately, Prolog has the capability to relate facts and to infer conclusions to questions on the basis of information provided without the user having to formulate explicitly all the relationships within the query window. In Prolog, this added power is achieved through predicate *rules.*

A rule is a Prolog structure that consists of two parts: (1) a conclusion that is known to exist, providing that certain conditions are true, and (2) the conditions (*goals*) that must be satisfied to draw that conclusion. Rules are closely related to IF . . . THEN [. . . ELSE] statements in more traditional procedural languages such as Pascal, where the statement takes the form

IF condition is true THEN do something [. . . ELSE do something else].

Interestingly, in Prolog the syntactical form of the rule more accurately represents a "then-if" statement of the form

THEN this conclusion is true IF
    condition 1 is true AND
    condition 2 is true AND
    . . .
    condition n is true.

The conclusion of a rule is also called the *head* of the rule, whereas the conditions taken together are called the *body* of the rule. The IF is represented in Prolog by the symbol :- (created by typing a colon followed by a dash), the AND is represented by the comma, and the period represents truth. In other words, when the Prolog query mechanism encounters a period, it declares the conclusion of the rule to be true. Notice that there is no logical OR implemented in a Prolog rule (analogous to the ELSE of a Pascal construct). Instead, Prolog relies on the built-in backtracking mechanism to enable multiple rule clauses to be tried one after another when searching for a solution. In a simplest sense, because every clause of a predicate acts as an alternative way of representing the desired logic, we can design clauses so that they function internally as groups of associations joined by the logic operator AND and collectively as a series of logical OR connections. In other words, we can define a series of clauses that would look something like those shown in figure 2.3.

In Prolog, anything appearing between the two symbol pairs /* and */ is treated as a comment to be ignored by the system. This form of comment can encompass any number of lines, which makes it very helpful for temporarily removing a predicate or clause from the program file without deleting the actual text. One working strategy for editing a clause is to duplicate it first and then comment out the original. If you find yourself getting into more trouble with the edited version, or if you simply want to remember what you had done the first time, having the original there can be very helpful. Additionally, the % symbol can be used to create a comment line that begins at the symbol and concludes automatically at the end of the current line.

Previously, we used a compound query to find which keys we could modulate to from C major using a G-major chord as a pivot chord. We can now construct a Prolog rule to perform the same set of heuristics. We will define a pivot chord as "the same chord present in two different keys." In Prolog, this rule could be written as shown in figure 2.4. A diagram of the `pivot_chord()` rule is shown in figure 2.5.

The `pivot_chord()` rule has an arity of three and will return values for `Chord`, `Key1`, and `Key2`. Notice that all the variables passed as arguments are duplicated at least once in the predicate calls embedded in the body of the rule. This point is very important because these variables achieve meaning only through instantiation

Figure 2.3   Prolog rules.

```
THEN  This conclusion is true IF       /* clause 1 */
      condition 1 is true AND
      condition 2 is true AND
      . . .
      condition n is true.
(OR)
THEN  This conclusion is true IF       /* clause 2 */
      condition 3 is true AND
      condition 4 is true AND
      . . .
      condition n is true.
```

Figure 2.4   The `pivot_chord()` predicate.

```
pivot_chord(Chord,Key1,Key2)  :-
key_member(Key1,Chord,_),
key_member(Key2,Chord,_),
Key1 \= Key2.
```

Figure 2.5   A diagram of figure 2.4.

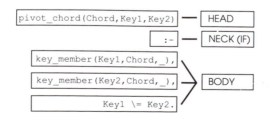

occurring in the body of the rule. If they are not bound before the end of the rule (period) is encountered, the rule passes back the variables in an unbound state, resulting in the conveyance of no meaning. Prolog assumes that variables passed into a rule are done so for a reason: either to pass in previously bound information for use within the rule or to collect new information through instantiation. Although failure to bind a variable will not cause a *fatal* program error, most Prolog interpreters will inform you that you have committed a *style* error, indicating that a variable was used only once. The message may initially seem a bit circuitous to the problem at hand, yet it is nonetheless accurate. Obviously, if a variable appears only once in a rule, it is either not being bound or not being used after it is bound. Because Prolog cannot be expected to deduce your logic, this observation is the best it can do at inferring a logic error on your part.

When a rule is called, Prolog strives to prove the head true by attempting to satisfy the body of the rule in the order that the goals are encountered (top to bottom). The first call to `key_member()` begins a search of the database in an effort to match the terms as described above. Once a match has been found, Prolog marks its place in the database (for backtracking if necessary) and begins the next call to `key_member()`. This second clause constitutes a new subgoal initiating a new search of the database, also beginning with the first entry in the database. Once the second goal is satisfied, Prolog compares the values bound to the variables `Key1` and `Key2`. If they are the same key, the comparison fails, and Prolog automatically backtracks in an attempt to find a new solution. If the keys (`Key1` and `Key2`) are different, then this subgoal succeeds, and the head is proven true. Prolog terminates the query by responding with the values bound to the three variables. As before, we can force Prolog to continue looking for other solutions (by typing a semicolon following the results of the initial query) or opt to discontinue the search. Clearly, what we have done is to transform our original query into the form of a rule, thus simplifying the amount of information required by the initiator of the query. In Prolog, there are generally few limitations to the size of rules, thus allowing us to express very complex relationships without losing the simple query access. In fact, rules can be nested many levels deep, enabling the body of one rule to incorporate another rule that in turn can contain additional rules, and so on.

Now we can query our new rule with the question posed earlier: "From C major, what keys can we modulate to using a G-major chord as a pivot chord?"

```
?- pivot_chord(gmaj,cmaj,Key2).
```

In this instance, we have limited the scope of our search to modulations from C major using only the G-major triad. When this query is posed and all the solutions are returned, Prolog responds with

```
Key2 = cmin;
Key2 = gmaj;
Key2 = dmaj;

no
```

Notice that the rule as defined does not exclude parallel functions (e.g., C major to C minor). To eliminate this possibility, we can amend the rule (from figure 2.5) as shown in figure 2.6. Because the same chord will have the same function in parallel keys, we can use that information to determine if such a relationship exists and thus exclude that choice if desired. Similarly, we can define a rule that will determine if a chord *is* borrowed from the parallel major or minor key by reversing the logic of the previous predicate. Because identical chords in parallel keys share identical functions, we can rely on the built-in pattern-matching prowess of Prolog to ensure that these conditions are met. This new rule can be written as shown in figure 2.7. On querying the system for all possibilities with

```
borrowed_chord(Chord,Key1,Key2,Function),k
```

Figure 2.6 The amended `pivot_chord()` predicate.

```
pivot_chord(Chord,Key1,Key2) :-
   key_member(Key1,Chord,Function1),
   key_member(Key2,Chord,Function2),
   Functional \= Function2,
   Key1 \= Key2.
```

Figure 2.7 The `borrowed_chord()` predicate.

```
borrowed_chord(Chord,Key1,Key2,Function) :-
   key_member(Key1,Chord,Function),
   key_member(Key2,Chord,Function),
   Key1 \= Key2.
```

Prolog will respond with

```
Chord = cmaj   Key1 = cmaj   Key2 = cmin   Function = tonic;
Chord = cmaj   Key1 = cmin   Key2 = cmaj   Function = tonic;
Chord = cmaj   Key1 = fmaj   Key2 = fmin   Function = subdominant;
Chord = cmaj   Key1 = fmin   Key2 = fmaj   Function = subdominant;
Chord = cmin   Key1 = cmin   Key2 = cmaj   Function = tonic;
Chord = cmin   Key1 = cmaj   Key2 = cmin   Function = tonic;
Chord = cmin   Key1 = fmin   Key2 = fmaj   Function = subdominant;
Chord = cmin   Key1 = fmaj   Key2 = fmin   Function = subdominant;

no
```

Notice that each answer is given twice, albeit in reversed order. This observation carries a logical explanation. Each time Prolog is queried for a new solution, it attempts to identify a possible solution for `Key1` *before* seeking a solution for `Key2`. In other words, once Prolog has backtracked to the first clause in our rule and substituted a new `Key1` beginning at the point in the list where it last succeeded, it moves forward to the next clause and looks at the entire list for *all* the possible solutions to `Key2` that match the value bound to `Key1`. Because our rule has made no provisions for remembering past combinations and comparing them with future choices, the rule continues finding *every* valid solution.

Forward and Backward Chaining

Rules in Prolog can function in one of two states, exhibiting either a forward-referencing or a backward-referencing structure, common referred to as *forward chaining* and *backward chaining*, respectively. More precisely, a rule is said to be forward chaining if it seeks to find an answer to a given question in which the steps to achieve the answer are defined in the body of the rule but the answer is unknown and will be determined as an outcome of the rule. Conversely, a rule is said to exhibit backward chaining if the answer to a problem is supplied in the head of the rule and the body of the rule defines the steps necessary to prove that answer. A forward-chaining model might take the form shown in figure 2.8a and a backward-chaining rule the form shown in figure 2.8b.

In reality, most Prolog rules can be used in both manners. In our previous examples generally, we have been using a forward-chaining query method or a mixture of both methods. By supplying unbound variables in a query, we are forcing a forward reference by asking the system to find an answer for us. In the last example, we defined the steps for finding borrowed chords. When queried, the system examined all the conditions and finally determined an answer. We

Figure 2.8   a) Forward chaining; b) backward chaining.

a. IF   condition 1 is true AND
      condition 2 is true AND
      . . .
      condition n is true
   THEN answer is found.

b. Answer is true IF
      condition 1 is true AND
      condition 2 is true AND
      . . .
      condition n is true.

can reverse the referencing direction by supplying symbols (or bound variables) instead of unbound variables as part of our query. By doing this reversal, we are now asking the system to prove whether our assertion is true on the basis of the deductive information contained in the body of the rule. For example, we can query the system with the question "Is a G major chord, the dominant of both C major and C minor, a borrowed chord?" We can posit the query as

```
borrowed_chord(gmaj,cmaj,cmin,dominant)
```

and the system will return

```
yes,
```

thus proving that our assertion is correct, obviously on the basis of the assumption that the body of our rule is an accurate reflection of the logic we wish to model. In this instance, as in other cases, if we do not care about certain items, we can simply omit them from the query without changing the reference. For example, if we do not care about the function of the chord, we can pose the query as

```
borrowed_chord(gmaj,cmaj,cmin,_),
```

and the function will be ignored. If we were to query the system with incorrect information, such as "Is an E-minor chord the mediant borrowed chord of C major and C minor?"

```
borrowed_chord(emin,cmaj,cmin,mediant)
```

then the system will respond with

```
no
```

and fail the rule.

Finally, we can easily mix forward and backward chaining within the same query. For example, the question "Is a G major chord a borrowed chord between C major and C minor, and, if so, what is its function?" can be posed as

```
borrowed_chord(gmaj,cmaj,cmin,Function),
```

and the result will be

```
Function = dominant.
```

Whenever the Prolog query mechanism responds with an instantiated value—in this case, the value bound to Function—it is assumed that the queried rule succeeded and that an implicit yes was given.

■ THE PROLOG LANGUAGE

Data Objects   Figure 2.9 contains a chart of the data objects and their hierarchical structure in Prolog. At the lowest level, objects are grouped into *atoms* and *numbers*. Atoms, also referred to as symbols, represent the smallest indivisible unit in the Prolog system. Prolog recognizes an object as an atom if it begins with a lowercase letter, consists of a string of special characters that do not have a predefined meaning, or if it is a series of characters enclosed in single quotes.

Figure 2.9   Prolog data objects.

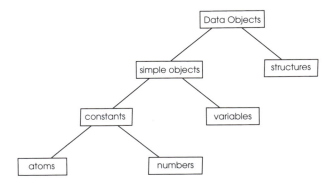

The following six examples are all considered to be atoms in Prolog:

```
Gmaj
x_or_y
_the_end
&&&
#@=~
'Mozart'
```

Prolog also supports the use of integers and real numbers. The range of acceptable integer and real number values is implementation dependent; however, a conservative range usually encompasses integer values equivalent to sixteen-bit precision and real values up to sixty-four-bit precision. All the examples in this book, however, assume a more traditional double-precision range of thirty-two bits, or +2,147,483,647 through −2,147,483,648. Prolog implementations also differ in the manner in which real numbers are stored and manipulated, and real-number computations may be inaccurate because of the particular rounding procedures implemented. In most Prolog systems, the treatment of real numbers is usually not carried out to a high degree of precision (the power of Prolog lies in its ability to manipulate symbols, not in its power as a number-crunching language) and thus should be used cautiously.

Atoms and numbers form *constants* in Prolog. These items are fixed and may not be changed within the program while the program is running (however, they may become bound to a *variable* as demonstrated in previous programs). Constants and variables form what are called *simple objects* in Prolog, meaning that they have only one component. We have also observed *structures* in the previous program. Structures are objects that contain several components, specifically a functor (which is an atom) and one or more arguments. It is possible, of course, for the arguments of a structure to be other structures in and of themselves, as arguments do not have to be atoms. The `key_member()` predicate is an example of just such a Prolog structure.

Arithmetic   Because Prolog is primarily a language of symbolic manipulation, it embodies a limited but nonetheless adequate number of arithmetic capabilities reflected in the standard predefined mathematical operators:

+	addition
−	subtraction
*	multiplication
/	division (results in a real number)
	{the numbers may be integers or real}
div	division (results in an integer)
mod	modulo

In the standard Edinburgh syntax Prolog, we can use these operators to express an equation using a traditional mathematical syntax prior to the assignment of a value to a variable, for example,

```
X is ((1+3)*(4/5))-1.5
```

Because Prolog actually implements all operators as functors, we can also express the same equation in the following manner:

```
is(X,-(*(+(1,3),/(4,5)),1.5)).
```

In this case, each of the mathematical operators appearing as a functor contains a pair of arguments that are themselves either constants, expressions, or additional functors. Whenever a functor is used as an argument, it is evaluated and must be true before the functor containing it as an argument can continue. In this case, +(1,3)   and /(4,5) must be solved before *(4,0.8) can be evaluated, and only then can −(3.2,1.5) be solved before assigning the result to X.

When making assignments to unbound atoms, such as variables, we use the term *is* instead of the equals sign, as Prolog treats the latter symbol solely as a boolean logic operator. If we were to attempt an equation such as

```
?- X = 3 + 4.
```

Prolog will promptly respond with

```
X = 3 + 4
```

The equals sign does not force Prolog to evaluate arithmetic equations. In Prolog, the equals sign undertakes equivalence operations on the basis of pattern matching, as demonstrated in the previous program examples. If two constants are equivalent, Prolog succeeds; if a variable and a constant are compared, the equal sign binds the variable to the symbol. In this case, X is bound to the symbol 3 + 4. Prolog also contains an equivalence operator that will evaluate two expressions and then compare them for equality. For example, if we queried

```
?- 1 + 2 = 2 + 1.
```

Prolog will respond with

```
no
```

because the symbol 1 + 2 is not the same as the symbol 2 + 1. However, if we change the operator from = to =:=, observe what happens:

```
?- 1 + 2 =:= 2 + 1.
yes
```

Prolog informs us that these two expressions are the same because each equation is evaluated *before* they are compared. So Prolog is actually comparing the equivalence of the expression 3 = 3 and therefore responds with yes. The opposite of this operator is the nonequivalent operator (=\=) that succeeds only when the values of the two terms do not equate. For example, presented with

```
?- 3 + 4 =\= 4 + 3.
```

Prolog will respond with

```
no
```

because the two terms are equal in value. As before, the *not equal* to operator evaluates the terms first and then does the comparison.

Prolog has an additional type of equality operator that is stricter than any of the other types. it is referred to as the *literal equality* operator (==). This operator compares two terms and succeeds only if they are absolutely identical, that is, if they exhibit the same structure and all the components of the structures are the same, even down to variable names. For example, querying Prolog with the following expression using the standard equivalence operator

```
?- key_member(gmaj,gmaj,tonic) =
   key_member(gmaj,gmaj,X).
```

will return

```
X = tonic
```

Prolog compares each element, and they either match or, as in this instance, a variable is bound (and yes is implied). Instead, if we try the same query with the liberal equivalence operator

```
?- key_member(gmaj,gmaj,tonic) ==
   key_member(gmaj,gmaj,X).
```

Prolog will respond with

```
no
```

because the symbol tonic and the variable X are not identical. All

Figure 2.10 Comparison operators.

A	=	B	A and B match
A	\=	B	A does not match B
A	>	B	A is greater than B
A	<	B	A is less than B
A	>=	B	A is greater than or equal to B
A	=>	B	A is equal to or less than B
A	=:=	B	The values of A and B are equal
A	=\=	B	The values of A and B are not equal
A	==	B	A is identical to B
A	\==	B	A is not identical to B

the comparison operators and equality operators are summarized in figure 2.10.

Characters and Strings

Characters and strings are purely implementation-dependent data types and are not part of the Edinburgh syntax; instead, they are treated as a list of ASCII-equivalent integers (a character would simply consist of a list with one value). Most Prolog implementations, however, realize some form of string representation and handling. In this book, strings and characters are defined as any ASCII-based symbol(s) appearing between double quotes and single quotes, respectively. For the sake of compatibility, we will avoid any excessive use of string manipulations but will include and discuss implementation-specific string handlers whenever we feel that they simplify the presentation of a code concept.

Lists

A *list* is one of the most powerful and flexible data structures in Prolog. Specifically, a list is a series of zero through *n* elements set off by square brackets [. . .] consisting of any combination of constants, variables, or structures, including other lists. Square brackets alone signify an empty list—in other words, a Prolog atom with *no* elements. Figure 2.11 shows several examples of Prolog lists. A list is extremely flexible because it can contain any number of elements and is limited only by the memory constraints of the system being used. The first item in a list is referred to as the *head*, and the remaining items in the list constitute the *tail*. Given

Figure 2.11   Prolog lists.

```
[fmaj,gmaj,amin]
[X,[hello,goodbye]]
[[[[X],Y],Z],letters]
[]
[[a.b.c],[D,E,F],[G,[h,i,j],K]]
```

```
        X = [cmaj,dmin,emin,fmaj,gmaj,amin,bdim],
```

the head of the list bound to X is cmaj, and the tail is bound to [dmin,emin,fmaj,gmaj,amin,bdim]. The head in this case is an *element* of the list, whereas the tail is a *list* of the remaining elements. In Prolog, we can separate a list into its head and tail by placing a vertical line at the point where we want to divide the list:

```
    [Head | Tail]
```

There are a number of different ways in which we can parse a list with the vertical divider. For example, using a list that incorporates a major scale

```
    ['D','E','F#','G','A','B','C#']
```

We can write a predicate to extract the tonic triad in several different ways. In the first example, we explicitly break the list into five heads and one tail and ignore all the unwanted elements by using anonymous variables:

```
    tonic_triad([Root,_,Third,_,Fifth |
        _],Root,Third,Fifth)
```

In the second example, we parse the list by removing individual heads from nested lists, again ignoring unwanted elements by using the anonymous variable:

```
    tonic_triad([Root | [_ | [Third | [_ |
        [Fifth[bar]_]]]]],Root,Third,Fifth).
```

We can query these predicates with either

```
    ?- X = ['D','E','F','G','A','B','C#'],
        tonic_triad(X,Root,Third,Fifth).
```

or

```
    ?- tonic_triad(['D','E','F#','G','A','B','C#'],
        Root,Third,Fifth).
```

and the result will be

```
Root  =  'D'
Third =  'F#'
Fifth =  'A'
```

In both examples, notice how the three unbound variables—`Tonic`, `Third`, and `Fifth`—appear twice in the argument list. Prolog always evaluates arguments in a left-to-right manner. In this case, the constant values appearing in positions 1, 3, and 5, of the list are bound to the three variables. Because these three bound variables happen to match the three arguments following the list, their values are immediately instantiated onto the latter three positions. In simpler terms, because the variables became bound on each of their first occurrences, those bound values carry over to their second appearance, thus supplying the necessary information to complete the task of determining the three pitches.

▧ Recursion: Operations on Lists

Now that we have defined the concept of a list, let us discuss more complex ways of manipulating the information within a list. Toward this end, we will define some of the standard operations on lists and use them as a model for investigating list structures and manipulations. One of the most fundamental tasks is to test for the existence of a given element within a particular list. Actually, this predicate is often predefined in various Prolog implementations; however, because it is valuable to explore the process, we have decided to include it in our discussion. We shall define the membership relation as follows:

```
membership(Element,L).
```

This goal will succeed if the item `Element` is located in the list (`L`). In defining this relationship, we can make several assumptions. First, we know that `Element` is present in the list if `Element` is the head of the list. Second, we know that `Element` is present in the list if `Element` is in the tail of the list. Because these are the only two elements of a list that can be checked, we can program the membership relation using two clauses reflecting these assumptions, as shown in figure 2.12. The first clause is a fact and the second clause a rule.

By querying Prolog with

```
?- membership(a,[a,b,c]).
```

we are questioning if the element `a` is present in the list `[a,b,c]`. Prolog begins searching the database for the first clause of the mem-

Figure 2.12 `membership()` predicate.

```
membership(X,[X | _]).  %fact: true if head of the list
membership (X,[_ | Tail]) :- %rule: true if tail of the list
    membership (X,Tail).
```

`bership()` predicate and attempts to match the terms, resulting in the following test:

```
membership(a,[a,b,c]) =
    membership(Element,[Element | Tail]).
```

Once Prolog internally matches the terms, the comparison becomes

```
membership(a,[a | [b,c]])
```

Because a is the head of the list `[a,b,c]`, the first clause of the relationship succeeds, and no further searching is necessary. Prolog returns with

```
yes
```

If we pose the query

```
?- membership(b,[a,b,c]).
```

Prolog will begin searching the database, attempting to match our query with the first clause of `membership()`. In this case, the internal matching will result in the following test:

```
membership(b,[a | [b,c]]) =
    membership(Element,[Element | Tail])
```

Obviously, this clause will fail because b (which is bound to `Element`) does not match the head of the list (a). Now Prolog automatically begins searching for the next instance of `membership()`. This rule states that `Element` is a member of the list (L) if `Element` is a member of the tail (`Tail`) of the list and is executed by calling the `membership()` clause again but this time passing only the `Tail` portion of the list rather than the complete list. At this point, Tail is bound to `[b,c]`, so the new call to `membership()` is in effect:

```
membership(b,[b,c]).
```

Because this is a new call to `membership()`, Prolog begins searching for the first occurrence of `membership()` in the database, finds our fact, and attempts to match b to the head of the new list `[b,c]`. Because this goal succeeds, Prolog returns the response:

```
yes
```

The second instance of `membership()` is defined as a *recursive* rule, a very useful principle in Prolog programming. In one sense, any rule that calls itself is a recursive rule. In another sense, a recursive definition is one where at least one part of the definition is explicit and the remaining solutions can be determined indirectly. We know that an item is a member of a list if it is the head of the list. This fact is the direct, explicit part of our definition. We also know that an item is a member of a list if it is in the tail of the list; however, the tail may contain an indefinite number of elements. This second clause represents the indirect portion of our definition. The recursive rule actually checks each element of the list against the first clause until it succeeds or until it reaches an empty list and fails.

More Recursive Operations

At some point, we may need to know the length of a list. To determine this information, we need to count the number of elements in that list. We can define the procedure

```
list_length(List,N).
```

so that N will return the number of elements in `List`. As with the `membership()` relation, we will use two clauses to define `list_length()` (see figure 2.13). We know that an empty list, by definition, has a length of zero because it contains no element. We also know that if the list is not empty, it can be divided into its head and tail (`List = [Head | Tail]`) and that its length is one plus the length of its tail. We can write a recursive definition of this operation in a very similar manner to that of the `membership()` relation above. If `List` is empty, our first `list_length()` clause will succeed. If `List` is not empty, however, `list_length()` will continue to recall itself, passing along the tail (`Tail`) of the list until the list is empty. When `List` is finally empty, the first clause of the `list_length()`

Figure 2.13 `list_length()` predicate.

```
list_length([],0).               %fact: if empty then length = 0
list_length([_ | Tail],N) :-     %rule: if not empty then
    list_length(Tail,N1),        %call list_length() with tail
    N is 1 + N1.                 %N counts until List is empty
```

Figure 2.14   Sample run of `list_length()`.

```
?- list_length([a,b,c],N).

Call #1:
      list_length([a,b,c],N) = list_length([],0).
    fail.

Call #1 (retry):
      list_length([a,b.c],N1)=list_length([_ | Tail],N1) :-
    succeed.
    (recursive call):
      list_length([b,c],N1),
    (place on stack):
      N is 1 + N1.

Call #2:
      list_length([b,c],N1) = list_length([],0).
    fail.

Call #2 (retry):
      list_length([b,c],N1) = list_length([_ | Tail],N1) :-
    succeed.
    (recursive call):
      list_length([c],N1),
    (place on stack):
      N is 1 + N1.

Call #3:
      list_length([c],N1) = list_length([],0) :-
    fail.

Call #3 (retry):
      list_length([c],N1) = list_length([_ | Tail],N).
    succeed.
    (recursive call):
      list_length([],N1),
    (place on stack):
      N is 1 + N1.

Call #4:
      list_length([],N1) = list_length([],0).
    succeed: N1 = 0
```

predicate will finally succeed on the next recursive call, thus causing the entire predicate to succeed. Now Prolog has to go back and finish, in reverse order, all the calls to `list_length()` that have already begun. Each time Prolog "backs out" of a recursive call, it will execute the final statement in the body of the rule and add one to N. Following the final iteration, the value in N will reflect the length of the list. To clarify this process, we can `trace` (or `step`) through a short example, shown in figure 2.14, and get the feel for how the recursion works by querying Prolog with the first line shown in the figure. We can tell by looking at our query that the length is three, but let us examine closely how Prolog determines the same information. The search begins by trying to match the first clause of `list_length()`; however, this fails because the list is not empty. Prolog then backtracks and looks for another relationship defining `list_length()` and finds the second (rule) clause. The second attempt succeeds and immediately calls `list_length()` recursively, saving a copy of the unfinished portion of the clause on the Prolog stack for later completion. The search begins again from the top of the database, the first clause failing and the second succeeding with the remainder of the code being placed on the stack. This process continues until the list is finally empty.

This time the call matches our factual clause and binds N1 to zero. Even though our rule has finally succeeded, Prolog has managed to "stack up" three unfinished portions of `list_length()` that must now be completed, always in the reverse order from which they were stored—in other words, "last in, first out." Because the successful call returns N1 bound to zero, the program now completes the body of Call #3: N = 1 + N1. The variable N (which was actually N1 passed in from the previous call) is now bound to one, and the rule succeeds. Now the program completes the body of Call #2, which again says that N = 1 + N1, binding N to two. This step completes Call #2 and allows the program to complete the body of Call #1 in the same manner. When all the recursive calls to the rule have succeeded, N is bound to three, which of course is the length of our list. Realize that although this takes a considerable amount of time to explain, Prolog executes the operation very quickly.

When we define a recursive procedure, it is often desirable to have one clause that is guaranteed to succeed at some point in the process. This clause is referred to as a *terminal clause,* which is a state that a recursive call is guaranteed to achieve, no matter how large the initial list, because the rule portion of our procedure will continue to make the recursive call until the tail is empty. In the `list_length()` procedure, our terminal clause is that fact binding the empty list with the length of zero. This procedure will not work properly if the order of the `list_length()` clauses is reversed. The order of the clauses in this case is of extreme importance. If the rule were placed before the fact, the fact would never succeed because it would never be called. The program would be caught in an infinite loop!

As we have defined it, the `list_length()` predicate has one significant drawback: it is not *tail recursive*. Because the recursive call is not the last line in the clause, it requires the system to save a copy of the unfinished portion of the code each time it is reiterated. This step may not cause problems for small lists, but imagine the memory requirements if we were to pass in a list with 5,000 elements! Clearly, routines that are non–tail recursive can be very memory intensive. On the other hand, if we write tail-recursive routines—in which the recursive call is the last call in the clause—there will be no code left to execute and therefore no code to store in memory after each call. We can reformulate the `list_length()` predicate (from figure 2.13) into a tail-recursive form with the code shown in figure 2.15. We can access it through a second predicate designed to set the initial value of CNT to zero:

```
find_list_length(L,N) :-
    list_length(L,O,N).
```

(This second step can be omitted and `list_length()` called directly if the user supplies a zero for the second argument of the predicate.) In this version of the predicate, each element of the list is tallied prior to each recursion, and the new value is passed along with the call. In a recursive structure such as `list_length()`, bound values passed into the recursive call will be restored to the value they were bound to prior to the call on "backing out" of the recursion. Even though no code is executed after each tail-recursive call, the iterations must still "unwind" themselves, and it is during this process that bound values are restored to their original values. In other words, even though CNT2 is incremented during each call, it will be similarly decremented on the way out, ensuring that the

Figure 2.15 The revised `list_length()` predicate.

```
list_length([],N,N).
list_length([_ | Tail],CNT,N) :-
    CNT2 is CNT + 1,
    list_length(Tail,CNT2,N).
```

value will be back to zero on exiting the call. To gain access to the incremented value without losing it on the way out, we can pass an unbound variable—in this case, N—through all the recursive calls, binding it only on achieving the terminal clause. Because the variable was never bound at any previous stage of the recursion, it will not lose the newly bound value on the way out to the calling routine.

Traversal Methods

Prolog list traversals can be generalized into two specific classes of algorithms: those looking for unknown information at a known location within a list and those looking for a known element at an unknown position within a list. Because nearly all recursive searches utilize one or the other of these strategies, we will examine the two models and develop a generalized predicate for handling each case.

We will define the first predicate, in which we will be looking for a known value at an unknown location within a list, as `search_unknown_pos()`. Unlike the previous examples that drew on two conditions, this predicate assumes three: (1) that we have searched the list and not found what we are looking for, (2) that we have found a match, or (3) that we must continue looking for the element in the remainder of the list. The first case will be used as a terminal clause. Obviously, if a match is not found, we will want the predicate to stop looking once the list is finally exhausted. The functor will have three arguments: the value we are looking for, which in this case is irrelevant and is replaced by the anonymous variable; the list we are going to search, which in this case is empty; and a variable to return the result, in this case to be bound to the symbol `not_found`. This factual clause is defined as

```
search_unknown_pos(_,[],not_found).
```

The second clause, also terminal, compares the variable `Val`, containing the value we are searching, against the head of the list. If a match occurs, the clause ignores the tail of the list and returns the symbol `found`:

```
search_unknown_pos(Val,[Val | _],found).
```

Finally, the third clause executes the recursive traversal through the list. Assuming that the first two terminal clauses fail (remember they are order dependent), the third clause truncates the head of the list and continues the recursive search by passing the tail:

```
search_unknown_pos(Val,[_ | Tail],X) :-
    search_unknown_pos(Val,Tail,X).
```

Figure 2.16   The `search_unknown_pos()` predicate.

```
search_unknown_pos(_,[],not_found).
search_unknown_pos(Val,[Val | _],found).
search_unknown_pos(Val,[_ | Tail],X) :-
    search_unknown_pos(Val,Tail,X).
```

Figure 2.17   The `search_known_pos()` predicate.

```
search-known_pos(_,[],not_found).
search_known_pos(1,[Val | _],Val).
search_known_pos(CNT,[_ | Tail],X) :-
    CNT2 is CNT - 1,
    search_known_pos(CNT2,Tail,X).
```

Again, notice that an unbound variable is passed both into and out of the recursive call so that the response bound to it in one of the two terminal clauses can be assessed after the recursion unwinds. The complete predicate appears in figure 2.16.

The second predicate, in which we are looking for an unknown value at a *known* location within a list, is defined as `search_known_pos()`, as shown in figure 2.17. Again, this model is defined through three conditions: (1) that the position we are seeking exceeds the length of the list, (2) that we have found the position we are looking for and can extract the value, or (3) that we have not yet arrived at the desired location in the list. In the first terminal clause, the empty list signifies that we have exhausted the search without finding the desired position. This code is defined identically to the corresponding clause in the previous example. The second clause determines that we have reached the desired position and will bind the appropriate value from the list with the unbound exit variable. Note that this clause succeeds by matching the numeral 1 in the first position, relying on a decrementing counter to keep track of our position within the list. On initially calling the predicate, we must supply a value corresponding to the position being sought, which is decremented with each recursive call until the counter indicates that we have moved recursively the desired distance through the list.

Additional Examples

We will use three additional examples to clarify the processes involved in list handling and recursion. Up to this point, we have dealt only with the deconstruction of a list; however, all the remaining examples will show several methods for reconstructing lists—replacing, omitting, or inserting elements in the process.

In the first example, we will demonstrate one method for undertaking an intervallic contour search of a melody by recursively traversing a list and examining all adjacent elements in that list—in other words, by comparing elements 1 and 2, then 2 and 3, and so on. We can create such a program by applying our understanding of the `search_unknown_pos()` predicate and slightly modifying it to compare all pairs in a list. The predicate `contour()` is built on two assumptions about traversing a list of elements: (1) that there are no more comparisons to be made because the list is either empty or has less than two elements left in it or (2) that there are additional comparisons that need to be made. Notice that the first assumption is really two assumptions signifying the same result and will be programmed as two separate terminal clauses. We begin our discussion with the third (recursive) clause because it embodies materials necessary for understanding the two terminal clauses.

We will utilize two methods for list reconstruction, the first of which appears in the recursive call itself (the last line of the clause). As can be seen in this example, the same method used for parsing a list into separate components can be used to reassemble a list as a parameter to be passed into or out of another call. The second method employs the relatively standard Prolog functor `append()`. The primary function of this predicate is to append two lists together into one combined list such that

```
?- append([1,2,3],[4,5,6],X).
X = [1,2,3,4,5,6]
```

Unfortunately, not all Prolog environments implement this procedure. The code shown in figure 2.18 is drawn from Clocksin and Mellish (1987) and can be used as a model for implementing the function in any Prolog environment.

This predicate is extremely useful when collecting information during the course of a recursive search, and we will utilize it in `contour()` to build a list of successive contour values. Initially, we will pass in an empty list, `TempContour`, to which we append a new contour each time we pass through the clause. Note that because the variable `NTVL` is not a list, it must be enclosed in square brackets—in other words, turned into a list of one element—for the call to

Figure 2.18   The `append()` predicate.

```
append([],L,L).
append([X | L1],L2,[X | L3]) :-
    append(L1,L2,L3).
```

Figure 2.19   The `contour()` predicate.

```
contour([],_,[]).
contour([_ | []],Contour,Contour).
contour([H1,H2 | Tail],TempContour,Contour) :-
    NTVL is H2 - H1,
    append(TempContour,[NTVL],NewTemp),
    contour([H2 | Tail],NewTemp,Contour).
```

function correctly. The resultant combined list `NewTemp` is then passed into the next recursive call. Also note that we are passing an unbound variable throughout the recursive calls. As before, this variable eventually becomes bound to the contour list in the terminal clause. The code for this predicate appears in figure 2.19.

In addition to the final clause, a first clause for this predicate is designed as a safety valve, with the sole function of handling an empty list (an invalid parameter) if it is accidentally supplied in the query. If this clause succeeds because of finding such a list (something that will not occur through the normal use of the predicate), it will return an empty list of contours and succeed. Obviously, if `contour()` is never called with an empty list, or if the query is designed to ensure against the possibility, this clause is superfluous. Because the real world is never so foolproof, we include the clause just in case.

The second clause acts as the functional terminal clause. For this clause to succeed, it must stop the search after examining the last interval. As we have shown, the last note examined is restored prior to the recursive call, which means that after we have examined elements $n - 1$ and n of the list (the last pair), element n is restored and passed through the recursion. If we attempt to call the recursive clause one more time, it will fail because it expects to find two heads in the list and we will have passed it only one. In other words, we need to stop the search when the list has only one head, that is, when the tail is empty. Our terminal clause includes in it the necessary code to instantiate the contour list (Contour) to the unbound output variable.

We might query this predicate with the following command, making sure that we initialize the second argument by supplying an empty list:

```
contour([1,3,5,4,3,6,2,5],[],X).
X = [2,2,-1,-1,3,-4,3]
```

The final two examples deal with the insertion and deletion of elements from within a list. Again we can utilize one or the other of the basic search algorithms discussed earlier, depending on the particular requirements of the search. The first example will demonstrate how to remove an element from a list. We will assume that we are attempting to remove a matching element from the list, so we will need to make the following three assumptions: (1) the element we are looking for is not present in the list, (2) the element has been found and must be removed from the list, and (3) we need to continue looking. As in several of the previous examples, delete_element() will have two terminal clauses and one recursive clause. The first clause should look familiar by this point (note that we are using an anonymous variable in the first position in place of the value we have been searching). Its primary function is to return an exact duplicate of the list sent into the search when no match is found:]

```
delete_element(_,[],List,List).
```

The third, or recursive, clause assumes that no match has yet been found and proceeds by appending the current head of the list (that does *not* match the supplied value) to the existing list of heads (TempList) checked in previous calls. In other words, as we move recursively through the list, we pull off one element at a time and, if we do not want to delete it, append it onto a new list. Once this operation is completed, a recursive call is made, passing in the bound lists TempList and Tail and the unbound variable List, which will pass back out the final reconstructed list:

```
delete_element(Val,[H | Tail],TempList,List) :-
    append(TempList,[H],NewTemp),
    delete_element(Val,Tail,NewTemp,List).
```

The second clause succeeds when the item being searched is found to match the head of the list. At this point, all that is required is to append the temporary list TempList to the tail of the remaining list. Because TempList contains all the heads pulled off the original list in the recursive clause *prior to this call,* appending it to Tail effectively reconstructs the original list with-

Figure 2.20   The `delete_element()` predicate.

```
delete_element(_,[],List,List).
delete_element(Val,[Val | Tail],TempList,List) :-
  append(TempList,Tail,List).
delete_element(Val,[H | Tail],TempList,List) :-
  append(TempList,[H],NewTemp),
  delete_element(Val,Tail,NewTemp,List).
```

out the one item—the head of the remainder list—being searched. The final code appears in figure 2.20.

We may also desire to insert an element into a list. Essentially, this process is nearly identical to deleting an element. For variety, however, we will define the functor `insert_element()` so that it inserts at a specific point located immediately *before* the element being searched. As in previous examples, `insert_element()` can be defined in three states, two terminal and one recursive: (1) the insertion point is beyond the length of the list, (2) the insertion point is located and the element must be added to the list, and (3) the insertion point has not been found yet. The functor as defined has an arity of five: a counting variable (CNT), a variable bound to the value to be inserted (VAL), a variable bound to the list to be traversed, a variable bound to a temporary list used to construct the new list, and an unbound variable used to return the final reconstructed list. When querying this predicate, the inquirer must supply four pieces of information as well: a value to be inserted, the position after which the value is to be placed, the list to insert it into, and an empty list to initialize the temporary list. Let us assume that we want to insert a supertonic harmony before the third position (i.e., between the second and third positions) of a harmonic progression. We might query this predicate with

```
?- insert_element(3,ii6,[i,vi,v7,i],[],X).
```

and Prolog will return with

```
X = [i,vi,ii6,v7,i]
```

The first terminal clause of this predicate is nearly identical to that of `delete_element()` and functions exactly the same. The second terminal clause, reached when the counter is decremented to one, used the `append()` predicate to build a new list from the existing one and combines it with the item to be inserted. As can be seen in the code below, two calls to `append()` are required: the first call appends the value to be inserted onto the end of the temporary head list, and the second call appends the existing head and tail onto the list created in the first call, thus re-creating the existing list with the new element inserted. Finally, the third (recursive) call decrements the value of the counter (CNT), adds the current head (H) onto the temporary head list (TempList), and together with the Tail passes these values recursively. The complete code for this predicate appears in figure 2.21.

We can readily modify this predicate to have it insert *after* a given location by ensuring that the head of the list following the insertion point is appended back onto the list prior to appending the inserted value. By creating a modified version of the second clause, we can achieve that goal. We can even set up this predicate so that the user decides at the time of the query whether the insertion should occur before or after the element located at the insertion point. Essentially, we add one additional argument to the functor, ignoring it in the first and last clause but using it to direct Prolog to execute the appropriate middle clause. In other words, we rewrite the predicate with four clauses but enable only three at any given time. The new revised code (from figure 2.21) appears in figure 2.22.

Note that the additional argument is placed at the head of the list. In the outer clauses, we use the anonymous variable to signify that this argument is irrelevant to these stages; however, in the two middle clauses the user must supply a symbol in the query that will match one or the other of the two symbols *before* or *after*. We might choose to replace the symbol *after* in the third clause with an anonymous variable as well. Because the ordering of the clauses dictates that the clause containing *before* will be checked first, the symbol *after* is therefore implied in the next one. Actually, by replacing *after* with an anonymous variable, we can allow for any symbol other than *before*, thus enabling *after* as a default insertion mode when *before* is not specifically requested in the query. For the same reason, however, we must be careful not to remove the symbol *before* if we want to use that mode as the default because the order of the clauses will ensure that that clause always succeeds because of the anonymous variable. To enable *before* as a default, we simply reverse the order of the two middle clauses before removing the symbol.

Database Manipulation

As discussed earlier in this chapter, Prolog is actually a database filled with facts and rules. Some of these structures are of our own creation (i.e., our data), whereas some represent language con-

Figure 2.21   The `insert_element()` predicate.

```
insert_element(_,_,[],List,List).
insert_element(1,Val,OldList,TempList,List) :-
    append(TempList,[Val],NewTemp),
    append(NewTemp,OldList,List).
insert_element(CNT,Val,[H | Tail],TempList,List) :-
    append(TempList,[H],NewTemp),
    CNT2 is CNT - 1,
    insert_element(CNT2,Val,Tail,NewTemp,List).
```

Figure 2.22   The revised `insert_element()` predicate.

```
insert_element(_,_,_,[],List,List).
insert_element(before,1,Val,OldList,TempList,List) :-
    append(TempList,[Val],NewTemp),
    append(NewTemp,OldList,List).
insert_element(after,1,Val,[H | Tail],TempList,List) :-
    append(TempList,[H,Val],NewTemp),
    append(NewTemp,Tail,List).
insert_element(BorF,CNT,Val,[H | Tail],TempList,List) :-
    append(TempList,[H],NewTemp),
    CNT2 is CNT - 1,
    insert_element(BorF,CNT2,Val,Tail,NewTemp,List).
```

structs. The entire Prolog language is really a set of facts and relationships residing in the system database. In fact, Prolog is often referred to as a *side-effect* language, meaning that the actions we take with our program can have the side effect of reprogramming our rules and relationships during execution of a search. It is this quality that enables Prolog to *learn* new information as well as to restructure its current knowledge dynamically. For obvious reasons, it is very important to have access to and be able to manipulate the Prolog database.

Prolog implements two groups of predicates for manipulating the internal database. The first predicate `asserta()`—or simply `assert()`—and its variant `assertz()` are used for placing (*asserting* or *consulting*) a new predicate clause into the database. Because the order of clauses in a predicate is essential for organizing program logic relationships, the two variants enable different insertion points within the database. Specifically, `asserta()` places a clause at the front of the database, and `assertz()` places a clause at the end of the database. The complement of these two functors is `retract()`, which will remove the front-most matching occurrence of a given clause from the database.

These clauses are particularly useful for collecting, storing, and retrieving information during the execution of a program. For a ready example, we can expand on the predicate `contour()` discussed earlier. Let us assume that during the course of building a contour map we want to maintain a tally of intervals we encounter. We can append the goal `store_ntvl()` to the existing code so that it will be called with each recursive iteration of `contour()`. The revised predicate (from figure 2.19) is coded in figure 2.23. The function of `store_ntvl()` is to assert a given interval into the database and tally the number of occurrences for each interval size. We can define the properties of `store_ntvl()` with two conditions: (1) the given interval has been encountered previously and stored in `ntvl_type()` and (2) there is no record of having encountered the

Figure 2.23   The revised `contour()` predicate.

```
contour([],_,[]).
contour([_ | []],Contour,Contour).
contour([H1,H2 | Tail],TempContour,Contour) :-
    NTVL is H2 - H1,
    append(TempContour,[NTVL],NewTemp),
    store_ntvl(NTVL),
    contour([H2 | Tail],NewTemp,Contour).
```

Figure 2.24   The `store_ntvl()` predicate.

```
store_ntvl(NTVL) :=
    ntvl_type(CNT,NTVL),
    CNT2 is CNT + 1,
    retract( ntvl_type(_,NTVL) ),
    assertz( ntvl_type(CNT2,NTVL) ).
store_ntvl(NTVL) :-
    not ntvl_type(_,NTVL),
    assertz( ntvl_type(1,NTVL) ).
```

given interval before. We can accomplish this with the predicate shown in figure 2.24.

The first condition requires only that we get the current count for the designated interval size and add one more to it. Our first clause is specifically designed to succeed only if there is an existing clause for `ntvl_type()` that matches the passed-in value of NTVL. If the first goal succeeds, then we increment the value of CNT by one and replace the existing clause of `ntvl_type()` with the revised version. The second condition requires that we create a new clause if none already exists, in which case we will utilize the built-in Prolog *negation* function when checking for an existing match to `ntvl_type()`. The functor `not` preceding a goal will simply reverse the logic of that goal.

For those conditioned by more traditional procedural languages, it should be apparent by this point that Prolog does not allow for the reassignment of variable values. For example, in Pascal the following code is completely acceptable:

```
procedure change_x (var X: real);    {X is passed the value 2}

begin
  X := X + 1;                        {X = 2 + 1 = 3}
  X := ((X * 2) / (X + 1)) * 4;      {X = ((3 * 2) / (3 + 1)) * 4}
end;                                 {X = (   6    /      4 ) * 4}
                                     {X =             6          }
```

Assuming that X is passed into this procedure already assigned the value two, X will be reassigned the value three and then reassigned the value six before being passed back out of the procedure. Prolog, however, would fail at the very first of these operations. Once X becomes bound to a value, it cannot be changed except through backtracking. If Prolog were to attempt an additional assignment statement, it would fail because it would treat the equation as

```
2 = 2 + 1
fail
```

Getting around this constraint is relatively easy if we use `assert()` and `retract()` to store and change the value of a variable (actually a clause stored in the database). The code in figure 2.25 shows how to reassign the value of a variable clause defined as `our_value()`. As can be seen here, we emulate the assignment of a variable by asserting the assigned value into a database clause. When we want to alter that information, we retrieve the current value by instantiating it into a new variable, retract the original database clause, com-

Figure 2.25   Reassigning a variable value.

```
begin_example :-
    X is 2,
    asserta( our_value(X) ),          %store the initial value
    emulate_pascal_example.             %call 2nd pred to vary X

    emulate_pascal_example :-
        our_value(X),                 %get prev value for X
        Y is X + 1,
        Z is ((Y * 2) / (Y + 1)) * 4,
        retract( our_value(_) ),      %remove old value for X
        asserta( our_value(Z) ).      %replace with new value
```

pute the new value and bind it to a second variable, and finally assert it back into the database.

Granted, this process is rather lengthy, but it does the job quite effectively. In fact, we can use this technique to avoid memory shortage problems with highly recursive predicates. Let us assume that while using the predicate search_unknown_pos() defined earlier we need to send in a rather lengthy list. Each time a recursive call occurs, the entire list is stored in memory for later retrieval as the recursion backs out through the previous calls. If our list is 10,000 elements long, search_unknown_pos() will require millions of bytes of memory even for undertaking its rather rudimentary task. On the other hand, if we use assert() and retract() to store and retrieve a copy of the list each time through a recursive call, and as long as we do not need access to the list on the way back out of the recursion, we need store only one copy of the information regardless of how many iterations occur. The code in figure 2.26 shows this predicate (from figure 2.16) rewritten so that the list is not passed recursively but is instead stored in and retrieved from the system database in the predicate our_list().

Before this predicate can be used, however, we must ensure that at least one valid clause of our_list() is asserted into the database. This assertion can occur in a previously called predicate, or we can simply assert it as part of a compound query such as

```
?- asserta(our_list([1,2,3,4,5])),search_
    unknown_pos(3,X).
    X = found
```

Figure 2.26   The revised `search_unknown_pos()` predicate.

```
search_unknown_pos(_,not_found) :-
  our_list([]).
search_unknown_pos(Val,found) :-
  our_list([Val | _]).
search_unknown_pos(Val,X) :-
  our_list([_ | Tail]),
  retract( our_list(_) ),
  asserta( our_list(Tail) ),
  search_unknown_pos(Val,X).
```

Figure 2.27   The `retract_all()` predicate.

```
retract_all(X) :- retract(X),fail.
retract_all(X) :- retract((X :- _)),fail.
```

Also very useful, but not always implemented in every Prolog environment, is the functor `retractall()`, which is designed to remove *every* clause matching the supplied arguments. This functionality is particularly desirable when we want to remove an entire predicate (i.e., all the relevant clauses) from working memory. By supplying a predicate functor with anonymous variables for every argument, `retractall()` will eliminate every clause of the predicate in one call. An often-used strategy is to employ `retractall()` for every retraction as a means of ensuring that no accidentally created duplicates of a predicate are left in memory—in essence, allowing a program to proceed with a "clean slate." Because `retractall()` is not part of the standard Edinburgh Prolog syntax, we show the code for one possible definition (Clocksin and Mellish 1987) in figure 2.27.

Control Mechanisms

Up to this point, the direct processes of backtracking and recursion have been the only control mechanisms we have discussed. Prolog offers us additional tools, however, that enhance the procedural and logical aspects of programming; the three most frequently employed are the built-in predicates `fail`, `repeat`, and `!` (*cut*). Specifically, `fail` is a predicate that can never succeed—in other words, it always `fails`—whereas `repeat` is a predicate that always suc-ceeds. This property of the latter predicate is of particular value because not only will `repeat` succeed when passing through it in a forward-directed search but it will also force a new forward-directed search when it is reached through backtracking. By using `repeat` and `fail` together, we can imitate a recursive loop without using any real recursion. However, avoid using them together at the same goal level within the same predicate because they will become locked in an infinite loop that cannot succeed.

As an example of using this pair of predicates, let us assure that we desire to traverse a list and store each element separately in the database. As the program searches forward through the `repeat` goal, it will eventually arrive at the `fail` predicate, at which point backtracking moves the search back up to the `repeat` predicate and the forward motion begins again. Because the loop will con-tinue indefinitely unless we break the succeed-fail cycle, we have provided a terminal clause for `do_search()` that enables the predicate to succeed without encountering the `fail`. The code for `search_list()` is defined in figure 2.28. In this program, we will rely on two predicates to achieve our goal. The first predicate, `search_list()`, controls the backtracking process, and the sec-ond one, `do_search()`, takes care of manipulating the list stored in `our_list()` and asserting the individual items into the database as `list_item()` clauses. Prior to entering the repeat-fail cycle, we use the `retractall()` predicate to remove any previous clauses left in memory from prior executions because they are not removed from the database when a query is finished. Any predicate clauses asserted during the course of a query will remain in the active data-base until you either exit the Prolog system or remove them explic-itly with `retract()` or `retractall()`.

On encountering `repeat` and succeeding to the next goal, `search_list()` calls `do_search()`. This predicate is designed so that the first clause will succeed only when it finds an empty list stored in `our_list()`; otherwise, the second clause is called to remove the head of the list, store it in the database in a `list_item()` clause, and then replace the current list with only the tail of the list. To ensure that the procedure loops back for additional tries, this clause must not succeed. To accomplish this, the clause ends with a `fail`, thus guaranteeing that the goal cannot succeed. Unfor-tunately, the built-in backtracking mechanism of Prolog will cause the search to back up one goal in an attempt to find a different solu-tion for the predicate (a process that we do not want to happen here because it will keep trying to assert a new list into the database). To disable backtracking, we employ the Prolog cut (!). Essentially, this predicate stops the backtracking mechanism from going further back in the goal list. In other words, it tells Prolog that "if you cannot find a solution beyond this point, do not bother backtracking past it as no other alternatives exist prior to this point." In this example, the cut (!) and `fail` force Prolog to return to the calling predicate, backtracking there for a new solution—which, of course, is found when

Figure 2.28   The `search_list()` predicate.

```
search_list(L) :-
  retractall(our_list(_)),
  retractall(list_item(_)),
  assert(our_list(L)).
repeat,
do_search.
do_search :-
  our_list([]).
do_search :-
  our_list([H | Tail])),
  assert(list_item(H)),
  retract(our_list([H | Tail])),
  assert(our_list(Tail)),
  !, fail.
```

Figure 2.29   Frequently used Prolog I/O functions.

`see`(file name)	file becomes the current input stream
`seen`	closes the current input stream
`tell`(file name)	file becomes the current output stream
`told`	closes the current output stream
`read`(Term)	input Term from the current input device
`write`(Term)	output Term to the current output device
`put`(CharCode)	output character with the given ASCII code
`get0`(CharCode)	input next character as an ASCII code
`get`(CharCode)	input next "printable" character
`nl`	output a new line break
`tab`(N)	output N blanks
`consult`(file name)	read all clauses in file name, adding them to the database
`reconsult`(file name)	as above, but removes previously defined relations

the `repeat` goal is encountered and succeeds, thus forcing the goal search to move forward into `search_list()` once again. This process continues until `search_list()` succeeds. No further back-tracking will occur, and the query will succeed.

Input/Output

Although not essential to logic programming in Prolog, the understanding of basic input/output functions, particularly with regard to printing information to the screen, is still necessary for understanding some of the code examples provided in the book. For this reason, we have included a brief summary of some frequently used I/O Prolog functions, as shown in figure 2.29.

THREE

Introduction to Logic Programming

■ INTRODUCTION

In this chapter, we discuss basic principles underlying knowledge-based programming models, specifically as to how they are understood and manipulated within a Prolog environment. We examine how to go about defining a problem in terms of *state spaces*. We then explore how to interact with that model through standard search strategies employing *depth-first, breadth-first,* and *best-first* models. We conclude with an overview of AND/OR strategies designed to integrate these various models.

■ BASIC PROBLEM-SOLVING STRATEGIES

State Spaces   In seeking a solution to a knowledge-based problem, we must begin by codifying how to define the nature of the problem to be solved—both how we represent relevant information (*states*) and how we relate that information (*paths*). In other words, we want to view most knowledge-based problems as a set of factual, or known, pieces of information that are related through various associational assertions. For example, when looking out our window, we can conceptualize an answer to the question "Is that a bird that I see?" by comparing a number of facts in a manner that leads us to a credible

Figure 3.1   A sample state space.

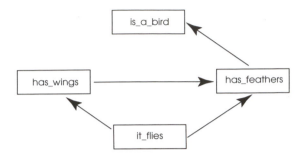

answer. In designing a heuristic for answering this query, we might choose to identify those traits or characteristics that we strongly associate with birds. Does it have feathers? Does it have wings? Does it fly? To a human way of thinking, any one of these three questions should suffice to define the questionable object if we were, in fact, looking at a bird and could draw on our past associations to reinforce our conclusion. On the other hand, a knowledge-based program has no such capacity and must be taught to draw on associations we frequently take for granted. Obviously, we might assume that something we see flying is likely to be a bird, but it could also be an airplane. Because airplanes do not have feathers, we can rely on our interrelating these two facts to draw a logical conclusion: *if* it has feathers *and* it flies, *then* it must be a bird. We need to be careful, though, or risk falling into additional logical traps. For example, because we know that not all birds can fly, our previous assertions will fail to identify the object as a bird if it is sitting on the ground. We might solve this dilemma simply by stating a second relationship: *if* it has feathers *and* it has wings, *then* it must be a bird.

When dealing with various logical states and the associative paths that bind them, it is helpful for us to think about the collective states as belonging to a *state space,* such as that shown in figure 3.1. To make our state space function as a problem solver, however, we must define all the possible paths, or logical connections, between the various nodes and incorporate relevant ways into and out of the model, thus completing a working model of our problem domain. For this purpose, we must define two additional states: *start nodes* and *goal nodes* (although there are several specific types of states, the term *nodes* will be used to refer generically to all states). As their names imply, these objects represent logical places to enter the state space (questions) and logical ways to exit that space (answers). Actually, these two nodes can be represented by any of the existing nodes in the state space. We need simply to define any states that can be representative of a query and any states that imply a resolution to that query. By allowing a number of states to function as start and goal nodes we are able to build into our model the power to deal with multiple problems or even different approaches to the same problem. For example, we may pose several other questions to our domain such as "Does the object have feathers?" or "Does it have wings?" and arrive at conclusive answers simply by defining different entry and exit points.

Finding Solutions

Finding solutions to problems represented in a state space requires three steps. Refer for the moment to the state space of figure 3.1. First, we must identify a goal node, or exit point from the space, that corresponds to the information we are seeking. In the case of the question "Is that a bird that I see?" the goal state corresponds to is_a_bird. Second, we must identify an appropriate start node, or entry point into the space. In this instance, we can enter the state space at any point other than the goal state, although all entry points may not lead logically to an appropriate conclusion. Finally, we need to seek a path that yields the desired answer by traversing the space so that we connect the start node with the goal node. For any given problem there may be several paths that would yield acceptable results, in which case it behooves us to develop additional strategies for identifying a *best* solution (or the *easiest* or *shortest*). In a sense, the path that we choose through the space becomes the *explanation* of that solution. We not only arrive at an answer to our query but also have the ability to examine the series of steps (states) that leads to that conclusion. In other words, we have not only an answer but also a means of explaining and re-creating the heuristic process that leads us to that answer.

Using this information, we can trace the logic that we draw on to find the answer. For example, by beginning at the state it_flies, we might arrive at the goal is_a_bird through either of the two paths shown in figure 3.2.

Additional paths can be explored by starting with the states has_wings or has_feathers, as shown in figure 3.3.

In trying to define a *best* way through the state, we must go through the process of determining just what constitutes a desirable strategy. In this instance, we might define the simplest way as being the best. If we pay attention to the defined state space, we should notice that in every case the only approach to the goal state is through the state

Figure 3.2   State-space traversals.

Path #1

Step #	State	Conclusion
1	it_flies	True
2	has_feathers	True
3	is_a_bird	True

Path #2

Step #	State	Conclusion
1	it_flies	True
2	has_wings	True
3	has_feathers	True
4	is_a_bird	True

Figure 3.3   Additional state-space traversals.

Path #3

Step #	State	Conclusion
1	has_wings	True
2	has_feathers	True
3	is_a_bird	True

Path #4

Step #	State	Conclusion
1	has_feathers	True
2	is_a_bird	True

has_feathers; or, more to the point, we could decide to eliminate all the other states because only one state is required to answer our query. Obviously, doing this would destroy the flexibility of the state space to deal with other pieces of information. For example, we can infer information from the state space that may not be explicitly defined within that state. Can we not assume that, if only birds and airplanes have wings and can fly, any failed attempt to assert that the object is a bird must conclude that the object is an airplane? Obviously, we cannot because we do not know why the query failed, leaving us with too many unresolved variables. For example, we do not know whether the object was flying or whether it had wings. Because each of our two associational paths required *two* pieces of information to be true, we need to know if either one *or* the other assertion in each path is true to deduce any usable information. With this *partial* information, however, we can draw conclusions only implicitly expressed

Figure 3.4 Chart of tonal progressions (from S. Kostka et al., *Tonal Harmony*, 3rd ed., 1997, McGraw-Hill. Produced with permission of The McGraw-Hill Companies).

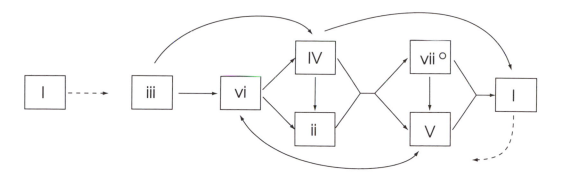

in the path. If our failed path shows that the object does have wings (implying that it has no feathers), for example, we can feel certain about identifying it as an airplane. Similarly, if it has feathers but still fails (in other words, it has no wings), we can definitely assert that it is neither a bird nor an airplane.

The ability to draw both direct and indirect associations from such a model makes it very powerful but also leaves it fraught with the potential to let us misread our logical intentions. Computer models cannot deduce rational assertions from irrational ones unless we teach them to do so in a manner that excludes all ambiguity. It is imperative that we define our assertions in a comprehensive manner that accounts for *all* the questions we are likely to ask of it. In other words, to ensure a successful design, we must limit the scope of our model to a specific area, or *domain,* of inquiry. Once we identify and achieve domain specificity, we are in a much better position to define all the relevant states and weigh all the possible paths that can function within that domain. In other words, effective knowledge-based systems must strive to work with *domain-specific* problems that can be comprehensively defined. Clearly, our initial question about the bird is fraught with ambiguity because the chosen domain is so broad as to include every possible living or human-made object that is perceived to fly, have feathers, or have wings!

Fortunately, music theory offers us several domains that are significantly more definable. We will focus our discussion around one such domain—diatonic tonal harmony—and develop more specific strategies for dealing with problem solving. Stefan Kostka and Dorothy Payne (1989) offer a simple and interesting way to model

Figure 3.5   a) A sample tree structure.

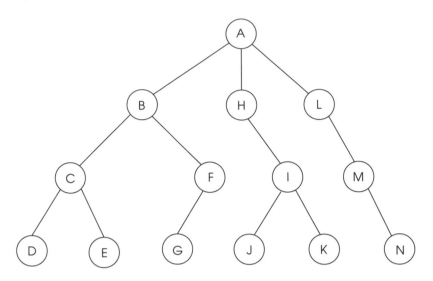

diatonic progressions using a diagrammatic representation quite similar—in fact, identical—to a state space. Figure 3.4, drawn from their book *Tonal Harmony,* shows this representation. To use the model, we need simply to start at any given point in the diagram and follow the arrows until reaching a desired state. (Dotted lines represent a motion to any other point in the diagram.)

■ SEARCH STRATEGIES

We can observe from our previous discussion that the process of determining an answer, or deducing the validity of a piece of information, is carried out by searching a path through a state space. For this reason most general knowledge-based heuristics are referred to as *search* strategies. The remainder of this chapter deals with four such heuristic models: *depth-first, breadth-first, iterative deepening,* and *best-first* search strategies.

Depth-First Search Strategies

In dealing with any given state space, we must first seek to organize our node structure in such a way as to clarify the process of seeking

Figure 3.5   b) A tree structure after figure 3.1.

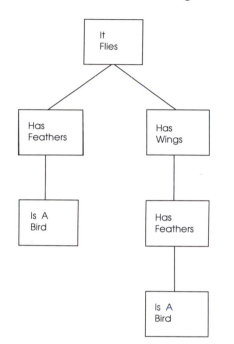

an answer. In a more complex state space, such as one we might model after those in figures 3.1 and 3.2, we can quickly get lost in the process of working through the various combinations of pathways. In other words, the exponential nature of the search quickly proves a significant hurdle for us when working in such an unfocused way. To facilitate our quest, we can redesign our state space into a series of downward-branching *trees,* where we first assign descending entry paths into the top of each relevant node and then assign any number of possible descending branches leading out of that node and into additional lower nodes. Several examples of this can be seen in figures 3.5. The top of the tree (*root*) represents the one possible start state for that domain, and any bottom node represents a possible goal state. Because any given query may have more than one goal, or because the same start state may be used to trace answers to different queries, our tree can have more than one bottom branch. Since these conceptualized trees are structures that enable us to seek answers by employing consistent "downward" paths from top (query) to bottom (goal), we refer to such searches as *depth first,* meaning we find a successful path by simply moving down to the bottom.

Figure 3.6 A tree diagram after Kostka and Payne (1989).

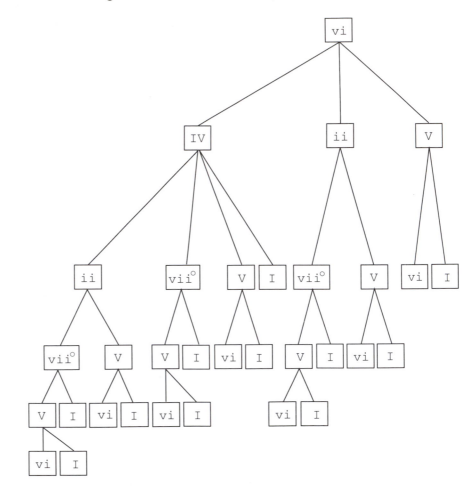

■ **Defining Searches**   If we attempt to build a tree structure for the tonal diatonic model in figure 3.4, we might have an extremely difficult time because there are any number of entry points into the diagram and numerous sets of interrelated and backward-pointing links. We can use *separate* trees, however, to represent different queries within that model by defining each tree as a set of possible progressions starting from *one* harmony (entry state) and leading to all acceptable culminations (goal state). In other words, we define a tree for each possible start node that incorporates all the possible paths leading to a goal note—the tonic harmony in this instance. Figure 3.6 show an example of such a tree beginning with the submediant (vi) harmony.

Traversing this tree in a depth-first manner is relatively straight-forward. Let us assume, for example, that we want to find any acceptable progression from the submediant (vi) to the tonic (I). We begin at the top of the tree and follow the *left-most* path (we could just as easily do a *right-most* search) until we reach a terminal node. If that node represents the tonic, then the search is complete and the nodes encountered through the descent represent an acceptable progression. If the terminal node does not constitute a tonic then a different path must be found. Because depth-first strategies demand that we seek always to go down, any motion back up the tree must be seen as counterproductive. Our search, therefore, should go backward only so far as to find the *next possible downward path*—in this case, usually one node above the current location. This process of *backtracking* is essential to the mechanisms of tree searching because it enables us to achieve, not only *an* answer but *all* possible solutions. In this example, if we follow the left-most branches throughout, we quickly arrive at a terminal node through the progression vi-IV-ii-vii°-V-vi. This answer, unfortunately, is not the one we are seeking, since it fails to arrive at a tonic harmony. Backtracking forces the search to move up one node at a time until another possible downward path can be found. In this instance, we need go back only one node to the dominant, where we find a different downward path. Without further backtracking, we move down the new path, this time arriving at a terminal node (a tonic chord) and our search is completed. The path we took (vi-IV-ii-vii°-V-I) represents one possible choice for a successful solution to our query.

If we want to find numerous solutions to the query, we can search using two additional steps: first, when reaching a terminal node, we store that progression and second, we cause backtracking to occur regardless of the answer we just acquired. This way, we cause our search to find all the possible solutions in the tree. Because we use the left-most rule, when we are done searching we arrive at the ordered list of progressions shown in figure 3.7.

Notice that different branches and nodes of the tree shown in several of the previous examples share a significant amount of duplicated information. One of the ways we can remove the redundancy—and in effect "tighten up" our logic—is to allow trees and nodes to be treated as synonymous. Instead of examining a node solely on the basis of the data in it, we must successfully traverse a subtree down to a subgoal before taking one of the paths leading down from it. In other words, instead of assuming the validity of a

Figure 3.7   Ordered list of progressions.

```
vi-IV-ii-vii°-V-vi
vi-IV-ii-vii°-V-I
vi-IV-ii-vii°-I
vi-IV-ii-V-vi
vi-IV-ii-V-I
vi-IV-vii°-V-vi
vi-IV-vii°-V-I
vi-IV-vii°-I
vi-IV-V-vi
vi-IV-V-I
vi-IV-I
vi-ii-vii°-V-vi
vi-ii-vii°-V-I
vi-ii-vii°-I
vi-ii-V-vi
vi-ii-V-I
vi-V-vi
vi-V-I
```

Figure 3.8   A three-dimensional tree.

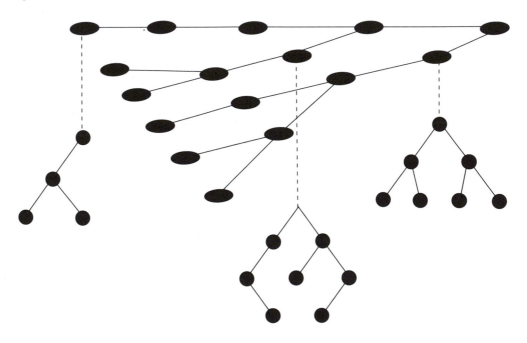

node solely on the basis of the data it represents, we must assume validity on the basis of the result of a subtree traversal. If the subtree reaches an acceptable subgoal, the parent node is validated. Likewise, if an acceptable subgoal is not met, the node is invalidated and backtracking occurs within the parent tree. The goal of a subtree may even represent the goal of the entire query, thus terminating the search without returning to the parent tree.

We can attempt to visualize this concept as a multidimensional structure, for example, representing any primary tree in a vertical plane and any subtrees in a horizontal plane. A three-dimensional example can be seen in figure 3.8.

Complexities leading to more than three dimensions, however, make this model quite difficult to conceptualize. We can draw an easier correlation simply by laying trees beside one another and drawing links between them or even simply by referring to them by an index or a name. In reality, when programming trees and subtrees, we usually represent them as separate blocks of program code that are called from one another when required. Figure 3.9 shows the three-dimensional tree of figure 3.8 in this new manner.

Essentially, we can follow the same strategy and break the previous tree of example 3.6 into one parent tree and two subtrees, thus avoiding a lot of duplicate information. One of our subtrees contains all those relationships common to progressions from the dominant and leading-tone harmonies (V/vii°), whereas another subtree contains the first subtree *plus* all the additional relationships from the subdominant and supertonic harmonies (IV/ii). The parent tree contains relationships from the vi chord as well as the two previous subtrees. The results of our reworked model appear in figure 3.10.

Going even further, we can see that there is additional duplication within the first subtree that can be separated into an additional subtree, as is shown in figure 3.11.

Undertaking a search for a possible path through this model is straightforward. Let us assume that we are seeking any allowable progression from the submediant triad (vi) to the tonic triad (I). We enter the state at the top node shown in the first tree of figure 3.6 and choose a possible path to take. Assuming that the search always goes left-most first, we begin by moving down to that node representing the subtree of the subdominant/supertonic (IV/ii). Once again, the search takes us down the left branch of that subtree, where we encounter first the subdominant node (IV), then the supertonic node (ii), and finally another subtree. Our query ends when we traverse the remainder of the second subtree, finding that

Figure 3.9   A three-dimensional tree.

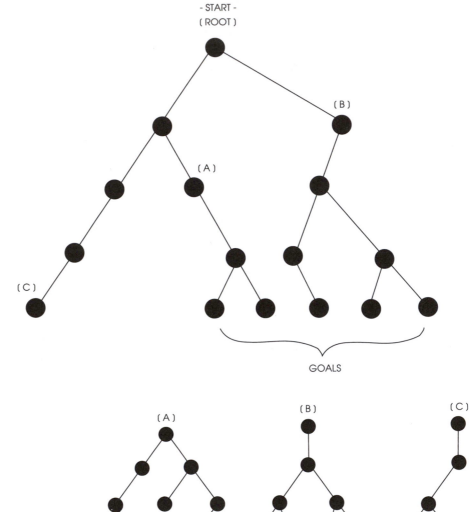

Figure 3.10   A three-dimensional tree after figure 3.6.

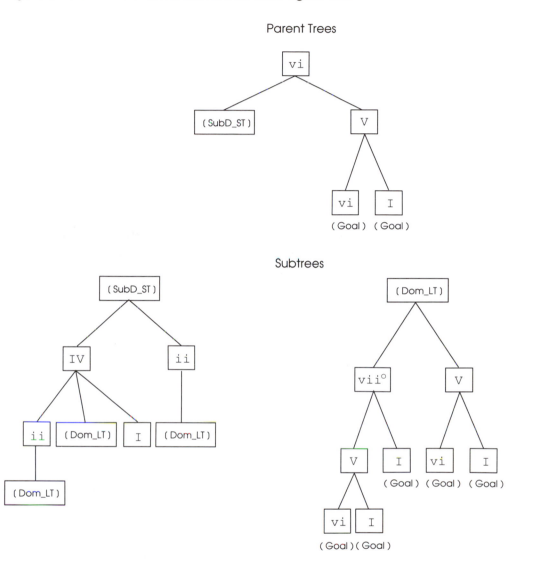

Figure 3.11   A further reduction of figure 3.10.

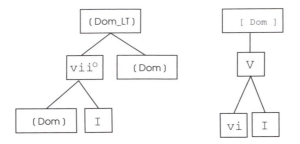

we have successfully reached a terminal node. Because the goal we attain is a submediant and not a tonic, we backtrack one node within the current subtree and attain an acceptable solution with the progression vi-IV-ii-vii°-V-I.

▧ Forward and Backward Chaining

In the examples that we have seen so far, our searches have always looked down the tree in search of an answer, taking paths without really knowing what solution will be found. This process is referred to as *forward chaining.* Such a strategy can cause us significant problems when searching for not just any but some specific answer. So far, however, we knew the answer that we wanted (the tonic triad) and we were really looking for a way to solve the steps needed to validate that answer. This second process is referred to as *backward chaining.* In a sense, forward and backward chaining can be thought of as a question seeking an answer and an answer seeking a question, respectively. One way to alter our tree of figure 3.6 to reflect the backward-chaining nature of our inquiry is to flip the data on the vertical axis. In this way, the top node represents the tonic, and the bottom goal nodes represent possible entry points, or queries. Because we know where we want to end up, we can derive a valid path to the question by traversing down the tree to a goal node, just as we do in a forward-chaining model, and then reverse the results to obtain an appropriate solution. A reversed version of this tree is shown in figure 3.12.

In this instance, using a backward-chaining model has a distinct advantage: it requires significantly fewer steps to complete a query because it requires no backtracking when looking for a specific solution, unless we limit the goal nodes we deem acceptable. On the downside, our tree is no longer able to support multiple answers

Figure 3.12   a) Backward-chaining models from figure 3.6.

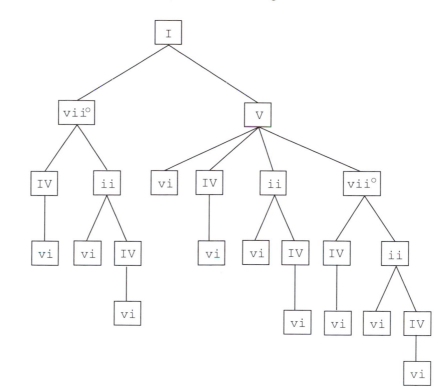

(root nodes); however, we now have the option of discovering different starting points instead—in essence, just the opposite of the forward-chaining tree. Our answers might be considerably different, however, without sufficient heuristic controls to guide the query. If, for example, we use the same left-most approach to search the tree in figure 3.12a that we used with figure 3.6 earlier, we get vi-IV-vii°-I (the reverse of I-vii°-IV-vi). This different result is directly attributable to the changed nature of the tree: the top-to-bottom ordering is reversed, but the left-to-right ordering is not. In other words, we have not completely reversed *every aspect* of the tree as we do in the tree shown in figure 3.12b. The same left-most search of this tree results in vi-IV-ii-vii°-V-I (the reverse of I-V-vii°-ii-IV-vi), the same as that found in the previous left-most forward-chaining search of the tree in figure 3.6. This complete reversal is not essential; indeed, only if we choose to use a search

Figure 3.12   b) Backward-chaining models from figure 3.6.

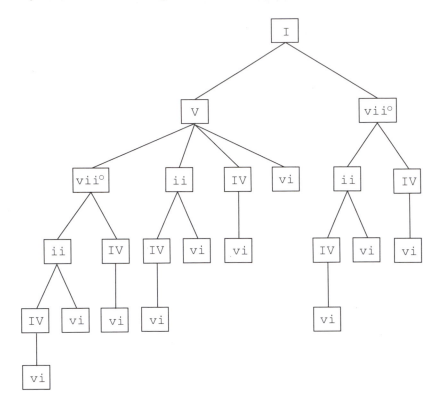

heuristic that is *tied to the structure of the tree* do we run the risk of inconsistent results. As long as our heuristics deal with the data and relevant interrelations on the basis of those data, we should have no problems with mixing forward- and backward-chaining queries. In reality, we do not need to think about backward-chaining trees at all because the Prolog backtracking mechanism enables both forward and backward chaining to take place without any of the reversal problems shown earlier.

■ **Programming Depth-First Searches**   When we program searches in Prolog (or any other applicable language for that matter), it is important to bear in mind that trees are simply representational models of state diagrams, which are themselves only conceptual models of how we attempt to comprehend a particular domain. Our data models and actual search heuristics

Figure 3.13 Factual predicates of harmonic progressions.

```
from_to('I','ii').        from_to('I','iii').
from_to('I','IV').        from_to('I','V').
from_to('I','vi').        from_to('I','vii°').
from_to('ii','V').        from_to('ii','vii°').
from_to('iii','IV').      from_to('iii','vi').
from_to('IV','I').        from_to('IV','ii').
from_to('IV','V').        from_to('IV','vii°').
from_to('V','I').         from_to('V','vi').
from_to('vi','ii').       from_to('vi','IV').
from_to('vi','V').        from_to('vii°','I').
from_to('vii°','V').
```

need only emulate the conceptual nature of the tree and not the tree itself. Fortunately, the structure of Prolog *predicates* strongly represents both the structure of trees and the depth-first searching strategy they are inherently designed to facilitate yet does it without some of the inherent structural limitations.

Prolog also simplifies the process of literally having to predesign trees for every possible path through the domain. Usually, we need only to define each data node once and identify only those immediate paths related to that node and its adjacent neighbors. For example, we might define a node to represent the submediant triad (`vi`) and then define the three possible paths leading down from it: `vi-IV`, `vi-ii`, and `vi-V`. Similarly, a definition of the paths leading from the supertonic harmony (`ii`) would include `ii-vii°` and `ii-V`. In a sense, we are enabling the construction and manipulation of numerous trees without the need to replicate the data because Prolog is designed to build treelike search structures for us as long as we supply the appropriate data connections. In a sense, even though we rely on such structures as the tree in figure 3.6 to inform our logic, we can now concentrate on defining our data and not on the structure of the tree. Whether we choose to rely on trees (figure 3.6) or networks (figure 3.2), as long as our links are the way we want them, Prolog will manage the structure for us. For the remainder of this discussion, we will utilize this form of data model, shown in its entirety in figure 3.13.

For accessing these data, we define a domain-traversal heuristic `get_progression()`. This predicate requires two arguments: an indicated starting harmony (`StrtChord`) and an unbound variable (`Prog`) for returning the completed progression. Also, `get_progression()` must accommodate three separate states of the list

Figure 3.14   The `get_progression()` predicate.

```
%empty list

    get_progression(StrtChord,[],Prog) :- !,
        get_progression(StrtChord,[StrtChord],Prog).
%completed
    get_progression('I',Prog,Prog) :-
        list_length(Prog,N),
        N > 2,
        write(Prog),nl,!.

%not done

    get_progression(StrtChord,OldProg,Prog) :-
        from_to(StrtChord,NextChord),
        check_for_deceptive_cadence(NextChord,OldProg,Test),
        Test \= done,
        append(OldProg,[NextChord],NewProg),
        get_progression(NextChord,NewProg,Prog).

%utility clauses

    check_for_deceptive_cadence('vi',['V','vi'|_],done) :- !.
    check_for_deceptive_cadence(Chord,[_|Tail],X) :-
        check_for_deceptive_cadence(Chord,Tail,X).
    check_for_deceptive_cadence(_,[],notdone) :- !.

    list_length([],0).                          % from Ch. 2; figure 2.13
    list_length([_|Tail],N) :-
        list_length(Tail,N1),
        N is 1 + N1,!.
```

`Prog`: (1) the list is empty, (2) the list contains a complete progression, and (3) anything else. The complete code for `get_progression()` is shown in figure 3.14.

The first clause deals with the empty list. Assuming that the progression list we supply is empty, this clause appends our requested starting chord onto the end of the list because it is this location from where harmonies are drawn for future comparisons. The second clause is used to terminate the predicate, assuming that we have a progression with more than two chords and the last chord selected. From this location, we can print out the resultant progression (as we do here), store it for later, process it, or do anything else we might choose to do with it. The third clause is where we process all other conditions of the list. Essentially, this clause emulates a tree traversal by matching acceptable pairs of harmonies with the factual database instances of the predicate `from_to()`. When Prolog finds an acceptable pair by binding a new match to the last harmony in the progression list, the newly selected chord is appended to the end of the list and becomes the next chord for comparison following a recursive call to `get_progression()`. In this clause, we must watch out for one problematic aspect of the harmonic model. Because the dominant chord (`V`) essentially can move "backward" in the state space by progressing to the submediant harmony (`vi`) instead of the tonic (`I`), we run the risk finding ourselves in an endless loop where `V` progresses to `vi`, which in turn progresses to `V`, which then progresses to `vi`, ad infinitum! The way we choose to avoid that problem here is to check for the deceptive cadence (`V-vi`) and make sure it occurs only once in the progression. If it occurs a second time, the choice is thrown out and a backtracking solution sought—in this case, `V-I` because the dominant has only two possible avenues of progression. Our predicate `check_for_ deceptive_cadence()` recursively searches the existing progression list, checking for the specified pair of harmonies. If one is found to exist—in other words, a progression was previously encountered and appended to the progression list—then a flag is set to `done`, causing the calling predicate to `fail`. Notice that the very first statement of the first clause is the Prolog *cut* (`!`). We place this here so that this entire clause will be bypassed if any backtracking occurs. Without the cut, backtracking into the clause causes the program to unbind the variable `StrtChord` and make a new recursive call, passing in the unbound variable. When the second clause is executed as a result of the recursion, it simply binds any valid values (i.e., valid to Prolog, not to our logic) to `StrtChord` and generates progressions that are not restricted to starting with the user-specified harmony.

Using the data from figure 3.13, we can follow a hypothetical execution of `get_progression()`. We can step through the process by following the trace shown in figure 3.15. We have added line numbers to aid the process. We begin by calling the predicate at #1.

This call succeeds on the first clause because the list we supply is empty. The chord from the first argument is then inserted into the list and the predicate is called recursively as in line #2. The second time around the third clause succeeds by calling the predicate at line #3 and having it returning line #4. After we check that these chords are not part of a deceptive cadence, `NextChord` is appended to the end of the list, and the predicate is called recursively once again with `NextChord` now substituted for the original starting chord. This process greatly facilitates the functioning of the predicate because pulling an element off the end of a list is very

Figure 3.15   Trace of `get_progression()`.

```
#1:   get_progression('IV',[],Prog).
#2:   get_progression('IV',['IV'],Prog).
#3:   from_to('IV',NextChord)
#4:   NextChord = 'I'
#5:   get_progression('I',['IV','I'],Prog)
#6:   from_to('I',NextChord)
#7:   NextChord = 'ii'
#8:   get_progression('ii',['IV','I','ii'],Prog)
#9:   get_progression('V',['IV','I','ii','V'], Prog)
#10:  Progression = ['IV','I','ii','V','I'].
```

computationally intensive. Storing it separately and passing through the call in this way allows it to be accessed without having to parse the list to get to it. The recursive call appears in line #5. The next call, line #6, repeats the process, returning the results bound as in line #7. After checking for deceptive cadences, the next two recursive calls, lines #8 and #9, bring us to our first encounter with the second clause. Since our current chord matches 'I' and the progression is longer than two chords, the predicate succeeds, binding the variable `Prog` as in line #10.

By inserting one or more chords into the list prior to the call, we can get the predicate to build onto these predetermined data, giving us greater initial flexibility than what we might gain simply by supplying a starting chord. To make it work, though, we must include the starting chord (actually the last chord in the preexisting progression) at the end of the supplied list. For example,

```
get_progression('ii',['iii','IV','ii'],Prog).
```

This predicate brings out one of the inherent problems with emulating trees in Prolog: the language automatically attempts left-most searches and therefore always arrives at the same answers in the same order. In reality, because we do not build actual trees, the order that clauses are asserted into the working memory dictates the order that they are accessed by Prolog. Or, to put it another way, the first, or top-most, element in a list is analogous to the top-most, left-most node in a tree. Because our data (as shown in figure 3.13) are arranged differently than in the tree of figure 3.6, our answers will be different as well. Reorganizing the data in a tree-specific manner requires that we manually traverse the entire tree in a left-most fashion and organize our Prolog data accordingly. We can

Figure 3.16   Rearranged data from figure 3.13.

```
from_to('I','ii').              from_to('I','iii').
from_to('I','IV').              from_to('I','V').
from_to('I','vi').              from_to('I','vii°').
from_to('ii','vii°').           from_to('ii','V').
from_to('vi','IV').             from_to('vi','ii').
from_to('vi','V').              from_to('iii','vi').
from_to('iii','IV').            from_to('IV','ii').
from_to('IV','vii°').           from_to('IV','V').
from_to('IV','I').              from_to('V','I').
from_to('V','vi').              from_to('vii°','V').
from_to('vii°','I').
```

Figure 3.17   The `generate_progressions()` predicate.

```
generate_progressions(StrtChord)  :-
   get_progression(StrtChord,[],Progression),
   evaluate_progression(Progression),
   fail.
generate_progressions(_).
```

rearrange the data from figure 3.13 to reflect a direct correlation with the tree of figure 3.6, as shown in figure 3.16.

To force our predicate to do something else, we need to use additional control heuristics, the simplest being the built-in `fail` predicate. By appending a `fail` to the end of the second, or terminating, clause we force backtracking to occur until all possible solutions are found, essentially undertaking a traversal of the entire tree. Moreover, because we may wish to evaluate each solution after it is found, a better method dictates that we create a second predicate that calls the current one, undertakes any required evaluations, and executes the `fail`. In this way, our predicate `get_progression()` is left untouched, yet we still can generate and evaluate every possible progression derived from the search. This new predicate, `generate_progressions()`, is shown in figure 3.17.

Another way to ensure a variety of answers—albeit one fraught with its own potential inefficiencies—is to rearrange the tree during the execution of the program. By using the side effect properties of Prolog (in other words, the ability for the program to rewrite itself during its own execution), we ensure a number of different and often unpredictable solutions. To facilitate this process, we need only to insert these two lines of code into the last clause of the predicate `get_progression()` immediately preceding the `append()` command:

```
retract(from_to(StrtChord,NextChord)),
assertz(from_to(StrtChord,NextChord)),
```

As each pair of chords is tested, that pair is removed from its current location and placed at the end of the list, and the result is a reordered tree. Ideally, this method sounds like a useful way to infuse a sense of randomness into the process. Unfortunately, because only one set of `StrtChord` values are moved and the others are not, our altered procedure ends up repeating certain progressions. In addition, by moving nodes around, our `fail`-based traversals no longer guarantee that searches will encounter each node, thus negating our ability to generate *all* possible paths. Essentially, some nodes may be moved that do not effect the next search, whereas others may get moved numerous times, creating a situation for us that causes some possibilities to be avoided altogether. For this reason particularly, we do not encourage the widespread use of side-effect strategies. We do offer one exception to this rule, however: when testing and debugging a heuristic for which you want apparently random data for generating a variety of test situations. As long as the routines are removed from the program once the testing is done and the data are restored to the original tree-based order, we can use them to our advantage.

Before moving our discussion to other search strategies, one more example should help to solidify our understanding of tree-based models. Up to this point, our searching has relied on a tree structure in which every downward path terminates with either a tonic (I) or a submediant (vi) harmony. It is a simple matter for us, however, to define any point in the tree as a terminal node without having to restructure new trees to reflect the change. When we recall our statement that trees are not true structures but only conceptual models, it becomes a simple matter for us to conceptualize various stopping points in one tree, thus gaining a significant degree of flexibility. Carried to its fullest, we can then formulate a domain model consisting simply of *one* tree, in which we can enter and exit at any point we desire. In other words, we conceive of any complete traversal between two points in the tree as being analogous to a subtree traversal.

We can explore this model simply by restructuring our predicate `get_progression()` to take into account not only variable starting points, `StrtNode`, but also variable ending nodes; `EndNode`. We

Figure 3.18 The `generate_var_progressions()` predicate.

```
generate_var_progressions(StrtChord,EndChord) :-
  get_var_progression(StrtChord,EndChord,[],Prog),
  evaluate_progression(Prog),
  fail.
generate_var_progressions(_,_).

  get_var_progression(StrtChord,EndChord,[],Prog) :- !,
    get_var_progression(StrtChord,EndChord,[StrtChord],Prog).
  get_var_progression(EndChord,EndChord,Prog,Prog) :-
    list_length(Prog,N),
    N > 2,
    write(Prog),nl,!.
  get_var_progression(StrtChord,EndChord,OldProg,Prog) :-
    from_to(StrtChord,NextChord),
    check_for_repeat(StrtChord,NextChord,OldProg,Test),
    Test \= done,
    append(OldProg,[NextChord],NewProg),
    get_var_progression(NextChord,EndChord,NewProg,Prog).

  check_for_repeat(Strt,Next,[Strt,Next|_],done) :- !.
  check_for_repeat(Strt,Next,[_|Tail],X) :-
    check_for_repeat(Strt,Next,Tail,X).
  check_for_repeat(_,_,[],notdone) :- !.
```

call this variant predicate `get_var_progression()`. The code appears in figure 3.18.

You should immediately note several changes. First, we pass in values for *both* starting and ending harmonies. Second, we replace the predicate `check_for_deceptive_cadence()` with the predicate `check_for_repeat()`. Within the limited scope of the Kostka and Payne's model of figure 3.4, the original check presents a particular problem when ending a progression on something other than the tonic. It is possible to continue looping through chord pairs without ever encountering a deceptive cadence, and, because tonics do not stop the search, we run the risk of entering into an infinite loop, such as would happen with the following pattern:

$$['ii','V','I','ii','V','I','ii','V','I','ii','V','I',$$
$$'ii','V','I','ii','V','I', \ldots \ldots \text{etc.}]$$

One possible way to circumvent the problem would be to look for any pair of repeated harmonies, allowing no more that one repetition of any

Figure 3.19   Revision of `check_for_repeat()` from figure 3.18.

```
check_for_repeat(StrtChrd,NextChrd,OldProgression,Test) :-
  check_for_3rd_repeat(1,StrtChrd,NextChrd,OldProgression,Test).

%previous deceptive cadence

  check_for_3rd_repeat(_,'V','vi',['V','vi'|_],done) :- !.
  check_for_3rd_repeat(3,_,_,_,done) :- !.
  check_for_3rd_repeat(CNT,StrtC,NextC,[StrtC,NextC|Tail],X) :-
    CNT2 is CNT + 1,
    check_for_3rd_repeat(CNT2,StrtC,NextC,Tail,X),!.
  check_for_3rd_repeat(CNT,StrtC,NextC,[_|Tail],X) :-
    check_for_3rd_repeat(CNT,StrtC,NextC,Tail,X).
  check_for_3rd_repeat(_,_,_,[],notdone) :- !.
```

pair. This strategy, however, raises additional problems because it fails to recognize many of the valid progressions found with `get_progression()` that *do* have repeated pairs, such as the following:

['ii','V','vi','IV','ii','V','I']

The problem is easy to understand. In our first predicate of figure 3.18, we still had a check-and-balance system in place that terminated the progression consistently, even though we had repetitions of certain progressions. Without the tonic termination, we must rely on some other criteria to get us out of the loop—in this case, by looking at *all* duplicated progressions.

There are other ways we can do this that will lead us closer to an equitable solution. For example, we might revise the predicate `check_for_repeat` to allow for a maximum of two repetitions instead of one, canceling the search only on reaching a third attempt. This strategy restores the bulk of the progressions found previously and adds a great deal more. Unfortunately, many of the additional progressions are the result of allowing multiple occurrences of the deceptive cadence. By putting in a separate clause specifically to allow only one occurrence of the deceptive progression, our code comes even closer to achieving a better balance, allowing repetitions of most progressions yet avoiding excessive V-vi progressions. The code for this revision appears in figure 3.19

Or we might choose to search for recurring tonics because the lack of a tonic completion fouls the previous approach. We can limit the progression so that it contains a maximum of two tonic iterations and/or one deceptive cadence, whichever comes first. The

Figure 3.20   Revision of `check_for_repeat()` from figure 3.19.

```
check_for_repeat(StrtChord,NextChord,OldProgression,Test) :-
  check_for_3rd_repeat(1,StrtChord,NextChord,OldProg,Test).

    check_for_3rd_repeat(_,'V','vi',['V','vi'|_],done) :- !.
    check_for_3rd_repeat(3,_,_,_,done) :- !.
    check_for_3rd_repeat(CNT,'I',NextChord,['I'|Tail],X) :-
      CNT2 is CNT + 1,
      check_for_3rd_repeat(CNT2,'I',NextChord,Tail,X),!.
    check_for_3rd_repeat(CNT,StrtChord,NextChord,[_|Tail],X) :-
      check_for_3rd_repeat(CNT,StrtChord,NextChord,Tail,X).
    check_for_3rd_repeat(_,_,_,[],notdone) :- !.
```

Figure 3.21   Final version of `generate_var_progressions()`.

```
        generate_var_progressions(Lnth,StrtChord,EndChord) :-
          get_var_progression(Lnth,StrtChord,EndChord,[],Prog),
          evaluate_progression(Prog),
          fail.
        generate_var_progressions(_,_,_).
          get_var_progression(Lnth,StrtC,EndC,[],Prog) :- !,
            get_var_progression(Lnth,StrtC,EndC,[StrtC],Prog).
          get_var_progression(Lnth,EndC,EndC,Prog,Prog) :-
            list_length(Prog,N),
            N = Lnth,
            write(Prog),nl,!.
          get_var_progression(Lnth,StrtC,EndC,OldProg,Prog) :-
            from_to(StrtC,NextC),
            list_length(OldProg,N),
            N < Lnth,
            append(OldProg,[NextC],NewProg),
            get_var_progression(Lnth,NextC,EndC,NewProg,Prog).
```

revised code for this routine appears in figure 3.20. Or we might choose to search for recurring tonics because the lack of a tonic completion fouls the previous approach. We can limit the progression so that it contains a maximum of two tonic iterations and/or one deceptive cadence, whichever comes first. The revised code for this routine appears in figure 3.21. Finally, we might choose to limit the total length of the progression, enabling the user to supply that information as part of the query. Because this sort of routine is most likely used in consideration with other musical parameters (such as melody or bass harmonization, which are metric considerations), we stand a much better chance of arriving at acceptable results by incorporating more intuitive heuristics. In this instance, the predicate is redesigned so that we can specify a starting harmony, an ending harmony, *and* a progression length. The final revised heuristic is shown in figure 3.21.

Essentially, we eliminate all checking for repeated progressions, relying instead on knowing fixed starting and ending points and knowing what length to accept. If the length of the progression does not fit the value we supply with our query, it simply employs backtracking until a suitable solution, if any, is found. Notice that we duplicate a length check in two different clauses of get_var_progression(). We need the double check because we set the heuristic up to accept only a harmonization of the specified length (Lnth). The first check occurs in the third clause, ensuring that our search does not go beyond the limit set in the query. Because progressions might arrive at the ending chord through a progression of fewer harmonies, we also have to make sure that they are deemed unacceptable, hence the additional length check in the second clause. Without this latter check, our predicate would return all appropriate progressions *less than or equal to* the specified length—perhaps a desirable characteristic but not the one we set out to achieve.

Breadth-First Search Strategies

Despite the flexibility of manipulating tree structures and conceptualizing traversal schemes, depth-first searching is not without its drawbacks. For example, because downward paths are always preferred over lateral choices, longest paths are often found first or, at least, are equally possible options to shorter ones. In fact, if we are not careful when deploying various search strategies, depth-first searches may be subject to potentially infinite downward iteration when dealing with trees of unknown depth. One way to solve this problem is to move laterally "across" the tree before traversing down. This type of search strategy is termed *breadth first* because lateral motion is *always* preferred over vertical motion within any tree. For example, we can do a partial alphabet tree in a manner that reflects breadth-first ordering as opposed to depth-first order. This tree appears in figure 3.22

Unlike depth-first searches, breadth-first ones will always find the shortest path first. This phenomenon results from *all* the choices at a given level being evaluated before searching down to another

Figure 3.22   A breadth-first search tree.

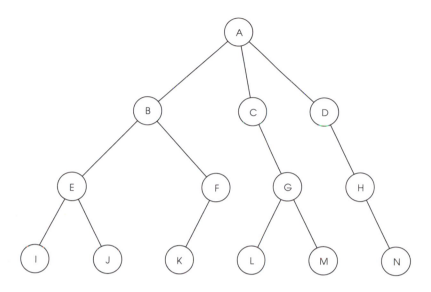

level. Although finding the shortest solution can be to our advantage in certain situations, implementing breadth-first searches is not without its own difficulties because the design complexity level takes a significant leap over that of depth-first searches. Prolog is built around a depth-first model and, obviously, works easiest in that manner. We can, however, implement a breadth-first search in Prolog without undue difficulty *if* we have the memory capability in our computer to handle the addition recursive data storage requirements imposed by the model. As we search through our domain, we must keep track of every possible path from the starting node to the current level each time we move one level down the tree. This record keeping is the only practical way to enable the program to return to a previous path, if necessary, and continue searching down from where it left off.

Let us assume for the moment that we are implementing a breadth-first search heuristic to find a harmonic progression beginning on a supertonic chord (ii) and ending on a submediant (vi). To facilitate the search, we first need to keep track of every possible "next step" from the supertonic. Assuming the same tree data used previously, our search begins with

```
['ii', 'viiº']
```

Before we continue, this partial progression is placed into storage while the heuristic returns to the initial node and seeks an additional solution. The second time, we find

```
['ii','V']
```

At this point, and only because we have searched and found *every acceptable path* from the supertonic, we continue to the next level. Before doing that, however, we need to restore our original progression, hence the need for a lot more computer memory to store and recover *every* progression our heuristic will generate.

Continuing, our search moves down one level, restores the first of the original search paths, and again seeks out every additional acceptable path beginning from that previous search. In this case the search restores

```
['ii','vii°']
```

and now generates and stores the following additional paths:

```
['ii','vii°','V']
['ii','vii°','I']
```

These are followed by a restoration of

```
['ii','V'],
```

which in turn generates and stores

```
['ii','V','vi']
['ii','V','I']
```

At this point, it is clear that we have finally attained an acceptable solution, having searched and stored a total of six possible paths. If we had used a depth-first approach, we would have arrived at an equally acceptable but longer solution,

```
['ii','vii','V','vi'],
```

albeit one that would be found on the *very first attempt,* thus negating any storage needs other than for this one progression.

Programming Breadth-First Searches

To facilitate an actual programming heuristic, we need to translate the "search, store, and restore" cycle into an effective recursive predicate. We approach this problem by thinking of a cyclic storage structure—in this case, a list—in which we can remove a progression from the front of the list and check to see if it is already an acceptable solution. If it is not acceptable, we search for all next-level extensions and finally store any new progressions at the end of the list. By following these steps, we progressively work through a list, attempting to extend every progression in that list. Because all successful extensions are added to the end of the list, they will eventually work their way to the head of the list for future evaluation as well.

As an example, let us revisit the same problem we just examined but now implemented with this newly proposed list model. We call our algorithm with an initial list (each progression is represented as its own list) containing one progression representing the beginning, or current, state of our query. This progression, which is actually just a single chord at this point, represents the root node of our search. For this example, we begin with the harmony:

```
[ ['ii'] ]
```

The initial step of the algorithm instructs us to remove the first progression from the list—in this case, the progression consisting of the ii chord we supplied initially—leaving us with a null list:

```
[ ]
```

Next, we check to see if the extracted progression is an acceptable solution. Because it has not yet arrived at our desired terminal harmony (vi), we search for all acceptable progressions emanating from this progression, finally inserting them at the end of the list. Because at the moment the primary structure is a null ([ ]) list, appending the two new progressions results in

```
[ ['ii','vii°'] , ['ii','V'] ]
```

We now repeat this process by once again removing the first progression;

```
['ii','vii°']
```

leaving the original list with

```
[ ['ii','V'] ].
```

We now check to see if the removed progression is acceptable, and because it is not, we search for all acceptable extensions, in this case

```
['ii', 'vii°', 'V']
['ii', 'vii°', 'I']
```

Because several are found, we insert them at the end of the original list:

```
[ ['ii','V'],['ii','vii°','V'],['ii','vii°','I'] ]
```

This process again repeats itself. First, we remove the head progression and check it for acceptability (in this case, it is not). Then we generate any new possible extensions (there are two) and append them to the end of the list, resulting in

```
[ ['ii','vii°','V'],['ii','vii°','I'],['ii','V','vi'],
    ['ii','V','I'] ]
```

According to the algorithm, we continue to examine each of the three-note progressions, checking them for acceptability, deleting them from the list, looking for acceptable four-note extensions, and adding them to the end of the list. The process ends (succeeds) when our list appears as

```
[ ['ii','V','vi'] ,['ii','V','I'] ,
    ['ii','vii°',  'V','vi'],
['ii','vii°','V','I'],['ii','vii°','I','ii'],
['ii','vii°','I','iii'],['ii','vii°','I','IV'],
['ii','vii°','I','V'] ['ii','vii°','I','vi'],
['ii','vii°','I','vii°'] ]
```

because the progression

```
['ii','V','vi']
```

finally achieves the head of the list, is removed, and is determined to be an acceptable solution. An actual implementation of this heuristic appears in figure 3.23.

We engage this heuristic by calling the predicate `breadth_first()`, supplying bound values for `StrtChord` and `EndChord`, and returning

Figure 3.23 The `breadth_first()` predicate.

```
%main predicates

breadth_first(StrtChord,EndChord,Progression) :-
  process_lists(EndChord,[[StrtChord]],Progression),
  write(Progression),nl,
  fail.
breadth_first(_,_,_).

  process_lists(EndChord,[[EndChord|Tail]|_],[EndChord|Tail]).
  process_lists(EndChord,[[CrntChord|SubTail]|Tail],X) :-
    build_lists(CrntChord,L2),
    append_all(L2,SubTail,[],NewList),
    append(Tail,NewList,TempList),
    process_lists(EndChord,TempList,X).

%utilities

  build_lists(Node,L) :-
    bagof([NewNode,Node],from_to(Node,NewNode),L).

  append_all([],_,NewList,NewList).
  append_all([H|Tail],SubTail,TempList,NewList) :-
    append(H,SubTail,Temp),
    append([Temp],TempList,TempList2),
    append_all(Tail,SubTail,TempList2,NewList).
```

a solution bound to `Progression`. The inclusion of the `fail` simply enables us to seek all possible solutions. Next, the recursive predicate `process_lists()` removes the last chord (`CrntChord`) from the current progression, builds a list of all possible extensions to that chord (`L2`), appends the results to the front of the exiting progression `SubTail`, appends the newly extended progressions to the end of the main list (`TempList`), and completes the task with a recursive call. The predicate succeeds when the last chord of the current progression matches the user-specified harmony, passing the result back out (bound to `X`) through the recursive calls.

Two aspects of this heuristic are of particular interest. Notice first that the progression lists are built backward. This reversal is done to facilitate the removal of the last chord from the progression. If the lists were not reversed, we would have to traverse each one in its entirety to gain access to the last element because Prolog can only deconstruct a list into its head. By reversing the chords in the progression, the most recently found one will always be at the head of the list, thus greatly simplifying the process of removing it.

Also interesting is the use of the built-in Prolog predicate `bagof()`. Essentially, `bagof()` saves a lot of effort when searching for multiple answers to a particular problem because it is designed to find all possible solutions to a user-specified predicate and bundle the composite solutions into one comprehensive list. In this heuristic, the call

```
bagof([NewNode,Node],from_to(Node,NewNode),L).
```

causes Prolog to seek out all possible solutions (`NewNode`) to the predicate `from_to()` when supplied with a bound value to `Node`—in this case, `Node` is bound to the *last* chord found in the current progression being examined (actually, the first chord in the list). The resultant pairs, specified as the first parameter of the call, are returned as the list `L`. Notice that the order of the stored pairs is reversed from their position in the `from_to()` call. This switch is implemented to conform with the previously discussed aspect of the heuristic: namely, that all progressions are stored in reverse order (i.e., reading right to left).

When breadth-first searches are programmed, the requirements of passing ever-larger amounts of data recursively can be astronomical. In the case of this example, we would be lucky to reach progressions of greater than eight or nine harmonies on a machine with a Prolog stack of several megabytes! One way to circumvent this problem is to use the built-in predicates `assert()` and `retract()` to store lists in memory as opposed to passing them recursively. Essentially, the last line of each recursive clause stores the current list in working memory and then makes the recursive call *without* passing the list. Upon reentering a clause, we retract the list from memory, manipulate it, and then repeat the process. By relying on working memory, as opposed to recursively using stack space, we can reduce our computational demands by many factors.

Integrated Search Strategies

Clearly, we can see that each of the two strategies we have discussed—depth-first and breadth-first searching—have their advantages and disadvantages. Depth-first searching is inherently faster and more efficient yet potentially suffers from a lack of depth control. Breadth-first searches, on the other hand, emphasize depth control at the expense of computational efficiency. Assuming that we have problems that are guaranteed not to exhibit any excessive depth tendencies or that may have depth potential yet most likely contain short answers, we can use either strategy effectively. The real world, unfortunately, is not always so kind. More often we are not able to anticipate all the behavioral characteristics of a state space and so need to identify strategies for controlling our searches. Two such strategies are those that employ *iterative-deepening* and *best-first* search strategies.

■ Iterative Deepening

Iterative deepening represents a strategy for embodying the best of both methods into one heuristic model. Essentially, it utilizes depth-first searching yet forces a periodic progress check at predetermined, incremental depths. If a suitable depth-first solution is not found by the time the first designated depth limit is reached, the heuristic imposes a `fail` and forces additional depth-first searches. By mandating more searches, we effectively imitate through backtracking the lateral movement of a breadth-first approach. Ideally, an acceptable solution will be found within that depth limit. Only if an answer is not found do we allow the search to continue incrementally past our current limit. In other words, we try for any depth-first solutions within a given depth range, moving deeper only if no successful solution is found.

Iterative deepening, though, is not without its problems. In attempting a melding of the two strategies, we gain a level of control absent from either of them individually, yet we end up compromising each of their strengths. For example, the computational efficiency of a typical depth-first heuristic is partially compromised by the need to store search information when causing lateral movement. If no solution is found, we must restore our previous search information and then continue from there. There is also a risk that the computational demands of too many incremental checks—and the resultant lateral searches associated with them—could keep us from effectively reaching a solution that lies very deep in the structure. Similarly, the depth efficiency of breadth-first strategies is somewhat diminished by limiting the number of depth checks. We are no longer checking *every* level, only those at incrementally defined depths. These points notwithstanding, we can still use this technique to its advantage once we determine that it represents the best possible approach to traversing the particular domain in question. In other words, the problem must dictate the means for solving it, not the other way around.

Programming Searches with Iterative Deepening

Let us approach our discussion by returning to the same harmonic domain we were using earlier. Specifically, let us again assume that we are searching for an acceptable harmonic progression beginning and ending with user-specified harmonies and that we prefer to find a relatively short progression but not at the expense of using up excessive computational resources. Because our domain is relatively small to begin with, we might want to check our progress fairly often, say, every two harmonies. In this manner, we are just as likely to find a successful four-note harmony as we are one with three notes. On the other hand, we guarantee an exhaustive search for a three- or four-note progression before looking at any of five or more chords. Essentially, we have just defined an ideal candidate for implementation through an iterative-deepening search. An example of this approach is shown in figure 3.24.

Our strategy for undertaking this search uses some of the methods we employed in previous examples. Most notable is our technique for storing unsuccessful depth-first searches for later reuse. We implement this method in a manner similar to that used in our breadth-first model (in figure 3.21), relying on the existing codes. On reaching the maximum specified depth (Depth) without having reached a suitable solution, our reworked predicate get_var_prog() appends the unsuccessful progression to the end of a storage list, prog_list(). If no solution is found after exhausting all possible progressions of length Depth, the following line of code in generate_var_prog() causes the search to fail:

```
TorF = true
```

Our heuristic then removes the first progression from prog_list(), extracts the last chord in that progression to use as a new starting chord (StrtChord), and continues searching to a new depth limit determined by the formula Depth + Diff. In other words, as we restore each incomplete search from the list, we use the last-found chord of the progression as a new root node to begin searching for suitable extensions. These extended progressions, if unsuccessful, are similarly appended to the end of prog_list() as part of the recursive process. If at any point in the search a successful solution is found, the heuristic halts and returns with an answer that is assumed to be the best choice drawn from the compromise between efficiency and length. In keeping with the spirit of increased efficiency, we take advantage of the built-in predicates assert() and retract() to store our partial-progression list in memory,

Figure 3.24   The `iterative_deepening()` predicate.

```prolog
iterative_deepening(Diff,StrtChord,EndChord) :-
  assert(prog_list([])),
  generate_var_progressions(Diff,Diff,StrtChord,EndChord,[]),
  fail.

% main heuristic

generate_var_prog(Depth,_,StrtChord,EndChord,TempProg) :-
  get_var_prog(Depth,StrtChord,EndChord,TempProg,TorF),
  TorF = true.
generate_var_prog(Depth,Diff,_,EndChord,_) :-
  NewDepth is Depth + Diff,
  get_next_prog(NewStart,NewProg),
  generate_var_prog(NewDepth,Diff,NewStart,EndChord,NewProg).

  get_var_prog(Depth,StrtChord,EndChord,[],TorF) :- !,
    get_var_prog(Depth,StrtChord,EndChord,[StrtChord],TorF).
  get_var_prog(_,EndChord,EndChord,CrntProg,true) :-
    list_length(CrntProg,N),
    write(CrntProg),nl,
    N > 2,!.
  get_var_prog(Depth,_,_,CrntProg,false) :-
    list_length(CrntProg,Depth),
    add_to_list(CrntProg),!.
  get_var_prog(Depth,StrtChord,EndChord,OldProg,TorF) :-
    from_to(StrtChord,NextChord),
    check_for_repeat(StrtChord,NextChord,OldProg,Test),
    Test \= done,
    append(OldProg,[NextChord],NewProg),
    get_var_prog(Depth,NextChord,EndChord,NewProg,TorF).

% additional utility clauses

  add_to_list(Prog) :-
    prog_list(L),
    append(L,[Prog],NewL),
    retract(prog_list(_)),
    assert(prog_list(NewL)),!.

  get_next_prog(NewStart,NewProg) :-
    prog_list([NewProg|Tail]),
    retract(prog_list(_)),
    assertz(prog_list(Tail)),
    reverse(NewProg,[NewStart|_]).
```

thus avoiding much of the excessive recursive stack requirements. In this case, the list tends to be smaller than that used in the breadth-first heuristic, but recursion by its nature demands a greater level of processing and is avoided when not really necessary.

In addition to the predicates used to implement the bulk of the search, we include a calling predicate, `iterative_deepening()`, to facilitate a `fail` procedure that will find all possible solutions to the given problem.

Best-First Search Strategies

All the search strategies addressed so far rely primarily on predetermined models for working through a state space. Essentially, we have to be knowledgeable enough about our domain before defining a search model to pursue the best approach. Once the heuristic is developed, the method then remains rather fixed, and flexibility suffers. For example, the problem of combinatorial explosion resulting from working through a large tree often dictates the need to rethink our strategies "on the fly" to maximize our searching, essentially demanding a malleable methodology.

One way to approach this problem is through the application of *best-first* strategies. Specifically, this model demands that we compute a cost of moving from the start of our search to a point representing a satisfactory conclusion. That cost can be based on any number of factors. For example, finding the shortest distance through a state while accounting for various cost-factor considerations such as data value and level of relevance represents a typical scenario. Considering the problem of generating harmonic progressions, one factor we might wish to consider is the value of various root progressions. Weighing such factors and then assigning some value to them might allow us to evaluate a progression on the basis of a preponderance of one or another class of root motions. For example, we might chose to define three classes on the basis of motions of fifths or fourths, seconds, and thirds or sixths.

Alternatively, we might create a scenario where we need to concern ourselves with the distance it takes, measured in chord changes, to arrive at a full cadence. When generating a harmonic progression, for example, we are typically constrained by stylistic issues of harmonic rhythm and the need to constrain our progression to a fixed length. Although any of our previous examples can be modified to reject progressions of the wrong length, they do not constrain the search process itself. The result is a lot of potentially wasted effort generating and then rejecting progressions that do not fit the criteria.

Clearly, a better method would allow us to control every stage of the search so that we can regularly reevaluate our potential for success, in other words, to look *first* for the "best" path for solving a problem. What the strategy requires is a method of record keeping that maintains an awareness of both the *actual cost* of the search from the beginning to the current state of the search and the *potential cost* of achieving the desired goal from that point. Expressed more formally, we can define a cost (X) as the *sum* of the actual cost from the start node (A) to the current node (n) and the potential cost from the current node (n) to the goal node (Z):

```
cost(X) = actual_cost(A . . . n) + potential_cost
(n . . . Z).
```

Programming Best-First Strategies

Because we generally want to seek out the best potential solution path at each level of a search, developing best-first strategies that work in conjunction with breadth-first searches proves most effective. Just as when we move down to each new level of a search tree in a breadth-first search, we want to move laterally before descending any further, checking each possible downward path as we progress. In best-first searches, however, we want to assess the potential cost of traversing *each* path and focus finally on *only one best choice*. Once an assessment is made, our search moves down that path to the next level and proceeds to explore laterally for another "ideal" path, continuing the process until a solution is found. Obviously, the decision that looks the best at one level may not ultimately lead us down what ultimately would be the best-solution path, as each descent locks out other downward paths that may prove better overall. Nonetheless, what results is a path that will *tend* to have a higher-than-average likelihood of being successful while being derived through a less-than-average number of searches. In certain situations, the notion of what constitutes a best path may actually change over time. It is critical, therefore, that any best-first heuristic we create always maintains some awareness of what makes up an acceptable path. It may be the shortest or the longest path, or it may represent some average value. Whatever the criteria, we must keep a constant eye on each level to maintain a desired *average* as we progress toward our defined goal. For example, if we are looking specifically for a path through a state that strives to visit as close to thirteen nodes as possible, then we would maintain a list of potential distances and seek that path coming closest to matching the desired distance. If the potential cost at one level is slightly lower than preferred, or vice versa, we might then seek a slightly opposite value at the next level to compensate for our skewed average, ideally coming as close as possible to our desired goal value.

What is difficult in this process is to determine a suitable criterion and methodology for assigning cost. Even when we *can* determine that information, the process of computing a potential cost without actually undertaking any searches to their logical conclusions can prove very elusive. Obviously, best-first strategies cannot be universally applied as models for efficient problem solving, but they can be quite useful when we can codify acceptable strategies for refining a search.

For the sake of example, let us consider again the problem of generating a fixed-length progression. Further, let us assume that we want to end any progression we generate with a I chord. In a rather trivial sense, we can alter our progression data to reflect the *average* number of moves it would take to achieve a tonic chord. We derive this figure by ascertaining the lengths of all possible paths to the tonic, averaging them, and then storing that figure with the data. Obviously, this preprocessing strategy would be very difficult with a large amount of data, where we would inevitably have to rely on much more complex heuristics, but for the sake of example it will suffice to show the type of programming steps required to implement a best-first search. Using our previous programs, we can quickly generate all the possible progressions derivable from our model, beginning on chord *X* and ending on a tonic arrival, tally the length of each, and derive an average value for traversing from *X* to I, as shown in figure 3.25. We can then take that information and alter our data to incorporate it. The computed results and altered data are shown in figure 3.26. Note that we have chosen to round off the computed values because we do not need any greater level of precision.

Before traversing our structure, we must also define our desired length. To achieve our goal, we alter the breadth-first program of figure 3.18 to select only one downward path at each level by taking these values into account. Specifically, we set a counter to our desired length and decrement it by one as we move down each level of the tree. Once that level is attained, we move laterally, looking for the *one* path that, when its average value is added to our current counter, comes closest to matching our desired length. Clearly, we will not always arrive at a progression of the desired length because these values represent only averages, but those that we do generate will always come close to that value, if not necessarily matching it. And we have the added benefit of significantly reducing the problems of combinatorial explosion because, after testing, only one path is followed at each level. Essentially, we make only *one* trip through the tree. The code for the best-first search using the revised data from figure 3.26 appears in figure 3.27.

Figure 3.25   Average distance from x to tonic (I).

X	Distance
I	7.7
ii	5.62
iii	7.48
IV	6.13
V	4.13
vi	6.7
vii°	5.13

Figure 3.26   Progression data altered to reflect probabilities.

```
from_to('I','ii',5).
from_to('I','iii',7).
from_to('I','IV',6).
from_to('I','V',4).
from_to('I','vi',6).
from_to('I','vii°',5).
from_to('ii','vii°',5).
from_to('ii','V',4).
from_to('iii','vi',6).
from_to('iii','IV',6).
from_to('IV','ii',5).
from_to('IV','vii°',5).
from_to('IV','V',4).
from_to('IV','I',2).
from_to('V','I',2).
from_to('V','vi',6).
from_to('vi','IV',6).
from_to('vi','ii',5).
from_to('vi','V',4).
from_to('vii°','V',4).
from_to('vii°','I',2).
```

Figure 3.27   The revised `best_first()` predicate.

```
best_first(StrtChord,EndChord,Ideal,Progression) :-
  retractall(values(_,_,_,[])),
  assertz(values(1,999,Ideal,[])),
  process_lists(EndChord,[StrtChord],Progression).
best_first(_,_,_,_).

  process_lists(EndChord,[EndChord|Tail],[EndChord|Tail]).
  process_lists(EndChord,[CrntChord|Tail],X) :-
    build_lists(CrntChord,L),
    find_best(L,L2),
    append(L2,Tail,NewList),
    update_values,
    process_lists(EndChord,NewList,X).

  build_lists(Node,L) :-
    bagof([Val,Y,Node],from_to(Node,Y,Val),L).

  find_best([],L2) :-
    values(_,_,_,L2).
  find_best([Head|Tail],L2) :-
    values(CrntSoFar,BestGuess,IdealTotal,_),
    check_values(CrntSoFar,BestGuess,IdealTotal,Head),
    find_best(Tail,L2).

    check_values(CrntSoFar,BestGuess,Ideal,[Val|Head]) :-
      fabs(Ideal - (CrntSoFar + Val)) <
                      fabs(Ideal - (CrntSoFar + BestGuess)),
      retractall(values(_,_,_,_)),
      assertz(values(CrntSoFar,Val,Ideal,Head)).
    check_values(_,_,_,_).

  update_values :-
    values(CrntSoFar,_,Ideal,_),
    CrntSoFar2 is CrntSoFar + 1,
    retractall(values(_,_,_,_)),
    assertz(values(CrntSoFar2,999,Ideal,[])),!.
```

FOUR
Programming Knowledge-Based Systems

■ INTRODUCTION

In chapter 1, we discussed several characteristics of knowledge-based programs, including their use of domain-specific knowledge, their ability to solve expert problems, their use of symbolic rather than numeric representations of knowledge, and their ability to solve ill-structured problems. Besides embodying most of these characteristics, *expert systems* also have the potential to share one additional feature: namely, if well designed, they can possess the ability to explain whatever reasoning they use to reach a solution to a problem. In this sense, the expert system, like a real-world expert, can present the reasoning behind the solution it reaches. These explanative mechanisms reinforce a user's confidence in the system, especially in complicated and uncertain knowledge domains. In addition to having explanative mechanisms, expert systems, it may be argued, also should possess the ability to learn. Research into machine learning is progressing down several promising avenues, but few (if any) researchers currently developing expert systems place machine learning as a requirement for an expert system. Rather, as new knowledge is developed, a well-designed knowledge base can be modified to reflect such dynamic changes efficiently and expediently. Therefore, we acknowledge the possibility that expert systems may indeed learn from their own mistakes but will not make machine learning a required part of our definition of expert systems.

Actually, expert systems represent a subclass of knowledge-based systems. All expert systems are knowledge-based programs, but not all knowledge-based programs are expert systems, as is shown in chapter 6. Because the boundaries between the more specifically defined expert system and the more generally defined knowledge-based system are vague at best—as are the distinctions between other types of knowledge-based systems, such as *models* and *simulations*—we tend to prefer the use of the more general term for describing any such system. We rely, however, on the more specific term when we feel it is necessary to draw a specific distinction between the various uses of each subclass system.

The remainder of this chapter details the basic components and design strategies for implementing an expert system. For demonstration purposes, we chose the relatively simple and straightforward task of identifying nonharmonic tones within a purely diatonic tonal syntax.

■ MAIN COMPONENTS OF A KNOWLEDGE-BASED SYSTEM

A typical system, as shown in figure 4.1, contains three primary components: a *knowledge base,* an *inference engine,* and a *user interface.* The knowledge base in an expert system contains domain-specific information such as that possessed by an acknowledged expert in some field. Such information is often encoded through the use of one or more knowledge-representation methods, often consisting of facts, irreducible particles of knowledge, and rules and relationships among those facts.

A typical programming problem presented to students of AI programming is to develop an application that can play chess. Defining the moves permitted within the context of the game is a relatively straightforward process. For example, a pawn can move only forward, except when capturing another piece. When capturing a piece, it may move only diagonally by one space. Furthermore, a pawn may move forward two spaces when leaving its opening position and only one space thereafter. These simple descriptions, together with those for all the other players, can be written into a program constituting a knowledge base that contains all the necessary "rules" for playing chess.

A simple musical example is to develop a program that can identify nonharmonic tones. The domain, in this case, represents a specific subfield of traditional western tonal theory. The knowledge necessary to the domain includes the definition of all nonharmonic

Figure 4.1   Parts of a knowledge-based system.

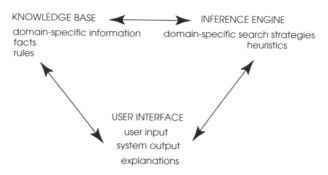

tones as well as the possible contexts in which they may occur. These definitions can in turn be translated into rules that constitute the knowledge base of an expert system for identifying nonharmonic tones. But, without some limitations on the context, the knowledge base for this example becomes extremely large and difficult to manage because we must essentially define a complete accounting of every possible juxtaposition of every element of the diatonic tonal universe within which these tones function—an arguably impossible task!

Knowledge alone is not sufficient to solve problems associated with many of the various manifestations of the domain data. Once the necessary information is identified and encoded in the knowledge base, we need a series of strategies, or heuristics, for searching that information so that we can find solutions to any specific domain-specific question or query. This inference engine, then, searches through such information to find solutions to our questions. To make it as efficient and manageable as possible, we must encode domain-specific strategies that reduce the number of testing possibilities when looking for each solution. In the case of a chess program, the total number of possible moves has been calculated to be 10^{120}! Of course, many of these moves are strategically useless, so it is the job of the inference engine to use domain-specific strategies to find only those moves that are appropriate within the context of the current situation. These heuristics are an integral part of any knowledge-based system and they reflect the rules of thumb—those uncodified, sometimes subconscious strategies—that experts develop over extended periods of time with their subject.

In a music theory, the inference engine would most likely resemble an analytical process. The knowledge base would contain specific facts and rules defined within the domain of a specific theory, whereas the inference engine would imitate the actual process that an analyst engages in when applying those musical rules—the inference engine must encode many of the same strategies an analyst employs when creating musically plausible observations. In our nonharmonic tone example, we as analysts might decide that a dissonant tone a ninth above the bass is treated as a passing tone in one context (e.g., in Mozart) and as a chord tone in another (e.g., Bruckner). As analysts, we also use domain-specific criteria to limit the number of possibilities; and, likewise, these heuristics must be incorporated into the inference engine for a program to function in an analogous manner.

With a knowledge base and an inference engine to guide searches through the problem domain, an expert system should be able to generate solutions to queried problems within that domain. But, without a means to convey that information to a user of the system or to accept information from that user, the expert system is essentially useless—after all, it is for *our* benefit that we design and use such systems. The user interface is that part of the program where the end user interacts with the system. A user may query the system for answers to specific questions, give the system additional information if requested, and ask the system to explain how it arrived at the solutions it presents. The complexity of an interface depends, obviously, on the system design and the nature of the encoded knowledge. Some user interfaces communicate through natural languages such as English, adding a considerable amount of programming complexity, whereas other interfaces may be less user friendly yet be capable of conveying essentially the same information, assuming that we know how to access it. In some cases, the expert system works in tandem with another computer program and therefore needs only to interface with the other program. Although interfaces vary according to the task and environment, they are essential parts of such systems and must be afforded considerable design attention to succeed at the tasks they were intended for.

■ A SAMPLE EXPERT SYSTEM: NONHARMONIC TONES

Having worked through the basics of the Prolog language (chapter 2) and having had an introduction to logic programming (chapter 3), we are now sufficiently prepared to begin developing a working

Figure 4.2   Nonharmonic tone classes.

	Approached by	Resolved by	Registral Directions
Passing Tone	scale step	scale step	same
Neighbor Tone	scale step	scale step	returned
Appoggiatura	skip	scale step	reversed
Escape Tone	scale step	skip	reversed
Suspension	unison	scale step	down
Retardation	unison	scale step	up
Pedal Tone	unison	unison	lateral

knowledge-based example. In this section, we present a small yet completely functional knowledge-based program.

The first step in generating such a program is to define precisely the domain of the data under consideration. For this task we develop a simple expert system that identifies the type of nonharmonic tone found in a particular three-note melodic pattern. To constrain the knowledge domain and thereby simplify the example for explanatory purposes, we make a few assumptions. First, we expect the system to identify only the type of nonharmonic tone (e.g., passing tone, neighbor tone, suspension, . . .), not any other information about linear or harmonic implications. Second, we limit the input to three pitches from the same voice, assuming that the first and third pitches are consonant and that the second pitch is the dissonant note—in other words, the nonharmonic tone. Third, we limit the pitches to the diatonic notes in C major and for only one octave (C–B). Although these constraints are certainly confining, they allow us to present the process of building a simple expert system clearly and also afford us the opportunity to discuss how the program can be modified to embrace a larger knowledge domain.

Domain-Specific Knowledge

The specific knowledge needed to determine the type of nonharmonic tones given the constraints previously discussed is relatively easy to define. If we consider all relevant passages to consist of a preparation, a nonharmonic pitch, and a pitch of resolution, we can limit our domain to seven nonharmonic tones, as shown in figure 4.2. These definitions fit the conventions found in Bruce Benward's *Music: In Theory and Practice* (1993) and Kostka and Payne's *Tonal Harmony* (1995).

According to our chart, a passing tone is a nonharmonic pitch approached by step and resolved by step while maintaining the registral direction established by the first two pitches (either ascending or descending). A neighbor tone is also approached and resolved by step, but the registral direction established by the second and third pitches is the reverse of that created by the first two and returns to the original pitch. For appoggiaturas and escape tones, we indicate that the registral direction is also a reversal but does not need to return. Although in most cases the direction usually reverses itself, it not necessarily true for *all* cases, and so care should be used when including a specified direction because it could represent an unwarranted restriction. We could modify the model to account for both types of motions, but it would add undo complexity at this juncture. Notice also that the specific registral direction (*up* or *down*) for suspensions and retardations relates solely to the direction of resolution because these nonharmonic tones are approached laterally. We use these terms here to avoid confusion with the previous term *reversed,* which is used simply to imply a change of direction while avoiding any reference to the specific direction of resolution. Finally, notice that the pedal tone is approached by unison and resolved by unison and that the registral direction is lateral. We could define the registral direction, actually, as being the same, just as we did with passing tones and neighbor tones, but in each case we are trying to define the registral direction with the most specific term we can—without limiting the flexibility of the definition. In addition, our current formulation avoids some possible problems with the implementation of the inference engine later.

The Knowledge Base

After defining all the possibilities within our admittedly limited knowledge domain, the next step is to select a strategy for encoding that knowledge in a format usable by the program. In chapter 1, we presented and discussed several common knowledge representation strategies, including production rules, frames, and semantic networks. Because our examples are all written in Prolog and production rules based on predicate logic are inherently suitable for use in that environment, we will employ this method for our encoding scheme.

A production rule in which a specific action or known entity occurs given a specified set of criteria takes the form of an IF–THEN statement. IF the criteria are satisfied, THEN a specific condition exists. Production rules furnish a means for efficiently modifying the knowledge represented in our program and a format for expressing relationships among "factual" components of that knowledge. In our example, the definition of a passing tone can be represented as follows:

> IF the nonharmonic tone is
> approached by step and
> resolved by step and
> the registral direction continues in the same direction
> THEN the nonharmonic tone is a passing tone

If we recall our discussions from previous chapters, we see that the actual syntax of a Prolog representation of this same rule more closely resembles a THEN–IF construction:

```
nonharmonic_tone(passing_tone)  :-
    approached(step),
    resolved(step),
    registral_direction(same).
```

Actually, depending on what information we supply when calling the predicate, we can implement either form: passing a bound variable represents the latter, whereas passing an unbound variable reverses the logic. In other words, passing in a bound value such as "passing_tone" is the same as saying "*then* it is a passing tone *if* . . . are true." Conversely, passing in no value (unbound) is analogous to stating "*if* . . . are true, *then* it is a passing tone." In this example, the Prolog rule states that an unidentified nonharmonic tone is a passing tone if (:-) it is approached by step and (,) resolved by step and (,) the registral direction stays the same.

Production rules represent excellent data structure models for developing knowledge-based programs, particularly because they are self-contained independent structures. Modifications in one rule do not change the content of any of other rules. The nature of these structures allows us to modify the knowledge base as necessary because adding a new rule does not adversely affect other definitions of the same rule. Further, this design allows for expedient modifications to the knowledge base and permits easy editing of rules already contained in the knowledge base. Production rules are even easily adapted to generate the explanations required in our expert system.

All the data shown in figure 4.2 are defined as production rules and represented in the following Prolog clauses shown in figure 4.3.

Actually, we add one additional rule beyond those represented in figure 4.2. There are several other possible combinations of approaches

Figure 4.3   The `nonharmonic_tone()` predicate.

```
% Nonharmonic tones defined as production rules.

nonharmonic_tone(passing_tone) :-
  approached(step),
  resolved(step),
  registral_direction(same).
nonharmonic_tone(neighbor_tone) :-
  approached(step),
  resolved(step),
  registral_direction(returned).
nonharmonic_tone(appoggiatura) :-
  approached(skip),
  resolved(step),
  registral_direction(reversed).
nonharmonic_tone(escape_tone) :-
  approached(step),
  resolved(skip),
  registral_direction(reversed).
nonharmonic_tone(suspension) :-
  approached(unison),
  resolved(step),
  registral_direction(down).
nonharmonic_tone(retardation) :-
  approached(unison),
  resolved(step),
  registral_direction(up).
nonharmonic_tone(pedal_tone) :-
  approached(unison),
  resolved(unison),
  registral_direction(lateral).
nonharmonic_tone(undefined) :-
  approached(_),
  resolved(_),
  registral_direction(_).
```

and resolutions that are not defined in the traditional discussions of nonharmonic tones. We include a provision in our knowledge base specifically to handle any such nonmatching patterns.

The Inference Engine

Now that we now have codified the knowledge necessary to create plausible analyses (within our stated limitations) using production

Figure 4.4 Flowchart for determining nonharmonic tones.

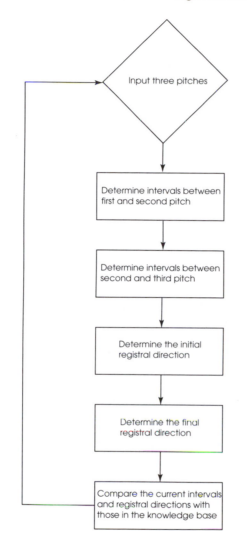

rules, we need to develop an inference engine that controls how we search through the information to arrive at a solution to various queries. The inference engine should parallel the process an analyst uses when confronted with a similar situation. Figure 4.4 shows a flowchart of a process we propose to use for determining the type of nonharmonic tone present within the context we outlined previously.

Figure 4.5 The `identify_nht()` predicate.

```
% Nonharmonic Tone Inference Engine

identify_nht(Pitch1,Pitch2,Pitch3,NHT) :-
    calculate_interval(Pitch1,Pitch2,Interval1),
    retractall(approached(_)),
    asserta(approached(Interval1)),
    calculate_interval(Pitch2,Pitch3,Interval2),
    retractall(resolved(_)),
    asserta(resolved(Interval2)),
    calculate_registral_direction(Pitch1,Pitch2,
                                    Pitch3,Register),
    retractall(registral_direction(_)),
    asserta(registral_direction(Register)),
    nonharmonic_tone(NHT),
    retractall(last_response(_)),
    asserta(last_response([Pitch1,Pitch2,Pitch3, Interval1,
                    Interval2,Register,NHT])).
```

Once we input the three pitches—representing the preparation, the nonharmonic tone, and the resolution—we need first to determine whether the intervals between the first two and last two pitches are steps and/or skips. Once we know how the nonharmonic tone is approached and resolved, we need to check the registral directions established by the same two groups of pitches. Armed with this information, the system is then able to compare the current information with the rules in the knowledge base and, if a match is found, stop searching and return an answer.

A Prolog predicate for implementing the analytical process outlined in figure 4.4 using the knowledge base we previously defined is presented in figure 4.5. The predicate `identify_nht()` takes four arguments (`Pitch1,Pitch2,Pitch3,` and `NHT`). To keep the user interface as intuitive and uncomplicated as possible, we design the inference engine to accept the letter names from C-B as the pitches. The nonharmonic tone returns or matches the nonharmonic tone names as defined in the knowledge base. The first predicate called in `identify_nht()` is `calculate_interval()`. The three clauses of this predicate are presented as figure 4.6. Note our use of the Prolog predicate `fabs()`, which is used to determine the absolute value of a floating-point number or, in this case, the result of an equation.

The `calculate_interval()` clause takes three arguments. The first clause compares the two pitches (`P1` and `P2`). If they are the

Figure 4.6   The `calculate_interval()` predicate.

```
calculate_interval(P1,P2,unison) :-
    P1 = P2.
calculate_interval(P1,P2,step) :-
    pitch(P1,N1),
    pitch(P2,N2),
    fabs(N2 - N1) < 3.
calculate_interval(P1,P2,skip) :-
    pitch(P1,N1),
    pitch(P2,N2),
    fabs(N2 - N1) >= 3.
```

same, the interval is a `unison`. The second clause calls the predicate `pitch()` with the variables `P1` and `N1`. Essentially, `pitch()` is a look-up table that converts the pitch entered by the user into a numeric value for calculating the interval between the two pitches. The values for `pitch()` are presented here:

```
% Pitch Look-up

        pitch(c,0)
        pitch(d,2).
        pitch(e,4).
        pitch(f,5).
        pitch(g,7).
        pitch(a,9).
        pitch(b,11).
```

Once the vale of a `N1` and `N2` are bound to integers, the absolute value of the difference between the numbers is compared against 3. If the value is less than 3 the interval is a step. The third clause checks to see that the interval generated is greater than or equal to 3, verifying that the interval is a step. Of course this check does not consider the possibility of an augmented second or a diminished third, but once the system is complete it easily can be modified to take such intervals into consideration.

One of these three clauses is guaranteed to succeed. We could write the third clause as `calculate_interval(_,_,skip)` because the order dependency of Prolog explicitly determines that we would already have eliminated the other two possibilities by the time we reached it. This definition, however, causes problems when switching from forward to backward chaining. (We discuss this problem in more detail in the next section.)

Returning to `identify_nht()`, this predicate retracts all references to the predicate `approached()` and asserts the value returned by `calculate_interval()` into the knowledge base. Because we may need this information again later for generating explanations, including it in the knowledge base now saves us from having to recalculate the information later. Although the computations in this particular program are not time consuming, a more complicated example may be. This caution is also compounded by the nature of the Prolog language, which is not very efficient at manipulating numbers.

Once both intervals are calculated and asserted into the knowledge base, the registral directions established by the first two and last two pitches are calculated and asserted in the knowledge base in a similar manner. The various clauses of the predicate `calculate_registral_direction()` are presented in figure 4.7.

The last two predicates in `identify_nht()` retract all references to the predicate `last_response()` and then assert all the currently bound variables into the knowledge base. This information is used to explain to the user how the solution is reached without having to recalculate all the information.

With the knowledge base complete and an inference engine prepared to search the knowledge base for solutions to posed questions, we have a complete program. We limited our knowledge domain (dramatically) and identified the basic information necessary to solve problems within this domain. The result is a knowledge base that encodes "expert" knowledge about nonharmonic tones in traditional Western tonal theory. We also identified a process that an expert analyst may use to apply that encoded knowledge to a piece of music, thereby identifying the type of nonharmonic tone. Now, with our completed program, we may begin posing questions to the system.

Querying the System

The top-level predicate in the inference engine is `identify_nht()`. This predicate takes four arguments: `Pitch1`, `Pitch2`, `Pitch3`, and `NonharmonicTone`. For example, given the pitches C, D, and E, we can type the following in the query window, and the program will determine the type of nonharmonic tone present:

```
?- identify_nht(c,d,e,NHT).
NHT = passing_tone
```

Figure 4.7 The `calculate_registral_direction()` predicate.

```
% lateral direction for pedal_tone
calculate_registral_direction(P1,P1,P1,lateral) :-
    pitch(P1,N),
    pitch(P2,N),
    pitch(P3,N).
% unison - down for suspension
calculate_registral_direction(P2,P2,P3,down) :-
    pitch(P2,N2),
    pitch(P3,N3),
    N3 < N2.
% unison - up for retardation
calculate_registral_direction(P2,P2,P3,up) :-
    pitch(P2,N2),
    pitch(P3,N3),
    N3 > N2.
% same registral direction for passing_tone (down)
calculate_registral_direction(P1,P2,P3,same) :-
    pitch(P1,N1),
    pitch(P2,N2),
    pitch(P3,N3),
    N1 < N2,
    N2 < N3.
% same registral direction for passing_tone (up)
calculate_registral_direction(P1,P2,P3,same) :-
    pitch(P1,N1),
    pitch(P2,N2),
    pitch(P3,N3),
    N1 > N2,
    N2 > N3.
% reversed (down-up)
calculate_registral_direction(P1,P2,P3,reversed) :-
    pitch(P1,N1),
    pitch(P2,N2),
    pitch(P3,N3),
    N1 > N2,
    N2 < N3.
% reversed (up-down)
calculate_registral_direction(P1,P2,P3,reversed) :-
    pitch(P1,N1),
    pitch(P2,N2),
    pitch(P3,N3),
    N1 < N2,
    N2 > N3.
```

continued on next page

Figure 4.7   (continued)

```
% returned
calculate_registral_direction(P1,P2,P1,returned) :-
    pitch(P1,N1),
    pitch(P2,N2),
    N1 \= N2.
```

This type of query represents an example of forward reasoning or forward chaining (discussed in detail in chapter 3). Essentially, forward chaining is a question seeking an answer. In this example, the question is, "What type of nonharmonic tone is present in the sequence of pitches C, D, E?" The inference engine proceeds to bind the constants (c, d, e) to the variables (Pitch1, Pitch2, and Pitch3) and begins searching through the knowledge base to find a solution to the query. The inference engine is designed with forward chaining in mind, that is, with the idea that a user will specify an initial set of conditions (data) and the program will search through the encoded knowledge and find a solution.

This program is also able to work with backward chaining, or cases in which answers seek questions. For example, if we want to know all the possible combinations of pitches that can generate a passing tone (within the constraints of our sample program), we can type the following in the Prolog query window:

```
?- identify_nht(X,Y,Z,passing_tone).
    X = c, Y = d, Z = e ;
    X = d, Y = e, Z = f ;
    X = e, Y = d, Z = c ;
    X = e, Y = f, Z = g ;
    X = f, Y = e, Z = d ;
    etc...
```

In this case, we provided three unbound variables (X, Y, Z) and the constant (passing_tone). As the inference engine works through the knowledge base, it attempts to match the constant, passing_tone, with any three pitches that can be assembled into a passing tone pattern. Once it finds a match, Prolog's relentless backtracking goes to work finding all the possible pitches that fulfill the criteria within the constraints of the system. In the case of backward chaining, the user provides the answer and the system searches to find valid data for asking a relevant question.

Figure 4.8   The `how()` predicate.

```
how :-
   last_response([Pitch1,Pitch2,Pitch3,Interval1,Interval2,
      Register,NHT]),
   write('The following pitches are currently being considered for analysis: '),
   write(Pitch1),write(-),write(Pitch2),write(-),
   write(Pitch3),write(.),nl,
   write('The first two pitches combine to create a '),
   write(Interval1),
   write('and the second two pitches create a'),
   write(Interval2),
   write('.'),nl,
   write('The registral direction established by the two intervals are: '),
   write(Register),write('.'),nl,
   write('According to the definitions in the knowledge-base, these criteria'),nl,
   write('identify the nonharmonic tone as a(n) '),
   write(NHT),write(.),nl.
```

Both forward and backward chaining are important components to consider in the development of all knowledge-based systems. Forward chaining involves moving through the state space, starting with data and moving toward a goal—in our example, starting with specific pitches and moving toward the goal, identifying the nonharmonic tone. Backward chaining, however, starts with a goal and moves backward through the state space to find valid data satisfying the conditions of the goal. In this sense, forward chaining is a data-driven search and backward chaining a goal-driven search. Most knowledge-based programs involve some combination of the two styles.

Explaining the Results

One of the more common types of questions posed to a knowledge-based program by a user might be "How did the program reach this conclusion?" The "how" explanations of a knowledge-based system trace the process that the program uses to generate a solution from the facts and relationships in the rule base. In the inference engine of our program, the last two predicates store the information generated during the process of finding a solution to the query. Essentially, we store all the information necessary to generate a how explanation. Our `how()` predicate is presented in figure 4.8.

In this case, we simply recall the information we stored in `last_response()` and format it on the screen in a manner that can be easily understood by the user. An example of a typical query may look something like this:

```
?- identify_nht(f,g,f,NHT).
   NHT = neighbor_tone

?- how.
```
The following pitches are currently being considered for analysis:
f-g-f.
The first two pitches combine to create a step, and the second two pitches create a step.
The registral direction established by the two intervals is: reversed.
According to the definitions in the knowledge base, these criteria identify the nonharmonic tone as a `neighbor_tone`.
```
   yes


?-
```

In other, more complicated cases, however, our program often has to make numerous decisions and traverse a number of both successful and failed branches before coming to a conclusion. Frequently, we want to know precisely just how the end result was arrived at. In other words, just what steps were taken, and what is the complete logic trail that the computer used to determine the answer it found? There are a number of ways that we could accomplish this goal, each requiring a specific strategy for determining the necessary information. The method we advocate is one of record keeping that can then be interpreted in a number of ways after the search is completed. This is precisely what we do in our simple example above. Our previous example, however, does not give us any insight into the various paths traversed and the resultant decisions being made. The program does not really need to in this case because the number and complexity of the rules are minimal. Let us assume, however, that we would like to modify our program so that it could emulate the record keeping necessitated by a larger knowledge base. For the sake of our example, we modify only one clause to demonstrate the method, which can in turn be transferred as a strategy to other, larger programs. For this example, we modify the clauses of the predicate `nonharmonic_tone()`, as shown in figure 4.9

Essentially, we add a call to the end of each clause that records successful attempts at finding an answer. Because the added record keeping is at the end of each clause, it is reached only if that particular

Figure 4.9 The revised `nonharmonic_tone()` predicate.

```
% Nonharmonic tones defined as production rules.

nonharmonic_tone(passing_tone) :-
    approached(step),
    resolved(step),
    registral_direction(same),
    record_data(['nht(passing_tone)',true]).
nonharmonic_tone(neighbor_tone) :-
    approached(step),
    resolved(step),
    registral_direction(returned).
    record_data(['nht(neighbor_tone)',true]).
nonharmonic_tone(appoggiatura) :-
    approached(skip),
    resolved(step),
    registral_direction(reversed).
    record_data(['nht(appoggiatura)',true]).
nonharmonic_tone(escape_tone) :-
    approached(step),
    resolved(skip),
    registral_direction(reversed).
    record_data(['nht(escape_tone)',true]).
nonharmonic_tone(suspension) :-
    approached(unison),
    resolved(step),
    registral_direction(down).
    record_data(['nht(suspension)',true]).
nonharmonic_tone(retardation) :-
    approached(unison),
    resolved(step),
    registral_direction(up).
    record_data(['nht(retardation)',true]).
nonharmonic_tone(pedal_tone) :-
    approached(unison),
    resolved(unison),
    registral_direction(lateral).
    record_data(['nht(pedal_tone)',true]).
```

Figure 4.10   The `record_data()` predicate.

```
record_data(CLAUSEdata)  :-
  data_list(LIST),
  append(LIST,CLAUSEdata,NewLIST),
  retractall(data_list(_)),
  assertz(data_list(NewLIST)).
```

Figure 4.11   The additional `nonhamonic_tone()` clause for figure 4.9.

```
nonharmonic_tone(_)  :-
  record_data(['nht(undefined)',fail]),
  !,fail.
```

clause succeeds. And because we write the new record-keeping clause so that it always succeeds, the predicate continues to function as it did before. The number and type of information stored depends on the needs of the program. In this case, we store only the identifying information and for the clause, together with the result of the clausal search, in an existing predicate, `data_list()`. Once a search is run and a solution found, the program can retrieve the data and do with it whatever the programmer chooses. The new predicate, `record_data()`, appears as figure 4.10.

Although this strategy works well for successful attempts, what do we do if all the clauses of a predicate fail? In our previous example, we added a fail-safe predicate designed to capture any failures as being "undefined" examples and to have them succeed. In larger systems, we usually will want any nonmatches to fail, so that the program will continue to search for other possible successful avenues. To deal with failures, we replace the existing successful "undefined" predicate with one that will record the failure while still keeping the predicate from succeeding, meaning that we must use the cut (!) and `fail` predicates to ensure failure without backtracking. The final additional `nonharmonic_tone()` clause appears as figure 4.11.

With these additions in place, we now are able to recover a complete trace of the program execution. In any given situation, we might wish to alter the amount and type of information we collect, and clearly we need to implement some rather complicated strategies for presenting that information in a meaningful manner. The beauty of the method, however, is that we do not need to concern ourselves with those details when designing the knowledge base. We simply need to set up a thorough method of collecting data.

Although the "how" type of explanation is important, another question is often asked of knowledge-based systems, specifically, "Why?" A "why" explanation usually happens during the course of running the program where the system may request additional information. It provides a means for the user to ask about the reasoning process the system is using to deduce its answers.

In our present example, there is little need for a "why" explanation because the rules in the knowledge base are categorical; that is, they are either true or false. There is no need in this simple model for the system to request more information given the constraint we defined. However, if we were to expand this program to include, for example, information about the harmony, the interval above the bass creating the dissonance, or the time period or the composer of the music, we would introduce more uncertainty into the process. There may be room for multiple interpretations, and the system may require more information than the three pitches to solve the problem. In such cases, "why" explanations help explain to the user why the additional information is needed and thereby explain its reasoning at that point in the solution process. We demonstrate a simple "why" explanation in the next section.

Uncertainty

Our present formulation and limitations of the nonharmonic tone program assume a view of the problem domain that the knowledge required to reach plausible conclusions is categorical, that is, that all the rules in the knowledge base are either true or false. Either a pitch is a passing tone or it is not. This, however, is not the most common type of knowledge. Rather, most conclusions within expert knowledge domains are accompanied by descriptions such as likely, possible, unlikely, and so on. These descriptors reflect the reality that knowledge is seldom categorical. Rather, rules are often applied within contexts, and it is the understanding of the complex interactions of general principles within specific circumstances at which experts excel. If we are to create knowledge-based systems that operate in a manner analogous to human experts, then we must be capable of accommodating these uncertainties within our programs.

Fortunately, through a few modifications, production rules are amenable to representing various types of uncertainty. For example, within the limited context we have outlined for the nonharmonic tone program, the rules state specific facts. The context has been limited to the point where the knowledge represented in the knowledge base is indeed "factual" within this limited domain. The production rule for a passing tone presented previously is a "factual" rule in this context—either the pitch in question is a passing tone or it is not. This type of purely logical relationship is particularly easy to represent with production rules. If, however, we broadened the context to the point where multiple interpretations of a particular nonharmonic are possible, production rules can handle this type of probablistic knowledge as well. For example, if we have a ninth above the bass, approached by step and resolved by step in the same registral direction in Mozart, the probability of the ninth being a passing tone and not a chord tone may be represented with a confidence factor of, say, 9 (out of 10). If the ninth above the bass is in a Bruckner symphony, the confidence factor may be considerably less, say, 6 or 7. By assigning confidence factors or certainty ratios to the knowledge in the program, we can approximate many of the uncertainties of real-world situations.

We can modify our nonharmonic tone program to begin taking some of these uncertainties into account. For the sake of illustration only, let us assume that we can assign confidence factors on the basis of the century that a composition was written—clearly, very much an overly simplistic view. We will need to modify several components of our program to accomplish this task. First, we need to expand the context of pitches available by at least another octave and provide a look-up for the particular bass note that supports the nonharmonic tone in question.

This step is necessary for calculating the interval under consideration. The new pitch look-up table is presented as figure 4.12. For illustrating the use of certainty factors, we consider only the relationship between the bass note and the passing tone and no others. Our actual production rules remain unchanged from their original versions, but the inference engine needs to be modified. Our new predicate for the inference engine is presented as 4.13.

The predicate `identify_nht_expanded()` contains two new arguments (`Bass2` and `Certainty`). `Bass2` is the actual bass note supporting the nonharmonic tone (the second pitch). A numerical value between 1 and 10, with 10 being the most certain, is assigned to the analysis of the nonharmonic tone on the basis of the information provided by the user. That information is the century within which the composition was written.

The predicate `calculate_interval_expanded()` is slightly modified from our earlier version. In addition to knowing if the nonharmonic tone is approached and resolved by step, skip, or unison, we need to know the precise interval between the bass pitch and the nonharmonic tone. The predicate takes two pitches and the bass pitch, returning a value of step, skip, or unison in the fourth

Figure 4.12   The revised pitch look-up table.

```
% Pitch Look-up—expanded
bass(c,0).
bass(d,2).
bass(e,4).
bass(f,5).
bass(g,7).
bass(a,8).
bass(b,11).

pitch(c1,12).          pitch(c2,24).
pitch(d1,14).          pitch(d2,26).
pitch(e1,16).          pitch(e2,28).
pitch(f1,17).          pitch(f2,29).
pitch(g1,19).          pitch(g2,31).
pitch(a1,20).          pitch(a2,32).
pitch(b1,23).          pitch(b2,35).
```

Figure 4.13   The identify_nht_expanded() predicate.

```
ɔnharmonic Tone Inference Engine—Expanded

ientify_nht_expanded(Pitch1,Pitch2,Pitch3,Bass2,NHT,Certainty) :-
   calculate_interval_expanded(Pitch1,Pitch2,Bass2,
                                        Interval1,Interval2),
   retractall(approached(_)),
   asserta(approached(Interval1)),
   calculate_interval_expanded(Pitch2,Pitch3,Bass2,
                                        Interval3,Interval4),
   retractall(resolved(_)),
   asserta(resolved(Interval3)),
   calculate_registral_direction_exp(Pitch1,
                                Pitch2,Pitch3,Register),
   retractall(registral_direction(_)),
   asserta(registral_direction(Register)),
   nonharmonic_tone(NHT),
   check_century(NHT,Interval2,Certainty),
   retractall(last_response_expanded(_)),
   asserta(last_response_expanded([Pitch1,Pitch2,
                         Pitch3,Interval1,Interval2,
                         Interval3,Interval4,Register,
                         NHT,Certainty])).
```

Figure 4.14 The `calculate_interval_expanded()` predicate.

```
calculate_interval_expanded(P,P,_,_,unison,0).
calculate_interval_expanded(P1,P2,B2,step,NHT_Int) :-
     pitch(P1,N1),
     pitch(P2,N2),
     bass(B2,N3),
     (integer(fabs(N2-N1))) mod 12 < 3,
     NHT_Int is ((N2-N3) mod 12) + 12.
calculate_interval_expanded(P1,P2,B2,skip,NHT_Int) :-
     pitch(P1,N1),
     pitch(P2,N2),
     bass(B2,N3),
     (integer(fabs(N2-N1))) mod 12 > 2,
     NHT_Int is ((N2-N3) mod 12) + 12.
```

argument and returning the actual numerical interval in the fifth argument. The code for `calculate_interval_expanded()` is presented as figure 4.14

Our routines for calculating the registral direction are essentially the same as in the original version of the program. We reiterate this code in figure 4.15.

The predicate `check_century()` (figure 4.16) is our one new piece of program code. We design it first to check if the pattern is a `passing_tone` (or whatever particular nonharmonic tone you chose to look for). If so, it tests to see if the interval above the bass is a ninth by checking the value bound to `Interval` to determine if it is a member of the list [13,14]. These interval numbers represent the distances above the base note of minor and major ninths respectively. Excluding chromatic alterations, these will be the only possibilities. Next, the system prompts the user for more information (specifically asking them for the century in which the composition was written), the user response is bound to the variable `Response`, and the predicate `check_response()` is called.

The first four `check_response()` clauses compare the user response against the century and return a certainty factor based as shown. The fifth `check_response()` clause is an example of a "why" type of explanation. The last clause simply checks for valid responses from the user. A sample query appears in figure 4.17.

There are a variety of difficulties that surface when we attempt to handle uncertainty. It should be apparent to us, even from this small example, that the number of possibilities that need to be

Figure 4.15 The `calculate_registral_direction_ exp()` predicate.

```
% lateral direction for pedal_tone
calculate_registral_direction_exp(P1,P1,P1,lateral) :-
    pitch(P1,N),
    pitch(P2,N),
    pitch(P3,N).
% unison - down for suspension
calculate_registral_direction_exp(P2,P2,P3,down) :-
    pitch(P2,N2),
    pitch(P3,N3),
    N3 < N2.
% unison - up for retardation
calculate_registral_direction_exp(P2,P2,P3,up) :-
    pitch(P2,N2),
    pitch(P3,N3),
    N3 > N2.
% same registral direction for passing_tone (down)
calculate_registral_direction_exp(P1,P2,P3,same) :-
    pitch(P1,N1),
    pitch(P2,N2),
    pitch(P3,N3),
    N1 < N2,
    N2 < N3.
% same registral direction for passing_tone (up)
calculate_registral_direction_exp(P1,P2,P3,same) :-
    pitch(P1,N1),
    pitch(P2,N2),
    pitch(P3,N3),
    N1 > N2,
    N2 > N3.
% reversed (down-up)
calculate_registral_direction_exp(P1,P2,P3,reversed) :-
    pitch(P1,N1),
    pitch(P2,N2),
    pitch(P3,N3),
    N1 > N2,
    N2 < N3.
% reversed (up-down)
calculate_registral_direction_exp(P1,P2,P3,reversed) :-
    pitch(P1,N1),
    pitch(P2,N2),
    pitch(P3,N3),
    N1 < N2,
    N2 > N3.
```

continued on next page

Figure 4.15   (continued)

```
% returned
calculate_registral_direction_exp(P1,P2,P1,returned) :-
    pitch(P1,N1),
    pitch(P2,N2),
    N1 \= N2.
```

Figure 4.16   The check_century() predicate.

```
check_century(passing_tone,Interval,Certainty) :-
  member(Interval,[13,14]),
  write('In what century was this piece written (17,18,19,20)? '),
  read(Response),nl,
  check_response(Response,Certainty).
  check_response(17,9).
  check_response(18,8).
  check_response(19,7).
  check_response(20,5).
  check_response(why,Certainty) :-
    write( 'Composers in the 17th and 18th centuries typically treated 9ths as' ),nl,
    write( 'passing tones. In the 19th century 9th chords became more common.' ),nl,
    write( 'As a result the certainty that a 9th is a passing tone is reduced. In the' ),nl,
    write( '20th century the certainty that a 9th is a passing tone is further reduced' ),nl,
    write( 'due to their use in nontonal contexts.' ),nl,
    nl,
    write( 'In what century was this piece written (17,18,19,20)? ' ),
    read(Response),nl,
    check_response(Response,Certainty).
  check_response(X,Certainty) :-
    write(X),write( 'is not a valid response.' ),nl,
    nl,
    write( 'In what century was this piece written (17, 18, 19, 20th)? ' ),
    read(Response),nl,
    check_response(Response,Certainty).
```

Figure 4.17   A sample query of identify_nht_ expanded().

```
?- identify_nht_expanded(c2,d2,e2,c,NHT,Certainty).
In what century was this piece written (17,18,19,20)? 18 .
    NHT = passing_tone, Certainty = 8
?- identify_nht_expanded(c2,d2,e2,c,NHT,Certainty).
```

continued on next page

Figure 4.17   (continued)

In what century was this piece written (17,18,19,20)? `why`.

Composers in the 17th and 18th centuries typically treated 9ths as passing tones. In the 19th century 9th chords became more common. As a result the certainty that a 9th is a passing tone is reduced. In the 20th century the certainty that a 9th is a passing tone is further reduced due to their use in nontonal contexts.

In what century was this piece written (17,18,19,20)? `20`.

```
    NHT = passing_tone, Certainty = 5
?-
```

accounted for can be tremendous. We see the number of possibilities explode combinatorially, depending on the complexity of the problem and the number of possible solutions. This problem often necessitates simplifying a problem to some degree or modeling only some smaller portion of a larger system to reduce the number of possibilities adequately. Also, many uncertainty schemes represent, at best, ad hoc systems. Often, the certainty factors provided by an expert are not mathematically reliable; rather, they tend to be based on intuition and experiences that are not easily quantified. In addition, mathematically sound formulas often require information that is not available. To be truly complete with our brief example, we would need to analyze all the passing tones occurring a ninth above the bass written between the year 1600 and the present and categorize them by their uses to find certainty values that may be mathematically sound. Even basic statistical sampling represents a tremendously time-consuming exercise. Even if this could be done, there are many places in the music literature where experts disagree on the "function" of the ninth. There are no easy solutions to the ad hoc nature of certainty factors, but their use can improve the performance of our systems on an intuitive level and help provide a more realistic expression of the real-world complexities in knowledge-based systems—as long as we are truly aware of their limitations!

Figure 4.18   A nonharmonic tone graph.

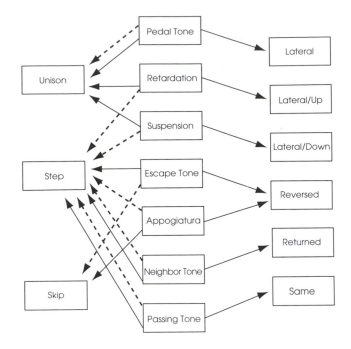

■ SEMANTIC NETWORKS

Throughout the proceeding examples, we programmed our knowledge base using production rules. We can also represent other knowledge using other representation strategies as well. We feel it would be helpful to examine very briefly several other strategies.

As we discussed in chapter 1, a semantic network is series of facts and relations between those facts. Semantic networks are customarily portrayed as graphs, with individual nodes or facts represented and the relationships of links shown as arcs. Figure 4.18 shows a graph of the nonharmonic tone information found in the knowledge base of our program.

We can represent this information in the knowledge base as a series of predefined constants—one for each possible nonharmonic tone. These clauses are shown in figure 4.19.

Figure 4.19   The `nonharmonic_tone()` predicate.

```
% Knowledge-base
% Nonharmonic tones defined as Prolog facts.
    nonharmonic_tone(passing_tone, [step,step,same]).
    nonharmonic_tone(neighbor_tone, [step,step,reversed]).
    nonharmonic_tone(appoggiatura, [skip,step,reversed]).
    nonharmonic_tone(escape_tone, [step,skip,reversed]).
    nonharmonic_tone(suspension, [unison,step,down]).
    nonharmonic_tone(retardation, [unison,step,up]).
    nonharmonic_tone(pedal_tone, [unison,unison,lateral]).
    nonharmonic_tone(undefined, [skip,skip,_]).
    nonharmonic_tone(undefined, [skip,step,same]).
    nonharmonic_tone(undefined, [step,skip,same]).
```

Figure 4.20   The revised `identify_nht()` predicate.

```
% Inference Engine

identify_nht(Pitch1,Pitch2,Pitch3,NHT) :-
   calculate_interval(Pitch1,Pitch2,Interval1),
   calculate_interval(Pitch2,Pitch3,Interval2),
   calculate_registral_direction(Pitch1,Pitch2,Pitch3,Register),
   nonharmonic_tone(NHT, [Interval1,Interval2,Register]),
   retractall(last_response(_)),
   asserta(last_response([Pitch1,Pitch2,Pitch3,Interval1,
                                Interval2,Register,NHT])).
```

By changing only one line of our predicate `identify_nht()`, we can use this alternative representation of the knowledge to generate our nonharmonic tones analyses. In this example, we still compute the intervals and registral direction, but, instead of utilizing a number of predicate clauses to calculate an appropriate answer, we use the predetermined data representations shown in figure 4.19 and simply rely on the built-in pattern matching power of Prolog to bind our calculations to an appropriate match. Of course, this representation still works within the same set of constraints as the previous one does. The new inference engine is presented in figure 4.20.

Figure 4.21   A frame-based example.

```
nonharmonic_tone ::
  [name: passing_tone,
  approached: step,
  resolved: step,
  registral_direction: same].
nonharmonic_tone ::
  [name: neighbor_tone,
  approached: step,
  resolved: step,
  registral_direction: reversed].
nonharmonic_tone ::
  [name: appoggiatura,
  approached: skip,
  resolved: step,
  registral_direction: reversed].
nonharmonic_tone ::
  [name: escape_tone,
  approached: step,
  resolved: skip,
  registral_direction: reversed].
nonharmonic_tone ::
  [name: suspension,
  approached: unison,
  resolved: step,
  registral_direction: down].
nonharmonic_tone ::
  [name: retardation,
  approached: unison,
  resolved: step,
  registral_direction: up].
nonharmonic_tone ::
  [name: pedal_tone,
  approached: unison,
  resolved: unison,
  registral_direction: lateral].
```

■ FRAMES

Another knowledge representation scheme used in developing expert-system programs is referred to as *frames*. As discussed in chapter 1, frames represent stereotypical "place holders" for infor-

Figure 4.22   A frame-based inference engine.

```
% Inference Engine

identify_nht(Pitch1,Pitch2,Pitch3,NHT)  :-
   calculate_interval(Pitch1,Pitch2,Interval1),
   calculate_interval(Pitch2,Pitch3,Interval2),
   calculate_registral_direction(Pitch1,Pitch2,Pitch3,Register),
   nonharmonic_tone:: [name: NHT,approached: Interval1,resolved:
                  Interval2, registral_direction: Register],
   retractall(last_response(_)),
   asserta(last_response([Pitch1,Pitch2,Pitch3,Interval1,
                  Interval2,Register,NHT])).
```

mation. These places holders, called *slots,* tend to be filled with either a single matching item or a list of items spanning a *range* of possible values. We present a frame representation for the nonharmonic tone knowledge base in figure 4.21.

In each of the nonharmonic tone frames, there is a list of values that identify the name of the nonharmonic tone, together with slots for how it is approached and resolved as well as for the registral direction. Again, by changing one line in the original `identify_nht()` predicate, we can access the knowledge represented in the frames. The modified `identify_nht()` predicate is presented as figure 4.22.

Notice the difference in Prolog syntax from what we used in our previous examples. We make this change here to help clarify the nature of frames, namely, that they are a collection of nested item names linked to lists of values that can successfully represent those items. In Prolog, all predicates are of the following form:

prefix_operator ([argument-1], . . . [argument-n])

For clarity, our logic statements often read better when we place *prefix* operators between our arguments, thus turning them into *infix* operators. For example, the statement showing the symbols + and * as infix operators

3 + 7 * 4

reads much better than if we treat them as prefix operators

*(4 , +(3 , 7)).

Actually, Prolog treats *all* operators as prefix operators but allows us to write designated ones (e.g., most mathematical operators) in an infix format. Prolog also allows us to define our own operators and to specify both the hierarchical status of each and whether it should be treated as a prefix or an infix operator. In our frame example, we could have chosen a more traditional Prolog representation such as

```
item([nonharmonic_tone,item([name,passing_tone]),
    item([approached,step]),item([resolved,step]),
    item([registral_direction,same])]).
```

When written this way, it is not overly clear just where the distinction lies between what is a *name* and what is a possible *value* for that name. In this case, the first item of a list is the name and the second one a value. We could choose to use the name of the slot as the predicate name, but we would then have no symbolic access to that name unless we duplicated it in the list:

```
nonharmonic_tone(
        [nonharmonic_tone,name([name,passing_tone]),
        approached([approached,step]),
        resolved([resolved,step]),
        registral_direction([registral_direction,
        same])]).
```

By defining a new infix operator, we can effectively separate the two arguments of each list so that the first one precedes the operator and thus acts both as an item in the list and as an identifier—without having to be duplicated elsewhere. Because the purpose of the operator in this case is simply to delimit our arguments, we define a new operator using the : symbol with the following Prolog statement (note that this statement *must* appear in our program prior to using the operator):

```
:- op(800,xfx,':').
```

Syntactically, this operational call tells the Prolog system to define (:-), a symbol (:) that will be used as an infix operator (f) between two arguments (x x) and that it should be assigned a precedence value of 800—an arbitrary number for determining if and when it should appear prior to other symbols when appearing in a nested statement. We now restate our list of nonharmonic tone attributes with the new infix operator as shown in figure 4.23.

Figure 4.23   The revised `nonharmonic_tone()` predicate.

```
nonharmonic_tone(nonharmonic_tone,
        [name : passing_tone,
         approached : step,
         resolved : step,
         registral_direction : same]).
```

Figure 4.24   Infix operators.

```
a. nonharmonic_tone ::
        [name:passing_tone,
         approached : step,
         resolved : step,
         registral_direction : same].
b. ::(nonharmonic_tone,
        [:(name,passing_tone),
         :(approached,step),
         :(resolved,step),
         :(registral_direction,same)]).
```

In our frame example, we also define a second, higher-level infix operator to delineate between the name of the nonharmonic tone with its list of attributes and the names of each attribute with their possible value(s). The higher-level infix operator is defined as

```
:- op(900,xfx,'::').
```

Once we have both operators defined, we rewrite each predicate clause in the syntax shown in figure 4.24a (actually, the same syntax we used initially). As a final way of clarifying how these newly defined operators work, we show you how Prolog actually interprets them on execution in figure 4.24b (remember, Prolog treats all operators as prefix operators).

■ CONCLUSION

In closing, we see that knowledge-based systems present us with a number of useful models for codifying our knowledge and compiling it into a useable format. Depending on the extent of the knowledge we are trying to deal with, our systems can strive for total comprehensibility or simply model some small component of the domain. Once encoded, these expert systems have the ability to explain their logic and to allow us the flexibility to change and manipulate it. As an important caveat, however, we do not wish in any way to imply that these systems are intelligent or even that they represent and access knowledge in any way that is similar to what we as humans do. To the contrary, what we advocate is a type of system capable of working as extensible tools—systems that work *with* us, not *instead* of us. We advocate a style of working in which we extend our thinking into the computer environment and then rely on that abstraction to serve as a window into our own formal processes. We present in the final two chapters of this book just such a working example of how to encode musical scores as well as how to model a complex system using these techniques. We also detail the ways in which such a system can work to our great advantage.

FIVE
A Generalized Model for Encoding Musical Data

INTRODUCTION

In this chapter, we propose a musically based generalized data model suitable for use in a declarative language such as Prolog. We develop a set of minimum criteria to ensure its suitability for most analytical needs, in other words, that it embodies enough information to make it valuable for studying musical meaning as well as for simply re-creating a score or for playing through a synthesizer. We also spend a significant amount of time detailing the design and creation of the structure and present strategies for encoding a score and translating it into the structure. The chapter concludes by examining a number of basic heuristics for traversing the structure and extracting salient information.

Nature of the Problem

Although previous computer-aided analysis studies have offered a great deal to our current understanding of theoretical paradigms, a significant number of past computer applications have been predominantly task specific and procedurally based. In other words, they were designed with a specific analytical task in mind and set about accomplishing that goal through the implementation of an algorithmic series of discrete procedures. We do not intend here to imply that this approach is inherently poor. In fact, most of these strategies accomplish their tasks quite effectively. To the contrary, these programs continue to be very effective tools for theoretical study. Procedurally based programs, however, do embody some inherent limitations, one of the most obvious being their difficulty in achieving a significant level of task independence. Because procedural approaches are usually designed to accomplish specific tasks, any significant refocusing of program functions tends to lead to major restructuring of the program itself. The more monumental the change, the greater the amount of effort that must be expended to accommodate it. In many cases, the change becomes significant enough that starting over from scratch proves more productive.

Obviously, because a computer program is really nothing more than a collection of data and a set of heuristic methods for manipulating those data, we can benefit greatly from a more flexible data model capable of overcoming the problems associated with more rigidly defined ones, and incorporating such a structure into a Prolog system can only serve to enhance that flexibility. We might begin by designing such a model around the following set of ideals: (1) our model should utilize a significantly flexible data structure to enable it to adapt to a multitude of different musical styles and genera; (2) our model should be powerful enough to enable the data to be manipulated in a flexible manner—one that can facilitate a number of different analytical strategies; and (3) our model should be able to implement various heuristic search mechanisms, thus enabling flexible and potentially interactive updating during the course of analysis. In other words, the paradigms we use to undertake an analysis should be determinable, and alterable, by us without significantly modifying the basic structure of our program.

Such an ideal system would have many additional benefits, not the least being its suitability to the declarative power of the Prolog system. Prolog offers us the ability to define declarative strategies using symbolic referencing and undefined data structures such as lists and predicates. These strengths enable us to develop a generalized data structure that can remain independent of any particular problems we are trying to solve. By maintaining a level of program independence, our structure should be applicable in a variety of different musical situations without needing to be redefined or restructured because it is the data that are being manipulated by the program and not the program that is driving the design of the data. This data model can offer us other advantages as well, such as the ability to interchange and share information between various programs and even between different languages and input/output mediums such as MIDI. In the most basic sense, we propose a music-representational data model that attempts to remain totally independent of any particular programming strategies yet maintain a sense of musical meaning and integrity general enough to encompass most musics that we might wish to study. Our proposed structure remains within the broad domain of our standard musical systems yet leaves it up to the individual application to define the specific domain within which the data are to operate.

We devote the remainder of this chapter to examining in depth the development and exploration of our proposed generalized data representation model. We begin by examining Alexander Brinkman's (1986a, 1990) excellent Pascal-based work in this area.

■ FORMAL OVERVIEW OF THE DATA MODEL

Background   In the fall of 1986, Alexander Brinkman of the Eastman School of Music published a significant article entitled "Representing Musical Scores for Computer Analysis." This article, which was later expanded and incorporated in his excellent text on Pascal programming (1990), details the development of a Pascal-based generalized data structure for computer-aided music analysis. The input for Brinkman's data generator consists of music encoded in DARMS code and subsequently parsed into rows of encoded musical events together with their associated parameters. DARMS, standing for *Digital Alternate Representation of Musical Scores*, is a text-based coding language used for describing the visual appearance of a musical score. Developed in the early 1970s by Raymond Erickson (1975, 1976), DARMS became one of the most frequently employed schemes for older text-based computational systems. Despite being slowly supplanted by other input schemes such as MIDI and SCORE, DARMS contains a comprehensive vocabulary for describing musical events and is still widely represented in various music research projects. A sample of a DARMS-encoded score and Brinkman's corresponding encoded list of musical events is included in figures 5.1 and 5.2, respectively. We discuss details of the DARMS language and elements within the encoded list later in this chapter. (For a thorough discussion of DARMS, see Brinkman [1990].)

From his encoded lists, Brinkman creates interesting two-stage models that transform the text-encoded representations of musical scores into a Pascal-based data structure consisting of overlapping representational strata interconnected through large numbers of pointer-based links. These links function to interconnect each musical event to all other events that might possibly relate to it in some

Figure 5.1   A DARMS coding example.

Mozart, Piano Sonata in B flat major, K333 (Mvt. III)

!G !K2- !M2:2 9Q.L,VP 7E 5Q 5 / 8L 30 4 RQ /
(6L 5) (7L 6) (8L 7) (9L 8) / 7Q.L1 ((8 7)) 6EL2

analytical manner. In essence, sound events whose durational span
and/or attack and release points coincide with any other event(s)
are linked together. Central to Brinkman's model is the notion of a
time spine. Specifically, this structure is a linear succession of connected time points marking the locations of starting and ending
times for every temporal event in the encoded musical score.
Linked vertically to every initiating time point is a list of one or
more nodes whose attack begins at that point in time. Other links
are connected from that node to all other event nodes that coincide
with it as well as to an additional point on the time spine indicating
the termination of that event. Additionally, DARMS *part codes* allow
musical events to be linked together with other events indicated as
belonging to the same part, a distinction whose meaning is left completely to the whim of the person doing the encoding. To account
for this aspect, Brinkman sets up multiple layers of events that are
linked vertically to their respective time points and horizontally to
other events belonging to the same part. In essence, every event in
a score is connected to every other adjacent event that could possibly relate to it in any analytical sense. By traversing the time spine
from beginning to end, a program will encounter a node representing every point in time that some event begins or ends. By traversing down any branch from a time point, the program can determine
what events begin or end at that point, and by traversing secondary
links the program can find all those events that are sounding at that
point (regardless of whether their attack or release points coincide)
as well as the next event belonging to the same part. An excerpt of a
completed score structure for the musical example appearing in figures 5.3a is shown in figure 5.3b.

Figure 5.2   Encoded score list modeled after Brinkman (1990).

p1   new instrument number
c Meter signature: 2 / 2   beats: 2;   beatnote: 1 / 2
m1.0   0.0000   1.0000   1.0000   1.5000

1	2	3	4	5	6	7	8	9	10	11	12	13
i1.0	0.0000	0.3750	1.0000	1.3750	5053	3 / 8	0	0	1	x	50	5
i1.0	0.3750	0.5000	1.3750	1.5000	5021	1 / 8	0	0	2	x	50	x
i1.0	0.5000	0.7500	1.5000	1.7500	4106	1 / 4	0	0	0	x	50	x
i1.0	0.7500	1.0000	1.7500	2.0000	4106	1 / 4	0	0	0	x	50	x
b1.0	1.0000		2.0000	2.0000								
i1.0	1.0000	1.2500	2.0000	2.2500	5032	1 / 4	0	0	1	x	50	x
i1.0	1.2500	1.5000	2.2500	2.5000	5074	1 / 4	0	0	2	x	50	x
i1.0	1.5000	1.7500	2.5000	2.7500	4095	1 / 4	0	0	0	x	50	x
i1.0	1.7500	2.0000	1.7500	2.0000	-1	1 / 4	0	0	0	x	50	x
b1.0	2.0000		3.0000	3.0000								
i1.0	2.0000	2.1250	3.0000	3.1250	5000	1 / 8	0	0	1	x	50	x
i1.0	2.1250	2.2500	3.1250	3.2500	4106	1 / 8	0	0	2	x	50	x
i1.0	2.2500	2.3750	3.2500	3.3750	5021	1 / 8	0	0	1	x	50	x
i1.0	2.3750	2.5000	3.3750	3.5000	5000	1 / 8	0	0	2	x	50	x
i1.0	2.5000	2.6250	3.5000	3.6250	5032	1 / 8	0	0	1	x	50	x
i1.0	2.6250	2.7500	3.6250	3.7500	5021	1 / 8	0	0	2	x	50	x
i1.0	2.7500	2.8750	3.7500	3.8750	5053	1 / 8	0	0	1	x	50	x
i1.0	2.8750	3.0000	3.8750	4.0000	5032	1 / 8	0	0	2	x	50	x
b1.0	3.0000		4.0000	4.0000								
i1.0	3.0000	3.3750	4.0000	4.3750	5021	3 / 8	0	0	1	x	50	x
i1.0	3.3750	3.4375	4.3750	4.4375	5032	1 / 16	0	0	0	x	50	x
i1.0	3.4375	3.5000	4.4375	4.5000	5021	1 / 16	0	0	0	x	50	x
i1.0	3.5000	3.6250	4.5000	4.6250	5000	1 / 8	0	0	2	x	50	x
	etc…											

As powerful as Brinkman's model is, however, we feel his structure has several characteristics that inhibit its use in declarative Prolog or Lisp applications. First, because of the inherent design of the Pascal language, the pointers linking his structure can be saved to a disk (or other storage media), but the score cannot be automatically re-created when it is read back into the computer. These pointers store only the actual memory location within the computer of each event at the time it is created and are meaningless to the actual structure of the data. It is virtually impossible for us to ensure that the same locations will be reused when the structure is loaded back into the machine, particularly on a different one. Therefore, the

Figure 5.3   a) A short score example.

structure is essentially unretrievable. Only through extremely elaborate and "smart" algorithms that essentially write the structure to a disk without the pointers yet that continue to maintain the organization of the data can we re-create Brinkman's model from storage without forcing it to be rebuilt from scratch each time it is retrieved. Second, Brinkman's model employs an extremely large number of pointers. Manipulating and traversing pointers is certainly not outside the ability of a good Pascal programmer, yet maintaining a constant awareness of where you are within the structure given the plethora of possible avenues and junctures at any given point is no easy task. In addition, there is a certain amount of memory overhead required for every pointer. If, for example, each event in a musical score had eight pointers associated with it, encoding a large score could require a significant increase in memory usage, an acceptable situation *only* if memory limits are not a constraint. Third, the inherent cohesiveness that makes the structure so powerful also serves to constrain flexibility by rigorously keeping the data within the structure. In other words, it is impossible to disassociate the data from the structure that contains those data. If, for example, we wanted quick and easy access to several isolated and perhaps unrelated musical events, we must traverse the entire structure to get to them. Normally, this presents no real problem. Consider, however, a situation in which we were developing a model for examining hierarchical relationships within a score. Might we not find it desirable to take higher-level nonadjacent events and link them in such a manner as to facilitate direct access from one event to the next? Although these first three issues may seem rather trivial, the final one is not. Because most Prolog and Lisp systems do not support the concept of pointers at all, Brinkman's data model is in effect, unusable in these environments without significant restructuring.

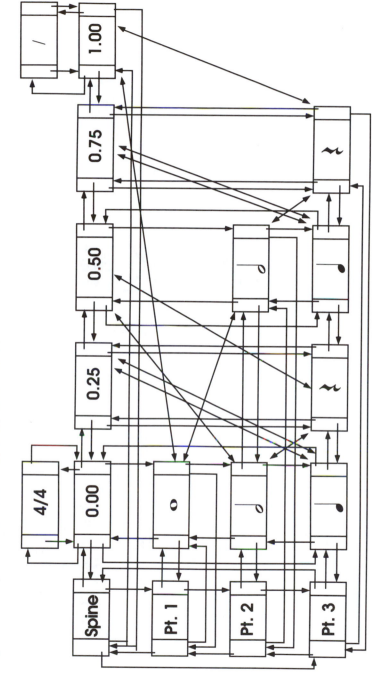

Figure 5.3 b) Brinkman's list-based representation.

Figure 5.4   A simplified list representation.

```
time_spine([[0.00, o, ♩, ♩],[0.25,(♩),♩],

           [0.50,(♩),♩,(♩),♩],[0.75,(♩),♩],

           [1.00,(o),(♩),(♩),/,(/)]] ).
```

NOTE: Events in parentheses represent termination points

The remainder of this chapter discusses how some of the basic ideas of Brinkman's model can be transferred to a list-based Prolog model that maintains and expands the flexibility of the original, yet with the added flexibility and simplicity inherent to Prolog programs and data structures.

Basic Criteria

The first step we must take in developing a working model is to identify the basic conceptual goals that will guide our development. Specifically, we wish to highlight those ideals that are central to the nature of the model. In other words, regardless of the specific details of the actual implementation, we want to maintain the following general guidelines above all else. Because we will be using Brinkman's model as a point of departure, we begin by clarifying strategies for overcoming the pitfalls identified earlier.

1. *We should significantly modify the structure to avoid Pascal-like pointers.* Fortunately, Prolog's list-based data structure offers us a simple solution. Replacing a group of events connected by pointers with a Prolog list containing that same group of events enables us to relate events together similarly. Because Prolog lists can contain any data types, *including other lists*, we can generate a structure of any complexity that we desire. Figure 5.4 shows in a simplified manner how the set of linked lists seen in figure 5.3 can loosely be restructured as a set of lists. In this instance, Brinkman's time spine converts to our outermost list, and his vertical pointer lists become our nested lists.

Initially, this conversion may seem rather simple and straightforward, but the transference is not quite so easy when we add the additional layers of overlapping links. In our rather simple example

Figure 5.5   An enhanced view of figure 5.4.

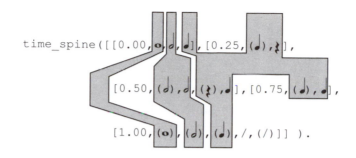

above, each small structure can be completely subsumed within an outer structure. This is not the case, however, if we use the excerpt from figure 5.3a. Although all the events within the vertical spines are subsumed within the horizontal time spine, not all the events in each horizontal part can be drawn together within the same sublist. To facilitate a list-based structure that accounts for this complexity, we would have to create a type of list that could include some elements but bypass others (see figure 5.5), a capability that is incompatible with Prolog's rigid hierarchical nesting requirements. Fortunately, the solution becomes rather simple because we have disassociated the data from the structure that organized them.

2. *We should disassociate the data from the structure to enable random access to all information and to enable greater flexibility in the design of the data structure.* Obviously, we will have to duplicate a certain amount of data to overcome the kind of problems exhibited in figure 5.5, although Prolog enables us to keep the amount of information we duplicate to a minimum. If we could conceptualize our musical events as simple integers, we would be able to reconstruct our nested lists (from figure 5.5) into a *series* of nested lists, each representing different perspectives on the same data—in this instance, the part spines (figure 5.6). Throughout this process, we inevitably must replicate certain data, but because each event is only one integer, the amount of overhead is greatly reduced. Even with a structure of 50,000 events, the overhead would be only 2 bytes per replication, or in this case 100,000 bytes, assuming that every single event is duplicated. This much memory is not trivial. However, considering that most scores contain significantly fewer elements and that the data for such a large score alone would probably take several million bytes of memory, we are really considering a worst-case increase of only 5% to 10%.

Figure 5.6   Part spines.

```
part_spine(1,[[0.00,o],[1.00,(o)]]).


part_spine(2,[[0.00,♩],[0.50,(♩),♩],[1.00,(♩)]]).


part_spine(2,[[0.00,♩],[0.25,(♩),𝄾],[0.50,(𝄾),♩],

     [0.75,(♩),♩],[1.00,(♩)]]).
```

We can expand on this notion by creating actual Prolog structures representing individual musical events, each assigned a unique index value. Essentially, we will store the actual data separately from any of our structures and use their assigned integer values as indices to link the data to the structure through simple instantiation, thus emulating the linking capability of Pascal pointers within a significantly simpler model. Prolog can then access the data apart from the structure yet simultaneously link them to any number of structures simply by virtue of including an appropriate index number at each location in the structure where an event is to be referenced. On traversing a structural list, we can access any event by binding the index numbers in the structure with those in the actual event nodes. Once instantiation is complete, all the data relevant to that event become accessible to the program. We examine this model in figure 5.7.

3. *Our structure must be dynamic and malleable.* As with designing any good exploratory tool, if we do not know the results of our labors before we begin them, how can we possibly anticipate all our needs before we even begin? Obviously, a highly malleable structure that can be easily manipulated is essential. Fortunately, the disassociation of data from the structure and the use of lists for our primary structural components give us the flexibility we need. Built into the Prolog environment is the ability to perform a number of constructive and deconstructive list procedures, such as insertion and deletion from a list, truncation and concatenation of lists, other mapping functions between lists, and various sorting and reordering operations. Our ideal structure should be able to execute many of these functions as we parse a composition into some sort of analytical structure. Fortunately, Prolog offers us just such power. Our data

Figure 5.7   Time spines.

```
time_spine([[0.00,1,2,4],[0.25,-4,5],[0.50,-2,3,-5,6],
           [0.75,-6,7],[1.00,-1,-3,-7,8,-8]]).
```

Events:

Index: 1	𝅝	Part: 1	Start: 0.00 End: 1.00		Index: 5	𝄽	Part: 3	Start: 0.25 End: 0.50

Index:		Part:	Start: 0.00		Index:		Part:	Start: 0.25
1	𝅝	1	End: 1.00		5	𝄽	3	End: 0.50
2	𝅗𝅥	2	Start: 0.00 End: 0.50		6	𝅘𝅥	3	Start: 0.50 End: 0.75
3	𝅗𝅥	2	Start: 0.50 End: 1.00		7	𝅘𝅥	3	Start: 0.75 End: 1.00
4	𝅘𝅥	3	Start: 0.00 End: 0.25		8	/	0	Start: 1.00 End: 1.00

NOTE: Negative index numbers represent termination points

should also remain safe because our structure will include only data references and not the actual data. Any destructive operations we undertake on our structure will not have any adverse effect on our data, and for the most part the opposite is true as well. As mentioned above, the creation of multiple and diverse structures is also a benefit of data abstraction, with the only additional overhead resulting from the replication of integer indices.

4. *Our data will generally adhere to structural aspects of the DARMS encoding scheme.* The choice of DARMS as a representational scheme is meant in no way to imply that other schemes are unacceptable or inferior; rather it is merely the choice that we have made for this project. A number of analytical programs (both past and present) have used this scheme, and there exists a significant body of previously encoded musical examples. Actually, we will not be incorporating much of the basic *representational* nomenclature because DARMS is designed to represent musical symbols as they appear on the printed page and not to convey any sense of musical meaning. Instead, we follow a number of the standard DARMS *organizational* schemes, such as the designation and use of parts, the general adherence to the inclusion of appended modifiers and

library codes, and the odd-even scheme for pairing tie and slur indicators. On the other hand, we do not expect users to learn and understand the entire DARMS language, and throughout this book we will undertake every effort to supply all the relevant information necessary to create and work with the structure.

Because much of our methodology for encoding musical information will not utilize actual DARMS code, we will rely heavily on some of the work previously developed by Brinkman (1986a, b, 1990), who offers several excellent strategies, particularly for encoding rhythmic and pitch information. Brinkman (1990) includes the complete Pascal source code for a DARMS interpreter for generating a text-based tabular listing of encoded information, derived from the original DARMS, that is nearly identical to that shown in figure 5.2. For those who know the code or who have access to DARMS-encoded scores, this program can be of great value. This intermediate translation process is extremely useful because it gives us a DARMS-independent interpretation of musical events that is easily translated into a number of computational environments, including Prolog. Consequently, we have chosen to use this format as a guide for organizing our own data, and because we do not wish to duplicate Brinkman's work, the information in the tabulated output is where we will begin to derive our model for data encoding.

5. *Our data should not be restrictive as to the type of musical events being encoded.* Because it is impossible to account for every possible musical event, our model will accommodate two classes of data types. The first, or *defined*, type will include notes, rests, bar lines, and all those elements that can modify them. The second, or *undefined*, type consists of user-defined and interpreted events where the user assigns their meaning when they are first created and is responsible for interpreting and maintaining them.

6. *The data and, to whatever extent possible, the structure should be as language independent as possible.* Ideally, the information encoded in the data and the organizational design of the structural components should be transferable to other media with as little effort—and with the least amount of information loss—as possible. To this end, we have relied on Brinkman's score format for the basic organization of encoded events. In other words, our data will be organized as a simple categorical list of relevant data qualifiers. Because the structure itself consists of nothing more than integer-based indices organized in nested lists, translating this information to some other medium through straight text translation becomes quite feasible. Ideally, we should be able to convert our data into standard MIDI files for playback or for importation into notation programs, or we might

wish to translate the complete structure into the Lisp programming environment. In other words, unique Prolog structures should be used as little as possible in the design of the data.

Coding the Data Structure

We devote this section of the chapter to describing in detail the specific design features of the data-encoding scheme and the various organizational structures.

■ Nodes

Our data structure consists of two classes of primary elements: *nodes* and *spines*. Nodes represent all discrete dynamic objects—musical events and user-defined objects—that can be *asserted* into or *retracted* from the Prolog database, whereas spines are those list-based structures that temporally organize the nodes. The most important nodes in the system are those representing individual events such as notes and rests. In addition, we will utilize a temporary node type designed to store the indices of all events occurring at any given time point prior to compiling the complete set of time spines.

Event nodes contain all the stored information relevant to an individual event. The information we can store in each `event()` node adheres quite closely to the score-code output from Brinkman's DARMS parser. Included in each event are the following: (1) a unique index integer in the range of 1 . . . *n*; (2) the user-defined DARMS part number; (3) a list of the starting and ending times of the event expressed in terms of whole-note divisions (Brinkman 1986a) as well as the placement of the event within the notated metric scheme; (4) the event name encoded in Brinkman's *Continuous Binary Representation* (1986b); (5) the event name encoded as a text string; (6) the duration of the event expressed as a fraction; (7) a list of related events such as ties, slurs, articulation marks, and dynamics; (8) a list for storing user-defined object information; and (9) an unused list for future expansion (and for use by various routines in the Threader program discussed in appendix 1).

Obviously, there are several redundancies within our data model, such as the starting and ending points within the time frame of the entire piece and within the appropriate measure and the expression of durations both as a decimal (deduced from comparing starting and ending points) and as a fraction. We decided, however, that the frequently required math-intensive operations necessary to compute durational and temporal values—something at which Prolog definitely does *not* excel—can be avoided with the small amount of

Figure 5.8 The event() predicate.

```
/*********************************************************************
* This predicate defines a musical event.
*********************************************************************/

event(INDEX,PART,[Strt,End,Mmnum],CBR,NAME,[DURnum,DURden],
    [Tie,Art,Slur,Dyn],[ObjectInfo],[Extra])
```

overhead created through duplication. Users can feel free to add or subtract parameters as they wish to fit their specific needs, as the arity of the functor will have no effect whatsoever on the functionality of the structure. Again, we can see the beauty of disassociating the data from the structure.

At this point, we would like to discuss each of the nine arguments of event() individually, supplying all the relevant information needed for implementing complete events. The event node type can be seen in figure 5.8.

1. *INDEX*: The index value consists of a unique *positive* integer within the range of 1 . . . *n*, where *n* represents the largest allowable numeric value within your particular Prolog system. The numbers do not have to be consecutive. In addition, the integer order that you assign to each node is of no consequence to the structure, as each index value serves one and only one function: to link the data node to the list structure—there is no implicit or explicit relationship between the two. Obviously, it may be an advantage to order them in a manner that is meaningful to *you*. For example, you may choose to assign consecutive numbers in the range 1 . . . 9,999 to events belonging to part 1 and events belonging to part 2 within the range 10,000 . . . 19,999. Whatever works for you is inevitably the best way to manage your data!

2. *PART*: This number represents the DARMS *part* to which the given event belongs. All events must be assigned a part number within the range 0 . . . 64. Generally, pieces in only one part are assigned part number 1 (we use this as the default value). Although it is not necessary to assign consecutive values to each new part, convention suggests that it be done this way. In other words, pieces in one part will be assigned part 1 pieces in two parts will use parts 1 and 2, and so on. Actually, DARMS does not support a zero part number. We elected to use this number only for indicating bar lines and meters that do not have any individual part association. For those special cases in which different parts have nonaligned metric

structures, it is a simple task for us to add additional bar lines and alter part membership as necessary by not assigning these structures to individual parts.

3. [*Strt,End,MMnum*]: The first two arguments in this list represent the starting and ending points of the event expressed in terms of whole-note values from the beginning of the excerpt. Values will be within the range 0.0000 . . . *n.nnnn*. Brinkman (1986a) devised this scheme so that each event could be placed at an absolute point within the work regardless of metric associations. In other words, an event with the starting and ending values of 3.5000 and 3.7500, respectively begins three-and-one-half whole notes into the piece and end three-and-three-quarters whole notes into the piece. The event represents a duration equivalent to that of one quarter note (0.2500 of a whole note). Similarly, a note beginning on the downbeat of a composition would have a starting value of 0.0000. If we desire to know the metric position of the event, the third parameter supplies us with this information by indicating the starting point of that event within the current measure. The actual value expresses the current measure number together with the percentage of the measure occurring prior to the entrance of the event. For example, a note starting on beat 2 of the second 4/4 measure in the piece would be assigned the value 2.2500. We must note that this number is treated differently than those represented by the first two arguments. In the former cases, the decimal value expressed a percentage of whole-note values—a consistent value regardless of metric diversity. The decimal value of the third argument, however, represents a percentage of the current measure—a value that will change, depending on the meter. For example, the value 1.5000 assigned to an event occurring in a 4/4 measure indicates that it begins one half note into the measure. On the other hand, the same value assigned to an event in a 2/4 measure indicates that it begins the duration of only one quarter note from the beginning of the measure.

This mathematical scheme presents us with a significant problem. Prolog was never designed as a math-intensive language; instead, its power lies in symbolic manipulation. Consequently, most Prolog environments do not handle floating-point operations very well. In fact, generally the error level is unacceptable. To overcome this problem, we reinterpret all the floating-point values as long integers multiplied by a value of 10,000. The value 3.5000 is thus represented as 35,000, the number 17.1250 as 171,250, and so on. By storing our values in the database in this manner, we can carry out nearly any computation as an integer operation without dealing with any error factor. The final result can then be divided by 10,000

Figure 5.9   Converting durational values.

```
/*****************************************************************
 * These predicates convert a DURation code into the
 * whole-note (Whole) and fractional (Fraction) location
 * of an event in time, or visa versa.
 *****************************************************************/

convert_DUR_to_parts(DUR,Whole,Fraction) :-
   Whole is DUR // 10000,
   Fraction is DUR mod 10000.

convert_parts_to_DUR(DUR,Whole,Fraction) :-
   DUR is Whole * 10000 + Fraction.
```

to achieve a true value, and our error factor effectively becomes a negligible consideration. The Prolog code for carrying out these operations appears in figure 5.9.

4. *CBR*: This value encodes the event as a *continuous binary representation* (Brinkman 1986b). We employ this scheme because it offers us an extremely compact way to represent pitch-based events, incorporating letter-class, pitch-class, and octave information within one integer. We encode letter-class information as a range from 0 . . . 6, representing the notes C . . . B, respectively. Pitch-class information is represented by the range 0 . . . 11, with zero representing C-natural and all other enharmonic equivalents, such as B-sharp and D-double flat. Octave indications use the Acoustic Society of America's designation system for defining the ten-octave audible spectrum. Zero indicates the lowest audible octave register, beginning with C-natural and encompassing the registral space of a major seventh to B-natural. Octave 4 indicates the register beginning with middle C (figure 5.10).

Creating a CBR code is relatively easy: the *thousands* digit of the CBR number indicates the octave, the *tens* and *hundreds* digits represent the two possible digits of a pitch class, and the *ones* digit represents the letter-class information. For example, we can represent the note A♭4 with a CBR of 4085 (4 = octave, 08 = pitch class, and 5 = A), E♯3 with a CBR of 3052, and Bn5 with a CBR of 5116. The code for creating a CBR from the three discrete values and for segmenting a CBR into the same three discrete values appears in figure 5.11. We have chosen to use binomial representation values of zero, negative one, and negative two to stand for bar lines, rests, and meters, respectively.

Figure 5.10   Table of values.

Letter Classes (LC)	Pitch Classes (PC)		Octave (OCT)
C = 0	C / B# = 0	F# / G♭ = 6	0..9
D = 1	C# / D♭ = 1	G = 7	middle-C = 4
E = 2	D = 2	G# / A♭ = 8	
F = 3	D# / E♭ = 3	A = 9	
G = 4	E / F♭ = 4	A# / B♭ = 10	
A = 5	E#/ F = 5	B / C♭ = 11	
B = 6			

Figure 5.11   Manipulating Brinkman's CBR codes.

```
/******************************************************************
* These predicates encode and decode Brinkman's CBR
******************************************************************/

encode_CBR(OCT,PC,LC,CBR) :-
   CBR is (OCT*1000) + (PC*10) + LC.

decode_CBR(CBR,OCT,PC,LC) :-
   OCT is CBR // 1000,
   PC  is (CBR // 10) mod 100,
   LC  is CBR mod 10.
```

5. *Name*: This parameter is simply a string of text (defined as list of characters in some Prolog implementations) between two quotes indicating the event name or type. Valid values include such entries as the following:

"C#"   "rest"   "bar line"   "meter"   "object"

We incorporate this parameter to facilitate quick comprehension of any data that we are examining. A significant amount of computational energy is required to convert numeric values into meaningful textual representations. By supplying a textual representation, we are able to eliminate this process altogether.

6. [*DURnum,DURden*]: These two parameters express the duration of an event as a fraction of a whole-note value, with the first argument indicating the numerator and the second the denominator. We

include these values to add precision to the decimal values assigned to the third argument of the predicate. Although we believe that these decimal values carried to four decimal places (one ten-thousandth of a whole note) are generally sufficient, triplets and certain other values will exhibit small but real rounding errors. Fractional representations permit us to express durations such as a triplet quarter-note as 1/6, a factor with no error, versus 0.1667, which has a small but obvious rounding error.

7. [*Tie,Art,Slur,Dyn*]: These four parameters indicate the presence of such elements as ties, slurs, articulation marks, and dynamics. We have generally followed the DARMS conventions for defining these values. DARMS indicates both the starting and the ending points for ties and slurs by employing odd-even pairs of integers, with an odd value, *n* (e.g., 1, 3, 99, 289), representing the beginning of the link and an even value, *n + 1* (e.g., 2, 4, 100, 290), the termination of that link. Any valid integers can indicate the start and end of a tie or slur as long as they follow the *n . . . n + 1* convention. Articulations and dynamics are simply assigned numeric values coded to a list of standard modifiers. Besides the standard articulations, DARMS accommodates a *library* of additional modifiers. This extension enables us to define any additional parameters such as *Hauptstimme* or other nonstandard articulations that we may desire to use. Although a thorough accounting of these articulation and dynamic values appears in Brinkman (1990), we have chosen to replicate some of the more common ones for your information and use in figure 5.12.

8. [*ObjectInfo*]: We include this argument for the storage of user-defined object information. Essentially, we would like a user to be able to define an event as an object and to give that object any meaning desired. The supplied list (normally empty when the event is a standard event type such as a note, rest, or bar line) can be filled with any valid Prolog symbol(s). For example, we might want to undertake a melodic analysis of a composition for voice and accompaniment for which we need to know the harmonic structure of the piece yet do not really need to encode every note of the accompaniment. Instead, we might choose to create objects that specify harmonic regions and store chord symbols and inversion information in this list. Generally, it is a good idea to treat any information stored in this argument as text; otherwise, Prolog will impose its normal restrictions for identifying symbols, variables, and key words. For example, if we were to store the following information,

[V7]

Figure 5.12   Select DARMS codes.

Articulations / library codes*			Dynamics			Extended dynamics**		
Staccato	=	1	ppppp	=	0	sfz	=	1000
wedge accent	=	2	ppppp	=	10	decrescendo		
tenuto	=	4	pppp	=	20	(over 1 note)	=	2000
accent (horiz.)	=	8	ppp	=	30	crescendo		
accent (vert.)	=	16	pp	=	40	(over 1 note)	=	3000
fermata	=	32	p	=	50	decrescendo		
arco	=	64	mp	=	60	(begin)	=	4000
pizzicato	=	128	mf	=	70	decrescendo		
snap pizzicato	=	256	f	=	80	(end)	=	5000
down bow	=	512	ff	=	90	crescendo		
up bow	=	1024	fff	=	100	(begin)	=	6000
Hauptstimme	=	2048	ffff	=	110	crescendo		
Nebenstimme	=	4096	fffff	=	120	(end)	=	7000
end Hupt/Neben	=	8192	fffff	=	130			
harmonic	=	16384						
mute	=	32768						
am steg	=	65536						

* These values are designed so that they can be added together so that more than one articulation can be present at the same time. When viewed from a binary perspective, each integer value represents a binary value with one bit active (1); all the others are off (0). For example,

16 (decimal)	=	00010000 (binary)
64 (decimal)	=	01010000 (binary)
16 + 64 = 80	=	01010000 (binary)

** Dynamic and Extended dynamics can be added together as well, in a manner similar to the CBR codes. In this case, the first three digits of a decimal number represent the current dynamic level; the fourth and fifth digits represent the presence of an extended code. For example,

4090 (decimal)	=	dynamic level ff (80)
		beginning decrescendo (4000)

Prolog will treat it as an unbound variable (remember that all variables begin with a capital letter) and not as the symbol we perceive it to be. If we place the same information within quotes or use lowercase letters,

["V7"]   or   [v7],

Prolog will not attempt to interpret the information and we will be free to do with it as we please. When an event is *not* defined as an object type, this list may be used for any purpose.

9. [*extra*]: This list is included for expansion and can be used for any purpose. However, if you are using the Threader program discussed in appendix 1, you cannot use this list because it stores information the program requires for manipulating the event on the screen.

■ **Spines**   Spine types, although technically dynamic objects similar to nodes, function to link together collections of discrete event nodes by storing the index numbers of these nodes in an event-time ordered list (or lists). The two basic spine structures we propose appear in figure 5.13.

Specifically, the time spine consists of a single list containing from 1 . . . *n* sublists. Each sublist represents one point in time and contains first a reference to that point followed by the index number of every event that begins or ends there. Positive index values represent the initiation of an event and negative index values the termination of that event. Let us assume for the moment that we have a short composition with three pitch events consisting of two sequential quarter notes, indexed as events 2 and 3, sounding simultaneously with a sustained half note, indexed as event 4. A half rest follows both parts and will be encoded with indices 5 and 6. Finally, the excerpt ends with a bar line encoded as event 7. We also include a meter event encoded as event 1. This excerpt, together with the coded `event()`s and part definitions, is shown in figure 5.14. The `time_spine()` for this excerpt consists of a list containing three sublists representing the three points in time that events occur. The first sublist indicates the time point zero and references the initiation of both events 1 and 3. The second time point, indicating 2500 (or one quarter of a whole note into the excerpt), signifies the termination of event 1 as well as the initiation of event 2. The third sublist, indicating 5000 (or one half of a whole note into the excerpt), identifies the termination of events 2 and 3 as well as the initiation of the two rests. Finally, the fourth sublist includes the termination events for the two rests as well as the initiation and termination events for the bar line—an event with no duration because it begins and ends at the same point in time. The complete `time_spine()` appears as

```
time_spine([[0,1,-1,2,4],[2500,-2,3],[5000,-3,
    -4,5,6],[10000,-5,-6,7,-7]]).
```

Figure 5.13   Spine definitions.

```
/* * * * * * * * * * * * * * * * * * * * * * * * * * * * * * * * * * * * * * * * * * * * * * * * * * * * *
 * The two primary spine structures
 * * * * * * * * * * * * * * * * * * * * * * * * * * * * * * * * * * * * * * * * * * * * * * * * * * * * * */

time_spine([[TimePoint#1,Event#1,...Event#n],...
    [TimePoint#n,Event#n1,...Event#nn]]).

part_spine(PartNUM,"name",[[TimePoint#1,Event#1,...Event#n],...
    [TimePoint#n,Event#n1,...Event#nn]]).
```

Figure 5.14   Examples of event().

```
event(1,0,[0,0,10000],-2,"meter",[3,4],[0,0,0,-1],[],[]).
event(2,1,[0,2500,10000],5000,"C",[1,4],[0,0,0,-1],[],[]).
event(3,1,[2500,5000,13333],4075,"G",[1,4],[0,0,0,-1],[],[]).
event(4,2,[0,5000,10000],4042,"E",[1,2],[0,0,0,-1],[],[]).
event(5,1,[5000,10000,16667],0,"rest",[1,4],[0,0,0,-1],[],[]).
event(6,2,[5000,7500,16667],0,"rest",[1,4],[0,0,0,-1],[],[]).
event(7,0,[5000,7500,20000],-1,"barline",[1,4],[0,0,0,-1],[],[]).
```

Although the time_spine() is non–part specific, our part_spine() structures contain only those events associated by the same DARMS part code. Because we may not desire all parts of the structure for a given analysis, the part_spine() structures offer us an alternative to the time_spine(), effectively reducing the overhead of dealing with extraneous information we may not wish to use. Because a large number of analytical inquiries can in fact be made with voice-delimited data, the part_spine() lists enable us to use the system more efficiently by reducing memory requirements and eliminating potential parsing procedures that we would need to undertake if we were working with the entire structure yet desiring only one part's worth of data. These constraints may not be necessary on a large and fast computer. However, memory and speed constraints of most midsize microcomputers are magnified significantly from those of larger systems. Any effort that we can make to reduce the amount of information treated during any typical operation becomes very desirable. A sizeable list of elements will eat up computer resources quickly when parsed recursively— and, in the case of musical scores, these lists may number in the thousands of events. We want to emphasize that these part-specific structures are in no way essential but are merely there to facilitate succinct analytical inquiry when this type of data restriction is acceptable. In certain situations, however, `part_spine()`s may be of no value. Obviously, if a selection of music is encoded in only one part, such as a solo piano piece might be, the `time_spine()` and the one `part_spine()` created would in essence be identical and no savings realized. In other cases, DARMS part distinctions might be encoded in a manner that does not reflect analytically significant musical parameters. Assuming that we were to construct the music shown in figure 5.14 into `part_spine()` structures as well as the `time_spine()`, we would end up including the following:

```
part_spine(1,"upper",[[0,1,-1,2],[2500,
    -2,3],[5000,-3,5],[10000,-5,7,-7]]).

part_spine(2,"lower",[[0,1,-1,4],[5000,
    -4,6],[10000,-6,7,-7]]).
```

■ Assembling the Structure

Prior to building any time-spine list, we will utilize a temporary predicate with the functor `time_spine_node()` to compile short lists of all events occurring at any single time point. This predicate can be seen in figure 5.15. Essentially, the EventLIST from each `time_spine_node()` will become a sublist in the final structure. Our routines for linking the `time_spine_node()`s and their associated `event()`s into a `time_spine()` and `part_spine()`s are relatively simple. The complete Prolog code is included as figure 5.16 with a detailed description following.

Our first predicate, `create_TimeSpine()`, is set up to coordinate the other operations used in building the structure. Before beginning the construction process, we must take care of some basic housekeeping by clearing the database of all `time_spine()` clauses and the utility predicate `time_spine_node()` left over from previous work. We also wish to initialize these two predicates by asserting the `time_spine()` with a *null* list and setting up a temporary dummy clause for `time_spine_node()`. Both of these operations enable our other predicates to be defined in a more general style by not having to check for the existence of these struc-

Figure 5.15 The `time_spine_node()`.

```
/*********************************************************
* Temporary predicate used when building a time_spine()
*********************************************************/

time_spine_node(TimePoint,[Event#1,...Event#n])
```

tures—acting differently depending on whether there are previously defined clauses.

The actual linking process is accomplished through the two additional predicates `create_TimeSpine2()` and `link_spine()`. To create the master list, we will engineer `create_TimeSpine2()` as a `fail`-generated loop that examines one event every time through the loop until every event in the database has been assessed. By using this repeat mechanism instead of a simple iterative recursive loop, we are able to collect events with discontiguous and unordered indices. An iterative loop, on the other hand, requires a counter of some sort that would look for each value as the loop increments regardless of whether any valid data are present in the database—a significant waste of time if all the indices are widely separated. Additionally, the algorithm would have no way of knowing when it has exhausted all the possible events without being informed of a maximum loop count. Our solution maximizes the efficiency of the program by guaranteeing that no unassigned numbers are checked, and because the `fail` mechanism simply forces Prolog to search through the database for every clause of a given predicate, it will automatically stop when no more are encountered, offering us a significant gain in flexibility.

As each event is accessed, the predicate `create_TimeSpine3()` is called, which in turn calls the predicate `search_TimeSpine()` to insert the current index number into that existing clause of the `time_spine_node()` matching the given time of the event. If no match is found, we create a new node reflecting the current event time. Once the start time is processed, the index number of the event is negated to indicate the end of the event, and `search_Time-Spine()` is called again, this time looking for the terminating time point. In addition to creating a `time_spine_node()` for each time point in the piece, the predicate `spine_insert()` calls the predicate `timeSpine_insert()` to incorporate the actual time point value (without the event indices) into the time spine. On exiting these predicates, `create_TimeSpine()` sorts the list into ascending order.

Figure 5.16 The `create_time_spine()` predicate.

```
/**************************************************************
*     This predicate controls construction of the time_spine()
**************************************************************/
      create_TimeSpine :-
          retractall( time_spine_node(_,_) ),
          assertz( time_spine_node(-1.0,[]) ),
          retractall( time_spine(_) ),
          assertz( time_spine([]) ),
          create_TimeSpine2,
          time_spine(X),
          sort(X,X2),
          retractall(time_spine(_)),
          assertz(time_spine(X2)),
          link_spine(_),
          retractall( time_spine_node(_,_) ).
/**************************************************************
*     These routines create individual time_spine_node()s
*         that associate all the events with their respective
*         time links.
**************************************************************/
      create_TimeSpine2 :-
          event(NUM,_,[Strt,End,_],_,_,_,_,_,_),
          create_TimeSpine3(NUM,Strt,End),
          fail.
      create_TimeSpine2.

      create_TimeSpine3(NUM,Strt,End) :-
          search_TimeSpine(NUM,Strt),
          Neg_NUM is (NUM * -1),
          search_TimeSpine(Neg_NUM,End),!.

      search_TimeSpine(CNT,Time) :-
          time_spine_node(Time,LIST),
          append(LIST,[CNT],LIST2),
          retractall( time_spine_node(Time,_) ),
          assertz( time_spine_node(Time,LIST2) ),
          timeSpine_insert(Time).
      search_TimeSpine(CNT,Time) :-
          assertz( time_spine_node(Time,[CNT]) ),
          timeSpine_insert(Time).

          timeSpine_insert(Time) :-
              time_spine(L),
              retractall( time_spine(_) ),
              append(L,[Time],L2),
              assertz( time_spine(L2) ).
```

Figure 5.16   (continued)

```
link_spine(_) :-
    time_spine(X),
    retractall( time_spine(_) ),
    assertz( time_spine([]) ),
    insert_node_info(X).
insert_node_info([]).
insert_node_info([H|Tail]) :-
    time_spine_node(H,L),
    retractall( time_spine_node(H,_) ),
    time_spine(X),
    append([H],L,L2),
    append(X,[L2],X2),
    retractall( time_spine(_) ),
    assertz( time_spine(X2) ),
    insert_node_info(Tail).
```

Through this last step, we are able to take the entire `time_spine()` structure (having been built by taking any event time in any order and appending it to the end of the list) and rely on the standard Prolog predicate `sort()` to arrange the list in ascending order—a process that would not work if all the indices were also included with the time points in the list. Inserting the event indices becomes a simple matter, as our predicate `link_spine()` calls the predicate `insert_node_info()` to extract information recursively from the `time_spine_node()`s and insert it into the `time_spine()`. When the operation is completed, the `time_spine_node()`s are retracted from the database because they are now redundant.

■ **Building the Part Spines**   Once the `time_spine()` is created, either of two additional predicates, `create_PartSpine()` or `create_all_PartSpines()`, can be called to create part-specific time spines. The heuristics for creating these lists are coded into Prolog and appear in figure 5.17.

Because our program routines have no way of knowing how many different parts are encoded in a score, and because parts do not have to be assigned contiguous numbers, we can simplify our heuristics considerably, particularly for `create_all_PartSpines()`, by including a user-specified predicate, `part()`, to define each DARMS part included in the score. Specifically, the `part()` predicate stores a part number and a symbolic (text-based) description of the part. For example, the two parts encoded in the short musical excerpt appearing in figure 5.14 might appear as

```
part(1,flute).
part(2,violin).
```

To build all the required lists, `create_all_PartSpines()` progresses through a `fail`-generated loop, systematically accessing each `part()` clause in the database—we simply supply the `create_PartSpine()` predicate with the desired part to create. Once a particular part is designated, both of these predicates call `create_PartSpine2()`, which in turn calls `link_part()` to create a `part_spine()` and then inserts `assertz()` into the completed structure into the database. Our actual part structures are created by traversing the previously created `time_spine()` and duplicating every element belonging to the designated part in the new structure. The predicate `link_part()` calls two other predicates to evaluate the time spine. As each time point is extracted from the complete `time_spine()` structure, `find_all()` is used to traverse all the elements occurring in the corresponding sublist, pulling out any relevant indices and inserting them into the temporary list `TempList2`. On exiting `find_all()`, the predicate `check_list()` is called to determine whether the newly created `TempList2` is empty (having no events belonging to that part relating to that time point) or has valid data in it. `Link_part()` then continues recursively to examine every time point in the original structure. We have elected to include bar lines and meters when creating `part_spine()` structures even though these events may not specifically be associated with any part. It is a simple matter to eliminate them from the part structures by deleting the third clause of `find_all()` in the code appearing in figure 5.17.

■ Saving and Retrieving the Structure

One of the powers of the Prolog system is revealed after the structure is created. As alluded to earlier, Prolog enables us to assert dynamic instances of a predicate into or out of any external data file. Once our program creates all the desired structures, it is a simple matter to save them as complete units to a text-based (ASCII) file and then consult them back into the system later using the built-in predicates `tell()`, `listing()`, `told()`, and `reconsult()`. In other words, all our analytical structures need to be created only once. What might take several minutes of computational time to create often can be retrieved from the file in a matter of seconds. In addition, because the information saved in the file is text based, it can be opened for examination, editing, or even printing from any word processor or text editor.

Figure 5.17   The `createPartSpine()` predicate.

```
/*****************************************************************
*      These routines create the part_spine()s,
*****************************************************************/

        create_PartSpine(Part) :-
            retractall( part_spine(Part,_,_) ),
            time_spine(SpineList),
            part(Part,Name),
            create_PartSpine2(Part,Name,SpineList),!.

        create_all_PartSpines :-
            part(Part,_),
            create_PartSpine(Part),
            fail.
        create_all_PartSpines.

        create_PartSpine2(PART,Name,SpineList) :-
            link_part(PART,SpineList,[],PartList),
            assertz( part_spine(PART,Name,PartList) ).
        create_PartSpine2(_,_,_).

        link_part(_,[],PartList,PartList).
        link_part(PART,[[H|Tail1]|Tail2],TempList,PartList) :-
            find_all(PART,Tail1,[],List),
            check_list(List,TempList,[[H|List]],TempList2),
            link_part(PART,Tail2,TempList2,PartList).
        find_all(_,[],List,List).
        find_all(PART,[H|Tail],TempL,List) :-
            H2 is integer(fabs(H)),
            event(H2,PART,_,_,_,_,_,_,_),
            append(TempL,[H],TempL2),
            find_all(PART,Tail,TempL2,List).
        find_all(PART,[H|Tail],TempL,List) :-
            H2 is integer(fabs(H)),
            event(H2,0,_,_,_,_,_,_,_),
            append(TempL,[H],TempL2),
            find_all(PART,Tail,TempL2,List).
        find_all(PART,[_|Tail],TempL,List) :-
            find_all(PART,Tail,TempL,List).

        check_list([],TempList,_,TempList).
        check_list(_,TempList,X,TempList2) :-
            append(TempList,X,TempList2).
```

Figure 5.18   The `save_the_structure()` predicate.

```
%---------------------------------------------
%      These routines save or reconsult the
%         Database containing the event nodes
%         and the ordered traversal list(s).
%---------------------------------------------
save_the_structure(FileName) :-
       nl,write('SAVING: score & all_spine(s)'),nl,
       save_score(FileName).

       save_score(FileName) :-
          tell(FileName),
          listing(part/2),
          listing(event/9),
          listing(time_spine/1),
          listing(part_spine/3),
          told.

       load_score(FileName) :-
          reconsult(FileName).
```

Specifically, `save_the_structure()` relies entirely on these built-in Prolog predicates for accomplishing the task of transferring the data. When supplied with a valid system (e.g., DOS or Finder) file name, `tell()` will create and open a text file for writing. The predicate `listing()` writes one or more predicate clauses to the file. If we supply specific data as a parameter, binding ensures that only the clause containing the specific match will be written. However, we can save all the clauses of a particular predicate by supplying only the functor of the desired predicate, followed by a forward slash (/) and the arity of the predicate. Finally, the predicate `told` closes the currently open system file. If we should desire to create and save additional structures, all we need to do is add the appropriate additional `telling()` clause(s) to the predicate `save_the_structure()`.

To recover the structure from a file, Prolog supplies us with the predicate `reconsult()`. Amazingly, this one predicate opens the specified file, reads all the information into the Prolog database, and closes the file when it is done—how could it be any simpler!

Traversing the Structure

In the final section of this chapter, we introduce a few basic heuristics for traversing the spine structure. We examine a number of complex ways for manipulating this data in the next several chapters and do not intend for these procedures to represent an exhaustive collection of methodologies. On the other hand, we do feel that a short exploration of several basic linear and vertical traversal strategies will be helpful in solidifying an understanding of the basic structure. To simplify matters, we have elected to use one short musical excerpt drawn from J. S. Bach's Chorale no. 5 for all the traversal routines. The score for the excerpt and the complete `event()` and `part()` data used to encode it appear in figure 5.19. Although the excerpt is short and relatively simple, it does exhibit several characteristics that render it a less than trival subject. First, the score is in four distinct DARMS parts, which enables us to explore the idiosyncracies of multipart structures. Second, the score exhibits representative examples of intravoice syncopation, or rhythmic displacement, rending vertical traversals more complicated.

■ Linear Traversals

The first of our linear traversal routines uses a simple-brute-force approach that allows us to traverse the spine by following one specified DARMS part from start to finish. As the spine is traversed, the part-specific pitch(es) encountered in each sublist are collected before moving on to the very next sublist, completing the search when the end of the spine is encountered. The code for this heuristic appears in figure 5.20.

Specifically, the predicate `brute_force_linear()` is called to access the time spine and to pass it to a second predicate, `linear_traversal1()`, consisting of two clauses. The first clause stops the recursive process of building the part-specific melody list and binds it to the unbound variable MELODY to pass it back out through the nested recursive calls. The second clause recursively extracts one sublist at a time from the time spine; passes it to a second parsing predicate, `collect_linear_events()`, to collect all the events belonging to the DARMS part specified by the variable PART; and then adds a list of any found events to TempMEL. The result of a query specifying DARMS part 1 appears in figure 5.21

Conceptually, the process we developed in the brute-force approach is simple and straightforward, yet it embodies one specific weakness: it ignorantly searches every sublist in the time spine even though many time points may not contain any events belonging

Figure 5.19   A Bach Chorale example.

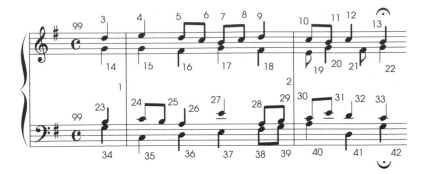

```
part(1,soprano).
part(2,alto).
part(3,tenor).
part(4,bass).

event(1,0,[10000,10000,20000],0,"barline",[0,0],[0,0,0,-1],[],[]).
event(2,0,[20000,20000,30000],0,"barline",[0,0],[0,0,0,-1],[],[]).
event(99,0,[0,0,1000],-2,"meter",[4,4],[0,0,0,-1],[],[]).
event(3,1,[7500,10000,17500],5021,"D",[1,4],[0,0,0,-1],[],[]).
event(4,1,[10000,12500,20000],5042,"E",[1,4],[0,0,0,-1],[],[]).
event(5,1,[12500,13750,22500],5021,"D",[1,8],[0,0,0,-1],[],[]).
event(6,1,[13750,15000,23750],5000,"C",[1,8],[0,0,0,-1],[],[]).
event(7,1,[15000,16250,25000],4116,"B",[1,8],[0,0,0,-1],[],[]).
event(8,1,[16250,17500,26250],5000,"C",[1,8],[0,0,0,-1],[],[]).
event(9,1,[17500,20000,27500],5021,"D",[1,4],[0,0,0,-1],[],[]).
event(10,1,[20000,21250,30000],5000,"C",[1,8],[0,0,0,-1],[],[]).
event(11,1,[21250,22500,31250],4116,"B",[1,8],[0,0,0,-1],[],[]).
event(12,1,[22500,25000,32500],5000,"C",[1,4],[0,0,0,-1],[],[]).
event(13,1,[25000,27500,35000],4116,"B",[1,4],[0,6,0,-1],[],[]).
event(14,2,[7500,10000,17500],4074,"G",[1,4],[0,0,0,-1],[],[]).
event(15,2,[10000,12500,20000],4074,"G",[1,4],[0,0,0,-1],[],[]).
event(16,2,[12500,15000,22500],4063,"F#",[1,4],[0,0,0,-1],[],[]).
event(17,2,[15000,17500,25000],4074,"G",[1,4],[0,0,0,-1],[],[]).
event(18,2,[17500,20000,27500],4063,"F#",[1,4],[0,0,0,-1],[],[]).
event(19,2,[20000,21250,30000],4042,"E",[1,8],[0,0,0,-1],[],[]).
event(20,2,[21250,23750,31250],4074,"G",[1,4],[0,0,0,-1],[],[]).
event(21,2,[23750,25000,33750],4063,"F#",[1,8],[0,0,0,-1],[],[]).
event(22,2,[25000,27500,35000],4074,"G",[1,4],[0,6,0,-1],[],[]).
event(23,3,[7500,10000,17500],3116,"B",[1,4],[0,0,0,-1],[],[]).
event(24,3,[10000,11250,20000],4000,"C",[1,8],[0,0,0,-1],[],[]).
event(25,3,[11250,12500,21250],3116,"B",[1,8],[0,0,0,-1],[],[]).
event(26,3,[12500,15000,22500],3095,"A",[1,4],[0,0,0,-1],[],[]).
```

Figure 5.19   (continued)

```
event(27,3,[15000,17500,25000],4042,"E",[1,4],[0,0,0,-1],[],[]).
event(28,3,[17500,18750,27500],3095,"A",[1,8],[0,0,0,-1],[],[]).
event(29,3,[18750,20000,28750],3116,"B",[1,8],[0,0,0,-1],[],[]).
event(30,3,[20000,21250,30000],4000,"C",[1,8],[0,0,0,-1],[],[]).
event(31,3,[21250,22500,31250],4042,"E",[1,8],[0,0,0,-1],[],[]).
event(32,3,[22500,25000,32500],4021,"D",[1,4],[0,0,0,-1],[],[]).
event(33,3,[25000,27500,35000],4021,"D",[1,4],[0,6,0,-1],[],[]).
event(34,4,[7500,10000,17500],3074,"G",[1,4],[0,0,0,-1],[],[]).
event(35,4,[10000,12500,20000],3000,"C",[1,4],[0,0,0,-1],[],[]).
event(36,4,[12500,15000,22500],3021,"D",[1,4],[0,0,0,-1],[],[]).
event(37,4,[15000,17500,25000],3042,"E",[1,4],[0,0,0,-1],[],[]).
event(38,4,[17500,18750,27500],3063,"F#",[1,8],[0,0,0,-1],[],[]).
event(39,4,[18750,20000,28750],3074,"G",[1,8],[0,0,0,-1],[],[]).
event(40,4,[20000,22500,30000],3095,"A",[1,4],[0,0,0,-1],[],[]).
event(41,4,[22500,25000,32500],3021,"D",[1,4],[0,0,0,-1],[],[]).
event(42,4,[25000,27500,35000],3074,"G",[1,4],[0,6,0,-1],[],[]).
```

Figure 5.20   The `brute_force_linear()` predicate.

```
brute_force_linear(PART,MELODY) :-
    time_spine(Spine),
    linear_traversal1(Spine,PART,[],MELODY).

    linear_traversal1([],_,MELODY,MELODY).
    linear_traversal1([[_|Tail1]|Tail2],PART,TempMEL,MELODY) :-
        collect_linear_events1(Tail1,PART,[],Temp),
        add_newEvents(TempMEL,Temp,TempMEL2),
        linear_traversal1(Tail2,PART,TempMEL2,MELODY).
    collect_linear_events1([],_,TempMEL,TempMEL).
    collect_linear_events1([H|Tail],PART,Temp,TempMEL) :-
        get_part1(H,PART),
        append(Temp,[H],Temp2),
        collect_linear_events1(Tail,PART,Temp2,TempMEL).
    collect_linear_events1([_|Tail],PART,Temp,TempMEL) :-
        collect_linear_events1(Tail,PART,Temp,TempMEL).
    add_newEvents(TempMEL,[],TempMEL).
    add_newEvents(TempMEL,Temp,TempMEL2) :-
        append(TempMEL,[Temp],TempMEL2).
        get_part1(H,_) :-                    % get rests/meters
            event(H,0,_,_,_,_,_,_,_).
        get_part1(H,PART) :-                 % get events
            event(H,PART,_,_,_,_,_,_,_).
```

Figure 5.21   A sample `brute_force_linear()` query.

```
?- brute_force_linear(1,MELODY).
MELODY = [[99],[3],[1,4],[5],[6],[7],[8],[9],[2,10],[11],[12],[13]]
```

to the designated part. A more elegant approach allows us to access the end point of the current event and to use it to guide us directly to the start of the next event. This approach assumes, of course, that all the events occurring in a given voice at any one time end together and that the next event(s) will begin when the previous events end. Unfortunately, because multiple events with different ending points may appear simultaneously in the same part, the algorithm becomes more complex because we need to keep track of multiple sets of end connections. We can accomplish this task by maintaining a separate list of ending time points. As our algorithm proceeds through each time point list, the END point of every relevant event is stored in temporal order (first to last) and used later to access the future events. In certain situations, however, a score may contain discontiguous events within a part—in other words, there may be a gap in which no events occur in a given voice. Because our end traversal algorithm is designed to deal primarily with contiguous or overlapping events, we must rely on the brute-force method to get us through those sections if the chosen part has ceased to exist temporarily. Essentially, if there is no end point to follow, our algorithm will proceed by examining each time point until the errant part returns, at which point the end traversal takes over again. The code appearing in figure 5.22 takes just such an approach to traversing the list.

Essentially, our predicate `elegant_linear()` functions similarly to the `brute_force_linear()` predicate we discussed earlier. After collecting the time spine, `elegant_linear()` calls `linear_traversal2()`, which in turn recursively calls `collect_linear_events2()` to gather all the events in each time point list (in TempMEL) associated with the designated DARMS part. At this point, however, the similarity between the two algorithms ends, as `collect_linear_events2()` must also maintain a list of the end points (ENDpts) for each event collected in Temp-MEL. On exiting `collect_linear_events2()`, our algorithm appends the new events onto the existing melody list (TempMEL3), sorts the list of end points into temporal order, appends any valid events to TempMEL3(), and calls the predicate `find_next_Time-Point()` to truncate the Tail of the time spine recursively until

Figure 5.22 The `elegant_linear()` predicate.

```
elegant_linear(PART,MELODY) :-
   time_spine(Spine),
   linear_traversal2(Spine,PART,[],[],MELODY).

   linear_traversal2([],_,_,MELODY,MELODY).
   linear_traversal2([[STRT|STail]|Tail],PART,TempENDpts,TempMEL,MELODY) :-
      collect_linear_events2(STail,PART,TempENDpts,ENDpts,[],TempMEL2),
      sort(ENDpts,[ENDpt|ENDptsTail]),
      revise_theList(TempMEL,TempMEL2,TempMEL3),
      find_next_TimePoint(STRT,ENDpt,Tail,NewTail),
      linear_traversal2(NewTail,PART,ENDptsTail,TempMEL3,MELODY).

   collect_linear_events2([],_,ENDpts,ENDpts,TempMEL3,TempMEL3).
   collect_linear_events2([H|Tail],PART,TempENDpts,ENDpts,TempMEL,TempMEL3) :-
      get_part2(H,PART,ENDpt),
      append(TempMEL,[H],TempMEL2),
      append(TempENDpts,[ENDpt],TempENDpts2),
   collect_linear_events2(Tail,PART,TempENDpts2,ENDpts,TempMEL2,TempMEL3).
   collect_linear_events2([_|Tail],PART,TempENDpts,ENDpts,TempMEL,TempMEL3) :-
      collect_linear_events2(Tail,PART,TempENDpts,ENDpts,TempMEL,TempMEL3).
   revise_theList(TempMEL3,[],TempMEL3).
   revise_theList(TempMEL,TempMEL2,TempMEL3) :-
      append(TempMEL,[TempMEL2],TempMEL3).

   find_next_TimePoint(_,_,[],[]).
   find_next_TimePoint(STRT,STRT,NewTail,NewTail).
   find_next_TimePoint(_,END, [[END|Tail1]|Tail2], [[END|Tail1}\Tail2].
   find_next_TimePoint(STRT,END,[_|Tail2],NewTail) :-
      find_next_TimePoint(STRT,END,Tail2,NewTail).

      get_part2(H,_,END) :-                          % get rests/meters
         event(H,0,[_,END,_],_,_,_,_,_,_).
      get_part2(H,PART,END) :-                        % get events
         event(H,PART,[_,END,_],_,_,_,_,_,_).
```

the first time point in the ENDpts list is encountered. The newly
truncated lists (NewTail and ENDptsTail) are then passed recursively through linear_traversal2() until the time spine traversal is completed. Throughout the operation of this algorithm, the
list of end points will expand and contract dynamically, depending on how many different staggered events are found at any
given time point. If each point contains one and only one event,
ENDptsTail will be null ([]); otherwise, it will contain all the

Figure 5.23   Several sample `elegant_linear()` queries.

a.
```
?- elegant_linear(2,MELODY).
   MELODY = [[99],[14],[1,15],[16],[17],[18],[2,19],[20],[21],[22]]
```
b.
```
?- elegant_linear(1,MELODY).
   MELODY = [[99],[3,14],[1,4,15],[5,16],[6],[7,17],[8],[9,18],
            [2,10,19],[11,20],[12],[21],[13,22]]
```

remaining end points that need to be traced. By sorting the list as each entry is entered, we are able to remove duplicate values as well as guarantee that the first element of the list will always be the next required time point.

Two sample traversals can be seen in figure 5.23. In figure 5.23a, we simply search one part with no simultaneous events. To test the effectiveness of the algorithm, however, we can alter our data so that all the events belonging to DARMS part 2 are changed to part 1, thus giving us a variety of staggered simultaneous events. The sample traversal for the altered data appears in 5.23b.

■ **Vertical Traversals**   Our simplest form of vertical traversal uses a strategy similar to that used in the previous `elegant_linear()` predicate. Essentially, we must not only examine every event that begins at a given time point but also keep track of any events that have different durations because we must account for their presence in later vertical segments. We can accomplish this task by maintaining a list of every event that is active at any given point in time. As we traverse the structure to collect vertical slices, our algorithm needs to undertake four primary operations: (1) it must stop at each time point and collect all the events beginning at that point, (2) it must record each of their ending times in a list for future reference, (3) it must account for those previous events that are still active, and (4) it must remove terminating events at the current time point from the reference list. The result of the algorithm is to create an exhaustive list of vertical segments: any time a new event occurs or an old event ends, a new segment is derived. Obviously, our strategy with this algorithm is to avoid making any preanalytical decisions while parsing the data. Ideally, we want to strive for nearly total data abstraction; in other words, our data should be as free of processing influences as possible. We should leave it up to later analytical heuristics, not to our parsing routines, to decide what to do with the

Figure 5.24 The `simple_verticals()` predicate.

```prolog
simple_verticals :-
      retractall(vertical(_)),
      time_spine(Spine),
      vertical_traversal1(Spine,[]).

      vertical_traversal1([],_).
      vertical_traversal1([[_|HTail]|Tail],Temp) :-
         process_events(HTail,Temp,NEWTemp),
         save_vertical(NEWTemp),
         vertical_traversal1(Tail,NEWTemp).

         process_events([],NEWTemp,NEWTemp).
         process_events([H|Tail],Temp,NEWTemp) :-
            add_or_deleteEvents(H,Temp,Temp2),
            process_events(Tail,Temp2,NEWTemp).

            add_or_deleteEvents(H,Temp,Temp2) :-      % add event
               H > 0,
               append(Temp,[H],Temp2).
            add_or_deleteEvents(H,Temp,Temp2) :-      % remove event
               H < 0,
               remove_event(H,Temp,[],Temp2).

            remove_event(H,[H2|Tail],NEWTemp,Temp2) :-
               H2 =\= integer(fabs(H)),
               append(NEWTemp,[H2],NEWTemp2),
               remove_event(H,Tail,NEWTemp2,Temp2).
            remove_event(_,[_|Tail],NEWTemp,Temp2) :-
               append(NEWTemp,Tail,Temp2).

      save_vertical([]).
      save_vertical(NEWTemp) :-
         sort(NEWTemp,NEWTemp2),                      % optional
         assertz(vertical(NEWTemp2)).
```

data. Clearly, we can add and refine this process in any number of ways, depending on our analytical needs, but we strongly promote the notion that the more levels of processing that strive for data abstraction, the less unique programming that will have to be created every time a new project is undertaken. The code for our first vertical traversal is shown in figure 5.24.

The predicate `simple_verticals()` begins first by initializing the data type `vertical()`—the structure we will use to store vertical

Figure 5.25 A sample `simple_verticals()` query.

```
?- simple_verticals.
   yes
?- vertical(X).
   X = [3,14,23,34] ;
   X = [4,15,24,35] ;
   X = [4,15,25,35] ;
   X = [5,16,26,36] ;
   X = [6,16,26,36] ;
   X = [7,17,27,37] ;
   X = [8,17,27,37] ;
   X = [9,18,28,38] ;
   X = [9,18,29,39] ;
   X = [10,19,30,40] ;
   X = [11,20,31,40] ;
   X = [12,20,32,41] ;
   X = [12,21,32,41] ;
   X = [13,22,33,42] ;
   no
```

slices—and purging the database of any occurrences left from previous runs and then by calling the recursive predicate `vertical_traversal1()`. To make the algorithm more efficient, we have structured this particular traversal so that all the vertical slices are stored as separate elements within the Prolog database. Because the results of most vertical traversals will include every event in the structure, this approach can save substantial computing overhead by avoiding the stack requirements necessary for passing large data structures recursively. As `vertical_traversal1()` works through the time spine (`Spine`), it maintains a list (`Temp`) of every event that is active at any given time point. Specifically, if the predicate `add_or_deleteEvents()` finds an event index that is positive (initiating an event), it is added to the list. Conversely, if the event index is negative (terminating an event), the index is deleted from the list. Any events that have been previously added to the list but have not yet reached their termination points remain in the list. Once all the events for a specified time point have been processed, the predicate `save_verticals()` is called to sort the vertical list and store it in the database. A sample call to `simple_verticals()` can be seen in figure 5.25.

To aid in understanding the workings of the algorithm, we can observe in figure 5.26 a trace of the values present in the `Temp` list

Figure 5.26   A data dump of `Spine` and `Temp`.

Position	Spine (sublist)	Temp	Action to Temp	
0.7500	(3,14,23,34)	(3,14,23,34)	add:	3,14,23,34
1.0000	(−3,4,−14,15,−23,24,−34,35)	(4,15,24,35)	remove:	3,14,23,34
			add:	4,15,24,35
1.1250	(−24,25)	(4,15,25,35)	remove:	24
			add:	25
			keep:	4,15,35
1.2500	(−4,5,−15,16,−25,26,−35,36)	(5,16,26,36)	remove:	4,15,25,35
			add:	5,16,26,36
1.3750	(−5,6)	(6,16,26,36)	remove:	5
			add:	6
			keep:	16,26,36
1.5000	(−6,7,−16,17,−26,27,−36,37)	(7,17,27,37)	remove:	6,16,26,36
			add:	7,17,27,37
1.6250	(−7,8)	(8,17,27,37)	remove:	7
			add:	8
			keep:	17,27,37
1.7500	(−8,9,−17,18,−27,28,−37,38)	(9,18,28,38)	remove:	8,17,27,37
			add:	9,18,28,38
1.8750	(−28,29,−38,39)	(9,18,29,39)	remove:	28,38
			add:	29,39
			keep:	9,18
2.0000	(−9,19,−18,19,−29,30,−39,40)	(10,19,30,40)	remove:	9,18,29,39
			add:	10,19,30,40
2.1250	(−10,11,−19,20,−30,31)	(11,20,31,40)	remove:	10,19,30
			add:	11,20,31
			keep:	40
2.2500	(−11,12,−31,32,−40,41)	(12,20,32,41)	remove:	11,31,40
			add:	12,32,41
			keep:	20
2.3750	(−20,21)	(12,21,32,41)	remove:	20
			add:	21
			keep:	12,32,41
2.5000	(−12,13,−21,22,−32,33,−41,42)	(13,22,33,42)	remove:	12,21,32,41
			add:	13,22,33,42

and `Spine` sublist for each vertical segment in the piece. (For the sake of clarity, we omit references to bar lines and meters.)

A second and certainly different approach is to segment the score into temporally determined vertical slices, in other words, verticals containing all the events occurring within a durational segment. For example, we might choose to explore the ramifications of imposing a quarter-note harmonic rhythm onto a piece of music, in which case we would segment the score into verticals

Figure 5.27   The `durational_verticals()` predicate.

```
durational_verticals(DUR) :-
   retractall(vertical(_)),
   retractall(temp_vertical(_)),
   assertz(temp_vertical([])),
   time_spine([[Time|HTail]|SpineTail]),
   vertical_traversal2([[Time|HTail]|SpineTail],0,DUR,[]).

   vertical_traversal2([],_,_,Temp) :-
      save_vertical2(Temp,_).
   vertical_traversal2([[CRNTtime|HTail]|Tail],Time,DUR,Temp) :-
      CRNTtime >= Time + DUR,
      NEWtime is Time + DUR,
      save_vertical2(Temp,NEWtemp),
      vertical_traversal2([[CRNTtime|HTail]|Tail],NEWtime,DUR,NEWtemp).
   vertical_traversal2([[_|HTail]|Tail],Time,DUR,Temp) :-
      process_events2(HTail,Time,DUR,Temp,NEWTemp),
      vertical_traversal2(Tail,Time,DUR,NEWTemp).

      process_events2([],_,_,NEWTemp,NEWTemp).
      process_events2([H|Tail],Time,DUR,Temp,NEWTemp) :-
         add_events(H,Temp,Time,DUR,Temp2),
         process_events2(Tail,Time,DUR,Temp2,NEWTemp).

         add_events(H,Temp,Time,DUR,Temp2) :-          % add event
            H > 0,
            not event(H,_,[X,X,_],_,_,_,_,_,_),
            append(Temp,[H],Temp2),
            add_events2(H,Time,DUR).
         add_events(_,Temp,_,_,Temp).

            add_events2(H,Time,DUR) :-    % check for longer DURs
               event(H,_,[_,END,_],_,_,_,_,_,_),
               END > Time + DUR,
               temp_vertical(X),
               append(X,[H],X2),
               retractall(temp_vertical(_)),
               assertz(temp_vertical(X2)).
            add_events2(_,_,_).

      save_vertical2([],[]).
      save_vertical2(Temp,NEWTemp) :-
         sort(Temp,Temp2),
         assertz(vertical(Temp2)),
         temp_vertical(NEWTemp),
         retractall(temp_vertical(_)),
         assertz(temp_vertical([])).
```

Figure 5.28   A sample `durational_verticals()` query.

```
?- durational_verticals(2500).
   yes
?- vertical(X).
   X = [3,14,23,34] ;
   X = [4,15,24,25,35] ;
   X = [5,6,16,26,36] ;
   X = [7,8,17,27,37] ;
   X = [9,18,28,29,38,39] ;
   X = [10,11,19,20,30,31,40] ;
   X = [12,20,21,32,41] ;
   X = [13,22,33,42] ;
   no
```

on the basis of that durational value. The predicate `durational_verticals()` aims to do just that. In a manner similar to that undertaken in the previous predicate, `simple_verticals()`, this algorithm maintains a vertical list by storing all events that it encounters at each time point. Here the similarity ends, however, as `durational_verticals()` does not remove any events until it has reached the next durational boundary, at which point it removes every event from the list, except for those that sustain into the next durational group. The code for this algorithm appears in figure 5.27.

The predicate `durational_verticals()` begins by initializing the data predicates `vertical()` and `temp_vertical()` and then calling the recursive predicate `vertical_traversal2()`. This predicate is defined with three clauses. The first is a terminal clause that stops the recursion once the complete `SpineTail` has been traversed and saves the final vertical in the database. The second clause checks the current point in the time spine against the specified durational span (`DUR`) and takes one of two actions, depending on the result: (1) if the current time point (`CRNTtime`) exceeds that point (`Time + DUR`), a new durational end point is created (`NEWtime`), and the current vertical is stored in the database, or (2) if the current time point is still within the current span, the second clause will `fail` and the third clause will be called. The third clause calls the predicate `process_events2()` to add any events to `temp()`. In addition, `add_events2()` checks for events lasting beyond the end of the current durational span and stores them in the data type `temp_vertical()` to be included in the next span. A sample run of this algorithm can be seen in figure 5.28.

■ Combined Linear/Vertical Traversals

The final four traversals we present here are perhaps the easiest to understand and program because they incorporate the least amount of decision making. The first of the three predicates, `combined_simple_traversal()`, simply traverses the time spine between defined starting and ending points, collecting all the intervening events. The code for this algorithm can be seen in figure 5.29a. Our predicate, `combined_simple_traversal()`, is called with three parameters: (1) a starting point in the structure, (2) and ending point in the structure, and (3) an unbound variable to return the segment. Before we enter the recursive predicate `combined_simple1()`, we first call `set_start_point()` to truncate the `Spine` by removing all events starting prior to `STRT`. Note that we do not take into account those events that are initiated prior to the designated starting point but do not terminate until after it. We are assuming in this case a scenario in which the music exhibits staggered voices and we cannot count on finding a clean break between desired segments. We can resolve this situation relatively easy by altering `set_start_point()` to keep track of every prior event sustaining past the starting point and then adding them to `TruncSpine()` prior to calling `combined_simple1()`. The revised portion of the code appears in figure 5.29b. The predicate `combined_simple1()` is defined in three clauses. The first two clauses function to terminate the recursion either when the end of the spine is reached or when the current time point is equal to or greater than the designated end point. The third clause simply collects all the events and passes them through the recursive call.

Two sample calls to the predicate can be seen in figure 5.30, each utilizing different versions of `set_start_point()`.

The second traversal method combines one or more DARMS parts together into one large segment. We call the predicate `combined_part_traversal()` by supplying it with a list of parts we wish to acquire (`PartLIST`), and it returns a segment (`Segment`) with the results. Our algorithm for this predicate is nearly identical to that of `combined_simple_traversal()` except that it restricts event selection to those belonging to the specified part(s). In addition, it does not allow us to designate starting and ending points in the spine. Rather than discussing this predicate in detail, we suggest you examine the code for `combined_simple_traversal()` in figure 5.30 and explore how to incorporate that option into the code for `combined_part_traversal()` shown in figure 5.31. A sample run of the predicate requesting parts 3 and 4 is shown in figure 5.32.

Our final two algorithms are extremely simple. Specifically, they work by calling on the previously designed predicates for doing vertical traversals and compile their results into one large segment.

Figures 5.29 Two variations of the `combined_ simple_traversal()` predicate.

a.
```
combined_simple_traversal(STRT,END,Segment) :-
   time_spine(Spine),
   set_start_point(STRT,Spine,TruncSpine),
   combined_simple1(TruncSpine,END,[],Segment).

set_start_point(STRT,[[H|HTail]|Tail],[[H|HTail]|Tail]) :-
   H >= STRT.
set_start_point(STRT,[_|Tail],TruncSpine) :-
   set_start_point(STRT,Tail,TruncSpine).

combined_simple1([],_,Segment,Segment).
combined_simple1([[H|_]|_],END,Segment,Segment) :-
   H >= END.
combined_simple1([[_|HTail]|Tail],END,TempSEG,Segment) :-
   collect_simple_events(HTail,[],Temp),
   append(TempSEG,Temp,TempSEG2),
   combined_simple1(Tail,END,TempSEG2,Segment).

collect_simple_events([],TempSEG,TempSEG).
collect_simple_events([H|Tail],Temp,TempSEG) :-
   event(H,_,_,_,_,_,_,_,_),
   append(Temp,[H],Temp2),
   collect_simple_events(Tail,Temp2,TempSEG).
collect_simple_events([_|Tail],Temp,TempSEG) :-
   collect_simple_events(Tail,Temp,TempSEG).
```
b.
```
combined_simple_traversal(STRT,END,NewSegment) :-
   time_spine(Spine),
   set_start_point(STRT,Spine,[],Segment,TruncSpine),
   combined_simple1(TruncSpine,END,Segment,NewSegment).

set_start_point(STRT,[[H|HTail]|Tail],Segment,Segment,
                              [[H|HTail]|Tail]) :-
   H >= STRT.
set_start_point(STRT,[[_|HTail]|Tail],Temp,Segment,TruncSpine) :-
   get_select_events(STRT,HTail,Temp,Temp2),
   set_start_point(STRT,Tail,Temp2,Segment,TruncSpine).

get_select_events(_,[],Prefix,Prefix).
get_select_events(STRT,[H|Tail],Temp,Prefix) :-
   event(H,_,[_,END,_],_,_,_,_,_,_),
   END > STRT,
   append(Temp,[H],Temp2),
   get_select_events(STRT,Tail,Temp2,Prefix).
get_select_events(STRT,[_|Tail],Temp,Prefix) :-
   get_select_events(STRT,Tail,Temp,Prefix).
```

Again, we have made no attempt to truncate the time spine with a starting and ending point but encourage you to explore that possibility. The code for these two traversals appears in figure 5.33 and sample queries can be found in figure 5.34.

Figure 5.30 Two sample `combined_simple_ traversal()` queries.

a.
```
?- combined_simple_traversal(13750,20000,Segment).
   Segment = [6,7,17,27,37,8,9,18,28,38,29,39]
```
b.
```
?- combined_simple_traversal(13750,20000,Segment).
   Segment = [16,26,36,6,7,17,27,37,8,9,18,28,38,29,39]
```

Figure 5.31 The `combined_part_traversal()` predicate.

```
combined_part_traversal(PartLIST,Segment) :-
    time_spine(Spine),
    combined_part1(Spine,PartLIST,[],Segment).

    combined_part1([],_,Segment,Segment).
    combined_part1([[_|HTail]|Tail],PartLIST,TempSEG,Segment) :-
        collect_part_events(HTail,PartLIST,[],Temp),
        append(TempSEG,Temp,TempSEG2),
        combined_part1(Tail,PartLIST,TempSEG2,Segment).

    collect_part_events([],_,TempSEG,TempSEG).
    collect_part_events([H|Tail],PartLIST,Temp,TempSEG) :-
        event(H,Part,_,_,_,_,_,_,_),
        member(Part,PartLIST),
        append(Temp,[H],Temp2),
        collect_part_events(Tail,PartLIST,Temp2,TempSEG).
    collect_part_events([_|Tail],PartLIST,Temp,TempSEG) :-
        collect_part_events(Tail,PartLIST,Temp,TempSEG).
```

Figure 5.32 A sample `combined_part_traversal()` query.

```
?- combined_part_traversal([3,4],Segment).
   Segment =
      [23,34,24,35,25,26,36,27,37,28,38,29,39,30,40,31,32,41,33,42]
```

Figure 5.33   Two collection predicates.

a.
```
combined_simple_vertical_traversal(Segment) :-
    simple_verticals,
    collect_verticals([],Segment).

collect_verticals(Temp,Segment) :-
    vertical(V),
    retract(vertical(V)),
    append(Temp,[V],Temp2),
    collect_verticals(Temp2,Segment).
collect_verticals(Segment,Segment).
```
b.
```
combined_durational_vertical_traversal(Duration,Segment) :-
    durational_verticals(Duration),
    collect_verticals([],Segment).

collect_verticals(Temp,Segment) :-
    vertical(V),
    retract(vertical(V)),
    append(Temp,[V],Temp2),
    collect_verticals(Temp2,Segment).
collect_verticals(Segment,Segment).
```

Figure 5.34   Two sample collection queries.

a.
```
?- combined_simple_vertical_traversal(Segment).

Segment = [[3,14,23,34],[4,15,24,35],[4,15,25,35],[5,16,26,36],
          [6,16,26,36],[7,17,27,37],[8,17,27,37],[9,18,28,38],
          [9,18,29,39],[10,19,30,40],[11,20,31,40],[12,20,32,41],
          [12,21,32,41],[13,22,33,42]]
```
b.
```
?- combined_durational_vertical_traversal(5000,Segment).

Segment = [[3,14,23,34],[4,5,6,15,16,24,25,26,35,36],
          [7,8,9,17,18,27,28,29,37,38,39],
          [10,11,12,19,20,21,30,31,32,40,41],[13,22,33,42]]
```

SIX
A Knowledge-Based Intelligent Tutoring Engine

■ INTRODUCTION

In recent years, music theorists have made considerable progress in their efforts to put microcomputers to pedagogical use. However, much of our current theory software relies too strongly on "drill-and-practice" strategies, a group of related approaches that, although good for assisting in the rote learning of tangible skills, are often far from ideal for tutorial uses and thus fail to fulfill recognized instructional potentials of computers. Most drill-and-practice environments attempt only to reinforce through repetition those concepts already learned and conceptualized elsewhere. In the majority of cases, they do not provide the motivation that a more explorative, knowledge-driven tutorial environment might. To the contrary, our mental capacities as humans allow not only for the ability to acquire knowledge but also for the power to comprehend and manipulate a level of understanding from that knowledge often only implied by the knowledge itself—something that no computer has the ability to do. Yet, if we could design a teaching machine that somehow could be endowed with human understanding, insight, and reason, the result of our efforts might not be a better machine but would certainly be something that might relate to and interact with us in a manner significantly closer to the way a human teacher does.

As we have mentioned, the notion of a knowledge-based system is that a *humanlike* response can be drawn from a computer if the computer contains domain-specific knowledge in the form of factual data and relational rules associating that data and if the computer is programmed to provide access to that knowledge through human-emulating heuristics-based mechanisms. A simple yet insightful definition of such a system was given by Igor Aleksander (1984), who proposed that "the focal point of artificial intelligence has been the realization that an intelligent response by *human* standards implies the storage in computers of *human* knowledge. . . . If the knowledge of an expert can be encapsulated in a program, and the program stored . . . then this knowledge can be made available to non-experts" (p. 117).

The educational implication is clear: knowledge-based computer technologies present us with a potentially significant vehicle for disseminating the knowledge of experts (such as teachers and scholars) to those without such knowledge or expertise (such as students). It follows logically, then, that these programs are often referred to as Intelligent Tutoring Systems (ITSs) or Intelligent Computer-Assisted Instruction (ICAI). Although it should be immediately clear to all of us that no computer system can truly be called "intelligent," with the aid of such properly designed and implemented systems students could have much greater access to the expertise of others than might ever be practical in today's typical classroom-oriented educational environment. It is our strongly held belief that knowledge-based models offer us one of the significantly better ways of implementing core knowledge engines for such systems.

The very nature of many music-theoretical concepts in some ways makes them highly conducive to implementation in an ITS environment. Particularly well suited are those aspects from which rules can, for the most part, be readily drawn but that often require some limited level of subjectivity in their application. In the teaching of tonal harmony, for example, textbooks often present sets of precepts defining the correct succession of harmonies within a tonal progression. In a confined learning environment (in other words, under the direction of a knowledgeable human tutor), the potential to apply the rules effectively with desirable results is greatly enhanced. Without such expert guidance, however, the student is apt to flounder. Taking a generalized rule structure proposed in one particular undergraduate harmony text as an example, an unguided student could derive the harmonic progression III-IV-I-V^6-VI-IV-I. Most knowledgeable musicians trained in the workings of the European art-music tradition would probably view this as an inferior progression, yet, as awkward as it seems, this particular progression is technically allowable according to the precepts in many harmony texts (we drew this specific progression from a set of relational rules presented by Kostka and Payne [1995]). A student might be able to identify it as odd but without quite knowing why the progression sounds unusual. With the explanatory properties of a properly designed intelligent tutorial, the student could explore the possibilities of this rule structure through instructive interaction and begin to develop a better grasp of the more subjective and elusive properties of the tonal harmonic language.

Envision the following scenario. A student, sitting down at an ITS, expresses a desire to compose a harmonic progression for a previously composed melody. The student continues by directing the tutorial to frame the progression with a perfect-authentic cadence and tonic incipit. Up to this point, the computer has been relatively quiet, as the student appears to be in control of the situation. The student, however, now a little unsure of how to proceed, queries the tutorial for some advice. The tutorial gives the information that nearly any diatonic root-position or first-inversion chord can follow the opening tonic. The student, put off a little by the vast number of choices, responds hesitantly. At this point, the tutorial narrows the choices by presenting the student with the possibility of creating a passing six-four progression. The student, now slightly relieved, wonders why the tutorial suggested that particular progression. The tutorial, having been programmed to expect such responses, explains that this particular progression is an especially good choice for two reasons: first, this progression helps to emphasize the opening tonic triad and, second, despite the relatively static tonic orientation, it creates a strong sense of melodic motion. A similar banter continues between student and tutorial until a satisfactory progression is completed.

It is important to emphasize the hypothetical nature of this example. Yet, despite the language limitations, current expert system technology supplies us with the tools necessary to develop highly effective but less expansive microcomputer-based tutorials capable of nearly all the functions displayed in the example above. Depending on the scope of the encoded domain, these programs may or may not lack some the sophistication, flexibility, and insight present in the above example. They will, however, still be able to store and codify a significant amount of rule-based knowledge and gain access to it in a logical and pedagogically sound manner.

It is beyond the scope of our study to delve into all the workings and nuances of such systems—we simply have neither the space nor the expertise. Yet, no such system can function without a working knowledge representational model capable of storing and retrieving the necessary domain information in a suitable manner. Such a core knowledge base is often referred to as the knowledge-based *engine* because it is used to drive the workings of the tutorial's knowledge. Our purpose for this chapter, then, is to explore the basic workings of a knowledge-based engine for use in a typical ITS. Specifically, we discuss the three key elements central to the development of a working system: (1) the knowledge representational scheme; (2) the heuristics, or basic organizational strategies, for bringing a higher level of meaning to the knowledge; and (3) the inference engine developed to coordinate the interaction of these rules.

■ HARMONY COACH: A KNOWLEDGE-BASED ITS FOR DIATONIC HARMONY

Overview   The nonmodulatory, tonal harmonic knowledge-based model (THM) we propose here is designed to work with a system for coaching a student in the creation of an acceptable harmonic progression for an existing unfigured bass line (in other words, a bass line with no prior indications as to voice-leading motion). It is essential that any well-designed knowledge base contain sufficient information to represent effectively the complete domain of the knowledge being tutored. The implementation of such a structure, however, also requires us to develop appropriate heuristic strategies to utilize and access the representative knowledge effectively. Unfortunately, because knowledge-based systems are capable of encapsulating facts, rules, and relationships only within and between each other, and because our understanding of harmony and its numerous intricacies is not wholly solidified, the knowledge domain of the tutorial, by definition, cannot be complete. It can, however, be fairly comprehensive within the scope of our existing precepts. Obviously, we could not use our proposed THM to analyze thoroughly all extant diatonic compositions because numerous precept variants and undefined anomalies will always be present. In reality, this limitation does not represent a serious hindrance for us, as tutorials utilizing this THM model would most likely be used to teach the normative fundamental precepts and not to analyze actual "messy" compositions. This strategy fits with what many teachers do all the time: teach those things that are definable first, saving the anomalies and exceptions for later stages of study. Intelligent tutorials cannot usually deal effectively with the intangible aspects of a domain but can usually be designed to aid in coaching the normative conventions.

Defining an expert model also can prove problematic because every theorist tends to view harmonic practices through their own tinted glasses. Ideally, we should be able to put five theorists in a locked room and have them pool their collective knowledge, with the result being one comprehensive point of view. Human nature being what it is, this approach would most likely be quite unproductive! Traditional harmony textbooks, however, do exhibit a surprisingly high level of correspondence. To test the effectiveness and thoroughness of the knowledge base, as well as the ability of the THM to actually model a comprehensive body of knowledge, we use textbooks as our primary source of expertise. We drew our materials from six books, each representing a distinctive approach. These works were digested, correlated, and codified, with the result being a comprehensive rule base—comprehensive, that is, within the confined domain delineated by the textbook precepts. The specific books we examined were Edward Aldwell and Carl Schacter's *Harmony and Voice Leading* (1989), Bruce Benward's *Music: In Theory and Practice* (1993), Allen Forte's *Tonal Harmony in Theory and Practice* (1979), Stefan Kostka and Dorothy Payne's *Tonal Harmony* (1989), Robert Ottman's *Elementary Harmony* (1983), and Allen Winold's *Harmony: Patterns and Principles* (1986).

Parts of the System

■ The Knowledge Structure

Our THM inference engine is designed around a heuristically driven *three-tiered* model (figure 6.1). The lowest two tiers of the model represent the precepts of diatonic harmonic progressions; the lower of these two tiers expresses the broader concepts of classifying harmonies into general chord classes, and the other structures the information specific to distinctive chord groups, or *pairs*. This part of our knowledge base contains all the factual and relational information necessary to represent the knowledge domain we are working with. We must emphasize that this knowledge gives us the ability not only to assess the viability of any existing harmonic choices but also to generate solutions on its own. It is precisely this ability that separates such a model from other forms of instructional systems. Not only can our system judge an answer to be right or wrong, but it can offer suggestions in the forms of suggested solutions. It can even offer explanations for its actions by presenting the logical progression by which it arrived at any given solution.

Figure 6.1   Diagram of the three-tiered TMH inference engine.

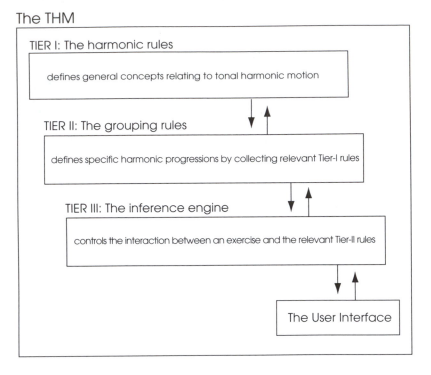

Unlike the lowest two tiers, which embody the factual and relational knowledge of the program, our third, or highest, tier constitutes a forward-referencing inference engine operating on a reverse-
looping design. This context-dependent tier is employed to trigger
control of those particular knowledge structures from the lower two
tiers appropriate for dealing with a given student query. This con-
text-based two-part "patterning" scheme forms the foundation for
modeling a common and effective student strategy for learning complex musical tasks. Allen Winold, in the preface to his text (1986),
describes the patterned approach as one that

> involves the presentation of a limited number of basic chord progres-
> sions as the core materials . . . After learning to analyze, write, play, and
> hear these progressions in their basic form, the student learns to adapt
> them and to integrate them into longer, more varied musical contexts.
> This approach is similar to modern methods of teaching foreign lan-

guages, in which students learn basic phrases and then learn to vary them and use them in longer patterns of thought. (p. vii)

Specifically, by starting with small atomic elements and coalescing them into larger conceptual packets, or patterns, a student is able to reduce the amount of information required at any given stage, thus simplifying the conceptualization process. Similarly, just as patterns are formed and associated by students during the course of learning a complex task, a knowledge structure designed to coach those same students also can be defined around such principles. Clearly, a well-constructed cognitive learning strategy should translate into an effectively organized expert model capable of the same sort of flexible yet simple level of comprehension.

■ The Three-Tiered Rule Base

Tier 1: The Harmony Rules

The first, or lowest, of our levels asserts facts and precepts that define specific aspects of harmonic structure and interaction. These precepts, in essence, represent a collection of all those commonly held tenets that make up the bulk of most theory textbooks. (As an aside, it is unfortunate that these elements are too often taught to beginning theory students in a manner that simply informs them of the "what" but, due to lack of instructional time, are not always followed up with the "how" and "why" of the application of that information. One primary role of an ITS is to do just that, namely, to coach the application of a previously learned skill in a way that imitates the subtle help an observant teacher might give a student in a focused individual tutoring session.) Through evaluating the cumulative materials of the theory texts previously mentioned, eleven general rule categories defining the textbook conventions of diatonic (in other words, nonmodulating, or music that remains within one key) harmonic progressions emerged. We present a list of these categories in figure 6.2.

Because many of these categories deal with well-defined concepts, they frequently can be translated into conceptually closed precepts. Other categories exemplify amalgamations of seemingly disparate facts pulled from various topical areas. For example, precepts about dominant-seventh chords are relatively self-contained. The harmonic and voice-leading functions of these chords are tightly defined and, within the limited domain of this ITS, tend to operate consistently regardless of their contextual situation. On the other hand, precepts defining the nature of inversions, for example, are often strongly contextual and must rely heavily on precept interaction, forcing our inference engine to monitor closely other factors

Figure 6.2   Harmonic precepts.

1. Phrase-level harmonic motion
2. General chord classifications
3. Root progressions
4. First-inversion functions
5. Second-inversion functions
6. General seventh chord functions
7. Dominant seventh chords
8. Other seventh chords
9. Harmonic rhythm
10. Harmonic succession
11. Linear harmonic functions

in a given exercise. For example, a cadential tonic six-four chord functions quite differently than a passing dominant six-four chord. Similarly, the bass note of a first-inversion triad may have a strong predilection to resolve by step unless the chord following it represents a different formulation of the same harmony, for example, a first-inversion tonic moving to a root-position, or second-inversion, tonic. In this case, the resolution would be by leap. In many cases, precepts at this level aim at being distinctly non–chord specific, instead generalizing on classes of chords.

Perhaps the most important and consistently restrictive structures of harmonic progressions are the beginnings and endings of phrases, in other words, *incipits* and *cadences,* respectively. Precept group 1, shown in figure 6.3, details these related issues.

As a foundation for structuring our ITS knowledge base, we draw on the notion of chord *classes.* Whereas many scholars throughout the twentieth century have relied on this convention of classification, we chose to use the four class categories as defined in Winold's (1986) text. Specifically, he identifies these as *tonic* class, *dominant* class, *subdominant* class, and *linear* class. Whereas some of our higher-tiered precepts relate to specific chords in specific juxtapositions, our lowest-tiered ones are designed around the notion of how chords of one class move to or from chords of the same or different classes. Once we have defined the classes to which each chord belongs, we can set out to define all the precepts relating to how classes interact. To make use of his model, we begin by assigning each chord to a class. The precepts shown in figure 6.4 implement this process.

Figure 6.3   Group 1 precepts: Phrase-level harmonic motion.

Regarding basic harmonic cadences, the following precepts apply:

1a: The last chord of a progression *must* be a tonic, dominant, or submediant.

1b: If the last chord of a progression is a tonic, then the next-to-last chord *must* be a dominant, subdominant, or leading-tone.

1c: If the last chord of a progression is a submediant, then the next-to-last chord *must* be a dominant chord.

Regarding incipits (beginnings), the following precepts apply:

1.1a: It is *preferred* but not essential that the first chord of a progression be a tonic or dominant.

1.1b: If the first chord is not a tonic, then the first bass note capable of supporting a tonic chord *should* be harmonized by a tonic chord.

Figure 6.4   Group 2 precepts: General chord classifications.

Regarding chord classifications, the following precepts apply:

2a: Root position and first-inversion tonic and submediant chords are considered to be (T)onic class.

2b: Dominant and leading-tone chords are considered to be (D)ominant class.

2c: Subdominant and supertonic chords are considered to be (S)ubdominant class.

2d: Mediant and second-inversion triads are considered to be (L)inear class.

Regarding general motion between classes, the following precepts apply:

2.1a: (T)-class chords *may* move to chords of any class.

2.1b: (S)-class chords *should* move to (D)-class chords. A subdominant chord may also move to a tonic chord.

2.1c: (D)-class chords *must* move to (T)-class (or IV6 in minor).

2.1d: A chord of one class *may* move to a different chord of the same class.

Note: Each (L)-class chord moves according to its own specific precept(s).

Most harmony texts seem to place a fair amount of weight on the notion of *root progressions.* In other words, the particular distance between the *roots* of two successive chords has a strong impact on both the strength and the character of a progression regardless of the actual position of the root note within the structure of a harmony. The preference of the descending-fifth motion from a dominant to a tonic chord, for example, remains relatively the same regardless of other, more specific voicing factors, such as those generated by particular inversions or spacings. The precepts in figure 6.5 attempt to clarify our weightings of each.

In addition to the more general relationships generated by successive root motions, the particular inversions of each chord within a progression imposes additional qualifications. These precepts appear in figure 6.6

In most cases, our preceding general precepts are sufficient to deal with root-motion and inversional requirements. However, the second-inversion, or *six-four,* chords have very specific and stringent requirements and must be dealt with individually. Of particular importance to us is the issue of rhythmic placement—in other words, where chord(s) lie within the metric structure of a piece of music. Because metric stress plays an important role, it is also necessary for us to define the level of accent associated with each beat in a measure (restricting ourselves in this case to *duple, triple,* and *quadruple* groupings). We propose the precepts shown in figure 6.7 to deal with these situations:

Seventh chords (chords with a note the interval of a seventh above the root) also require special handling both with regard to the way in which these chords interact with simple triads (chords without sevenths) and with regard to the specifics of individual seventh-chord types. Figures 6.8 to 6.10 address these two issues.

Figure 6.5   Group 3 precepts: Root progressions.

Regarding preference of root motions, the following precepts apply:

3a: Root motion down by a fifth is *preferred* to all other motions.

3b: Root motion up by a second is *preferred* to all motions except precept 3a.

3c: Root motion down by a third is *preferred* to all motions except precepts 3a and 3b.

3d: Root motion up by a fifth is *preferred* to all motions except precepts 3a–3c.

3e: Root motion down by a second is *preferred* to all motions except precepts 3a–d.

3f: Root motion up by a third is *least preferred.*

Figure 6.6   Group 4 precepts: First-inversion functions.

Regarding first-inversion chords, the following precepts apply:

4a: A progression from any root-position chord to the same chord in first inversion is *acceptable* and *desirable*.

4b: A progression from any first-inversion chord to the same chord is *acceptable* but *not preferred*.

4c: A progression from any first-inversion chord to a chord whose bass note lies stepwise above or below the current bass note is both *acceptable* and *desirable*.

Regarding specifically the first-inversion mediant and submediant, the following precept applies:

4.1a: These chords *should only* occur in descending stepwise root progressions (see specific precepts for each chord).

Figure 6.7   Group 5 precepts: Second-inversion functions.

Regarding the cadential six-four, the following precepts apply:

5a: A second-inversion tonic triad *must* move to a root-position dominant or dominant-seventh chord.

5b: A second-inversion tonic triad *should only* be preceded by a (T)onic- or (S)ubdominant-class chord, *never* by a (D)ominant-class chord or another second-inversion tonic chord.

5c: It is *preferable* for a second-inversion tonic triad to be approached by stepwise motion in the bass.

5d: A second-inversion tonic triad *should only* appear as part of the final cadence of the phrase but *never* as the last chord.

Regarding the rhythmic placement of a cadential six-four chord, the following precept applies:

5.1a: A second-inversion tonic triad *must* appear on a stronger beat than that of the next chord.

Regarding metric stress (accent), the following precepts apply:

5.2a: Beat 1 of a measure is *always* the strongest.

5.2b: The last beat of a measure is *always* the weakest.

5.2c: In quadruple meter, beat 3 is *always* stronger than beat 2.

Figure 6.8   Group 6 precepts: General seventh-chord functions.

Regarding triad/seventh-chord motions, the following precepts apply:

6a: Motion from a triad to a seventh chord built on the same root is *acceptable*.

6b: Motion from a seventh chord to a triad built on the same root is *not acceptable*.

Figure 6.9   Group 7 precepts: Dominant-seventh chords.

Regarding the dominant seventh, the following precepts apply:

7a: The dominant-seventh chord *must* resolve to a (T)onic-class chord or to another dominant-seventh chord.

7b: A tonic resolution of the dominant-seventh chord is *preferred* to a submediant (deceptive) resolution.

7.1a: When a dominant-seventh is approached by scale-degree 5 in the bass, the *preferred* preparation is by a dominant-seventh or tonic six-four.

7.1b: When a dominant-seventh is *not* approached by scale-degree 5 in the bass, the *preferred* preparations include the supertonic, subdominant, and submediant.

Regarding dominant-seventh chords in inversion, the following precepts apply:

7.2a: A first-inversion dominant seventh *must* resolve up by a half step to a root-position tonic chord.

7.2b: A second-inversion dominant seventh *must* resolve by step to either a root-position or a first-inversion tonic chord.

7.2c: A third-inversion dominant seventh *must* resolve down by step to a first-inversion tonic chord.

Figure 6.10   Group 8 precepts: Other seventh chords.

Regarding the supertonic seventh, the following precept applies:

8:    The supertonic seventh chord *must* resolve to a (D)ominant-class chord *or* a second-inversion tonic triad.

In addition to defining positions of metric stress as they affect the specific placements of cadential chords, we must also concern ourselves with the more general notion of *harmonic rhythm*. In other words, we need to understand that several metric and rhythmic precepts work to control chord-pair positions within a harmonization. Specifically, we choose to adhere to the two rules shown in figure 6.11.

Up to this point, we have been dealing nearly exclusively with chords of the three primary classes: tonic, dominant, and subdominant. Chords of the fourth (or linear) class, although occurring only infrequently, also need to be addressed. Actually, we include two rules: one relating specifically to the mediant chord (a linear-class chord) and the other dealing with progressions exhibiting a high degree of linear *motion* without being restricted to linear-class chords. These precepts are shown in figure 6.12.

Finally, we complete our rule structure by examining rules related specifically to individual second-inversion chord types (other than the cadential six-four dealt with previously in rules 5a–d; see figure 6.7). Like the dominant-seventh chords, harmonies voiced in this manner require very specific treatments. These rules are shown in figure 6.13.

Figure 6.11   Group 9 precepts: Harmonic rhythm.

Regarding harmonic rhythm, the following precepts apply:

9a: It is *preferable* that the harmony change with each note of the exercise.

9b: Two adjacent chords sharing the same root *should not* be separated by a bar line.

Figure 6.12   Group 10 precepts: Harmonic successions.

Regarding successions of inversions, the following precept applies:

10:    Any bass progression of three or more notes *descending by step* may be harmonized by first-inversion chords *regardless* of the resulting progression.

Regarding specifically the mediant chord, the following precept applies:

10.1: A root-position mediant chord *must* progress to a subdominant or root-position submediant triad.

Figure 6.13   Group 11 precepts: Linear harmonic functions.

Regarding *passing* six-four chords, the following precept applies:

11a: A second-inversion tonic or dominant chord *may* harmonize the middle note of a three-note stepwise progression *if* the outer two notes are harmonized by one root position and one first-inversion form of the same chord.

Regarding *neighbor* six-four chords, the following precept applies:

11b: A second-inversion tonic or subdominant chord *may* harmonize the middle note of a three-note progression *if* the outer two bass notes are the same as that of the middle note *and* the outer two notes are harmonized by the same root-position chord.

Regarding *both* six-four chord types, the following precept applies:

11.1:   All passing and neighbor six-four chords must appear on a beat weaker than the preceding beat.

Tier 2: The Grouping Rules

Our second (or middle) heuristic level acts essentially as a traffic manager for the first-tier precepts. Once we assign a specific chord to a chord class, the primary function of this level is to coordinate those first-tier precept(s) that we should apply and test for any given situation and to determine the order in which they will be evaluated (or *fired*). Our heuristic precepts at this level are designed specifically to function with adjacent chord pairs at positions Pos and Pos+1 (we will discuss this concept in detail later). Because the third, or highest, heuristic tier deals primarily with interrelationships between multiple harmonies, it is essentially the job of the middle-tier precepts to coordinate the individual *chord-pair* functions that subsequently link together during the final stage of our query. Figure 6.14 shows three examples of our middle-level precepts. (A complete precept listing of all middle-level heuristics appears in appendix 1.) In each case, the rule assumes the assertion of a user-supplied chord and then looks forward one position in the melody, bass line, or whatever is being harmonized to complete a chord pair for comparison.

Notice that our rules are set up in the form of Prolog predicates. This initial organizational method saves us a great deal of time when it comes to actually converting our ideas into program code. Even more significantly, we gain an additional level of maintainability by structuring our rules this way. Once we have code generated and tested, we can move back and forth between the real code and the pseudo code with very little need to translate our ideas in the process, as the two formats essentially mirror each other in structure. In other words, we can enter into an effective hypothesize-test-modify cycle whereby we create a harmonic rule, code it, observe the outcome, and modify it if necessary. Our altered code is then easily translated back into the pseudo code and vice versa.

The first of these three excerpted rules reads as follows: A root-position tonic triad may harmonize the given bass note IF the note can be harmonized by the chord in question (assumed) AND the next position in the exercise is *not* harmonized (either not done yet or we are on the last note of the exercise) AND the next note is capable of being harmonized by an appropriate chord (determined through third-tier heuristics); OR the resulting progression follows the rules controlling the motions of a (T)onic-class chord to chords of the same chord class AND the two adjacent chords are not separated by a bar line AND if either chord is the last chord of a progression (a cadence), the chord in question must be a tonic, dominant, or submediant; OR it follows the rules controlling the motions of a (T)onic-class chord to chords of the different chord classes AND the two chords do NOT share the same root AND if either chord is the last chord of a progression (a cadence), it must be a tonic, dominant, or submediant.

It might be obvious to assume that we could simplify things by determining four single rule structures capable of dealing with all root-position triads within a specific *class* instead of the *chord-*particular ones we show here. Some situations, however, demand greater specificity and would probably increase the complexity of the rule to a point where it begins to become unmanageable. For example, as stated earlier, a linear-class tonic six-four chord would require a significantly different treatment than a linear-class passing dominant six-four chord. Both chords are of the linear class, yet their functions cannot be united. Given this and similar situations, we deemed it more productive to isolate various subclass groups and assign specific middle-level heuristics where appropriate. Because this specificity is critical to the ability of the knowledge base to respond effectively to student inquiries, the more finite each of our precepts, the better able our program is to respond to individual queries.

Figure 6.14   Three pseudo-code samples.

"I" can harmonize a note IF
    the next note is not harmonized AND
    the next note is capable of supporting an acceptable chord
    OR
    it follows the rules for movement within a class (2.1d) AND
    it does not repeat across a bar line (9b) AND
    if relevant, it follows the rules about cadential chords (1a-c)
    OR
    it follows the rules of (T)onic-class movement (2.1a) AND
    it is *not* the same chord AND
    if relevant, it follows the rules about cadential chords (1a–c) AND
    if relevant, it is a proper preparation for a V7 (7.1a–b).

"I6" can harmonize a note IF
    the next note is not harmonized AND
    the next note is capable of supporting an acceptable chord
    OR
    it follows the rules for movement within a class (2.1d) AND
    it does not repeat across a bar line (9b) AND
    if relevant, it follows the rules about cadential chords (1a-c)
    OR
    it follows the rules of (T)onic-class movement (2.1a) AND
    it is *not* the same chord AND
    if a first inversion resolving in the preferred stepwise manner (4c) AND
    if relevant, it follows the rules about cadential chords (1a–c)
    OR
    it follows the rules of (T)onic-class movement (2.1a) AND
    it follows the rule about successions of inversions (10) AND
    if relevant, it follows the rules about cadential chords (1a-c)
    OR
    it follows the rules of (T)onic-class movement (2.1a) AND
    it is *not* the same chord AND
    if a first inversion resolving in the preferred stepwise manner (4c) AND
    if relevant, it follows the rules about cadential chords (1a–c) AND
    if relevant, it is a proper preparation for a V7 (7.1a, b).

"V7" can harmonize a note IF
    the next note is not harmonized AND
    the next note is capable of supporting an acceptable chord
    OR
    it progresses to the same chord AND
    the chord of resolution is not a triad of the same class (6b) AND

Figure 6.14   (continued)

> if relevant, the previous chord is a proper preparation for a V7 (7.1a, b) AND
> it progresses to the same chord in a different inversion (4a) AND
> it does not repeat across a bar line (9b)
> OR
> it must resolve to a (T)-class chord (7a).

Tier 3: The Inference Engine

Finally, our highest heuristic level triggers consultation decisions on the basis of the location of a specific chord-pair choice within the context of a given exercise. As we implied earlier, this tier contains no specific *factual* information. Instead, it functions to coordinate the specifics of an actual exercise with the lower two tiers of the rule structure. For example, regardless of chord classification (such as tonic or dominant), the positioning of a particular chord within a cadence—as opposed to elsewhere in a specific harmonic progression—might significantly affect which precepts need to be consulted as part of the determination process. Our heuristics at this level also must take into account previous successful harmonization choices. Obviously, our selection of a particular chord at a given position within a progression will be more restrictive if an adjacent position is harmonized than if it is not. Because we would like to allow students to harmonize an exercise in any order they wish, we cannot assume that each chord choice will have immediate successors or predecessors present in the progression. Whenever a new chord is inserted into the exercise, we need to recheck existing chords on both sides of the entry, taking into consideration the newest entry. By undertaking this action, we ensure that all previous choices are updated in relation to any new information in the knowledge base. If a previously acceptable harmonization now becomes problematic in relation to some new choice elsewhere in the progression, we should inform the students of the problem and give them the opportunity to correct it by changing either or both of the offending harmonies.

In developing our heuristic strategies for this level, then, we have to create a control heuristic capable of coordinating the middle-tier heuristics in a manner that can account effectively and efficiently for all these various situations. For example, a chord may appear at the beginning of the piece, in which case there will be no chord of preparation; likewise, the final chord of the exercise will have no chord of resolution. A harmony in the middle of the progression might or might not have a previously asserted harmony on either or both sides of it; and, if one of the adjacent notes is or is not harmonized, how many additional notes on either side of that one are or are not harmonized? Unfortunately, the list of possibilities is considerable, even when dealing solely with adjacent notes, as shown in figure 6.15.

When we expand beyond two notes, the possibilities grow at nearly an exponential rate, essentially doubling with each added harmony. For example, a progression of just three notes would generate eighteen possibilities, a progression of four would generate thirty-six, and so on!

To deal with this complex side effect, we propose a forward-referencing, reverse-looping inference engine that actually alleviates most of these problems and that does it in a rather straightforward manner. Recall that all the middle-level heuristics are chord-pair referenced. In other words, we compare each harmony with one and only one other harmony at any given point—the chord of resolution in nearly every case. Designing our precepts around a *forward-only* referencing scheme such as this eliminates much of the unnecessary complexity of a rule structure that would have to take into account all the various multidirectional situations outlined a moment ago. As we have already seen, each of our precepts needs to know only where it is going, not from where it is coming.

Conversant musicians, of course, should be able to see the weakness in this rather myopic view. If, however, our forward-referencing model is employed as part of a repetitive, reverse-looping design that sequentially shifts the chord-pair reference point forward and backward, all the notes necessary to evaluate the relevant portion

Figure 6.15   Table of two-note possibilities.

Preceding chord	Succeeding chord
Harmonized	Harmonized
Not harmonized	Harmonized
Harmonized	Not harmonized
Not harmonized	Not harmonized
(None)	Harmonized
(None)	Not harmonized
Harmonized	(None)
Not harmonized	(None)
(None)	(None)

of the progression can, in effect, be evaluated without adding an excessive amount of complexity to the process. This heuristic approach effectively accomplishes the task of looking forward and backward from any point in the progression while allowing us to maintain the simplicity of the original forward-referencing model. Figure 6.16 clarifies our process through a hypothetical example.

Figure 6.16 contains a typical introductory melody that our program might present to a student for harmonization. In this instance, every note of the melody is preset to an initial harmonization of *null* (not currently harmonized). Recall that our knowledge structure is explicitly designed to avoid any references to specific exercises. It is constrained solely by the domain of acceptable harmonic progressions and thus allows students to begin anywhere they choose. However, in this case our hypothetical learner begins at the beginning by asserting a root-position tonic chord as harmonization for the melodic D natural shown in figure 6.16a. The upper-level heuristic begins by calling the first relevant middle-level precept. Because all our functions deal with forward-referencing chord-pairs, our *asserted* chord is checked against the harmonization of the next position. In this example, finding a null harmonization causes two actions to occur. First, every time we encounter a nonharmonized position (the note in position 2), the note in question is checked in relation to the proposed chord preceding it (in this case, a tonic triad). Then, our program attempts to see if that note has the potential to support a harmonization suitable for the chord pair in question. Second, our control mechanism must reposition the reference pointer one position to the right and then check the next chord pair to ensure that any of the hypothetical solutions to the first null are also capable of progressing to the next harmony. In this instance, a second null in an adjacent position halts the forward succession of events and triggers a reverse loop that moves the reference position from its current location two positions to the left, ending up on the immediate predecessor to the original position on the first note. At this point, another middle-level precept is called to deal with the new chord pair. Because no note exists prior to the first one, the process is halted, and our program responds to the student that the choice is acceptable.

Next, as we show in figure 6.16b, the student asserts a root-position submediant chord as a harmonization for the second melody note. As in the previous assertion, a middle-level precept checks the chord pair in positions 2 and 3. Any further forward references are halted after testing the null in position 3 and checking it against that in position 4. Reverse looping is triggered again, and the chord pair starting in position 1 is now checked for acceptability.

Figure 6.16   A hypothetical example.

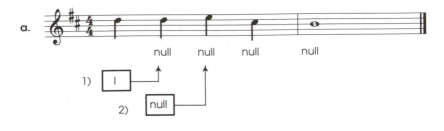

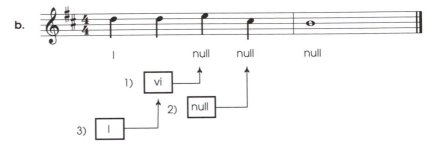

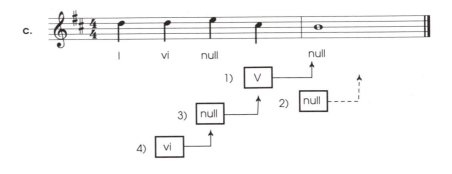

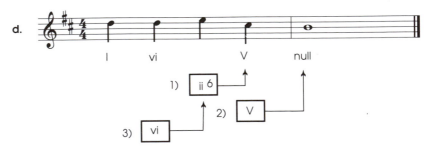

In figure 6.16c, the student next decides to jump ahead to the cadence and asserts a dominant chord in the penultimate position of the exercise. Again, a forward reference is made and halted at the null harmonization of the final chord. Reverse looping moves the reference point one position to the left, and another check is undertaken. At this point, a null in the first position of the chord pair causes an additional reversal to occur, which, in turn, checks the forward-referencing progression from the root-position submediant in position 2 against the null in position 3. This additional step is essential because any hypothetical solutions for harmonizing the E-natural in position 3 must form an acceptable progression with the existing chord preceding it. Two situations are possible at this point, both of which would stop the reverse looping. First, a null harmonization in position 2 would indicate a complete *null pair* between positions 2 and 3. Further checking beyond this point would be unproductive for us because the number of possibilities would expand exponentially, thus making any further concrete assertions unproductive. Second, the presence of a chord in position 2, as is the case here with the previously asserted submediant, indicates to us that checking has already occurred between chord pairs to the left of this position, thus making any further checks at this level redundant.

Finally, as seen in figure 6.16d, our student fills the middle gap by asserting a choice for the E-natural in position 3. A forward reference checks position 3 against position 4 and then position 4 against the null in position 5. A reversal occurs, and position 2 is checked against position 3. Finally, the student completes the exercise by supplying the tonic in the last position; the last checks are made and final evaluations undertaken.

Although this example is not meant to be comprehensive, it does show the potential ability of the forward-referencing, reverse-looping heuristic to deal with a number of different situations. The same principle could also be applied to the examination of larger musical gestures or more complex problems. Keeping in mind the phrase-level domain of our THM, however, such usage would be limited to a relatively small number of precepts. Again, a simple hypothetical example, shown in figure 6.17, will suffice.

On completion of an exercise such as the one shown throughout figure 6.17, we might want to undertake several checks to assess the overall performance of the student. One obvious point to examine might be the structural integrity of the phrase in terms of the final cadence, the early establishment of a key, and the motion from the incipit to the close of the phrase. Our check begins when a third-level heuristic triggers those precepts designed to deal with phrase structure and organization. Figure 6.17a shows the precept beginning its check between the final chord pair of the piece. Once satisfied that the cadence is in order, reverse looping takes place, and the position pointer is moved to the initial note of the exercise, as shown in figure 6.17b. At this point, forward-referenced chord pairs are examined sequentially until the precept is satisfied that the tonic of the exercise is established relatively early in the phrase. Again, only one check is required in this example. To ensure that our student has written an exercise exhibiting a satisfactory balance between repetition and variety yet not containing an excess of cadential material, the precept begins a forward-referencing look at the intermediary chords to determine if any additional dominant harmonies occur. If the chords do appear, they are examined as to their possible function in the progression. In figure 6.17c, our search encounters a dominant harmony fairly early on. Immediately, as in figure 6.17d, our pointer is moved forward to position 5, and a second forward-referenced search is undertaken to determine the nature of the remaining progression. This time, no tonic is found prior to encountering the final cadence. A quick scrutiny of the intervening harmonies determines that a larger-scale dominant prolongation has occurred between positions 5 and 9. Finally, satisfied that the cadential properties of the exercise are in order, the precept repositions the pointer to position 5—the beginning of the dominant prolongation—and initiates a simple forward-referencing, reverse-looping examination of the remaining harmonies. Our process continues in this manner until all desired assessments are made.

We hope it is obvious at this point that, by defining a relatively simple chord-pair model and using reverse-looping and forward-referencing techniques to apply it, we can effectively tackle any number of problems at numerous levels of complexity, albeit with a fair amount of preplanning still being required. With the forward-referencing model, we still need to be aware of several different general conditions, such as whether a chord is already harmonized. Nonetheless, our list of possible conditions is significantly reduced, as we can restrict ourselves solely to the nine possibilities shown in figure 6.15 and rely on the heuristic model to deal with the rest. For the sake of demonstration, we elect to simplify our heuristic model to make sure that the concepts are clear. It then becomes a relatively straightforward process to expand upon the simplified algorithm. Specifically, we limit ourselves to the immediate neighbors of the chord in question. In other words, we check the chord pair located at positions POS and POS+1 and then reverse-loop to check the pair at position POS−1 and POS. In this way, we can set up the

Figure 6.17   A second example.

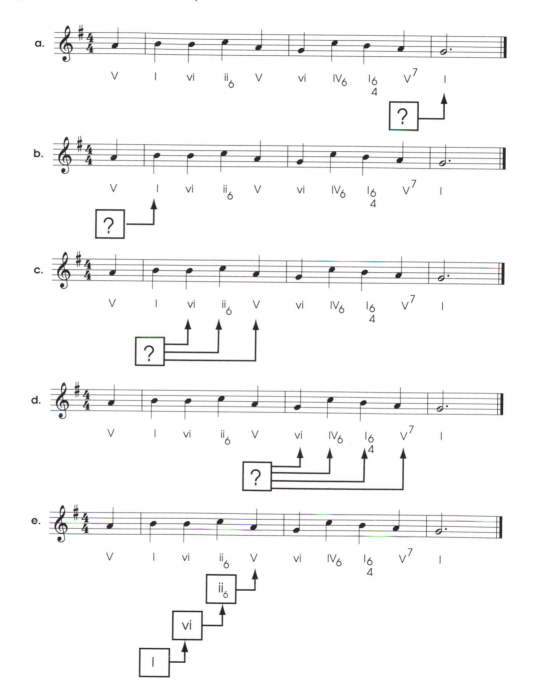

basic mechanism for looking in both directions (thus facilitating all the essential motions) without adding the complexity of including multiple forward and backward comparisons. Figure 6.18 shows the structure of the model we propose here.

Specifically, we segment the algorithm into three primary groups. First, we look to see if the student's choice is intended for the final position in the piece. If it is, and if it can successfully harmonize that note, we look backward one position. If the penultimate harmony is not null, we loop back and try the pair at POS–1; if it is null, we go no further but instead check to see if the chosen chord will work in a cadential setting. Our second group checks those harmonies intended for the first note of the exercise. In this case, we simply look at the one chord pair of positions 1 and 2. Finally, the third group deals with chord pairs appearing within the outer two pitches (positions 2 through length–1). In this situation, one of two actions can occur: either the previous chord is harmonized, in which case we check the chord pairs starting at both positions POS and POS–1, or the previous chord is null, and we check only the pair starting at position POS.

Notice that we do not check any chord pair when the *first* harmony of a progression is null. By doing this, we run the risk of harmonizing a chord at POS that cannot be preceded by any chord capable of harmonizing the note at position POS–1. Because our entire rule structure is defined in a forward-referencing fashion—in other words, so that it always looks forward from the chord in question—we would have to employ a fairly complicated heuristic to look for all possible harmonic choices for POS–1 and then check them one by one. It stands to reason that, because every note but one in an exercise is preceded by another one, the student will eventually get around to supplying a solution to the note at POS–1, and it is at that point that the forward-referencing model can undertake the evaluation. By doing this, we accomplish two goals: first, we keep the rule structure as simple and logical as we can and, second, we allow the student to make choices that may have future ramifications, even though they may present future problems. In other words, we advocate a situation in which the student can explore and experiment without excessive constraints. To some extent, the student will have to learn from his or her own mistakes!

■ **Coding the Knowledge Base**   We spend the remainder of this chapter detailing the actual code necessary to implement the THM. Although it is beyond the scope of this chapter to detail all the program code (it simply is too long)

Figure 6.18   Checking chord pairs.

```
Attempt to assert a chord at a given position IF
        the note is in the LAST position of the exercise AND        /* last position */
        the chord choice harmonizes the given note AND
        the previous chord is not NULL AND
        reverse loop and try position POS-1 THEN
        (success!)
        OR
        the note is in the LAST position of the exercise AND
        the chord choice harmonizes the given note AND
        the previous chord is NULL AND
        check for allowable cadence choices THEN
        (success!)

        OR
        the note is in the FIRST position of the exercise AND        /* first position */
        check the forward-referenced chord pair at position POS THEN
        (success!)

        OR
        the note is in the MIDDLE of the exercise AND   /* middle positions */
        the previous chord is not NULL AND
        check the forward-referenced chord pair AND
        reverse loop and check the chord pair at position POS-1 THEN
        (success!)
        OR
        the note is in the MIDDLE of the exercise AND
        the previous chord is NULL AND
        check the forward-referenced chord pair at position POS THEN
        (success!)

        OR                                                          /* failure */
        (failure!)
```

we do examine representative predicates of every necessary component of the system, including all the necessary data structures. A
complete code listing appears in appendix 2.

Basic Data Structures and Conditions

Central to any well-designed program is a data design capable of
supporting the kinds of task we wish to ask of our system. Or, put a
different way, the best designed programs are often ones where the
data design drives the development process and not the other way

around. For our THM, we decided on three important criteria and then incorporated them into our data structures:

1. We must keep track of the individual voices within each harmony. Because most instruction in harmonic practices is built around the standard SATB (soprano, alto, tenor, and bass) model, we utilize it in our structure.

2. Both metric position and stress play important roles in the determination of harmonic progressions. Therefore, we need to be able to either compute a metric position or have the information predefined as part of our structure. To simplify the THM, we opt for the latter by specifying both the meter type of an exercise and the position and duration of each note.

3. The very nature of our tonal domain is wrapped around the notion of "key." We decided to include specific information such as the key to which each note belongs and the scale degree within that key represented by the note at hand. We choose to associate this information with individual notes as opposed to the entire passages. This localization enables us to expand our rule structure to include modulations to other keys within an example. In other words, at the point of modulation we can simply change the key/scale-degree designators for all the remaining notes so that they match the new key.

Given these criteria, we define our final data structure as shown in figure 6.19.

Specifically, the predicate notes() contains the following information: (1) a list containing character representations of the selected pitches, including octave and duration, for the bass "B", tenor "T", alto "A", and soprano "S" voices, with "null" representing undefined entries; (2) an index number, ExPos, indicating the position of each note() within the exercise; (3) a scale-degree number, ScaleDeg, for each pitch, indicating its location within the designated key; (4) a string-based indication of the currently selected harmonization, CrntHarm; (5) an indicator, MetricPos, showing the position of the note within the measure where it is located; and (6) a character-based indicator, "Key", of the key to which the current note belongs. Within each data field, we adhere to the limitations presented in figure 6.20. We should note that our extensive use of character-based string representations is done to facilitate easy communication with the students using a program based around the THM (this is simply a decision we made and has no direct bearing on the structure of the model). Prolog treats these

Figure 6.19   The THM data structure.

```
notes( ["B","T","A","S"], ExPos, ScaleDeg,
"CrntHarm", MetricPos, "Key" )
```

Figure 6.20   Field contents from figure 6.19.

["B",…"S"]:	"DurationPitchnameOctave" where
	Duration = Q, H, T, or W
	PitchName = C, D, E, F, G, A, or B;
	with # for sharp, b for flat, and n for natural
ExPos:	integers from 1 to n, where n is the length of the exercise.
ScaleDeg:	integers from 1 to 7, where 1 = tonic, 5 = dominant, etc.
CrntHarm:	"ChordFigures" where
	Chord = I, ii, iii, IV, V, vi, viio (major)
	i, iio, III, iv, V, VI, viio (minor)
	Figures = 6, 6 / 4, 7, 6 / 5, 4 / 3, 4 / 2
MetricPos:	integers from 1 to 4
Key:	"KeyMode" where
	Key = C, D, E, F, G, A, or B
	with # for sharp and b for flat
	Mode = M, m (for Major and minor)

structures no differently than any other representations (in other words, symbolically), so it presents no real problem for us in using them with our rule structure. This feature can also facilitate writing any future input and output routines.

Figure 6.21 contains an actual sample coding of the melody appearing in figure 6.17. To complete the basic exercise-specific data we add three additional predicates: one to identify the metric structure (two, three, or four beats per measure), one to indicate the length of the progression, and one to point out whether we are harmonizing a melody or a bass line (1 = bass, 3 = melody). Because the exercises are relatively small and straightforward, these two additions can simplify our querying without really hindering our flexibility. If we later choose to allow for multiple meters within a phrase, we can simply append the metric information to each individual data node, as we do with key information.

In addition to our exercise-specific predicates, we also predefine certain unalterable information necessary to judge student queries. First, we define classes for each of the harmonies included in our

Figure 6.21   THM data for figure 6.17.

```
notes(["null","null","null","QA4"],1,2,"null",4,"GM").
notes(["null","null","null","QB4"],2,3,"null",1,"GM").
notes(["null","null","null","QB4"],3,3,"null",2,"GM").
notes(["null","null","null","QC5"],4,4,"null",3,"GM").
notes(["null","null","null","QA4"],5,2,"null",4,"GM").
notes(["null","null","null","QG4"],6,1,"null",1,"GM").
notes(["null","null","null","QC5"],7,4,"null",2,"GM").
notes(["null","null","null","QB4"],8,3,"null",3,"GM").
notes(["null","null","null","QA4"],9,2,"null",4,"GM").
notes(["null","null","null","TG4"],10,1,"null",1,"GM").
ex_length(10).
meter(4).
Lsn_mode(2).
```

domain. In addition, we find it useful to add information regarding the scale degrees for both the root of each chord and the actual bass note necessary to harmonize the particular inversion of the chord, which, of course, will be different. We also choose to include a symbolic class representation for each specific chord for later use by any interface routines we might want to add. Figure 6.22 shows the structural representation of the predicate class() as well as a partial listing of the necessary clauses (for a complete listing, see appendix 2).

Our next group of predicates are designed to aid us in determining the relative strength of each position within a particular meter type. For example, in a quadruple meter the first beat is considered to be the strongest of the four beats and is thus assigned a weighing value of four (4). Similarly, because the last beat of any metric type is considered the weakest, we always assign it a value of one (1). Figure 6.23 shows all the related predicates used to define structural weights.

Finally, as part of every query to the THM, we must first decide if the chord choice being offered is even capable of harmonizing a given note. In other words, does the note supplied by the exercise even belong to the chord being presented? Obviously, if it does not, it wastes our efforts to continue searching the remainder of the THM looking for acceptable harmonic progressions. Our predicates do_harmonizes() and harmonizes() are used to carry out this initial screening. Essentially, do_harmonizes() is called to check the status and mode of the current exercise (are we being asked to

Figure 6.22   The `class()` predicate.

a.
```
class("ClassSymbol","ActualChord",ClassName,Root,BassNote).
```
b.
```
class("I","I",tonic,1,1).
class("I","I6",tonic,1,3).
class("vi","vi",tonic,6,6).
class("i","i",tonic,1,1).
class("i","i6",tonic,1,3).
class("VI","VI",tonic,6,6).
class("V","V",dominant,5,5).
class("V","V7",dominant,5,5).
. . . etc.
```

Figure 6.23   Relevant metrical predicates.

```
has_quad_beat_val(1,4).
has_quad_beat_val(2,2).
has_quad_beat_val(3,3).
has_quad_beat_val(4,1).
has_triple_beat_val(1,3).
has_triple_beat_val(2,2).
has_triple_beat_val(3,1).
has_duple_beat_val(1,2).
has_duple_beat_val(2,1).
```

harmonize a bass or a melody note, and is the key major or minor?) and then to check the given note against all the possible notes that are part of the harmony. We choose to use the factual predicate `harmonizes()` for storing the relevant information for each harmony. We could have developed an algorithm for determining the various choices in each case, but the pattern-matching powers of Prolog make this "hard-wired" approach an ideal because it simplifies both the coding and the debugging process. The complete code for `do_harmonizes()` and a partial listing for `harmonizes()` appears in figure 6.24.

The initial clause of `do_harmonizes()` simply takes the first item in the list of all possible note choices for the given chord because this clause deals solely with bass-line harmonizations and the given note choice is dictated. If we are looking at a melody note,

Figure 6.24   The `do_harmonizes()` predicate.

```
do_harmonizes(bass,Chord,Note) :-
      harmonizes(Mode,Chord,[Note|_]).
do_harmonizes(melody,Chord,Note) :-
      harmonizes(Mode,Chord,List),
      member(Note,List).

      harmonizes(major,"I",[1,3,5]).
      harmonizes(major,"I6",[3,1,5]).
      harmonizes(major,"I6/4",[5,1,3]).
      harmonizes(major,"V",[5,7,2]).
      harmonizes(major,"V7",[5,7,2,4]).
      harmonizes(major,"V6",[7,5,2]).
      harmonizes(major,"V6/4",[2,5,7]).
      harmonizes(major,"V6/5",[7,5,2,4]).
      harmonizes(major,"V4/3",[2,5,7,4]).
      . . .etc.
```

however, any of the elements in the list could represent possibilities, and all must be checked for a match.

The Rule Base (the Lowest Tier)

We discussed earlier that the lowest two tiers of the THM contain the actual knowledge of the system. It is in the lowest one specifically that we define predicates covering the various relationships already discussed at some length and summarized in figure 6.2. It is beyond the scope of this discussion to cover every predicate in detail (a complete code listing appears in appendix 2). Instead, we choose to highlight several select predicates as models for understanding the remaining ones. We begin by examining the predicate clause shown in figure 6.25.

This particular set of precepts relates to the general motions of dominant-class chords. The first clause checks if the chord in question is a member of the dominant class. If it is, an additional check is made of the following chord to see if it happens to be a member of the tonic class. Because our rule 2.1c (see figure 6.4) states that dominant-class chords may proceed to tonic-class chords, this clause will succeed if these two conditions are met. Notice that we use a final call in the clause to store a record of the successful call. This information is stored for later use in reconstructing the logic of our search, as we discuss later in this chapter. Continuing, we see

Figure 6.25   Tier 1: the `d_class_movement()` predicate.

```
d_class_movement(Chord,Pos)  :-                    /* 2.1c */
        class(_,Chord,dominant,_,_),
        Pos2 is Pos+1,
        notes(_,Pos2,_,Chord2,_,_),
        class(_,Chord2,tonic,_,_),
        good_list("2.1c"),!.
d_class_movement(Chord,Pos)  :-
        Pos2 is Pos+1,
        notes(_,Pos2,_,Chord2,_,_),
        class(X1,Chord,dominant,_,_),
        class(X2,Chord2,dominant,_,_),
        X1 \= X2,
        good_list("2.1c"),!.
d_class_movement(Chord,Pos)  :-
        class(_,Chord,dominant,_,_),
        Pos2 is Pos+1,
        notes(_,Pos2,_,Chord2,_,_),
        member(Chord2,["IV6","iv6"]),
        good_list("2.1c"),!.
d_class_movement(Chord,Pos)  :-
        class(_,Chord,dominant,_,_),
        Pos2 is Pos+1,
        notes(_,Pos2,_,"null",_,_),
        good_list("2.1c"),!.
d_class_movement(_,_)  :-
        error_list("2.1c"),!,
        fail.
```

that the second clause seeks to match that condition, enabling a dominant-class chord to progress to a *different* dominant-class chord. As our search progresses through the predicate, it should become apparent that the individual clauses tend to be arranged in ascending order of specificity. In other words, we seek the most general solutions first. It is not until the third clause of this particular predicate that we begin to check for particular circumstances, in this case that one anomalous situation allowing for a violation of the more general rules. Finally, our fourth clause checks for a "null" condition. If the chord at `Pos2` is not harmonized, our chord choice is allowed. If we had wanted our algorithm to be more expansive, we could use this point in the predicate to begin our search for all *potential* harmonizations for the second chord. Again, for clarity we have omitted that operation.

If all the first four clauses fail during the course of a query, we cause the entire predicate to fail but not before we store that information as well. We can use several strategies for collecting information on our search. One method would be to wait until a search is completed, either successfully or not, and then to redo the search, collecting only the relevant data as we go. Because very few predicates are actually queried during any one search, we deem it easier to collect all the data the first time through, simply discarding the irrelevant data once we finish our query. The predicate shown in figure 6.26 is similar yet offers a different twist. Of initial interest here is the second clause. We have chosen to be more restrictive because this particular chord can progress to only one harmony group: the dominant/dominant-seventh chord. Even though the next chord may be null, we can very easily check the validity of the progression by checking the scale degree of the note given at that position. If that note is not scale degree 5, we simply cannot suc-

Figure 6.26   Tier 1: the i64_to_dominant() predicate.

```
    i64_to_dominant(Pos) :-               /* 5a */
    not ex_length(Pos),
    Pos2 is Pos+1,
    notes(_,Pos2,_,Chord2,_,_),
    member(Chord2,["V","V7"]),
    good_list("5a"),!.
i64_to_dominant(Pos) :-
    not ex_length(Pos),
    Pos2 is Pos+1,
    notes(_,Pos2,5,"null",_,_),
    good_list("5a"),!.
i64_to_dominant(Pos) :-
    Pos2 is Pos+1,
    notes(_,Pos2,_,"null",_,_),
    error_list("5a.2"),
    error_list("5a.1"),!,
    fail.
i64_to_dominant(_) :-
    error_list("5a.1"),!,
    fail.
```

ceed, and we duly note that information in the succeeding two clauses. The remaining clauses for the entire lowest tier heuristics appear in appendix 2.

The Rule Base (the Middle Tier)

Predicates designed for the middle tier deal solely with specific chord pairs. Generally, our predicates at this level function to organize and coordinate the firing of the various precepts defined at the lowest level. Again, we choose to highlight only several examples here because the complete code is too extensive to detail in its entirety (a complete listing is included in appendix 2). We begin by examining the code shown in figure 6.27.

Figure 6.27   Tier 2: The `can_harmonize()` predicate.

```
can_harmonize(C,Pos)  :-               /* Rule 19.1a */
    member(C,["I","i"]),
    notes(_,Pos,N,_,_,_),
    lsn_mode(M),
    check_mode(M,N,[1,3,5],1),
    empty_goodlist,
    Pos2 is Pos+1,
    notes(_,Pos2,_,"null",_,_),
    good_list("19null"),!.
can_harmonize(C,Pos)  :-
    member(C,["I","i"]),
    notes(_,Pos,N,_,_,_),
    lsn_mode(M),
    check_mode(M,N,[1,3,5],1),
    empty_goodlist,
    same_class_movement(C,Pos),
    not_across_barline(Pos),
    last_chord(C,Pos),!.
can_harmonize(C,Pos)  :-
    member(C,["I","i"]),
    notes(_,Pos,N,_,_,_),
    lsn_mode(M),
    check_mode(M,N,[1,3,5],1),
    empty_goodlist,
    t_class_movement(C,Pos),
    not same_chord(C,Pos),
    last_chord(C,Pos),
    cannot_precede_v7(Pos),!.
```

Essentially, these rules seek to find out if a given chord (C) can harmonize a note appearing at a specific position (Pos) in an exercise. In this particular instance, we are checking to see if a root-position tonic chord can be used successfully. Our first clause, designed to deal with a "null" successor, begins by checking if the supplied chord is a root-position tonic chord (in either a major or a minor key). If so, we then look to see if the note appearing in the exercise is in fact part of that chord. Before doing this, however, we must check the mode (M) of the lesson. Because this THM is designed to deal with either bass-line or melody harmonizations, we need to control our aspect accordingly. With a bass-line harmonization, we need only check the given note against the root of the chord, whereas melody harmonization requires checking all possible chord tones because any one of them might appear in a voice other than the bass. Once this step is passed successfully, a "null" check is executed. Assuming that these criteria are met, the predicate succeeds. If the next position of the exercise is already harmonized, however, we must then move on to the next clause and continue our query. The second clause begins in a manner similar to that of the first one. Instead of looking for a "null" condition, however, we now check those rules that dictate progressions emanating from the supplied choice. In this case, we check for movements within the same class (rule 2.1d) and for special cadential considerations (rule 1a). Additionally, as a special condition of same-class movement, we do not allow the same chord to be repeated across a bar line, hence the additional check. If our query encounters the third clause, we can assume that the next chord is neither "null" nor a member of the same class. If this is the case, we can then look at those precepts not bound by the previous conditions. Specifically, we examine for those general conditions regulating the movement of tonic-class chords to chords of other classes (rule 2.1a) as well as for any relevant special cadential considerations (rule 1a). In addition, we look to see if the next chord is a dominant-seventh chord (rules 7.1a and b). If it is, we must follow the restrictions relegating motion toward that chord.

Note that, prior to checking the lowest tiered rules triggered by any one of these clauses, we first call the predicate empty_goodlist() to clear out the storage of previous successful attempts. In this way, the list contains only those elements related to the one query that successfully approved the asserted chord choice.

The Inference Engine (the Highest Tier)

It is specifically the job of this highest tier to coordinate the testing of the various chord pairs in a harmonization. We apply the basic heuristic presented earlier in figure 6.18, with very little modification required to generate the actual Prolog code. We use the two clauses of our predicate `test()` to demonstrate the workings of the heuristic. This code, together with the related predicate `try_chord2()`, is shown in Figure 6.28 (a complete listing appears in appendix 2).

The first two clauses shown here are designed to test harmonizations proposed for any middle position in an exercise (in other

Figure 6.28   Tier 3: The `test()` predicate.

```
test(Chord,Pos)  :-                              % Middle POSition(s):
    not ex_length(Pos) ,                         % non-null predecessor
    Pos > 1,
    Pos2 is Pos - 1,
    notes(_,Pos2,_,Chord2,_,_),
    not Chord2 = "null",
    can_harmonize(Chord,Pos),
    try_chord2(Chord,Pos,Chord2,Pos2),
    record_chord_choice(Chord,Pos,on),
    record_answer(true),
    clear_variables2(Chord,Pos),!.
test(Chord,Pos)  :-                              % Middle POSition(s):
    not ex_length(Pos),                          %null predecessor
    Pos > 1,
    Pos2 is Pos - 1,
    notes(_,Pos2,_,"null",_,_),
    can_harmonize(Chord,Pos),
    record_chord_choice(Chord,Pos,on),
    record_answer(true),
    clear_variables2(Chord,Pos),!.
    try_chord2(Chord,Pos,Chord2,Pos2)  :-    % Test Other POSitions
        record_chord_choice(Chord,Pos,off),
        goodlist(List1),
        clear_variables2(Chord2,Pos2),!,
        can_harmonize(Chord2,Pos2),
        goodlist(List2),
        retract(goodlist(_)),
        retract(goodlist2(_)),
        assertz(goodlist(List1)),
        assertz(goodlist2(List2)),!.
```

words, neither the first nor last the position). The first clause, which assumes that the preceding chord is already harmonized, begins by calling the middle-level predicate can_harmonize() to test the chord pair beginning at Pos. If this call succeeds, our heuristic continues by calling the related predicate try_chord2() to test the preceding chord pair: that pair beginning at Pos2 (actually, Pos−1). If this call succeeds as well, the clause calls record_chord_choice() to record our acceptable chord choice, calls record_answer() to indicate a successful query, and finally calls clear_variables2() to reset the exercise environment (for a complete code listing of all the relevant code used by the THM, see appendix 2). The second clause works in manner similar to the first, except it does not attempt any solution to the chord pair at Pos−1. As we discussed earlier, one option for enhancing the power of the THM would be to insert a series of queries that would attempt to find all the possible hypothetical solutions for harmonizing the preceding position—in light, of course, of our original harmonic choice for Pos.

Our other predicate, try_chord2(), is used to test harmonizations at positions prior to the one actually being queried. We must include several important components, however, to keep it from interfering with our predicate test(). Recall that, during any call to the middle-tiered heuristics, our THM builds a list of all the rules that succeed while asserting an acceptable harmonization. This information is stored as a list of rules in the factual predicate goodlist(). Because try_chord2() now calls can_harmonize() for a second time, we effectively lose all the information collected during the first call. It is imperative, then, that we retrieve the original list and store it for safekeeping while testing the second chord pair. We now have the information necessary to re-create the entire query for both chord-pair queries, and the list of information for the pair at Pos is stored in goodlist() and the information for the latter search at Pos−1 in goodlist2().

■ The Student Module

It is beyond the scope of this study for us to go into all the details and nuances of developing a complete, intelligent tutorial. We do need to consider, however, the basic needs of students using our program. Do they need to be coached? Do we explain answers to them? Do we offer alternative solutions to their problems? These and other related tasks fall within the domain of a *student module*. We focus here on two specific aspects of a such an implementation.

The first deals with the two related issues of needing to know why or why not our choice of a harmonization was acceptable. The second deals with the notion of generating *other choices* for consideration as possible alternative solutions.

The ability of a knowledge-based program such as the THM to explain its actions is critical to separating it from the more rudimentary drill-and-practice types of programs that tend to respond in a simple right-versus-wrong manner. To this end, we can implement features designed to explain to a user why a particular query does or does not represent an acceptable choice. Actually, we already have all the information needed to express these ideas. At the end of every query, we have access to three predicates that contain the information we need: `goodlist()`, `goodlist2()`, and `errlist()`. The data in `goodlist()` and `goodlist2()` consist of lists identifying every rule that was part of our most recently undertaken successful search beginning after the last failed predicate (remember from our earlier discussion that we clear these lists after each failed attempt). The predicate `goodlist()` contains that information specific to the chord pair beginning at `Pos`, whereas the data in `goodlist2()` relate to the second chord pair tested, specifically, that pair beginning at `Pos-1`. Essentially, we can do whatever we choose with the information, but just by virtue of having the data we stand in a strong position to present it in a useful and meaningful manner.

Why? And Why Not?

The "why not?" function is the easiest of all the operations to facilitate because the information we need is stored in one easy-to-access location: the `errlist()`. Because the THM maintains only the information relevant to the last failed attempt, we will have a minimum of data to process. For example, assuming that we tried to assert a root-position mediant triad on an E-natural, preceded by a root-position tonic triad on C-natural and followed by a third leap to an unharmonized G-natural, we would find the following information in the database:

```
?- errlist(X).
   X = ["10.1", "cannot support"]
```

The information in this list tells us two things. First, we have violated rule 10.1, which states that a root-position mediant triad must progress to a subdominant, or root-position submediant triad. Second, the "null" note in `Pos+1` cannot support either of these chords.

With this information at our disposal, we can create whatever type of pedagogical presentation we deem relevant for conveying such information.

The "why?" function is a bit more complicated because we must convey the entire sequence of steps necessary to arrive at a successful harmonization, including the information relating to both progressions away from and toward the chord in question. Let us assume that, instead of the root-position mediant triad in the previous example, we chose to assert a first-inversion tonic chord. After receiving a successful response to our inquiry, we can query the database and derive the following information:

```
?- goodlist(X).
       X = ["19null"];
       no
?- goodlist2(Y).
       Y = ["9", "2.1d", "4a"];
       no
```

The information in X gives us the path we followed successfully to complete the progression from Pos, whereas the data in Y gives us the information related to determine our arrival from position Pos-1 to the chord in question. Specifically, rule "19null," found in the predicate goodlist(), states that because the next chord is not currently harmonized, for the time being the progression is acceptable. The data in goodlist2() tell us that three rules—9, 2.1d, and 4a—were all successfully traversed in the process of moving from Pos-1 to Pos. Again, with these data we have the ability to recreate and disseminate this information for whatever purposes we choose.

Help: Other Choices?

The "other choices?" feature requires a bit more programming to facilitate effectively. For the THM, we choose to implement a predicate, other_choices(), that repetitively calls the third-tier predicate test() to find all the possible solutions to a given exercise. The complete code for other_choices() appears in figure 6.29.

This predicate is set up to test all possible harmonizations for a note at a given position. By utilizing the fail predicate built in to Prolog, our heuristic is able successively to test every possible chord that it can bind to X. Regardless of whether the test is successful, fail will force backtracking to continue until all possible solutions for X have been exhausted, thus ensuring that we have a complete list of possible harmonizations. As each successful at-

Figure 6.29   The `other_choices()` predicate.

```
other_choices :-
    exercise_pos(Pos),
    other_choices_2(Pos).
    other_choices_2(Pos) :-
    retractall(good_chord_choice(_,_)),
        notes(_,Pos,Note,_,_,Key),
        get_mode(Key,Mode),!,
        do_harmonizes(Mode,X,Note),
        test(X,Pos),
        answer(true),
        process_solutions(X,Pos),
        fail.
    other_choices_2(_).

    process_solutions(Chord,Pos) :-
        goodlist(List),
        goodlist2(List2),
        append(List2,List,List3),
        assertz(
            good_chord_choice(Chord,List3)).
```

tempt is completed, our heuristic calls the predicate `process_solu-tions()` to garner the appropriate information from `goodlist()` and `goodlist2()` and store it with the successful chord choice in a new predicate, `good_chord_choice()`. On completing our "other choices?" search, we simply call all the instances of the `good_chord_choice()` predicate to derive the collected informa-tion. If for the moment we assume that we want to test all possible solutions for harmonizing the E-natural in the example mentioned earlier, we would set the position pointer to `Pos=2` and then call `other_choices()`. On completing the inquiry, we can query the database and find the following choice:

```
?- good_chord_choice(X,Y).
        X = "I6"
        Y = ["9","2.1d","4a","19null"]
        no
```

■ CONCLUSION

For all intents and purposes, the heuristic inference engine in the THM is sufficient to allow our program to fulfill successfully the basic criteria so essential to the functional ability of an intelligent tutoring system. The THM contains the domain knowledge in a manner consistent with our recognized teaching tools, and it can access that knowledge in a manner that allows it to solve domain problems, explain the logic behind *how* the problem was solved and *why* the choice is acceptable, and similarly explain *why* a choice is not acceptable. It can also explain the logic underlying that assessment. Because the inference engine in our THM functions in a teaching environment aimed specifically toward the development of relatively low level skills, it does not explicitly include extensive knowledge on larger-scale harmonic structures. As we showed in the previous examples, however, the pattern approach of grouping multiple smaller structures into a reduced number of larger patterns (a concept so integral to the heuristic model) would certainly be capable of supporting such expansion. Finally, although the particular knowledge base we discuss here is designed specifically for the storage and dissemination of principles related to harmonic progressions, the three-tiered organizational structure of pattern building is sufficiently flexible to allow for its use in numerous musical applications.

SEVEN

KIRS: A Knowledge-Based Simulation

▓ INTRODUCTION

Music theories can contain both objective and subjective elements. They may define principles or elemental structures—such as pitches, intervals, registral directions, and durations—for which there are objective means of identification and classification. These elemental definitions, however, often combine to generate precepts describing more complex objects—such as harmonies and counterpoints—that are also objective constructs in the sense that they are definitively defined; yet they are somewhat subjective in that the theories they are part of do not always define explicitly how they are to be applied. By using knowledge-based programming techniques, we can encode the rules of a particular theory as a working knowledge base. We can also define logical ways to apply those rules to given musical examples as part of an inference engine and thus strive to generate plausible analytical results. Applying the nuances of the inference engine as a strategic control for searching the knowledge base for problem solutions (in this case, a musical analysis) can provide us with an isomorphic model of a specific analytical process. By combining these two components (the knowledge base and inference engine) into a computer program, we are able to create a knowledge-based simulation of a music theory.

The process of constructing such a simulation provides a powerful tool for investigating and, subsequently, critiquing a music theory. This process includes extracting rules or relations and incorporating them into the knowledge base of a system. The extraction and codification process, called *knowledge engineering*, requires that we engage and scrutinize the underlying theoretical premises to a degree not necessarily required, although preferable, when manually applying those same assumptions. The process also includes our extracting and defining explicitly the manner in which the rules are applied to create an effective inference engine. Our computer simulation, therefore, is a model of some real process. In other words, the activities of a program have the potential to parallel actual human analytical processes, at least the rational ones, to an extent greater than is possible with other forms of models. We can often benefit greatly from this process because, even in simple, well-specified theories, it is possible to "watch" the analytical process unfold. Therefore, the computer should be able to generate plausible analytical results on the basis of the knowledge base and inference engine designed from the theory. If such analyses are not generated by the program, reasons for this must be explored and corrected resulting in our modifying the model and, subsequently, the theory.

Throughout this chapter we present the methodology for constructing a knowledge-based simulation of a music theory. Specifically, we develop a complete working system called KIRS (*K*nowledge-based *I*mplication *R*ealization *S*imulation). KIRS attempts to simulate the bottom-up cognitive primitives that form the foundation for Eugene Narmour's (1990, 1992) formalization of the implication-realization model for melodic analysis. The analyses generated by KIRS, combined with the knowledge gained through the process of generating the program, provide us with our basis for criticizing and reformulating certain aspects of his theory.

Specifically, we divide the remainder of this chapter into five sections. In the first section, we present some of the characteristics of traditional computer simulations and how they relate to knowledge-based simulations. In the second section, we present an overview of the processes employed in constructing KIRS and lay out in detail the actual construction of the model. Specifically, we discuss both those aspects of Narmour's theory we have chosen to incorporate into the model and those we have not. Throughout this section, we also build a detailed English-language model of the knowledge base. In the third section, we discuss the implementation of the model on a microcomputer system, concluding with explanations and examples of how we verify that the system operates as we expect it to. We then present two examples of the type of information and subsequent criticisms that can be generated through this type of investigation. The fourth section addresses some of the benefits and limitations of simulating music theories as a methodology for investigating them.

■ PART 1: FOUNDATIONS

Computer Models and Simulations

■ **Computer Models**   Most theories are sufficiently complex that a single model cannot be devised to represent an entire system adequately. For example, a single model of the global warming theory would be so immense in terms of the different ecosystems affected and the number of variables involved that it would be prohibitively difficult for us to simulate with our present tools. Fortunately, most theories can be divided into smaller components, relevant to more circumscribed situations, thus allowing us to make predictions on the basis of this information. Frequently, we can represent theories of music through models that, although often more restricted in their intent than the complete expressions of those theories, avoid most representational difficulties by applying themselves only to limited subsets of the phenomena they address. Any simplification we require of a model makes it less generally applicable than a complete theory, but it is usually very explicit with respect to the *specific* context the model addresses. To this extent, our models strengthen and extend the specifications of a theory while avoiding the complexities of the full range of processes covered in the complete theoretical statement.

There exists a variety of models, such as physical, mathematical, and language-based ones. Physical models (e.g. miniature models of cars or airplanes) resemble the structure of the object being modeled, often with great specificity. These models often can be built with more expediency and less effort than full-size productions and can be used to facilitate and test various aspects of design. Architects often create models of buildings or developments to help others visualize a project in terms of efficiency and aesthetics. Physical models may also be full-size models, such as the body of a car, which can be subjected to aerodynamic and stress testing without creating a finished vehicle.

We can represent observed or imagined relationships with mathematical models or formulas. The graph in figure 7.1 is a straight-line, or linear, graph representing a one-to-one correspondence of points on the X and Y axes of the model. This graph can be represented by the mathematical formula $Y = 2X$. For every point on the X axis there is a corresponding point on the Y axis equal to $2 \times X$. It is often easier for us to manipulate a mathematical description of a line ($Y = 2X$) than a verbal one. We frequently employ mathematical models to describe extremely abstract theories, but such models are often nearly as abstract as the phenomena they describe, making their comprehension difficult. Mathematical models also are often, but not always, static in that they tend to describe "snapshots" of some process in time rather than describing an entire process. This feature is desirable in some applications but can be detrimental in situations where it is important to observe whatever process is invoked to reach a specific point in time.

A model of a theory can also be constructed using natural languages such as English or German. Because a theory is generally a "loose" collection of verbal statements, it is frequently riddled with inconsistencies, ambiguities, and undefined aspects within specific contexts. A natural-language model must be more specific than a general theory within a specified context, something that is often accomplished by formalizing a portion of the theory into a series of discrete rules. The encoded rules reflect the premises of the theory and show how those premises are to be applied within the real-world context they model. A natural-language model uses language as the means to create a more complete representation of a theory within a specific context, even if the theory was originally presented in the same language. To this extent, the model serves to expand and clarify the prevailing theory.

Computers are frequently employed to implement models, whether the model is mathematical or built from a natural language. A computer implementation of a mathematical model can represent an element of the real situation not present in many mathematical

Figure 7.1   Graph of $Y = 2X$.

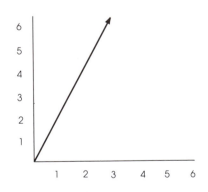

models, namely, the element of time. Real-world processes unfold over time in a dynamic and changing fashion. By observing thousands of mathematical "snapshots" in time, we can model the illusion of change in a manner analogous to that of a motion picture. A computer implementation of a natural-language model, then, allows us to examine the logic, consistency, and operation of the model over time. It also provides us an opportunity to adjust the model and test modifications in an expedient manner. We refer to this implementing and operating of a model by computer as a *computer simulation*.

■ Characteristics of Computer Simulations

Actually, we use the term "computer simulation" in two senses. In a general way, a computer simulation is a program that serves to model some theory. In a more specific way, it is the actual process of operating a computer program so that it runs parallel to the domain being simulated. We use a computer simulation, therefore, to *emulate* some real-world process (or theory) and to serve to clarify or explain that process. (There are a number of good introductions to computer simulation. Among those most often cited are Bratley, Fox, and Schrage [1983]; Bulgren [1982]; Neelamkavil [1987]; Spriet and Vansteenkiste [1982]; and the classic by Zeigler [1977]. Any of these will provide a thorough introduction to the concepts of simulation and are accessible to those with a modest background in computers and computer programming.)

Traditional computer simulations were frequently implemented using mathematical models and constraints, were usually written using procedural programming languages, and relied heavily on static algorithms to generate output. Once an algorithm was designed, the simulation used only that algorithm to solve relevant problems. Beause the simulations relied on algorithmic strategies, traditional simulations required that the data provided to the system be well defined; that is, the data had to be measurable in some tangible manner. The data also had to be comprehensive because the mathematical algorithms could not adequately handle ill-structured problems. Because theories are often partially defined and/or contain ambiguous elements, traditional computer simulations encouraged and often forced solutions to such ambiguities to create operational systems. Although the initial solutions may not have been the best ones, readjusting the ambiguous parts of theories to align with their real-world counterparts often did infuse additional clarity and refinement. Because the outputs (results) of simulations were expected to resemble or imitate the outcomes of the real-world processes they were attempting to emulate, traditional computer simulations commonly relied on statistical comparisons of the results with physical measurements from the real-world systems being modeled. Once the simulations accurately *resembled* the real-world systems, changes were able to be introduced into the simulations—affecting those observed changes—and predictions could be generated on the basis of the information gained.

Such considerations of the results of a model are important in assessing the validity of a simulation; but equally important is the *imitation* of the real-world process. A computer simulation is *not* an exact copy of some real system or process but rather a flexible imitation. This suggests to us that although the process can be regarded as similar or parallel, we cannot imply a one-to-one correspondence. This is an important distinction because the most significant aspect of a simulation is the similarity of process between itself and the real-world system it emulates, not any *presumed* similarity of structure. For example, often we employ simulations to study some kind of system and predict the effect of changes or alterations on the system. Usually, these are systems too large, too complex, or too expensive for us to reproduce and study as a whole. For example, we can investigate the effect of adding a new runway to an airport by simulating it on a computer before actually constructing it. It is less expensive in terms of time and money to model the airport system prior to construction than to observe the nature of the real system after it is too late to fix. One goal of this simulation might be to model the operation of the airport's traffic flow, modeling flight paths and ground traffic while watching for congestion patterns. Once this aspect of the model closely resembles the real operational characteristics of an actual airport, changes can be made to the simulation and the effects observed until the results are desirable. Because the model is built before the airport is constructed, it has to be modeled using data from other real-world situations and therefore is not a true representation, only a model. Nonetheless, it still has the potential to predict real behavior with a high degree of accuracy because it is based on the information gleaned from other sources (airports) sharing the same domain of knowledge.

Or, in other instances, models or partial models of the earth's environmental systems are used to predict the effects of various changes to the system, such as the impact of specific pollutants on a given ecosystem. Simulations are employed to model emergency equipment placements and response times within a community in an attempt to optimize the locations for the equipment within a given area. Economists often use simulations of national economies to make predictions concerning the impact of proposed fiscal policies, changes in lending rates, consumer spending patterns, and a host of other variables on the economy as a whole. Until recently, most of the applications have been scientific studies based primarily on the predictive powers of a model. The main purpose of the simulation has been to predict future events on the basis of data and relationships known to exist today.

Knowledge-Based Simulations

As already alluded to, traditional simulations had the same inherent limitations as other computer programs implemented with mathematically based languages. They used algorithms to simulate the operation of real-world systems, which meant that a simulation could use only a prescribed method (the algorithm) to reach a solution to a given problem. They also used numeric methods to represent the knowledge required of the simulation, often resulting in additional levels of abstraction when compared to AI knowledge-representation methods and making it difficult for them to handle ill-structured problems. Finally, the logic guiding the output of a program was often explained in terms of both the mathematical algorithm driving it and the statistics employed to verify its accuracy rather than in terms of the original problem or question the simulation was to answer. In the late 1980s, a number of researchers in computer simulation became acutely aware of the advantages of applying AI concepts to their programs. Likewise, some AI scientists began incorporating established concepts from computer simulation in their work, leading finally to the creation of a new genre representing a hybrid of the two fields: knowledge-based simulations. (Widman, Loparo, and Nielson [1989] present an excellent introduction to the integration of these two subfields of computer science. Their book is a collection of articles that discuss different aspects of the simulation process and how AI techniques, strategies, and concepts can be used to create better, more powerful, and more useful simulations by combining many of the principles developed within these subdisciplines.)

Many of the advantages that accrue to AI languages also accrue to knowledge-based programs. First, knowledge-based programming offers us several techniques for representing domain-specific knowledge, reflecting more accurately the manner in which such knowledge is understood by an acknowledged expert. Because AI languages are based on symbolic as opposed to numeric manipulations, they are clearly better suited for implementing our natural-language models than traditional ones. Second, knowledge-based programming offers us the advantage of dealing with incomplete, or ill-structured, information. A programmer can concentrate on describing the processes involved in the real-world system and allow the computer to search for solutions on the basis of those processes. Because they use encoded facts from a specific knowledge domain rather than defining explicit procedures to solve the problem, knowledge-based programs can also infer solutions for us on the basis of the knowledge provided. This *declarative* approach has the added advantage of facilitating model and simulation development more rapidly than programming simulations with procedural languages. Third, knowledge-based programs have the ability to explain how they arrive at the decisions they generate by reproducing the process for us. They also have the capability of generating solutions through more than one "path" in a manner analogous to humans. A similar explanative process is not available or necessary in traditional simulations because their solutions are generated through an explicit algorithm. The power of having the system generate solution paths allows the programmer to develop the model from a more declarative viewpoint and the program to work out many of the procedural details on its own. Fourth, knowledge-based programming strategies provide the end user with an explanation of its reasoning consistent with the knowledge encoded within the program. Because such knowledge is encoded in a manner similar to an end user's conceptualization of that knowledge, the system can justify its solutions in terms the end user can understand.

Constructing KIRS

As we mentioned at the beginning of this chapter, KIRS is a knowledge-based simulation of the "bottom-up" syntactic primitives from Eugene Narmour's theory of melodic implication-realization. The program simulates the theory as presented in *The Analysis and Cognition of Basic Melodic Structures* (1990) and *The Analysis and Cognition of Melodic Complexity* (1992). Before we build the actual simulation, it is helpful for us to examine some of the basic strategies involved in planning and implementing such a system.

In developing computer-based simulations, we advocate the use of the five primary steps frequently employed in the process of creating traditional computer simulations (see figure 7.2). It is important to understand this process because the development of KIRS parallels portions of it yet diverges considerably in two respects, which we will discuss shortly.

Figure 7.2   Steps in a simulation project.

1. Identify objectives of simulation
2. Construct the model
3. Verify the model
4. Validate the model
5. Interpret the output

1. *Identify objectives.* Because a model represents a specific aspect of a theory, it is important to determine what purpose the simulation is to serve. If our goal is to determine the optimum operating levels of a power plant, the design of the simulation must reflect this goal in terms of the model and the types of data employed. If our goal is to determine whether a new power plant will be profitable when built, another set of criteria and data may be deemed more important. If our goal is to determine the environmental impact of the new power plant on the surrounding area, yet another set of data and relationships will need to be introduced into the model. Our model should be designed with the stated purpose and the proposed outcomes in mind. This is not to say that the outcomes are predetermined; rather, the type of information deemed important to the study should and will influence the design of our model.

Our first two objectives for KIRS are to design and implement a knowledge-based computer simulation of the bottom-up component from Narmour's theory and to use the information generated during the process of designing, implementing, and running the simulation to provide a critique of that theory. While building KIRS, we have to deal with many of the incomplete, ambiguous, and undefined aspects of the theory for the simulation to run. The knowledge that guides the basic analytical premises (knowledge base) as well as the method or process of applying those premises to the music (inference engine) must be defined. Our final goal then sets out to use the results of the process to create a more comprehensive expression of Narmour's theory.

2. *Construct the model.* Constructing a model is probably the most time-consuming task involved in the project. Our models must accurately reflect (and perhaps expand) the specific portion of the theory under investigation. There are numerous ways to achieve this. First, we must isolate the parts of the theory relevant to the desired outcomes of the project, then we must determine relationships among the various parts of the system, that is, how those

parts operate and interact with one another. We must select knowledge-representation methods on the basis of the relevant data and then create a computer program to emulate the operation of the real-world system. Additionaly, our program needs to parallel the processes involved in the real system without necessarily duplicating them.

In many instances, we can divide music theories into two primary components: (1) the knowledge constituting the basic premises of the theory and (2) the procedures for applying those assumptions to the music (the actual process involved in the analysis). For this project, we wish to construct a model where the knowledge necessary to generate plausible analyses within the context of Narmour's theory is presented through declarative natural-language statements. Fortunately, Narmour's implication-realization theory already presents the basic premises in terms of formal definitions. We need only examine the definitions and translate them into rules in the form of "if-then" constructs, which in turn provide us with the foundation for our knowledge base. The analytical process—the order and manner in which these rules are applied to music to generate an analysis—constitutes the inference engine of our simulation. Because Narmour does not explicitly define his analytical processes, we must create this portion of the natural-language model by carefully charting the steps required to generate plausible analyses and anticipating possible decisions that could be made at given times throughout an analysis.

Another reason we generate the natural-language rule base includes simplifying the implementation of our model and thereby reducing the amount of debugging time required when actually writing the program. If we successfully codify our rules into appropriate if-then formats, implementing the knowledge base becomes a relatively simple translation process. Because we already know how the entire model should operate, we can select the appropriate programming structures and avoid the ad hoc code created when improvising during program development. Part 2 of this chapter provides a detailed account of the model construction process.

After building the natural-language model, we undertake a translation into an operating knowledge-based simulation. We first adopt the Prolog data structure presented in chapter 5 to represent the music we want to analyze. Because this structure affects how the natural-language model is translated into the knowledge base and the inference engine of the simulation, we define this aspect of the program first. Then, having selected our musical data structure, we first translate the rules from the natural-language model into a syntax appropriate for Prolog and then translate the analytical process into a series of control mechanisms guiding the application of the rules to musical examples. The process of implementing the knowledge base and inference engine are addressed in detail in part 3 of this chapter.

3. *Verify the model.* We must "verify" that our model works as it was meant to. Bratley et al. (1983) state that verification is "checking that the simulation program operates in the way that the model implementer thinks it does" and asking if the program is "free of bugs and consistent with the model?" (p. 8). There are no fixed methods for debugging a program, but some of the strategies we employ to debug any computer program may assist in the process. We may work out our logic by tracing through examples by hand and comparing the results with those of the computer program, or we may submit data to the program for which a solution is already known and compare it with the output of the simulation. We should then address any discrepancies by altering the program until it is capable of reproducing the results we desire. This process does not mean that our program is completely free of bugs (a debugging process is rarely ever completed), but if our program can produce correct output for known examples, the chances are good that it will operate properly.

When verifying KIRS, we implement the natural-language model and test each rule in the knowledge base and inference engine. Each time a rule does not yield the proper results, it is modified until we find the output satisfactory. Obviously, the greater the number and variety of test examples, the more likely it is that the system will operate correctly. When the system finishes analyzing a sufficient quantity of material satisfactorily and with predicted results, we deem the program to be functioning properly—in other words, the program is working as we intend it to. We verify KIRS by submitting specific melodic fragments and longer patterns to the system for analysis, knowing in advance what analysis the program should generate for the specific examples. Samples of the material used to verify KIRS are also discussed in part 3 of this chapter.

4. *Validate the model.* Validation is closely related to verification. Bratley et al. (1983) define validation as "checking that the simulation model, correctly implemented, is a sufficiently close approximation of reality for the intended application" (p. 8). Again, we have no fixed methods for determining the validity of a simulation. In most cases, we can compare the results statistically with data from the real-world system under investigation. If the results compare favorably, we consider our simulation to be a valid representation of the

real system. Once the system is validated, we can use the results to predict the future state of the real-world system on the basis of present information. Alternative future states can also be predicted by changing controllable variables within the simulation.

This portion of the process differs from the applications presented for traditional simulations. Because of the nature of most music theories, validation in terms of absolutes or statistical correlates is usually impossible. The simulation process for music theories, therefore, should not necessarily focus on the predictive powers of a theory, if such a thing exists. (Those who maintain a purely "scientific" conception of music theory will find traditional simulations appealing because of their emphasis on subdividing problems into quantifiable components. Those who conduct research in cognition will find knowledge-based simulations appealing for their prowess in simulating mental processes.) In light of our conceptualizations, the validation process can only confirm the *plausibility* of the analyses presented by KIRS. If the system presents plausible results, we deem it valid. On the other hand, if the simulation performs correctly in the verification phase and fails to generate analyses that match those of others, there is room for criticism of the simulation and/or the analyses of others. This observation, however, does not validate or invalidate our simulation. The interpretations of other observers concerning the same pieces of music are publicly validated only through their acceptance or rejection within the wider body of music criticism. The analytical results of KIRS, obviously, may also be criticized along the same lines.

5. *Interpret the output.* Interpreting the output of the simulation is the last step in a traditional computer modeling project. Often, we must translate the results of our simulation into a form useful to the people making decisions on the basis of that simulation. For example, the prospective owners of a power plant may need to know the results of certain scenarios to decide whether to build the plant, to determine how they can minimize damage to surrounding ecosystems, or to determine whether the new plant is feasible on the basis of the information obtained from the simulation. We can explain how certain constraints were implemented, how specific variables were changed, and how those changes affected the output of the simulation. Preferably, we can explain these things in terms of the problem and not in the programming or mathematical terms that form the foundation for the simulation.

As stated earlier, we generate output in KIRS by having the program analyze specific fragments of music for which an analysis was already known. If the output from the program matches our anticipated result, the system is deemed to operate properly within that context. This output also allows us to explore the validity of the theory by studying the analyses generated by KIRS and to determine whether they indeed represent plausible analyses. The information we gain from these studies, combined with the knowledge acquired throughout the development and implementation of KIRS, provides us with the foundation for our criticism and restructuring suggestions.

Obviously, we believe the most interesting and powerful data collected from simulations in music theory are found in the *process* and not necessarily in the *final output* or *product* of the system. Although both are important, we assert that more insight and understanding can come from the modeling and programming process than from observing the analyses generated by the simulation alone. We do not bring up this point simply to infer that the output of a computer simulation is of no value. On the contrary, we think this information is very useful. If a computer simulation is deemed adequately representative of a music theory and the output generated by the simulation is not musically plausible, it can and should raise questions about the very nature of the theory under investigation. Obviously, a computer simulation should not be used as a sole source for confronting or assessing a theory; it is only one method among many, and some of the many should be tried and applied before rendering a final verdict. The simulation provides only one perspective and should be taken as such.

■ PART 2: CONSTRUCTING THE MODEL

Narmour's Theoretical Premises

Narmour (1990) succinctly posits the question his theory purports to answer: "What are the specific, note-to-note principles by which listeners perceive, structure, and comprehend the vast world of melody?" (p. 3). He also strongly believes that his approach to implication-realization answers this question. To study and explain these aspects of melody, Narmour adopts a multiple parametric approach to the investigation of music. Specifically, he adopts Leonard Meyer's (1973) division of music into primary (melody, harmony, and rhythm/meter) and secondary (texture, tempo, register, and dynamics) parameters. Although Narmour states that all these parameters may be governed by specific sets of rules, his theory deals specifically only with those rules governing melody. He openly acknowledges the considerable influence of Meyer on his thinking, especially the ideas presented in *Explaining Music* (1973), and adopts many of his concepts and conventions, such as his views concerning conformant relationships, closure, diachronic analysis, and Gestalt principles, and his exclusive focus on the role of the musical listener.

Narmour, however, also makes a dramatic departure from Meyer's treatment of musical styles. Throughout Meyer's writings, musical style functions as a highly complex network of learned structures with which listeners reference and compare new experiences, forming expectations on the the basis of the conformance of the current auditory experience to some extant model in the mind. These expectations are either realized or denied, as the music continues creating new implications in a cyclic manner until the music ends. For Meyer, then, all implications and related realizations are based within a stylistic context that is never fixed but rather is dynamic, as each new experience adds to or modifies an individual's concept of a given style. But Narmour abandons style as a basis for his implication-realization model, believing for several reasons that style cannot function as a constant from which implications can arise. For example, Narmour (1990) claims that "we cannot adequately define style" (p. 19), and, because the definition of style changes with each generation of theorists, our understandings of style remain in a constant state of flux, making it impossible for us to use style as a formal foundation for a theory. Further, he claims that style is problematic because fixed definitions of style cannot adequately account for the variants of individual listeners. He goes on to explain that

> because the cognitive knowledge of style differs significantly from listener to listener—in terms of what stylistic structures a given perceiver possesses, in terms of varying strengths of cognitive structures from listener to listener, and in terms of individual abilities concerning how quickly a given subject can invoke a relevant style—style is, and will always constitute, an extremely problematic source from which to hypothesize *constants* in a perceptual-cognitive theory of implication. From the viewpoint of the individual listener, there is, cognitively speaking, no such thing as *a* style. (p. 22)

Narmour regards the use of styles and stylistic contexts as overly subjective—terms having negative connotations for him—and discounts the possibility of building a theory on such principles.

Because Narmour abandons style as a basis for his theory, he turns to cognitive psychology to provide a constant theoretical

Figure 7.3   Bottom-up processing.

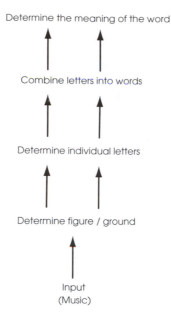

foundation, adopting a variation of a top-down/bottom-up process-ing model for this purpose. Figure 7.3 shows a diagram of how we can come to recognize the meaning of a word through bottom-up processing (we base this discussion on an explanation and series of examples originally presented by Glass and Holyoak [1985]). The input stimulus in this case is the word "music." When someone looks at the word, they immediately notice the contrast of black marks against a white page. Once the contrasts are observed, the mind distinguishes between figure and ground. Once the figure and ground are differentiated, the individual letters can be identified. Next, the letters are combined to form a word, which is then com-pared with a large list of words that the person knows. When a match is located, the corresponding definition, and therefore the meaning of the word, is obtained. Notice that each step builds up from the bottom. (Of course, this example represents a simplified version of what actually happens because several steps have been omitted for the sake of clarity.) Glass and Holyoak (1985) state that "the defining property of a strictly bottom-up process is that the outcome of a lower step is never affected by a higher step in the process" (p. 22). For example, in figure 7.3 the step of combining letters into words cannot influence the determination of individual letters or the figure and ground. Because the latter operations represent lower levels than combining the letters into words, they cannot be influenced by the higher-level operation in a strictly bottom-up process.

In contrast to the bottom-up process, figure 7.4 shows how we may determine the meaning of an unknown word through a top-down process. The input stimulus for this example is the sentence fragment ". . . the melodic archetype presents . . ." with the unknown word: "archetype." To determine the meaning of the word, we might select a potential meaning on the basis of other similar words for which we know the meaning. Such a list may consist of "architect," "archaeologist," "arch," and "archaic." We also know that "type" could mean a kind, class, or group. From the context of the sentence, we know that the word must be a noun, which eliminates "archaic," an adjective. Using "architect," "archaeologist," or "arch" in the sentence does not appear to make sense. However, we know that an archaeologist studies primitive or original cultures. By combining the definitions of "archaeologist" and "type" we obtain the definition of "archetype" as an original or primitive class or group of something—in this case, melodies. We often use top-down process-

Figure 7.4   Top-down processing.

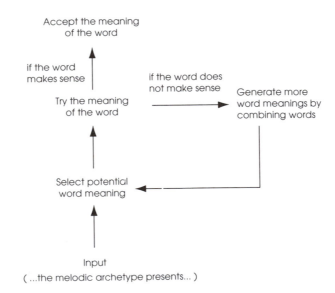

ing to model higher-order cognitive processes such as learning, reasoning, and inferencing. In a top-down processing model, the output of a higher step may influence a lower one. In figure 7.4, if a word does not make sense in a sentence, we generate more potential meanings and return cyclically to a "lower level" until an acceptable word meaning is found.

Top-down and bottom-up processes are not mutually exclusive; rather, they are used often in tandem to explain complex cognitive processes with information being understood through both bottom-up and top-down processes simultaneously. The results of one type of processing often influence the outcome of the other. Narmour employs such a *bidirectional* model for explaining the cognitive processes involved when we listen to music. He hypothesizes that there are specific innate, cross-cultural cognitive constants that operate subconsciously in human perception. These constants are always operating on auditory input and serve to group or segment stimuli into patterns. These *universals* are considered to be brute-force mechanisms existing in every person regardless of culture or background. They are "hard-wired" in our subconscious, allowing us to perceive and process aural information in general and musical information in particular. Narmour hypothesizes that these mechanisms segment stimuli into patterns on the basis of specific principles from Gestalt psychology, namely, similarity, proximity, and common direction. The patterns describe how these innate constants segment musical patterns subconsciously and function from the bottom up in Narmour's system, forming the "constants," or the cognitive foundation on which he builds his theory of implication-realization. Narmour (1990) calls these primitive mechanisms *style shapes* and defines them as follows:

> By style shapes I refer to the properties that individual parameters exhibit. In the parameter of melody, for instance, any pair of pitches displays a registral shape (it moves either up, down, or lateral); and a melody also has an intervallic shape (it spans some definable, nameable, relative distance). (p. 34)

Narmour believes that a series of innate cognitive mechanisms segments melodies according to registral direction and intervallic motions from the bottom up. He generates a series of basic shapes, based on registral and intervallic motion, that represent the way he believes these mechanisms partition the melody. He derives an analytical symbology to describe these segmentations, and it is a tacit assumption that this symbology (the analysis) informs an understanding of the music.

After abandoning style as a foundation for his theory, Narmour reintroduces style into his system as a top-down process. Narmour states that musical styles are learned structures that influence our perception of implications from the top down. He calls these *style structures*, by which he refers to

> complex patterns organized by many different parameters—a highly specific amalgam of melodic, harmonic, and durational patterning positioned metrically, texturally, timbrelly, and dynamically in a musical context characteristic of one particular style. (p. 34)

Narmour claims that musical sounds are processed from the bottom up and from the top down simultaneously. He states that the top-down component of his theory influences our perceived implications, depending on our knowledge and experience with a given musical style. Implications generated by top-down processes, however, cannot change the implications generated by the bottom-up mechanisms. In this regard, Narmour's formulation of the top-down/bottom-up model is at variance with the general model presented earlier.

Narmour painstakingly presents the foundations of his model in the two published volumes of his work under consideration here (1990, 1992) but admits that the theory is incomplete and that there is at least one additional volume forthcoming. Narmour presents his basic cognitive hypotheses concerning the style shapes, or *basic structures*, and their role in melodic implication. He discusses in considerable detail the role and effect of closure in the theory and how various levels of understanding are generated within his theory. He also discusses briefly how learned musical styles influence our expectation—in Narmour's terms, *style structures*—but there is not a thorough presentation of these principles, and the portions mentioned are scattered throughout his discussion of his basic structures or style shapes. Even though Narmour's theory represents work in progress, the bottom-up part of this theory is by far the most thoroughly discussed to date; therefore, the bottom-up portion of the theory will form the basis for our natural-language model and subsequent computer simulation.

Narmour presents three universal mechanisms as a foundation for his theory: similarity and differentiation, closure and nonclosure, and parametric scales. These mechanisms, part of Narmour's bottom-up processing model, operate on all aural input regardless of source or purpose. He claims that they are noninterpretive and that we cannot eliminate their control—they simply always operate. Narmour combines these mechanisms to generate his style shapes. The first general concept (similarity and differentiation) contains "two universal formal hypotheses" providing the basis for what constitutes implications of continuation (similarity) and differentiation. The first of these hypotheses (constants) states that

> when form $(A + A)$, intervallic patterns (A + A), or pitch elements (a + a) of a given melody are similar $(A, A,$ or a$)$, the listener subconsciously or consciously infers some kind of repetition of pattern, element, or form. (1990, p. 3)

That is, $A + A \rightarrow A$, A + A $\rightarrow$ A, and a + a $\rightarrow$ a, where "$\rightarrow$" is read as "implies." In this case, two similar elements, whether the elements are formal, intervallic, or pitch specific, imply that the following element will be similar to the first two. The second constant of this pair defines a reciprocal relation to the first, which Narmour presents as follows:

> When form, intervallic patterns, or pitch elements are different $(A + B,$ A + B, a + b), the listener subconsciously or consciously perceives some implied change in form, pattern, or element (C,C,c). (1990, p. 3)

That is, $A + B \rightarrow C$, A + B $\rightarrow$ C, and a + b $\rightarrow$ c. In this case, if the original two elements are perceived as being different, they imply that the third element will also be differentiated from the first two elements. These constants operate on all subparameters of melody (intervallic motion, registral direction, time point, time span, and specific pitch) independently.

Narmour (1990) defines his second general concept (nonclosure and closure) by stating that "[all] forms exhibit one of two universal functions, either closure or non-closure (in some degree)" (p. 3). He explains that nonclosure is equivalent to implication and that implications may occur with varying degrees of strength. Narmour employs the term "implication" in the same sense that Leonard Meyer (1973) uses the term, where an implicative relationship is defined as "one in which an event . . . is patterned in such a way that reasonable inferences can be made both about its connections with preceding events and about how the event itself might be continued and perhaps reach closure and stability" (p. 110). Although Narmour's discussion of melodic implication parallels Meyer's in the sense that he deals with connections between melodic events, he generates his bottom-up implications from his formal hypotheses of similarity and differentiation, whereas Meyer bases implications on an individual's knowledge and experience within a musical style. Closure is associated with the realization of an implication, and like nonclosure it may occur in variable degrees. Narmour uses the term "closure" in the same sense as Meyer; and following Meyer, Robert Hopkins (1990), states that "closure in music is the sense of satisfactory conclusion that comes with the anticipated arrival at a state of comparative repose following tension or activity" (p. 4). Likewise, Narmour claims that melodic closure occurs at a place in the music where several melodic subparameters achieve such repose simultaneously. He also states that each subparameter of melody may exhibit degrees of closure independently.

Because the degree of any given implication and realization may vary, Narmour (1990, p. 4) offers some assistance with his third general concept, that of *syntactic-parametric scale*. This scale determines whether any pair of comparative elements is considered to be similar or different. It also determines closural and nonclosural functions for these elements as well as the degrees of closure or nonclosure present in a given melodic pattern. The syntactic-parametric scales apply to the subparameters of melody: registral direction, intervallic motion, pitch specificity, time points (metric positions), and time spans (rhythmic durations). Narmour states that all the primary and secondary parameters of music are governed by these scales. The scales are used to measure the amount of closure or nonclosure in a given subparameter of melody at a given point in time. Even though all the subparameters of melody are governed by these scales, Narmour (1992, p. 15) admits that only two of these systems are relevant to the perception of melody—namely, those governing intervallic motion and registral directions. Narmour's intervallic scale is displayed in figure 7.5.

Narmour uses the scale in figure 7.5 to measure relative implicative strength within a given melodic excerpt. For example, assume that we play two successive melodic intervals, such as a major third and a major second. Because our pattern moves to the left on the parametric scale, this progression represents a motion to a relatively weaker implication, or simply motion toward closure. Conversely, if we play the successive intervals of a minor second and a major third, the pat-

Figure 7.5 Intervallic parametric scale.

u m2 M2 m3 M3 P4 TT P5 m6 M6 m7 M7 (P8) m9 . . . . . .
sameness . . similarity . . . . differentiation . . . .
               (threshold)
weak implication . . . . strong implication

tern moves to the right on the scale, representing a relative increase in the strength of the implication, or motion toward nonclosure. Given two successive intervals of a major second and a major second, we have no motion on the parametric scale (nil motion), meaning that no relative change in the strength of the intervallic implication has occurred. Narmour presents these syntactic-parametric scales as a primary component of his theory—they represent his conceptualization of a mechanistic input system for auditory stimuli—yet they play a relatively minor role in the actual analyses generated by his theory.

The Implication-Realization Model (Rule-Base)

In the following sections, we examine the implications of all the subparameters of melody that form the foundation for Narmour's implication-realization theory. We present the "facts" as Narmour defines them and then translate these principles and definitions into a natural-language model, forming the foundation for the computer simulation. The entire natural-language model appears in appendix 3.

■ Registral Implications

Narmour defines three kinds of registral motion—ascending, descending, and lateral—stating that an established registral motion implies continuation in the same direction. He adopts this concept from Meyer (1956) who felt that "a shape will, all things being equal, tend to be continued in its original mode of operation" (p. 92). According to this principle, the two notes played in figure 7.6a establish an ascending registral direction and thereby imply that the next note will continue the upward registral motion. The pitch of that note may be any pitch higher than the C5. The pitches in figure 7.6b establish a descending registral motion and therefore imply continuation of the descending registral direction—in this case, any pitch lower than C5. The pattern in figure 7.6c implies a continuation of

Figure 7.6 Registral Implications.

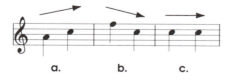

a.   b.   c.

the pitch C5 established by the lateral registral direction. From the definition of registral implications, we can place the following facts into the natural-language model:

1. ascending registral direction implies ascending continuation,

2. descending registral direction implies descending continuation, and

3. lateral registral direction implies lateral continuation.

Figure 7.7 shows Narmour's (1990, p. 284) syntactic parametric scale for registral direction, which mirrors his intervallic scale in terms of dividing registral directions into three types: *same, similar,* and *different.* Each pair of terms, such as lateral to lateral, represents the registral direction established by two successive intervals. For example, given three identical pitches, the registral direction established by the first two is lateral, as is the registral direction established by the last two. Narmour regards such a motion (lateral to lateral) as representing *registral sameness.* This scale, however, has a logical problem because registral direction represents an either-or situation: either the registral direction established by three pitches continues in the same direction (up/up, down/down, or lateral/lateral) or the direction changes. Narmour attempts to force a three-way scale on a two-possibility system in an attempt to maintain consistency with the remaining parametric scales (e.g. intervallic motion and duration).

In the intervallic *syntactic parametric scale* presented in figure 7.5, intervallic sameness is manifest in melodic motion by intervals of exactly the same size. Similarity represents a relationship where the intervals are not exactly equivalent but are perceived as similar, and intervallic differentiation occurs when the intervals are perceived as being different. In registral direction, ascent to ascent and descent

Figure 7.7   Registral direction parametric scale.

lateral to lateral	ascent to ascent descent to descent	ascent to descent descent to ascent ascent to lateral descent to lateral lateral to ascent lateral to descent
(sameness) A + A	(similarity) A + A	(differentiation) A + B

to descent are no less exact than lateral to lateral. All three cases represent registral motion in the same direction. Therefore, we will use the parametric scale found in figure 7.8 to define registral relationships. This scale preserves the integrity of the similarity relation as defined for intervals and represents a minor change in Narmour's theory. From the modified scale, *registral sameness* can be defined and added to the natural-language rule base as follows:

> IF the registral direction established by two intervals is in the same direction,
> THEN "registral sameness" is true.

▣ Intervallic Implications

Narmour (1990) presents his notion of intervallic implication with his definition of the syntactic parametric scale:

> In terms of subconscious expectations, [the syntactic parametric scale hypothesizes] that small melodic intervals generate registral and intervallic implications of similarity (A+A). And it says that large intervals generate intervallic and registral implications of differentiation (A+B). (p. 5)

Narmour posits the hypothesis that unisons, minor seconds, major seconds, and major thirds imply continuation of the established registral direction (up/down/lateral) and intervallic motion by a similarly sized interval. He asserts that melodic intervals of a minor sixth, major sixth, minor seventh, and major seventh imply a change of registral direction and motion by an interval of dissimilar size. Narmour considers the perfect fourth, tritone, and perfect fifth to be threshold intervals, lying somewhere between the clear continuation implications of the smaller intervals and the apparent reversal implications of the larger intervals. He considers the octave to be a

Figure 7.8 Modified registral syntactic parametric scale.

lateral to lateral	ascent to descent
ascent to ascent	descent to ascent
descent to descent	ascent to lateral
	descent to lateral
	lateral to ascent
	lateral to descent
(sameness)	(differentiation)
A	

special interval that functions primarily as a closed interval that has no implicative properties, reflecting the notion of a registral transfer, but that has an inherent tendency to imply a reversal because of its classification as a large interval. Compound intervals generate reversal implications, except for multiples of the octave, which are also treated as octave transfers. Figure 7.9 summarizes the "facts" generated by Narmour's hypotheses that we incorporate into the rules of the model.

Narmour (1990, p. 87) continues by defining *intervallic similarity*. Two successive intervals, *X* and *Y*, are considered similar if *Y* continues in the same registral direction as that established by *X* and if the difference between *X* and *Y* is less than that of a minor third. Figure 7.10a provides an illustration of this rule. The three notes in figure 7.10a create two intervals, marked *X* and *Y*. Because the pitches constituting interval *X* and *Y* are all ascending, registral sameness is true, thereby satisfying the first requirement for intervallic similarity. Interval *X* is a major second (2), and interval *Y* is also a major second (2). The difference between these intervals is a unison (0), or no difference—the intervals are the same size. Because a unison obviously is less than a minor third (3) in size, intervallic similarity holds true. (We use integers to facilitate the numerical manipulation of intervals and represent their absolute size. In this system, zero represents a unison, one a minor second, two a major second, ans so on. In this example, the difference between the intervals is determined by subtracting interval *Y* from interval *X*, resulting in zero. Because the difference between the intervals is less than a

Figure 7.9   Intervallic implications.

Unison implies continuation of sameness (unison); weakest implication.

m2 implies continuation.

M2 implies continuation.

m3 implies continuation.

M3 implies continuation.

P4 implies continuation; also weak reversal; threshold interval.

TT implies continuation of similarity and reversal equally; threshold interval.

P5 implies reversal; also weak continuation; threshold interval.

m6 implies reversal.

M6 implies reversal.

m7 implies reversal.

M7 implies reversal.

P8 implies a closed dyad prospectively, with an inherent potential to function retrospectively as a reversal.

Figure 7.10 Intervallic similarity with the same registral direction.

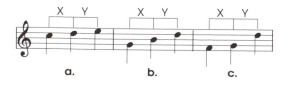

a.   b.   c.

minor third, the second of the two parts governing "intervallic similarity" is satisfied.) Figure 7.10b is also an example that satisfies the criteria for intervallic similarity, whereas figure 7.10c does not satisfy the requirement. In this case, the registral direction requirement is satisfied, but the difference between interval X (2) and interval Y (7) is that of a perfect fourth (5), which is larger than a minor third (3). In this case, the two intervals are considered to be differentiated, meaning they are simply perceived as nonsimilar. A rule defining intervallic similarity can be generated by building on the registral sameness rule previously defined:

> IF "registral sameness" is true,
> and the difference between two intervals is less-than or equal-to a minor third,
> THEN "intervallic similarity" is true;
> OTHERWISE "intervallic similarity" is false.

Narmour (1990, p. 129) presents a slightly different definition of intervallic similarity to cover those cases where the registral direction changes. He believes that listeners require less differentiation between the intervals to perceive them as being different when registral direction changes. If a change of direction between two adjacent intervals and the difference between the intervals is the space of a major second or less, the intervals are considered similar. If the difference between the intervals is a minor third or more, the intervals are considered nonsimilar. Figure 7.11 demonstrates this definition of intervallic similarity. Figure 7.11a presents two intervals where registral sameness is false: X is a major third (4) and Y a major second (2). The difference of these intervals is a major second (2) and, therefore, satisfies the second requirement of the new intervallic similarity rule. Figure 7.11b provides an example where registral sameness is denied because the difference between interval X and interval Y is a major third (4); therefore, the intervals are considered to be nonsimilar (differentiated). A rule reflecting the previous definition of intervallic similarity is formulated as follows:

Figure 7.11   Intervallic similarity with a change of registral direction.

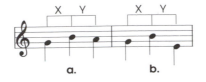

IF "registral sameness" is false,
and the difference between two intervals is less than or equal to a major
        second,
THEN "intervallic similarity" is true;
OTHERWISE "intervallic similarity" is false.

■ **Time Point and Time
Span Implication**

Narmour (1990) proposes that not only are the registral direction and the intervallic motion of a generative interval implicative, but so are the time points and the time spans of the next (implied) note—an event that is similarly implied by the time spans and time points of the preceding notes.

> All other things being equal . . . the pitches C-D in quarter notes imply that the next ascending tone will occur as a quarter note and, moreover, that that tone will take place at a time point exactly a quarter note away. (p. 92)

Figure 7.12a shows a melodic excerpt where the registral direction, intervallic motion, time point, and time span implications are all realized. The generative interval *X* implies that the next pitch will continue in the same registral direction (ascending) following a similarly sized interval. The pitch should occur at a time point exactly one quarter note away from the second pitch and should have a time span (duration) of a quarter note. In this case, all the implications are realized by the quarter note B4 on the third beat of the measure. Figure 7.12b displays a similar pattern. The generative interval *Y* creates the same implications as interval *X*, but in this case the timespan implication is not realized by the third note, even though registral sameness, intervallic similarity, and the time point implications are realized.

For realization to take place, implied location (time point) or implied duration (time span) must be satisfied. Narmour (1990, p. 431) states that any duration equal to or greater than the second note of a generative event can function as the "right" durational length for a

Figure 7.12   Time point and time span implications.

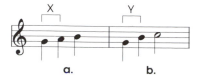

Figure 7.13   Specific pitch implications.

realization. He also states that any duration less than the second note of a generative event can function as the "right" time point for a realization.

■ Specific Pitch Implications

Narmour (1990, p. 92) states that "implied pitch specificity is dependent on the recognition of mode" where mode represents a specific collection of pitches. Given the initial pitches C4 and D4, there are a variety of different pitches that can satisfy continuation of the established registral direction and preserve intervallic motion by a similarly sized small interval such as E-flat4, E4, F4, F-sharp4, and G4. Narmour continues, "The listener's recognition of a minor mode . . . makes (1) E flat the probable implication of C-D, (2) makes E the confirmation of a major mode, and (3) makes F the continuation of a C-D-F-G-A pentatonic collection" (p. 92). Figure 7.13a shows an ascending scalar passage. Narmour points out that the next pitch should continue the ascending registral direction and realize the implied intervallic motion by a similarly sized small interval. Assuming the key of C major, the specific pitch implied by this melodic interval is the E4, representing diatonic continuation. Figure 7.13b shows the actual continuation as E-flat4 rather than E4, which results in the listener feeling a mild denial of specific pitch implication.

Narmour assumes that the recognition of "modes" represents an innate operation, an assumption he neither elaborates on nor supports.

If the recognition of major and minor modes (not to mention pentatonic and presumably any other diatonic "mode" we might imagine) is an innate process, why do many freshman music students (especially those with a limited range of musical experiences) initially have such difficulty aurally identifying major and minor modes? If modal recognition is innate, these students should correctly identify such modes automatically, but this has often not been the case. After being provided a wide variety of listening experiences and some theoretical instruction, our students achieve considerable facility for identifying such modes. (The theoretical instruction is optional, of course, but it does seem to accelerate acquisition of the skill. Identifying modes is most often learned by nonmusicians completely through listening experiences.) This observation suggests to us that recognizing musical modes is a skill *learned* through a variety of musical experiences and is *not* an innate universal. Because Narmour claims that learned structures are to be implemented in his bidirectional cognitive processing model from the top down, there is a contradiction in which the specific pitch sub-parameter of melody is incorporated into the theory—specific pitch implications should not be incorporated into the theory as a part of the bottom-up component of the theory.

Specific pitch implications may very well be generated through the modes employed in traditional Western musical practice, but these represent *style*-specific traits applicable to a circumscribed style of music. Such style structures must in turn be redefined for each style under consideration. Though specific pitch implications may be defined in terms of the general concepts of similarity, proximity, and common direction, the precise definitions will change from style to style.

Further, Narmour omits specific pitch implications and subsequent realizations from virtually all his analyses. Through his omission, he tacitly acknowledges the extremely limited influence any specific pitch has on implications and their subsequent realizations. Narmour (1992, p. 15) openly acknowledges that only intervallic motion and registral direction are relevant to the perception of melodic implication. Because of the top-down nature of specific pitch implications and Narmour's lack of emphasis on these, specific pitch implications are omitted from the model and simulation.

Melodic Archetypes

Narmour's (1990) universal hypotheses of similarity and differentiation, closure and non-closure, and the syntactic parametric scales combine to identify "five, and only five, kinds of melodic archetypes" (p. 4):

1. *process or iteration* (3 or more note groups, A+A, non-closural)
2. *reversal* (3 note groups, A+B, closural)
3. *registral return* (3 note groups, A+A, non-implicative)
4. *dyads* (2 note groups, may be closed or unclosed)
5. *monads* (1 note group, may be closed or unclosed).

Narmour's five melodic archetypes provide general frameworks into which his basic structures (discussed in the next section) can be classified. They are also considerably different than those presented by Meyer (1973) in terms of their organization and the spans of music involved. For Narmour, any melodic pattern reflecting similar motion in terms of registral and intervallic implications belongs to the *process* archetype. Figure 7.14a shows a pattern belonging to this archetype. Narmour states that such patterns are nonclosural: they imply continuation. Figure 7.14b presents an iterative pattern, also nonclosural, that, according to the theory, implies continuation of registral sameness and intervallic sameness. A duplicated pitch implies continuation of that pitch, representing a special member of the process archetype. Figure 7.14c shows a pattern belonging to Narmour's reversal archetype where registral sameness and intervallic similarity are false. Members of the reversal archetype do not project any open-ended implications of continuation like members of the process archetype. All of Narmour's basic structures of three or more notes can be classified as belonging to either the process or the reversal archetype. A pattern that Narmour terms *registral return* appears in figure 7.14d. These structures form an "aba" pattern with respect to pitch. Though registral returns are nonimplicative patterns in Narmour's system, they do create a mild sense of closure because they function as low-level closure patterns (these are discussed in more detail when we address closure later in this chapter). Figure 7.14e shows a two-note structure, or *dyad*, whereas figure 7.14f shows a one-note structure, or *monad*. Dyads usually arise

Figure 7.14   Basic melodic archetypes.

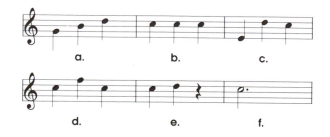

as the result of unrealized implications or from an interrupted melodic line caused by encountering a rest. Monads arise from single notes in the melodic line or arise on higher structural levels through transformation. (Narmour specifies a series of rules for transforming notes from a lower level to a higher one, thereby generating hierarchic levels. We discuss his transformation rules later in this chapter.)

These five melodic archetypes form the foundation for Narmour's sixteen basic structures (style shapes), which in turn form the building blocks, from the bottom up, of his theory of melodic analysis and cognition. These archetypes are designed to provide broad models into which the basic structures are classified.

Basic Structures

By combining the three possible registral motions (up, down, and lateral) with his hypothesized interval implications, Narmour derives several possible combinations for either complete or partial realization of the respective implications. For example, an initial ascending interval of a major second implies continuation of the ascending registral direction and continued intervallic motion by a similarly sized interval. We can realize both of these implications, realize one implication while denying the other, or deny both implications. Each of the four possible patterns represents a different *basic structure*, or *style shape,* in Narmour's theory. He defines sixteen basic structures resulting from various combinations of realized and denied registral and intervallic implications.

A *process* is one of the three most fundamental basic structures in Narmour's system. (Narmour uses the same term, *process*, to identify both a general melodic archetype and a basic structure generated by his cognitive mechanisms. Likewise, he uses the term *reversal* to represent both a general melodic archetype and a basic structure. Throughout the remainder of this chapter, we refer to the basic structures and not the general archetypes.) Figure 7.15a and b highlights several examples of this basic structure. For Narmour, a process is a series of pitches that realize both the registral and the intervallic implications established by an initial small interval. In each example, both the registral direction of the generative interval and the similarity of intervallic motion are realized. Processes represent "open-ended" structures in that they may contain more than three notes; in fact, a process theoretically can continue realizing both registral and intervallic implications indefinitely. A process ends when one of the implications (registral or intervallic) is denied or through one of the other rules of closure.

Figure 7.15 Narmour's basic structures.

We can define a process by using the registral sameness and intervallic similarity rules already defined and place them in the natural-language rule base as follows (larger intervals are discussed below):

> IF an initial interval is greater than or equal to a minor second,
>   and the initial interval is less than or equal to a tritone,
>   and "registral sameness" is true,
>   and "intervallic similarity" is true,
> THEN the structure is a "process."

A *reversal*, the second fundamental structure in Narmour's system, occurs when the registral direction changes, when between intervals there is nonsimilar motion, and when there is intervallic motion from a large interval (a minor sixth or larger) to a smaller interval. Figure 7.15c and d shows typical reversals. The initiating large interval implies that the following interval will be dissimilar and will articulate a change in registral direction. Because both of these implications are realized in figure 7.15c and d, they are considered reversals. Notice that in figure 7.15d the initial registral direction is ascending and the terminal motion lateral, therefore indicating a change in direction. Narmour's definition of reversal does not necessarily mean that the direction actually reverses, merely that it changes. We can also add a rule defining reversals to the rule base using previously defined rules, such as those governing registral sameness and intervallic similarity:

> IF an initial interval is greater than or equal to a tritone,
>   and the interval is not an octave or a duplication of the octave,
>   and "registral sameness" is false,
>   and "intervallic similarity" is false,
>   and the second interval is smaller than the initial interval,
> THEN the structure is a "reversal."

A *duplication*, the third basic structure presented by Narmour, occurs when registral direction continues laterally by the interval of a unison. Thus, a duplication consists of repeated pitches with an open-ended structure analogous to a process. Figure 7.15e and f presents two examples of duplications. A definition follows:

> IF an initial interval is a unison,
>   and "registral sameness" is true,
> THEN the structure is a "duplication."

The three basic structures described above represent patterns where the implied registral direction and intervallic motion of the initial interval are realized. The remaining basic structures represent patterns in which one or both of the initial implications is denied. Figure 7.15g shows an example where a small initial interval implies continuation in the same registral direction by means of a similarly sized interval. Intervallic similarity is realized, but the registral direction changes, denying the initial registral implication. Narmour calls this an *intervallic process*. The pattern in figure 7.15h illustrates the opposite combination of realizations. The generative interval established by C4 and D4 implies continuation of both intervallic similarity and registral direction in this example; however, the registral direction is realized, whereas intervallic similarity is not. Figure 7.15h represents an example of a *registral process*. (Narmour symbolizes interval with the letter *I* to mean an intervallic process (*IP*) but he uses the letter *V* for register because the letter *R* symbolizes a reversal. The *V*, according to Narmour, is a mnemonic for vector indicating registral direction. His choice is unfortunate because he also uses *V* to designate a chord built on the fifth scale degree. Perhaps a better choice for reversal would be a changing structure (*C*) because the registral direction does not necessarily reverse directions. This would allow *I* to represent interval and *R* to represent register.)

Before presenting the definition for an intervallic process, we first need to define a new rule for *intervallic sameness*: if two intervals are identical in size, they are considered to be equivalent. Although this precept is simple, we will use it in defining intervallic processes and *exact registral returns*. We can add intervallic sameness to the rule base as shown below:

> IF an initial interval is equal to a second interval,
> THEN "intervallic sameness" is true.

An intervallic process can be defined as follows:

> IF an initial interval is greater than or equal to a minor second,
>   and the interval is less than or equal to a tritone,
>   and "registral sameness" is false,
>   and "intervallic similarity" is true,
>   **and "intervallic sameness" is false,**
> THEN the structure is an "intervallic process."

The portion of the rule in bold type is a correction to Narmour's model. If intervallic sameness is true, then the structure is identical to an intervallic duplication (figure 7.15k and l). This limitation is added to maintain the integrity of the intervallic process as a separate and distinct structure—which appears to be Narmour's intent. A rule defining a registral process is displayed below:

> IF an initial interval is greater than or equal to a minor second,
>   and the interval is less than or equal to a tritone,
>   and "registral sameness" is true,
>   and "intervallic similarity" is false,
> THEN the structure is a "registral process."

Partially realized implications can be found when the initial registral and intervallic implications indicate a reversal. In figure 7.15i, the initial major sixth implies a change in registral direction, that the second interval will be differentiated from the initial interval (intervallic similarity is false), and that the second interval will be smaller than the initial interval. In figure 7.15i, the implied change in intervallic motion is realized and the expected change in registral direction denied. Narmour calls this an *intervallic reversal*. In this instance, intervallic similarity proves false, but registral direction does not change as the initial interval implies it should. Figure 7.15j presents a structure where the implied change of registral direction is realized while the intervallic motion continues to an interval larger than that of the generative interval. Narmour defines this pattern as a *registral reversal*. A rule defining an intervallic reversal is presented here:

> IF an initial interval is greater than or equal to a perfect fifth,
>   and the interval is not an octave or a duplication of the octave,
>   and "registral sameness" is true,
>   and "intervallic similarity " is false,
> THEN the structure is an "intervallic reversal."

A registral reversal is defined as follows:

> IF an initial interval is greater than or equal to a perfect fifth,
>   and the interval is not an octave or a duplicate of the octave,
>   and "registral sameness" is false,
>   and "intervallic similarity" is false,
>   and the second interval is larger than the initial interval,
> THEN the structure is a "registral reversal."

Narmour states that an *intervallic duplication* results when a small interval moves by an equivalent small interval in the opposite registral direction, as shown in figure 7.15k and l (a *registral duplication* is not possible). An intervallic duplication is defined as follows:

> IF an initial interval is greater than or equal to a minor second,
>   and the interval is less than or equal to a tritone,
>   and "registral sameness" is false,
>   and "intervallic sameness" is true,
> THEN the structure is an "intervallic duplication."

Narmour considers each of the eight basic structures described thus far to be *prospective structures* because at least one implication (registral or intervallic) is realized. But there are still several possible realization (or denial) combinations that have not been addressed. Narmour calls these remaining patterns *retrospective structures* because they must be reevaluated when the initial implications are left unrealized. Narmour claims that these structures require reflection as the music flows by in time. Narmour indicates retrospective structures in a score with the basic structure symbol enclosed in parentheses.

Figure 7.16a shows a *retrospective process*. The initial large interval implies a reversal of intervallic motion (from a large interval to a smaller interval) and a change in registral direction. In actuality, however, the second interval continues the ascending registral direction by means of a similarly sized interval. The implied registral direction and intervallic motion articulated by the first two notes are denied. Narmour calls this pattern a retrospective process because of its kinship with a prospective process: both registral sameness and intervallic similarity are true. A retrospective process can be added to the rule base as follows:

Figure 7.16   Narmour's retrospective basic structures.

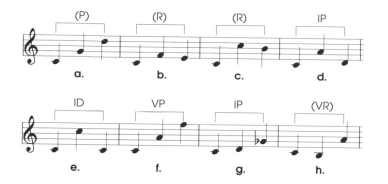

IF an initial interval is greater than or equal to a perfect fifth,
    and the interval is not an octave or a duplication of the octave,
    and "registral sameness" is true,
    and "intervallic similarity" is true,
THEN the structure is a "retrospective process."

An example of a *retrospective reversal* appears in figure 7.16b. The pattern begins with an ascending perfect fourth (generally considered a small interval by Narmour), implying continuation of both registral direction and intervallic motion by a similarly sized interval, yet both of these implications are denied. The registral direction changes, and intervallic similarity is false. Only intervals of a minor third, major third, and perfect fourth are large enough to realize a change in intervallic size (where intervallic similarity is false) and still be considered a small interval. Therefore, only these three initial intervals need to be included in this definition of a retrospective reversal. A rule defining a retrospective reversal can be added to the natural-language rule base as shown here:

IF an initial interval is greater than or equal to a minor third,
    and the interval is less than or equal to a perfect fourth,
    and "registral sameness" is false,
    and "intervallic similarity" is false,
    and the second interval is smaller than the initial interval,
    THEN the structure is a "retrospective reversal."

Figure 7.16c shows another type of retrospective reversal. The octave and duplications of the octave receive special treatment in Narmour's theory. Prospectively, Narmour considers an octave as a closed nonimplicative interval that functions as a register transfer.

But because the octave is a large interval, it has an inherent tendency to function as a reversal, at least retrospectively, which is precisely what happens in figure 7.16c. This type of retrospective reversal is defined in the rule base as follows:

> IF an initial interval is equal to an octave or a multiple of the octave,
>   and "registral sameness" is false,
>   and "intervallic similarity" is false,
>   and the second interval is smaller than the initial interval,
> THEN the structure is a "retrospective reversal."

Figure 7.16d illustrates a *retrospective intervallic process*. In this case, the initial large interval implies a change of registral direction and differentiated intervallic motion (intervallic similarity is false) from a large interval to a smaller one. The change of registral direction is realized, but the intervallic motion is by a similarly sized interval and thus denies the established intervallic implication. The definition of a retrospective intervallic process can be added to the rule base as displayed below. The criterion in bold type is added to Narmour's definition to preserve the integrity of the *retrospective intervallic duplication* (next) and parallels the correction we made to the prospective intervallic duplication earlier:

> IF an initial interval is greater than or equal to a perfect fifth,
>   and "registral sameness" is false,
>   and "intervallic similarity" is true,
>   **and "intervallic sameness" is false,**
> THEN the structure is a "retrospective intervallic process.

Figure 7.16e presents a *retrospective intervallic duplication*. This structure is closely related to the retrospective intervallic process, except here intervallic motion proceeds by an interval equivalent to the initial interval. The initial interval of a major sixth implies a change in registral direction and motion by a differentiated interval. Though the change in registral direction is realized, the intervallic motion proceeds by an equivalent interval, causing the structure to resemble an intervallic duplication. Because the initial intervallic implication is not realized, Narmour claims that this pattern can be perceived only through reflection. The definition for a retrospective intervallic duplication is as follows:

> IF an initial interval is greater than or equal to a perfect fifth,
>   and the interval is not an octave or a duplication of the octave,
>   and "registral sameness" is false,
>   and "intervallic sameness" is true,
> THEN the structure is a "retrospective intervallic duplication."

Figure 7.16f displays a pattern that Narmour defines as a *retro-spective registral process*. In this case, the initial large interval implies a change in registral direction and intervallic motion by a small interval, neither of which is realized. The registral direction continues ascending, and the second interval is actually larger than the initial one. Narmour does not specify that the second interval in such a process must be differentiated from the first (intervallic similarity is false), only that it must be larger than the initial interval. A retrospective registral process is defined as follows in the natural-language rule base:

> IF an initial interval is greater than or equal to a perfect fifth,
>   and "registral sameness" is true,
>   and the second interval is larger than the initial interval,
> THEN the structure is a "retrospective registral process."

Figure 7.16g presents a *retrospective intervallic reversal*. The initial interval implies continuation of registral direction and similarity of interval size because Narmour generally considers a perfect fourth to be a small interval. In this example, the register implication is realized, but the intervallic motion is differentiated. The only small interval large enough to continue registral direction and realize intervallic motion by a non–similarly sized interval (intervallic similarity is false) is a perfect fourth. The definition of this pattern appears in the natural-language rule base as follows:

> IF an initial interval is equal to a perfect fourth,
> and "registral sameness" is true,
>   and "intervallic similarity" is false,
> THEN the structure is a "retrospective intervallic reversal."

Figure 7.16h illustrates Narmour's *retrospective registral reversal*. The initial interval implies continuation of both the established registral direction and the intervallic motion by a similarly sized interval, but both of these implications are denied. The registral direction changes and the second interval is differentiated (intervallic similarity is false) from the initial interval. The definition of a retrospective registral process appears in the natural-language rule base as follows:

> IF an initial interval is greater than or equal to a minor second,
>   and the interval is less than or equal to a tritone,
>   and "registral sameness" is false,
>   and "intervallic similarity" is false,
>   and the second interval is a large interval,
> THEN the structure is a "retrospective registral reversal."

The only basic structure mentioned by Narmour not represented here is the *retrospective duplication*. Narmour claims that such a structure exists but that it occurs only as the result of stylistic influences, therefore representing an element from the top-down component of his theory. Because Narmour's discussion of it is fleeting, and because it represents a top-down rather than a bottom-up element, we omit it from both the model and the simulation. We do not believe that this adversely affects our model because it appears in only 3 of over 500 examples in the two volumes we consider.

Registral Return and Near Registral Return

After formulating his sixteen basic structures, Narmour informs his readers that there are, indeed, two more nonimplicative structures: *exact registral return* (aba patterns) and *near registral returns* (aba' patterns). Figure 7.17a contains an exact registral return, a phenomenon Narmour defines as a discontiguous pitch relation where the first and third pitches are equivalent, the intervals are equivalent, and the registral direction moves in either a down-up or an up-down pattern. A near registral return, shown in figure 7.17b, consists of a pitch relation where the first and third pitches are within a major second of each other, the intervals are within a major second of each other, and registral sameness is false. The rules defining exact registral return and near registral return can be added to the rule base as follows:

IF the first pitch is equal to the third pitch in a three-note pattern,
    and the initial interval is equal to the second interval,
    and "registral sameness" is false,
THEN the structure is an "exact registral return."

IF the difference between the first and third pitches in a three-note pattern
    is less than or equal to a major second,
    and the difference between the initial interval and the second interval
    is less than or equal to a major second,
    and "registral sameness" is false,
THEN the structure is a "near registral return."

Figure 7.17   Registral return and near registral return.

All intervallic duplications and most intervallic processes create aba patterns, but not all aba patterns create intervallic duplications or intervallic processes. Even though registral returns and near registral returns do not imply continuation, they do create a weak sense of closure. This particular closure is the weakest of Narmour's three types—*articulation*, *formation*, and *transformation*—and is confined to the level of its occurrence.

Dyads and Monads

Figure 7.18 shows several two-note structures referred to by Narmour as *dyads*. This pattern frequently results from unrealized registral and intervallic implications. In the first case, the opening interval is a descending major third, implying registral continuation by means of similarly sized intervals. The pattern, however, contains only two pitches—the initial implications are not realized. Narmour labels dyads with arabic numerals, indicating the size of the interval without regard for the quality of the interval (major, minor, diminished, augmented, or perfect). Thus, Narmour labels the interval (figure 7.18a) with a "3" because it represents a third. We follow the convention of labeling the absolute size of the interval using arabic numerals. Figure 7.18b shows an equivalent interval labeled with the arabic numeral "4," representing an absolute interval size of four semitones. We employ this labeling convention throughout the remainder of this chapter.

Narmour also defines a single-note structure, a *monad*, as shown in figure 7.18c. Monads are nonimplicative structures that account for individual notes. Monads and dyads are important structures when dealing with transformational levels; we discuss them again when addressing Narmour's rules for transformation later in this chapter.

Rules of Closure

Narmour (1990) defines closure as an event "whereby the termination, blunting, inhibiting, or weakening of melodic implication occurs" (p. 102). He recognizes three distinct forms of closure: articulation, formation, and transformation.

Figure 7.18 Dyads and monads.

Articulation typifies weak albeit noticeable melodic closure on a lower level. *Formation* . . . is a moderately strong closure that portends a higher level but nevertheless remains wedded to the level of its occurrence. *Transformation* represents strong closure in the usual sense of the term—one where a new hierarchical level comes to pass. (p. 11)

Closure is the opposite of implication (nonclosure), and just as implication occurs in varying degrees, so does closure. Narmour (1990) states that closure is created by

1) rests,
2) reversal of melodic direction,
3) reversal of motion to a small interval,
4) durational cumulation,
5) metric emphasis,
6) strong resolution of dissonance,
7) repetition,
8) the interruption of a pattern, or
9) some combination of the above. (p. 11)

Rests cause closure by interrupting the basic patterns in progress because they do not allow a melody to realize active implications. Figure 7.19 displays a short melodic fragment that we have analyzed as three separate processes. The process in measure 1 is closed by the quarter rest on beat 4 of the measure, representing transformational closure, the strongest type within Narmour's system. The process beginning on the downbeat of measure 2 is also closed by a rest—in this case, the eighth rest. Notice that the bracket circumscribes the boundaries of a process because processes may have variable lengths. This structure, along with duplications, represents the most open of Narmour's structures. The process beginning on beat 4 of measure 2 is also closed, this time by durational cumulation, which we discuss shortly. A rule defining this type of closure can be added to the rule base as follows:

IF the next event is a rest,
THEN "transformational closure" is true.

Figure 7.19   Rests and closure of basic patterns.

Narmour states that rests caused by articulation, such as would occur when playing a passage in a staccato style, may also enhance closure even though those rests are not notated in the score. Unfortunately, he fails to codify any means for determining how those rests enhance closure and gives us no way to measure the amount or type of closure they would generate. Rests caused by articulations represent the only part of the theory where Narmour does not rely on the printed score as the sole source of information in the analytical process. From his discussions, it appears that this type of closure would most likely be weak and therefore probably considered articulative. Narmour does not indicate closure caused by articulations, nor does he notate this type of closure in his analyses. For these reasons, closure caused by articulation is omitted from the model and the simulation.

Closure can also be created by changes in melodic direction. In measure 1 of figure 7.20, the three-note intervallic duplication beginning on the downbeat is closed on beat 3 because of the change in registral direction. This closure is reinforced by the quarter rest on beat four, though closure has already taken place prior to reaching that beat. The two processes in measure 2 are divided by the closure created when the melody changes direction on C5. We can add this rule to the rule base as follows:

> IF "registral sameness" is false,
> THEN "transformational closure" is true.

Narmour states that closure is also created by motion from a large interval to a small one. The first measure of figure 7.21 contains an intervallic reversal that is closed because of the motion from a large interval to a small interval and that is reinforced by the quarter rest on beat 4 of the measure. Measure 2 contains an intervallic reversal beginning on the downbeat and ending with G4 on beat 3 because of the intervallic motion from a large initial interval to a small interval. The remainder of measure 2 consists of a process that closes on C5 on beat 3 of measure 2. This rule can be added to the rule base as follows:

Figure 7.20   Closure by change of direction.

Figure 7.21   Closure by intervallic motion to a small interval.

IF an initial interval is a large interval,
    and the second interval is a small interval,
THEN "transformational closure" is true.

We previously defined reversals as closed structures, as they contain two characteristics that cause closure: a change of melodic direction and intervallic motion from a large to a small interval. Each of these motions, according to Narmour, causes transformational closure. Figure 7.22 exhibits a pair of reversals. The pattern in measure 1 is closed because the registral direction changes and there is motion from a large initial interval to a small interval. The closure is reinforced in this measure by the quarter rest on beat 4. In measure 2, the first three notes constitute a reversal, which is also closed according to Narmour's theory.

Narmour (1977) defines three terms to describe durational relationships: *additive*, *cumulative*, and *countercumulative*. An additive durational relationship occurs when successive notes have the same durational value, as shown in figure 7.23a. A cumulative relationship, where there is rhythmic motion from an initial note to one that is longer in duration, is presented in figure 7.23b. A countercumulative relationship is the opposite: rhythmic motion from a longer note to a shorter note, as shown in figure 7.23c.

Narmour states that a basic structure can become closed through durational cumulation. Figure 7.24 shows processes closed by durational cumulation. The whole note in figure 7.24a suppresses the implication of the line to continue rising by blunting the time span and time point implications present in the ascending quarter-note line. The A4 and B4 on beats three and four imply that the next note should be a quarter note. When the C5 lasts longer than that, it also begins weakening the implication governing the precise time point of the next event until transformational closure occurs and a new pattern is established.

Narmour defines *nonreleasable suppression* of a melodic pattern as that which occurs when a note exceeds the implied duration or location by 50 percent or more. Nonreleasable suppression causes

Figure 7.22   Reversals and closure.

Figure 7.23   Durational relationships.

Figure 7.24   Durational cumulation and closure.

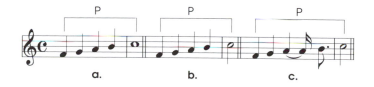

transformational closure. In figure 7.24a, the implied time point is realized by the C5, but the time span lasts for four beats rather than the implied one, a duration more than 50 percent longer than a quarter note. The pattern in figure 7.24b is also closed by durational cumulation because the C5 in this case is 50 percent longer than the quarter note implied by the A4 and B4 on beats 3 and 4.

Figure 7.24c presents an example of what Narmour calls *releasable suppression*. In this example, the A4 on beat 3 of measure 1 extends beyond the implied quarter-note time span by a sixteenth note. This causes durational cumulation, but by only 25 percent of the implied time span. The passage continues by realizing the initial registral and intervallic implications with a slight delay. Narmour defines releasable suppression as durational cumulation that is less than 50 percent of the implied time point or time span. It is releasable because continuation of the original implications, in terms of registral direction and intervallic motion, may be realized. Releasable suppression does create closure but is considered articulative, which is weaker than the transformational closure generated by nonreleasable suppression. These closure rules can be added to the rule base as follows:

> IF a note exceeds the implied location or duration by less than 50 percent, THEN "articulative closure" is true.
> IF a note exceeds implied location or duration by 50 percent or more, THEN "transformational closure" is true.

■ Meter and Closure

Narmour posits that metric emphasis causes transformational closure, but unfortunately he remains somewhat vague on the concept. He (1990) states that

> I do not refer to impulse, pulse, tactus, ictus, accent, stress, or beat (though *beat* is the mnemonic to help remember the symbol b). Rather, I mean to symbolize metric differentiation that is sufficiently emphatic in concert with some other parameter to partition a melodic line and thus transform a melodic tone, regardless of beat configuration (whether accent or nonaccent) and *regardless of level.* (p. 207)

Narmour continues to explain that any metric emphasis leading to a transformational closure in a melody is created through the interactions of the various parameters of music, especially melody, harmony, and duration. He views meter as the "summarized result of interactions among all operative parameters" (p. 208). This conception of meter, however, presents several problems within the context of Narmour's theory of implication-realization. First, he has not formalized harmonic and rhythmic implications. If meter is the summarized result of the interactions of these parameters, it seems that meter cannot be defined until all the other primary parameters have been clarified. Narmour is attempting to define metric emphasis formally in terms of the interaction of three parameters (melody, rhythm, and harmony), two of which have themselves not been formally defined. In addition, Narmour's theoretical treatment of meter is extremely weak. It seems apparent that even Narmour must realize just how problematic his "rules" governing metric emphasis are by his continual efforts to downplay their importance. Statements by Narmour such as the following are typical:

> The topic of meter and its effect on melody is a vast and elusive subject . . . We can thus do little more than maintain a hypothetical approach—postulate the possibilities, establish some guidelines, and then set about collecting the anomalies. (p. 219)

Narmour's vague notions about meter lead him to generate several metric rules that rely on concepts of harmony, dissonance, and an established sense of meter (all from a Western art-music perspective). According to Narmour, each of these rules leads to closure by establishing metric emphasis. We add none of them, however, to either the knowledge base or the simulation because we perceive each of these aspects (meter, harmony, and dissonance) as being defined and learned within a stylistic context and therefore consider them to be top-down structures. Although this causes some inconsistencies between the analyses generated by KIRS and those of Narmour, we believe that the resulting simulation more *accurately* models the melodic component of the theory. By isolating the melodic structures and observing whether they generate plausible analyses from the bottom up, we gain valuable information about the formulation of the melodic parameter of music and perhaps some insight into how such a system can be generated for rhythm and harmony. If the melodic structures cannot generate plausible analyses, the rules must be examined to determine why they failed.

■ Closure by Repetition and New Patterns

Narmour claims that closure is created when a repetition interrupts an implied pattern. Unfortunately, he does not give any examples of this type. If a pattern is interrupted by a repetition of a single pitch, the pattern would be a duplication and analyzed as such. This rule, therefore, appears redundant. Because Narmour presents no examples or explanations of this rule, it is omitted from both the rule base and the simulation. In light of Narmour's disinterest in describing this type of closure, we do not believe that leaving it out of the model adversely affects the simulation. Narmour also states that closure can be caused by the onset of a new pattern, which also seems redundant: for any new pattern to emerge, the previous pattern must be closed by one of the earlier rules (durational cumulation, change in registral direction, or motion to a small interval). He also does not give any examples or explanation of this type of closure, so we omit this rule as well.

■ Dyads, Monads, and Closure

Narmour asserts that dyads may exhibit properties of either closure or nonclosure. A dyad becomes closed through durational cumulation or through an ensuing rest (silence) in the same manner as the basic structures. Because they reach closure through the same rules as the basic structures, we see no need to redefine special closure rules just for them. Narmour (1990) goes on to state that monads can also become closed through the following means:

1) an ensuing silence,
2) undergoing a high degree of textural change (undefined),
3) undergoing a high degree of dynamic differentiation (undefined), or
4) some combination of the above. (p. 410)

Narmour states that a monad becomes closed through the same ensuing silence that has already been defined for the other basic structures, so we do not define a new rule for this aspect of closure. Unfortunately, Narmour does not define the meanings of "a high degree of textural change" or "a high degree of dynamic differentiation." These methods for closing a monad are not included in the model because they represent secondary parameters that remain undefined by Narmour. Further, he does not give any examples of this type of closure.

Rules of Transformation

Narmour (1990, p. 428) states that the initial and terminal notes of structures three or more notes in length function as the structural notes of melodic groupings and are consequently transformed to the next hierarchical level. We present in figure 7.25 a short melodic fragment analyzed with Narmour's previously discussed rules of structure and closure, together with the subsequent hierarchic levels resulting from the application of his transformational rules. The original melody is shown in figure 7.25a and consists of two parallel phrases in the key of G major. The first phrase contains two processes and an intervallic duplication and the second phrase two processes and an intervallic process. The level shown in figure 7.25b is created by transforming the notes from the beginning and end of each basic structure to the next hierarchical level. Once a new level is generated, we generate subsequent hierarchical levels by applying the rules of structure and closure to the remaining notes of each preceding level. Narmour (p. 235) states that this process is recursive, so that the rules are literally reapplied to each new set of notes. The transformation rules can be added to the rule base as follows:

IF a note is the initial note of a "basic structure,"
THEN it is transformed to the next level.

IF a note is the terminal note of a "basic structure,"
THEN it is transformed to the next level.

Figure 7.25   Transformation levels.

■ **Dyads and Transformation**   Dyads pose a slight problem when undergoing transformation because both pitches of a dyad are transformed if we rely on the two previous rules. Narmour, therefore, includes the following rules to address which pitch of a dyad is transformed:

> IF a "dyad" is countercumulative,
> THEN the initial note is transformed.

> IF a "dyad" is cumulative,
> THEN the terminal note is transformed.

> IF a "dyad" is durationally cumulative,
>   and stress is present,
> THEN the stressed note is transformed.

Figure 7.26 presents examples of each rule. In figure 7.26a, duration cumulates in the second pitch; C5 is therefore transformed to the next level. By contrast, in figure 7.26b the two pitches create a countercumulative durational pattern, meaning that the initial pitch, A4, is transformed to the next hierarchic level. Figure 7.26c shows an example where the durations of the dyad create a cumulative pattern. Here the initial pitch is stressed and therefore transformed to the next level. Narmour presents one more rule governing

Figure 7.26   Transformation of dyads.

the transformation of dyads, but because it involves the resolution of dissonance, it should be discussed in a top-down context.

■ **Monads and Transformation**

Narmour never states whether monads can be transformed to higher levels. However, because he does enumerate cases in which a monad is closed, it is assumed that they can. If a monad is closed on a lower level, it will be transformed to the next higher level to remain consistent with the other basic structures. An appropriate rule can be added to the natural-language rule base as follows:

> IF a note is a monad,
>   and the note is closed,
> THEN transform the note to the next level.

Time Tags

Narmour introduces a structure he refers to as a *time tag*. He hypothesizes that some implications extend beyond their initial denial—to be realized in a discontiguous manner. Narmour (1992) explains that "time tags result from small ascending and descending intervals whose inherent implications suffer interruption or delay" (p. 289). Time tags do not play a prominent role within Narmour's theory but rather form secondary structures. Because "time-tagged realizations . . . entail discontiguous realizations, they are always simultaneous secondary structures, functioning in subservience to the primary [basic] structures constructed of contiguous connections" (p. 264). Neither the initial nor the terminal note of a delayed process (PT) is transformed to a new level unless one of the notes corresponds to the simultaneous dominant contiguous realizations. Because the time tags are not primary components of the bottom-up implication system, they too are omitted from the model and the subsequent simulation. We do not feel that their omission affects the performance of the bottom-up basic structures.

Combining and Chaining of Basic Structures

The majority of Narmour's second volume (1992) is dedicated to the presentation and explanation of combining (*combinations*) two basic structures as well as binding three or more into longer structures (*chains*). He states that "the combining of structures occurs because metric non-closure causes two different structures to share intervals" (p. 47). At first glance this promises to provide the missing theory of metric implication-realization required to incorporate Narmour's metric rules of closure into the model. Unfortunately, Narmour does not provide a systematic explanation of meter or the possibilities of meter containing implications and subsequent realizations. Rather, he relies on several observations, learned through experience with Western music, to provide the foundation for his combinational and chaining structures.

Narmour (1992) states that there are only eight low-level conditions creating combinations or chains:

1. the occurrence of strong non-chordal dissonance on a metric accent in additive or weakly cumulative durations (provided the resolution itself is weak);
2. the presence of an ongoing metric context on any level (e.g., non-accents in 3/4 or 3/8 meter or metrically ambiguous passages in additive durations at the very beginnings of melodies);
3. the processive [P] envelopment of metric accent in additive patterns and countercumulative patterns (regardless of level);
4. the duplicative [D] envelopment of metric accent in additive patterns;
5. the harmonic processive (hP) envelopment of metric accent in additive or countercumulative contexts;
6. the durational processive (dP) envelopment of metric accent in additive or countercumulative contexts;
7. the dynamic processive (dynP) envelopment of metric accent in additive or countercumulative contexts; and
8. ongoing syncopation in additive contexts. (p. 46)

There are a variety of problems regarding combinations and chains of basic structures when looking specifically at the bottom-up component of the theory. First, Narmour's vague treatment of meter makes creating rules for guiding these decisions quite problematic. If we cannot define a metric accent, how can we envelope it in a process?

Also, several of the conditions for combining structures are based on learned, or top-down, rather than bottom-up processes. For example, Narmour incorporates dissonance in the first condition leading to combinational structures, but as previously mentioned, dissonance represents a top-down, stylistically learned phenomena. Likewise, in the fifth condition, he relies on harmonic processes (such as circle progressions in tonal music) to explain metric non-closure, but such harmonic progressions are learned within the context of Western tonal music and are not innate structures. Narmour similarly states that meter can remain open through durational or dynamic processes. A dynamic process refers to a crescendo or decrescendo, whereas a durational process refers to changes in tempo (accelerando or ritardando). Unfortunately, he does not formalize how to incorporate these musical processes in the analysis; and perhaps even more troubling, he relies solely on the printed score for such markings. If there are no markings in the score to correspond to these processes, they are not considered in the analysis! Finally, Narmour employs a number of grossly ambiguous definitions such as "ongoing syncopation" and "ongoing metric context."

Narmour's ideas regarding combinational and chain structures are interesting, and we do not mean to suggest that they are unimportant. On the contrary, Narmour draws out several interesting ideas while explaining these concepts, but they are based on learned stylistic structures that, in agreement with his own cognitive processing model, should be incorporated from the top down. Because the combinations and chains of basic structures represent top-down processes, they are beyond the scope of this project and are not included in the model or the simulation.

The Place of Style in the Theory

Style is of paramount importance to Narmour's theory. He promises to devote an entire chapter to intra-opus and extra-opus style in the forthcoming third volume of the series. He often mentions that style influences his decisions, but we are not privy to the guidelines he employs in making these decisions. In defense of his style omissions, the major premise of these books is to present and explain the bottom-up structures of his theory. These structures are not supposed to be based on any type of style structures, as he so emphatically insists. His sketchy treatment of style in these volumes may be forgiven if such matters are adequately addressed in future volumes. Because style schema are not systematically presented and since the focus of this project is the investigation of the bottom up, syntactic primitives of Narmour's theory, top-down style structures are left unimplemented until Narmour has given a sufficient enough exposition of his concepts to warrant their investigation.

The Analytical Process

Narmour does not discuss analytical processes in explicit detail, but we can deduce them by meticulously recording the steps required to generate analyses using the rules specified in the natural-language rule base. Figure 7.27 presents the opening two melodic phrases (violin I, mm. 2-6) from the first movement of Mozart's G-Minor Symphony. We use this melody (extracted from metric and harmonic contexts) to illustrate the specific steps involved in generating an analysis following Narmour's rules.

Narmour claims that his theory of musical perception is designed to explain how we subconsciously organize melodies "in time," thereby reflecting a diachronic perspective. In other words, we should generate an analysis by attending to a melody as if hearing the piece in chronological order. This requires an analysis of the melody in the strict temporal order in which the events (notes and rests) are presented.

Beginning with the first measure of the excerpt in figure 7.27, the two initial events are rests. Rests function as closural elements in the theory, but because there are no previous events in this case for the rests to close, the initial rests are ignored, being passed over in the analytical process until an audible event occurs. This may seem trivial, but it is an important consideration for implementing the simulation. The first audible sound in this excerpt is the E-flat5 occurring

Figure 7.27   Melody from Mozart's G Minor Symphony, violin I.

on the downbeat of beat 4 in measure 1. An individual note is, of course, nonimplicative, but for experienced listeners it generally implies that another note is likely because the piece has not reached any form of closure. The next event is the D5 in measure one. These two notes combine to imply that the next pitch will continue the descending registral direction and the established motion by small intervals. The next event should be located an eighth note away in time from D5 in the first measure and be an eighth note in duration. The D5 on the downbeat of measure 2 satisfies the implied motion by small interval (unison) and realizes the time point implication. This basic structure realizes closure through a change of registral direction marking the end of the pattern. By examining the three events, we observe that registral sameness is false and intervallic similarity true. These criteria correspond to those of an intervallic process, resulting in the analysis circumscribing the first three notes in figure 7.28.

On closing this pattern, we face a dilemma: Where does the next basic structure begin? Does it start with the quarter note D5 on the downbeat of measure 2? Does it begin with the first E-flat5 eighth note in the measure? The majority of Narmour's analyses treat durational closure as sufficient to close a basic structure *without* the terminal note simultaneously functioning as the initial note of the next structure—in other words, without sharing a note. Unfortunately, he never explains either the analytical process or the reasons for his choices. By treating durational closure as sufficient to eliminate overlapping notes between basic structures and applying this principle, we see that the next basic structure begins with the first E-flat5 in measure 2 of the excerpt. Applying the same analytical procedure described for the first structure to the music in measure 2 of the excerpt results in the remaining intervallic processes shown in figure 7.28.

If measure 2 of figure 7.27 were to be rewritten using only quarter notes, it would result in the analysis in figure 7.29. In this case, D5 on the downbeat of measure 2 closes the initial intervallic process while simultaneously operating as the initial note in the indicated intervallic duplication. This linking occurs because the notes in measure 2 are in direct relation (an additive relationship where the durations are equivalent) to one another. Our formulation for deciding where to begin a new basic structure parallels virtually all Narmour's analyses. We arrived at it through observing many analytical excerpts and attempting to codify the procedures employed.

Continuing our analysis, the D5 closes an E-flat5-D5-D5 intervallic process and simultaneously functions as the initial note of the next

Figure 7.28   First two measures, Mozart's G Minor Symphony.

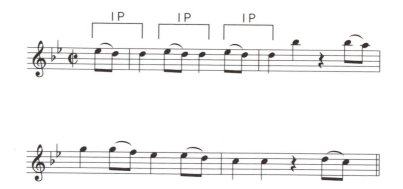

Figure 7.29   Modified Mozart.

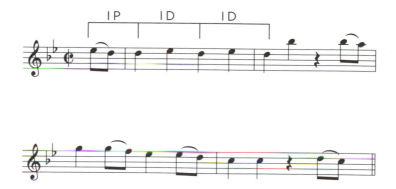

basic structure because the next note is also a quarter note. We realize that we have determined the function of a pitch that works as an end point and an initial point by "looking" ahead to see what the next event will be. For our listeners, this is not possible. They would actually process this information retrospectively in a manner analogous to the retrospective structures discussed previously. We have explained it in this manner because the simulation will have the ability to "look" forward, even though such structures will be understood by the listener retrospectively. This construction eases the implementation of this aspect of the model. This implementation reflects a case where the similarity of the listening/analytical process in terms of recognizing the pattern is preserved, but the underlying programming strategies for achieving this outcome does not correspond with the process in a one-to-one manner.

The next event is a rest closing the pattern—in this case, two pitches forming a dyad. Next we move to the first audible event beyond the rest and begin the analytical process again. The complete analysis is shown in figure 7.30.

Figure 7.31 displays a flowchart representing our analytical process as extracted from this analysis. This chart forms the foundation for the inference engine of our simulation. Beginning at the top left-hand corner of the chart, we begin by extracting the first event from the excerpt (Extract Event 1). If the first event is a rest, we simply ignore it and return to Extract Event 1. If the first event is a note, we continue on to examine the next event (Extract Event 2). If the second one is a rest, we check the structure for closure, record the analysis (in this case identifying it as a monad), check the transformation rules, adjust the third event to accommodate overlapping structures if necessary, and return to the top to extract the next event in the melody. If the second event is a note, we calculate the interval size (Compute Interval 1) and the registral direction articulated by the initial interval (Compute Register 1). We then move on to examine the third event (Extract Event 3). If this event is a rest , indicating a dyad, we check the closure rules, record the analysis, and so on. If the third event is a note, we calculate the interval size (Compute Interval 2) and registral direction (Compute Register 2) articulated by the second two notes. With the two intervals and registral directions, we can determine the basic structure

Figure 7.30   Completed Mozart analysis.

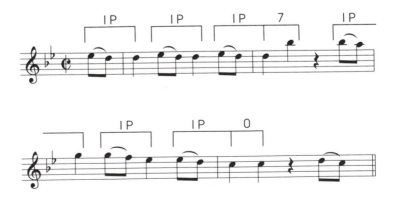

Figure 7.31 Flowchart of analytical process.

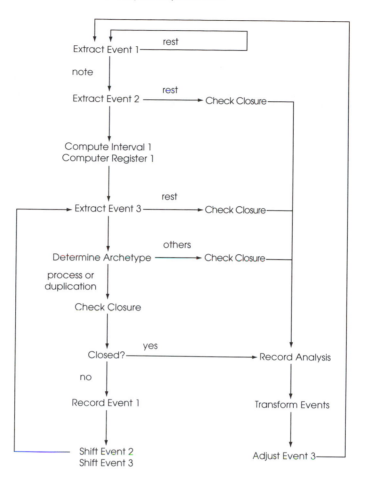

of the three notes currently under consideration (Determine Archetype). If the basic structure is either a process or a duplication, we check the closure rules. If the structure is closed, we record the analysis, apply the transformation rules, and adjust the third event if necessary. If the process or duplication is not closed, we record the initial note of the structure, shift the note in the event 2 position into the event 1 position, and likewise shift the note in the event 3 position into the event 2 position. Then we extract a new third event (Extract Event 3) and continue through the analysis. Returning to the Determine Archetype position in the chart, if the basic structure is not a process or duplication, we then check the closure rules, record the analysis, check the transformation rules, and adjust the third event if necessary. This process continues until there are no more events (notes or rests) left in the melody.

PART 3: IMPLEMENTING THE MODEL

Constructing an operational computer simulation from the natural-language model of Narmour's formalized theory requires several steps, as shown in figure 7.32. First, we select an appropriate programming language for the project and a computer platform that supports that language. Second, because the simulation works with musical data, we either choose or adapt an appropriate data structure for representing that data in the computer. The data structure must represent the musical information required to generate an analysis with Narmour's rules accurately. The next three primary steps (translating the rule base, translating the analytical process, and designing the output) actually occur in parallel. Although as humans we tend to be able to work on only one thing at a time, the complex interaction between these three aspects of the program frequently requires us to move between them throughout the implementation process. When generating the knowledge base, we translate each rule from the natural-language rule base into an appropriate syntax for the chosen programming language. We immediately test the rule to make certain that it has been translated "correctly"—that it is operating as we expect. Each aspect of the analytical process, constituting the inference engine, is likewise implemented and tested. The inference engine provides strategies for searching the knowledge base for solutions to proposed problems—in this case, an analysis of a specified melody. Because the output mechanisms are essential in assisting us with testing the rules, we develop them concurrently. Once the simulation is operating, we put the system through another series of tests to verify that the program is operating as we would like it to. This part is, in essence, the debugging stage of the project. Once the system is completely implemented and verified, it can be used to analyze a variety of musical examples. The output from the simulation, combined with the experience and knowledge gained from constructing the simulation, can then be used to correct, modify, and critique the theory.

Figure 7.32 Steps for implementing the model.

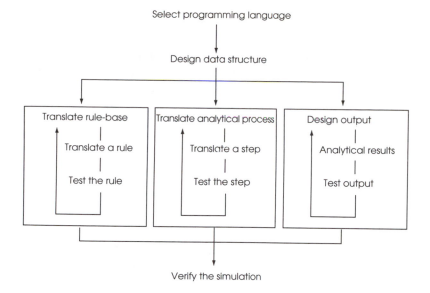

Implementing the Knowledge Base

KIRS is implemented with an Edinburgh-syntax Prolog programming language (discussed in chapter 2) and employs the generalized Prolog data structure (described in chapter 5) for representing musical examples in the computer. In part 2 of this chapter, we designed a natural-language model of specific aspects from Narmour's implication-realization theory and represented the rules in the form of if-then constructions. These rules closely resemble the "production rules" for representing knowledge in AI programming discussed in chapter 1. The if-then constructions forming the natural-language model are translated into appropriate Prolog syntax, creating the knowledge base of the simulation. For example, the definition of "registral sameness" from the natural-language model is reproduced here:

> IF the registral direction established by two intervals is in the same direction,
> THEN "registral sameness" is true.

Our Prolog implementation of this rule appears in figure 7.33. The Prolog predicate `register_same()` compares the registral direction articulated by the first two notes of a melodic pattern, and the registral direction is established by the second and third notes of the pattern. (Throughout this chapter, we use the term "predicate" to represent a general Prolog rule consisting of one or more "clauses." If a predicate has several clauses, each one corresponds to a different definition of the predicate. If we have a one-clause predicate, the terms "predicate" and "clause" can be used interchangeably. For example, the register_same() predicate contains only one clause, whereas the compare_reg() predicate has two clauses.)

The directions are computed from the specific pitch information embodied in the CBR of the individual events and stored as Prolog facts in the predicates register1() and register2() by the inference engine. When a call to the register_same() predicate is encountered, it retrieves the stored registral directions in the variables X and Y. Then the retractall() function removes all previous references to register_sameness() from the Prolog database. Finally, the predicate compare_reg() is called with the passed-in values stored in X and Y. The first clause of the compare_reg() rule tests to see if the two variables are the same. If the test succeeds, the predicate register_sameness() is asserted (asserta()) into the database with the value true; otherwise, the second clause of the rule automatically succeeds and stores the value false in register_sameness(). Once this fact has been stored in the Prolog database, it can quickly be retrieved by other predicates without recalculating the information required to determine the registral direction articulated by the pitches currently being considered by the system.

The rules we extracted from Narmour's theory can be divided into five primary groups: rules governing (1) registral direction, (2) intervallic similarity, (3) basic structures, (4) closure, and (5) transformation. We have already shown how the registral sameness rule is translated into Prolog. Next, we present examples from each of the remaining rule groups to demonstrate the translation process.

When implementing the simulation, we can use previously defined Prolog predicates in the definition of new ones, just as we did in the

Figure 7.33 The register_same() predicate.

```
register_same :-
    register1(X),
    register2(Y),
    retractall(register_sameness(_)),
    compare_reg(X,Y).

compare_reg(X,X) :-
        asserta(register_sameness(true).
compare_reg(_,_) :-
        asserta(register_sameness(false).
```

natural-language model. The definitions of intervallic similarity from the natural-language rule base follow:

> IF "registral sameness" is true,
>   and the difference between two intervals is less than or
>   equal to a minor third,
> THEN "intervallic similarity" is true;
> OTHERWISE "intervallic similarity" is false.

> IF "registral sameness" is false,
>   and the difference between two intervals is less than or equal to a
>   major second,
> THEN "intervallic similarity" is true;
> OTHERWISE "intervallic similarity" is false.

In the natural-language rule base, we define intervallic similarity in terms of registral sameness. In Prolog we can also use previously defined predicates as part of more complex rules. Each of the intervallic similarity clauses, for instance, refers to `register_sameness()`. Our Prolog implementation of Narmour's intervallic similarity rules appear exactly as shown in figure 7.34 in the knowledge base of the simulation.

Figure 7.34 The `interval_sim()` predicate.

```
interval_sim :-
  register_sameness(true),
  retractall(interval_similarity(_)),
  interval_diff(Difference),
  compare_int1(fabs(Difference)).

  compare_int1(X)  :-
    X =< 3,
    asserta(interval_similarity(true)).
  compare_int1(_)  :-
    asserta(interval_similarity(false)).

interval_sim :-
  register_sameness(false),
  retractall(interval_similarity(_)),
  interval_diff(Difference),
  compare_int2(fabs(Difference)).

  compare_int2(X)  :-
    X =< 2,
    asserta(interval_similarity(true)).
    compare_int2(_)  :-
    asserta(interval_similarity(false)).
```

When a call to the `interval_sim()` predicate is encountered, the first clause in the database is attempted by the Prolog system. The first call is to `register_sameness()` with the value `true`. The value located in `register_sameness()` was already stored by the `register_same()` predicate discussed previously. If the value in `register_sameness()` is in fact `true`, this Prolog call succeeds, and the system proceeds to the next statement, `retractall()`, removing all stored references to the predicate `intervallic_similarity()`. If the value stored in `register_sameness()` is `false`, the call fails, and the Prolog system skips to the second clause of the `interval_sim()` predicate and begins working on the statements located there. One of these two clauses is guaranteed to succeed. Returning to the first clause of `interval_sim()` and after removing all references to the relation `interval_similarity()`, the `interval_diff()` predicate computes the difference in size between the two intervals currently under consideration by the system. The difference is returned in the variable `Difference`, and the *absolute value* (`fabs`) of this difference is used as an argument in the call to the predicate `compare_int1()`. The first clause of this predicate checks to see if the difference in the size of the intervals is less than or equal to three semitones. If it is, it stores the value `true` in `intervallic_similarity()`. If this test fails, the second clause succeeds and stores the value `false` in `intervallic_similarity()`.

The rules governing registral sameness and intervallic similarity are used to define the basic structures of Narmour's bottom-up analytical/cognitive theory. The rules defining Narmour's basic structures are implemented in a manner analogous to the intervallic similarity and registral sameness rules. The definition of a process from the natural-language rule base follows:

> IF an initial interval is greater than or equal to a minor second,
>   and the initial interval is less than or equal to a tritone,
>   and "registral sameness" is true,
>   and "intervallic similarity" is true,
> THEN the structure is a "process."

Our Prolog implementation of this rule appears in figure 7.35. The predicate `structure_type()` is called with the unbound variable `Archetype`. There are sixteen different definitions or clauses for the `structure_type()` predicate corresponding to each of the basic structures Narmour employs in his theory. When the inference engine calls the `structure_type()` predicate, one of these definitions is guaranteed to succeed. Prolog attempts definitions in the

Figure 7.35   The process clause of the `structure-type()` predicate.

```
structure_type('P') :-                    % process
    interval1(A),
    member(A,[1,2,3,4,5,6]),
    register_sameness(true),
    interval_similarity(true).
```

order they are encountered—from top to bottom in the database—until one succeeds, at which point it will return to the location in the program where the call was initiated with the corresponding symbol (`'P'` in figure 7.35) bound to `Archetype`. This symbol reflects the analysis of the current "basic structure."

This rule states that essentially a structure is a "process" *if* the initial interval is a small interval, the registral direction is the same for both intervals, and the intervallic sizes are similar. The call to `structure_type()` begins by retrieving the size of the interval articulated by the generative event (the first two notes of the structure) and stored by the inference engine in he predicate `interval1()`. Once this interval is stored temporarily in the variable `A`, it is compared against an inclusive list of intervals spanning the range of a minor second to a tritone by half-step increments. If the number is a member of the list [1,2,3,4,5,6], the small-interval criterion is satisfied, and the clause continues to test for registral sameness. If the registral direction generated by the two intervals is the same, the call to `register_sameness()` with the value `true` succeeds, and the relation tests for intervallic similarity. If the call to `interval_similarity()` succeeds, the variable `Archetype` is *bound* to the symbol `'P'` signifying that the melodic pattern is a process. Once the clause succeeds, the Prolog system returns to the location where `structure_type()` was called, and no other versions of the predicate are attempted.

The rule defining a prospective reversal serves as another example of how we translated Narmour's basic structures from the natural-language rule base into the knowledge base of KIRS:

> IF an initial interval is greater than or equal to a tritone,
>   and the interval is not an octave or a duplication of the octave,
>   and "registral sameness" is false,
>   and "intervallic similarity" is false,
>   and the second interval is smaller than the initial interval,
> THEN the structure is a "reversal."

Our Prolog implementation of this rule appears in figure 7.36. The initial interval is retrieved and stored in the temporary variable A (stored in `interval1(A),`) and immediately checked to confirm that A represents a large interval (at least a perfect fifth or larger). Next, A is tested to determine if it is a multiple of the octave by employing the modulus (`mod`) function. If the interval is an octave or a multiple of the octave, the result is zero, and the test fails. The octave is treated separately in another definition of the reversal. If A is not an octave, `registral_sameness()` and `interval_simi-larity()` are checked for the proper criteria. If both are satisfied, the size of the second interval is retrieved (`interval2()`) and stored in the temporary variable B, which is then compared to A to make sure that B is smaller than A. If it is, this clause of the `struc-ture_type()` predicate succeeds, binding the variable Archetype to the symbol 'R'.

Note that the order of the statements in our Prolog definition follows the order presented in our natural-language model and by Narmour. We intentionally design our rules to adhere closely to Narmour's own organization. A programmer must decide how closely to make the Prolog rules resemble those being modeled. It is often possible to change the order of the conditions without necessarily changing the structure or function of a rule. Such changes may, in fact, significantly improve the operating efficiency of the simulation. These "trade-offs" between closely reflecting the appearance of the model and the speed of the simulation must be examined by the programmer when determining the construction of their Prolog rules. We choose to define our Prolog rules so that they remain as close to Narmour's basic structures as possible to maintain the essence of both our natural-language model and Narmour's original presentation. To facilitate this choice and minimize the number of computations, we design the inference engine to compute the regis-

Figure 7.36   The reversal clause of the `structure_type()` predicate.

```
structure_type('R') :-                    % reversal
    interval1(A),
    A >= 7,
    A mod 12   0,
    register_sameness(false),
    interval_similarity(false),
    interval2(B),
    B < A.
```

tral directions and the interval sizes currently under consideration by the system, which are then inserted into the Prolog database. Each `structure_type()` clause needs to know the size of the intervals and the registral directions. Because these values have been added to the database, they are quickly recalled and do not require the computations to be redone for each call to the clause. This aspect facilitates designing our Prolog rules in correspondence with their exposition in Narmour's theory without causing unnecessary operation delays in the course of running the simulation.

The closure rules are also implemented in the knowledge base. One of the most common methods of attaining transformational closure in Narmour's theory is through durational cumulation. The definition for closure by durational cumulation from the natural-language rule base is reproduced here:

> IF a note exceeds implied location or duration by 50 percent or more, THEN "transformational closure" is true.

Our Prolog implementation of the predicate `closure_by_durational_cumulation()` appears in figure 7.37. This predicate takes two event numbers as arguments (`En1` and `En2`). The starting and ending positions of these events are extracted in the first two lines of the clause and are bound to the variables `Start1`, `End1`, `Start2`, and `End2`. With this information, the duration of the second event is compared with the duration of the first event multiplied by a factor of 1.5. If the duration of the second event is greater than or equal to the factored duration of the first event, this clause succeeds, and it is deemed that closure by durational cumulation has occurred. If this clause does not succeed, transformational closure by cumulation is determined not to have occurred.

The rules governing the creation of hierarchic levels through transformation are also present in the knowledge base. Narmour states that the initial and terminal notes of structures of three or more notes function as the structural tones of the group and are transformed to the next hierarchic level. This statement was translated into the following rules in the natural-language rule base:

Figure 7.37   The `closure_by_durational_cumulation()` predicate.

```
closure_by_durational_cumulation(En1,En2) :-
    event(En1,_,[Start1,End1,_],_,_,_,_,_,_),
    event(En2,_,[Start2,End2,_],_,_,_,_,_,_),
    (End2 - Start2) >= ((End1-Start1) * 1.5).
```

IF a note is the initial note of a "basic structure,"
THEN it is transformed to the next level.

IF a note is the terminal note of a "basic structure,"
THEN it is transformed to the next level.

Our Prolog implementation of these rules appears in figure 7.38. The predicate transform() takes two event numbers representing the initial and terminal notes of a basic structure as arguments. The call to trans() recalls a list of events already transformed to the next level, storing this list in the variable OldList. If the current events represent the first events of a new level, OldList will be an empty list. The retractall() call removes all references to trans() from the database. Next, the new event numbers are appended to the end of OldList and stored in the variable TempList. Finally, trans() is added to the database with the new list (TempList).

We implement all the remaining rules from the natural-language rule base in a manner analogous to the examples in this section. Similarly, we omit some of the code here to save space and maintain a manageable chapter size. The entire Prolog computer code for KIRS, however, is located in appendix 4. Once the knowledge base is completed, the next major task is to implement the analytical process.

Inference Engine

The KIRS inference engine is that portion of the program controlling the application of the rules located in the knowledge base to melodies, thereby generating an analysis. It resembles the analytical process deduced in part 2 of this chapter and represented by the flowchart in figure 7.31 (please refer back to it for the remainder of this discussion). Our Prolog implementation of this process is manifest in three primary predicates: begin(), start_search(), and analyze(). The top-level predicate (begin) controls the operation

Figure 7.38   The transform() predicate.

```
transform(En1,En2) :-
    trans(OldList),
    retractall(trans(_)),
    append(OldList,[En1,En2],TempList),
    asserta(trans(TempList)).
```

of the simulation and is presented in figure 7.39 with English pseudo-code commentary describing the operation of each specific clause. Many predicates and clauses start with a pseudo-code representation that is transformed into a specific language syntax. Because pseudo code is often easier to read and understand than the programming syntax, in the code examples that follow, Prolog statements appear on the left and corresponding pseudo-code descriptions on the right.

The next primary predicate, `start_search()`, controls the chronological searching of the events during the analytical process. The actual Prolog code for this predicate appears with a pseudo-code explanation of each clause and statement in figure 7.40.

Figure 7.39   The `begin()` predicate with pseudo-code descriptions.

```
begin :-
```

`time_spine(L1,_),`	Retrieve time spine information for the current melody from the database.
`extract_event_num(L1),`	Extract the event numbers of the notes and rests and store them in a separate list.
`main_list(Event_List),`	Retrieve the event list from the database.
`start_search(Event_List),`	Begin searching the event list in chronological order, analyzing the events encountered (this is where most of the analytical work is done).
`analysis(X),`	Retrieve the analysis from the database.
`write(X),nl,`	Display the analysis on the screen.
`trans(Y),`	Transform the analyzed pitches to the next hierarchic level.
`write(Y),nl,`	Display the transformed pitches on the screen.
`transform1(Y).`	Repeat the analysis process with the pitches of the new hierarchic level until no more levels can be generated.

Figure 7.40   The `start_search()` predicate with pseudo-code descriptions.

`start_search([]).`	Check for an empty list. If the list is empty; the analysis is complete.
`start_search(Event_List) :-`	
`build_sublist` `(Event_List,SubList,Tail1),`	Build a sublist from `Event_List`. `SubList` should contain the first three events from `Event_List` or, if there are fewer than three events, all the remaining events in the list. It should also return the tail of `Event_List` because the remaining events still need to be processed.
`analyze` `(SubList,Tail1,Tail2),`	Send the sublist to be analyzed by the knowledge base. The tail of `Event_List` is sent into this clause because the system may need to look ahead to the next event. An unbound variable (`Tail2`) is also sent to this clause. After adjusting the last event encountered, the new tail is bound to `Tail2`.
`start_search(Tail2).`	Repeat `start_search`, sending `Tail2` into the call. This will repeat until the list is empty, which signifies the analysis is complete.

Finally, the actual predicate that most closely reflects the flow-chart of figure 7.31 is `analyze()`. Figure 7.41 shows the Prolog statements and a pseudo-code explanation of each clause, with the description on the right corresponding to the `analyze()` clause.

The interaction of the three predicates just described constitutes the bulk of the KIRS inference engine. Figure 7.42 shows a short melodic pattern that we use to demonstrate how the inference engine operates. Figure 7.43 contains the time spine and events that correspond to the melody in figure 7.42.

Once the time spine and events representing a melody are asserted into the Prolog database, the predicate `begin()` is entered at the query window, prompting the simulation to analyze the melody. The call to `time_spine()` retrieves the time spine information for the melody currently under consideration, returning the forward time spine information in the variable `L1`. Using the example in figure 7.43, `L1` is bound to the following:

```
[[0,11,-11,15],[2500,-15,16],[5000,-16,17],
    [7500,-17,18],[10000,-18]]
```

Figure 7.41   The `analyze()` predicate pseudo-code descriptions.

`analyze() % initial rest`	Check the first event of `SubList`. If it is a rest, then append the remaining two events to the tail and return to `start_search()`.
`analyze() % monad 1`	Check the first event of `SubList`. If it is a note and there are no other events, this event must be a monad.
`analyze() % monad 2`	Check the first two events of `SubList`. If the first event is a note and the second event is a rest, this event must be a monad.
`analyze() % dyad 1`	Check the first two events of `SubList`. If the first two events are notes and there are no other events, the structure is a dyad.
`analyze() % dyad 2`	Check the first three events of `SubList`. If the first two events are notes and the third event is a rest, the structure must be a dyad.
`analyze() % all but p, (p), d`	If all three events are notes and they are not processes or duplications, they are closed structures and identified by this definition.
`analyze() % p, (p), d`	If the events form either a process, retrospective process, or duplication, they are open structures and are identified by this definition.

Figure 7.42   Sample pattern for analysis.

Figure 7.43   Time spine and events for music in figure 7.42.

```
time_spine ([[0,11,-11,15],[2500,-15,16],[5000,-16,17],
             [7500,-17,18],[10000,-18]],
            [[10000,-18],[7500,-17,18],[5000,-16,17],
             [2500,-15,16], [0,11,-11,15]]).
event(11,0,[0,0,10000],0,"barline",[0,0],[0,0,0,-1],[],[]).
event(15,1,[312,2812,10312],4000,"C",[1,4],[0,0,0,-1],[],[]).
event(16,1,[2500,5000,12500],4042,"E",[1,4],[0,0,0,-1],[],[]).
event(17,1,[5000,7500,15000],4000,"C",[1,4],[0,0,0,-1],[],[]).
event(18,1,[7500,10000,17500],-1,"rest",[1,4],[0,0,0,-1],[],[]).
```

This list is sent to the clause extract_event_num(), where the event numbers of the notes and rests are stored in main_list(). The predicate extract_event_num() removes the time points, bar lines, user-defined objects, and release events from the list, leaving only the event numbers representing the attack points of the notes and rests in the order of their occurrence. The extract_event_num() predicate generates the list [15,16,17,18] from the time spine information in the variable L1 in this example.

The call to main_list() stores the abbreviated event list in the variable Event_List, which is used to analyze the melody. The heart of the inference engine is the call to start_search() and will be described in detail momentarily. After start_search() is completed, the call to analysis() retrieves the analysis of the melody, which has been stored in this predicate during the process of analyzing the melody. The call to write() outputs the analysis on the computer screen while nl advances the cursor in preparation for another line of information. The call to trans() applies the transformation rules to the analyzed melody, and the next call to write() prints a list of the event numbers that have been transformed to the next level. The call to transform1() restarts the analysis process using the list of transformed event numbers, reflecting the recursive generation of hierarchic levels. When no further transformation levels can be generated, the analysis is complete.

The primary second-level predicate, start_search(), is where much of the analysis actually takes place. The first definition of start_search() tests for an empty list. If the list sent into this predicate is empty, the first clause succeeds and exits because there are no more events to analyze. The second definition calls the predicate build_sublist(), which extracts the first three events from Event_List and stores them in the variable SubList. If there are fewer than three events remaining in the Event_List, Sublist will store the number remaining. The predicate build_sublist() also returns the tail of the Event_List (the items remaining in Event_List after the first one, two, or three events have been removed) in the variable Tail1. Event_List is bound to the list [15,16,17,18] on the basis of the data shown in figure 7.43. When this list is subjected to the build_sublist() predicate, SubList returns bound to the list [15,16,17], and Tail1 returns bound to the list [18].

The short list contained in SubList is sent to the analyze() predicate, where the majority of the analytical work takes place. One of the seven different definitions of analyze() (each was briefly described previously) is guaranteed to succeed with any combination of events. The `analyze()` clause that checks for all three note patterns, except "processes" and "duplications," is presented in figure 7.44.

The CBRs are extracted from each event in the first three lines of this rule. These pitches are sent to the `check_rule_base()` predicate with the unbound variable `Archetype`. In `check_rule_base()`, the registral direction and interval sizes are computed and stored in the database; then the knowledge base is called to determine the `Archetype` (basic structure) represented by the three notes in the pattern. (If there are fewer than three notes in the pattern, this call will not be attempted.) The next line of code checks the value in `Archetype` to verify that it is not a process or a duplication (these represent potentially open structures that are handled by another `analyze()` clause). If this call succeeds, there is a call to `check_closure()` to test the pattern for closure and return a code in the variable `Return`. Finally, there is a call to the `compare_dur()` predicate.

Figure 7.44 The process clause of the `analyze()` predicate.

```
analyze([En1,En2,En3|_],[Head|Tail],Tail2) :- %all but p,(p),d
    event(En1,_,_,CBR1,_,_,_,_,_),
    event(En2,_,_,CBR2,_,_,_,_,_),
    event(En3,_,_,CBR3,_,_,_,_,_),
    check_rule_base(CBR1,CBR2,CBR3,Archetype),
    not member(Archetype,['P','(P)','D']),
    check_closure(En1,En2,En3,Return),
    compare_dur(Return,CBR1,CBR2,En1,En2,En3,
        Archetype,Head,Tail,Tail1,Tail2),!.

compare_dur(duration1,CBR1,CBR2,En1,En2,En3,
    Archetype,Head,Tail,Tail1,Tail2) :-
    Archetype2 = dyad,
    compute_dyad_interval(CBR1,CBR2,Interval),
    record_analysis([En1,En2,Archetype2,Interval]),
    transform_dyad(En1,En2,Return2),
    transform(Return2),
    append([En3,Head],Tail,Tail1),
    Tail2 = Tail1.
compare_dur(_,_,_,En1,_,En3,Archetype,Head,Tail,Tail1,Tail2) :-
    record_analysis([En1,En3,Archetype]),
    transform(En1,En3),
    append([Head],Tail,Tail1),
    check_duration(En3,Tail1,Tail1,Tail2) ).
```

If the value in `Return` matches `duration1`, durational closure occurred, but it happened on the second note of the pattern. The first occurrence of `compare_dur()` analyzes the structure as a dyad and computes the interval (`compute_dyad_interval()`), records the analysis (`record_analysis()`), determines which note is to be transformed (`transform_dyad()`), transforms the dyad (`transform()`), and finally adjusts the third event by appending it to `Tail1` so that when the analysis continues the third event will become the first event of the next structure. The second clause of the `compare_dur()` predicate records the analysis (`record_analysis()`), transforms the initial and terminal tones of the basic structure (`transform()`), and adjusts the third event (`check_duration()`). If the third event is the same duration as the next event in the list, it will be treated as an elision and moved into the first position of the next structure. If the third event and the next event are not the same duration, no adjustment is made to `Tail1`.

Once the `analyze()` predicate is completed, it returns to the `start_search()` clause from which it was called. The next line in the `start_search()` clause is a call to `start_search()`, except this time it sends the events remaining in `Tail2` to the `analyze()` routine. This process continues until there are no events in `Event_List`, indicating that the analysis of this level is complete. The system then returns to the `begin()` predicate, where the call to `start_search()` was initiated.

Output   KIRS stores the beginning and ending event numbers of a structure it identifies along with a symbol representing the basic structure as determined by the knowledge base. The resulting analysis for the pattern in figure 7.42 follows:

```
[[15,17,'ID']]
```

This indicates that the pattern begins with event number 15 and ends with event number 17 and that KIRS identifies this pattern as an intervallic duplication, 'ID'. The symbols supplied by the knowledge base correspond to the symbols presented by Narmour. If more than one pattern is present, each is placed in a separate sublist. An analysis of a melody containing four intervallic duplications would appear somewhat as follows:

```
[15,17,'ID'],[19,21,'ID'],[22,25,'ID'],[27,29,
   'ID']]
```

Again, the beginning and ending point of each pattern is indicated by event numbers and the analysis of the pattern by the appropriate symbol. Such a list is followed by a list of the event numbers transformed to the next level. In this case, the transformed list would appear as follows:

```
[15,17,19,21,22,25,27,29]
```

This list of events is then sent to the `start_search()` predicate for continued analysis because the same rules are applied to the new hierarchic level, reflecting the recursive application of the analytical rules. The process of analyzing the list of events and transforming the indexed pitches continues until there are no events remaining to generate a new hierarchic level, indicating that the analysis is complete.

Verifying the Simulation

The verification stage of a simulation project is essentially where errors, or *bugs*, in the program are identified and rectified. We attempt to verify that the simulation is operating in accordance with the model and in the manner expected by the programmer. Separating implementation and verification aspects of programming a simulation is somewhat misleading because the testing and debugging processes occur simultaneously throughout the programming process, but we present implementation and verification here separately for the sake of clarity. Unfortunately, there are no fixed, tried, and true procedures one may follow to ensure error-free computer code, but there are some strategies that can reduce the quantity of bugs that often plague programmers. Before discussing these strategies, we should review the basic categories of errors that occur: *syntactical*, *run-time*, and *logical*.

Most programming languages consists of reserved words or symbols that have predefined meanings within the context of the language. Each language also has a series of grammar rules prescribing a format for statements within the language. The reserved words and the grammar rules combine to create the syntax for the language. For instance, in Prolog arguments in a factual clause must be enclosed in parentheses and separated by commas, and the clause must conclude with a period. The `event()` clause below is an example of a syntactically correct Prolog statement:

```
event(15,[0,2500,10000],4000,"C",[1,4],[0,0,0,
   -1],[],[]).
```

In the following statement, a comma is omitted between the fourth and the fifth arguments, and the closing period has been omitted:

```
event(15,[0,2500,10000],4000 "C",[1,4],[0,0,0,
    -1],[],[])
```

This type of error can be an insidious problem, but most programming packages available today have very good syntax checking and debugging tools. These tools make discovering and correcting syntax errors a much less problematic aspect of programming than was the case several years ago when such systems were not widely available.

Run-time errors occur when asking a computer to perform a task that it cannot possibly perform, such as requesting the computer to divide by zero or to take the square root of a negative number. The code will be syntactically correct, yet when executing the program statements errors will still result. In Prolog programs, run-time errors can also result from the Prolog system's relentless search for solutions to a question. When Prolog reaches a "dead end" by following one series of steps to find a solution, it automatically "backs up," attempting to solve a problem through an alternative series of steps. The language's insistent *backtracking* to find all solutions to a given query may result in erroneous execution. Fortunately, Prolog has predefined clauses (`cut` and `fail`) that allow the programmer to control backtracking and avoid this type of programming bug. The avoidance and recognition of run-time errors necessitates the programmer's familiarity with the procedural aspects of Prolog. Even though the majority of the programming may be done in a declarative manner, Prolog still follows some procedural conventions when it searches for query solutions. By remaining aware of these conventions and incorporating them into the order that certain clauses appear in the knowledge base and inference engine, we can prevent many run-time errors.

Logic errors are caused by incorrectly defining predicates and clauses despite the fact that they are syntactically correct—incorrectly defined clauses can give erroneous results. An example of a logic error is instructing the computer to add two numbers when they were supposed to be subtracted. These errors are often the most difficult to find and correct. Ideally, we should test every possible combination of interactions within a system, but this process is frequently impossible in terms of time and computing power because of the enormous number of potential interactions between the clauses in a moderately sized knowledge base. The next best way to verify that the system operates correctly (as the programmer expects) is to test the system with a variety of data for which correct responses are known. In KIRS, this may include test patterns of three or more notes, such as those presented by Narmour when introducing his basic structures.

An attempt should also be made to determine problematic types of data, introduce them to the system, and observe the system reactions. If they are unfavorable (e.g., if the program crashes), adjustments should be made to handle these data sets.

The first step in avoiding logic errors takes place by constructing the natural-language model. By meticulously investigating the theory and extracting its premises and relationships into if-then representations, we have the opportunity to work out a logical representation that provides an excellent model for translation into computer code. Further, this step allows us to determine the kinds of information to be included in the knowledge base and to design our Prolog structures in advance. In addition, by maintaining a close correlation between the natural-language model and the predicate code, we can find inconsistencies that much easier. Logic errors frequently arise when programmers attempt to write a program "on the fly" without carefully contemplating all the necessary components of the system. Once a natural-language model is completed, implementing that model is accomplished by translating its rules and the analytical process into the operating computer simulation.

While implementing the model, we can continually test individual clauses as they are constructed. Theoretically, if each clause functions properly, any remaining problems are generated within the inference engine, where they can be isolated, identified, and corrected. The clause `compute_int1()` from the inference engine appears in figure 7.45.

Figure 7.45 The `compute_int1()` predicate.

```
compute_int1(CBR1,CBR2) :-
  C11 is CBR1 // 10,
  C12 is (C11 mod 100),
  C13 is CBR1 // 1000,
  C21 is CBR2 // 10,
  C22 is (C21 mod 100),
  C23 is CBR2 // 1000,
  C31 is ((C13 - C23) * 12),
  compare_oct(C12,C22,X),
  retractall(interval1(_)),
  asserta(interval1(X)).
  compare_oct(C1,C2,X) :-
      C1 =\= C2,
      X is integer(fabs(C22 - (C12 + C31))).

  compare_oct(_,_,X) :-
      X is 12 * (integer(fabs(C23 - C13))).
```

This clause takes two CBRs as arguments, computes the interval between them, and stores this value in the database for later use by other predicates. This rule can be tested from the query window by typing the following:

```
? compute_int1(4000,4021).
yes

? interval1(X).
  X = 2
```

The clause `compute_int1()` is called with two CBRs (4000 and 4021) representing the pitches C4 and D4. During the execution of this clause, the value of the interval is stored in the predicate `interval1()`. From the query window, we can retrieve the value by calling the clause with an unbound variable (X). Because the interval between C4 and D4 is a major second, the value of X should be 2, which is confirmed by the system. A wide range of pitches and subsequent intervals must be attempted until the programmer is satisfied that the clause functions correctly. Each predicate may be checked in this manner with materials where the results are known in advance.

Once we are convinced that the individual rules are functioning properly, we begin submitting complete pieces of test data to the system for analysis. Again, the best available way to test the system is to submit a variety of examples for which the analysis is already known. In this case, we selected short melodic patterns and fragments similar to those Narmour used to demonstrate and explain his rules. If the computer replicates these analyses, we consider the system to be operating properly. The examples incorporate simple patterns (such as the basic structures) as well as more complex melodies containing rests and varied rhythms. We also prepare some examples that "tax" the system, just to see how it responds. We test KIRS with over fifty patterns and musical examples, the majority of which are taken from Narmour's explanation of the various basic structures and larger melodies incorporated into his discussions. These examples provide the ideal test material because they are short, well defined, and often constructed to explain the rule we are attempting to test. We present some of these examples along with the reasons for their inclusion in the test set.

Figure 7.46 presents a simple three-note pattern designed to check the operation of the inference engine to the extent that it extracts the correct event information and tests the knowledge base for correct identification of the basic structures. The analysis we expected (based on examples presented by Narmour) is indicated above the music and the analysis generated by the computer below the music. We generated examples like this for each basic structure and submitted them to KIRS for analysis.

Figure 7.47 shows a longer example with rests interspersed between the patterns. The purpose of this example is to test the ability of the inference engine to handle rests occurring in a melodic line. It also checks the operation of the dyadic structures and the computations involved with them. A variety of similar examples are analyzed by the computer until we are satisfied that the inference engine is in fact working correctly when it encounters rests.

Figure 7.48 presents a more extended example that we use to test the basic structures and the inference engine in terms of rests, and

Figure 7.46   Sample basic structure test pattern.

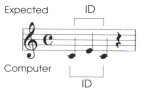

Figure 7.47   Test pattern with inserted rests.

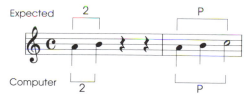

Figure 7.48   Extended reversal patterns.

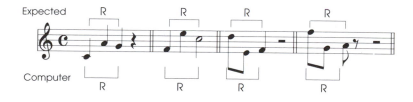

most important, to check the closure rules. We are primarily interested in testing for durational closure, as it occurs in the second and third measures of this melodic excerpt. A version of this test pattern is analyzed for each basic structure.

Processes are more open than the other structures, and KIRS must be capable of recognizing larger passages, such as that shown in figure 7.49. This example checks the ongoing characteristic of the process rule in the knowledge base. A variety of extended processes and duplications are analyzed with varied rhythmic patterns until we were satisfied that these rules operate correctly.

The final example (figure 7.50) is by far the most complex. We derive it from a melody used by Narmour to explain the various basic structures. The expected analysis appears above the music and the computer analysis below. A few other examples of this complexity are also submitted to the system for analysis.

Once a significant number of possibilities have been analyzed by the computer, the program may be considered verified, but this is rarely a completed process. We almost always encounter unanticipated situations when running later examples through the system. When such occurrences arise, we must determine whether the program is at fault or if the program has discovered a discrepancy in

Figure 7.49   Extended process.

Figure 7.50   Test melody after Narmour.

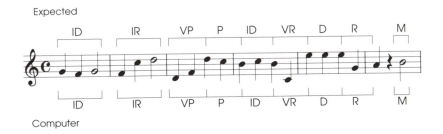

the theory that may be important for us to know about. If the problem is caused by a programming error, it must be corrected. If a discrepancy is found, the program should also be corrected, resulting in a modification or extension to the theory and not just a programming error. It should be remembered that the verification process does not mean that the program is valid but rather that the program works as we expect it to work. If the model has been carefully designed and implemented, the simulation should present plausible results, which is the most that can be expected in terms of validation as discussed in part 1 of this chapter.

■ PART 4: EVALUATING THE THEORY

In part 2, we discussed some minor problems with Narmour's theory and actually restructured the syntactic-parametric scale governing registral direction. The purpose of this section is to demonstrate similar types of information that can be generated from the knowledge-based simulation. This discussion includes examples where the criticisms of the theory are generated from the information learned in the process of designing, implementing, and running the simulation.

Transformations   Narmour claims that the main purpose behind his approach to music theory is the pursuit of low-level (surface-level) understanding and that he is not particularly interested in higher-level structures, yet he appears compelled to present rules governing the generation of higher transformational levels. Narmour (1990, p. 428) states that hierarchic levels are generated when the beginning and ending notes of a basic pattern are transformed to a new level. He also generates rules governing the transformation of melodic dyads. Further, he states that higher levels are generated *recursively* (p. 235). In other words, the same analytical rules are applied to subsequent levels, which in turn generate the next hierarchic level. Although this appears logical, Narmour's recursive rules do not function properly at higher levels. Figure 7.25 shows an analysis of a melody and the first four transformation levels generated by applying his rules. We generate this analysis to demonstrate the spirit of Narmour's transformation rules and believe that this interpretation adheres to the principles he intended. We also believe that we are applying Narmour's rules strictly when generating this analysis. We

Figure 7.51   Melody 1 analyzed by KIRS.

submit the same melody to KIRS for analysis with the results shown in figure 7.51.

There are a number of discrepancies between our application of the rules and the analysis generated by KIRS. In figure 7.51, KIRS follows Narmour's rules of transformation to the letter, generating level "b" in this figure without difficulty. The first two processes are broken by KIRS because it starts a new grouping when durational cumulation causes closure, occurring here on the downbeat of measure 2. When KIRS attempts to analyze the pitches in level "b," it stops processing when it encounters the repeated A4—Narmour does not account for repeated pitches on higher levels in his presentation of transformations. Also notice that closure on higher levels is still governed by surface durational relationships: D5 and A4 of level "b" are transformed to the next level because they have longer durations than the notes preceding them on the surface.

The analysis in figure 7.51 cannot be considered a plausible representation of the structure of this melody according to currently accepted transformational paradigms, whereas the analysis in figure 7.25 is plausible at least in terms of melodic contour. The discrepancy lies in the fact that we bring prior knowledge of other transformational theories to bear on our personal application of Narmour's rules. The computer has no knowledge beyond what it is programmed to do and hence cannot make the assumptions that we make. From our experience with Schenkerian theory, we assume that repeated pitches serve as prolongations of that pitch, meaning that they are treated as one pitch on subsequent levels. KIRS cannot make this assumption because this knowledge is not part of Narmour's transformation rules. In Schenkerian theory, rhythm is a subsidiary musical component to preferred scale degrees whether they are part of the *Urlinie* or the *Baßbrechung*. This knowledge guides our selection of transformational pitches on higher levels without regarding surface-level rhythmic durations. Again, Narmour does not generate such a rule when formulating his transformational grammar.

Fortunately, KIRS does provide an amenable environment for testing these assertions. We can reprogram KIRS, changing the knowledge base and modifying the theory to eliminate repeated pitches on higher levels. Figure 7.52 shows the analysis subsequently generated by KIRS. Level "b" is the same as in figure 7.51, but with the elimination of the duplicated A4, KIRS is able to complete the analysis of this level and generate the subsequent levels (the first four of which are shown in figure 7.52). This analysis is more plausible than that presented in figure 7.51 but still does not resemble more traditional hierarchic analyses, primarily because of the influence of the

Figure 7.52   Melody 1, eliminating duplicate pitches in higher transformation levels.

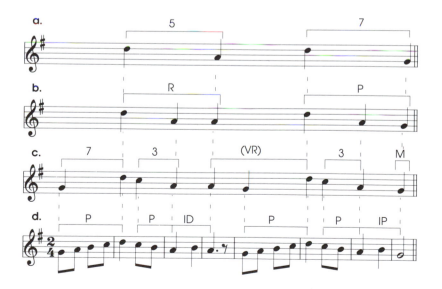

surface level durations on closure at higher levels. Because Narmour does not specify that the durations of notes on higher levels should be modified or ignored, KIRS recursively applies the rules to the surface-level notes to generate the higher levels.

We can also program KIRS to ignore the durations of notes on higher levels and eliminate the repeated pitches. Figure 7.53 shows the analysis generated by KIRS and represents the most plausible hierarchic analysis generated by the system. In this case, the basic contour of the melody is represented at level "c" and the tonic pitch at level "d." Of course, there are several problems with this analysis. For example, the D5s in measures 2 and 6, each representing the apex of a melodic contour, have been eliminated. Which G4 do we select as the pitch representing the level "d" monad? We select the closing G4 following generally accepted Schenkerian principles. The modifications of the transformation rules that create the analysis in figure 7.53 do not eliminate the problem of the eliding basic structures on level "a." This problem can be addressed only by the formulation of a more explicit analytical process where the criteria governing such elisions are explicitly presented.

The recursive generation of hierarchical levels presented by Narmour does not generate musically plausible analyses. His formula-

Figure 7.53   Melody 1, no duplicated pitches or durational closure at higher levels.

tion suffers from the same problem that all recursive rules suffer when creating transformational levels: one cannot assume that all the surface-level criteria are still operating in the same manner at higher levels, which is the tacit assumption made by Narmour when defining his transformation rules. As one ascends to higher levels, the rules for closure must be modified to reflect the larger scale of the passage under consideration, something Narmour fails to do. His transformational rules generally do not provide plausible results when compared with more traditionally accepted higher-level structures, such as those proposed by Schenker (1979) or Lerdahl and Jackendoff (1983). With some significant modification, Narmour's transformation rules may be capable of generating basic melodic contours, but we find the musical significance of such an enterprise limited at best. Perhaps Narmour feels obligated to generate such levels because of the present climate in current music-theoretical thinking, which for some reason is heavily invested in the twin concepts of "hierarchy" and "level." If he is interested in surface-level patterning and perception—which we believe to be a completely valid pursuit in and of itself—then he should abandon his higher-level transformational rules.

Studying Narmour's transformational rules highlights three strengths inherent in the examination of music theories through knowledge-based simulation models. First, the construction of a knowledge-based simulation often forces us to examine the prior knowledge we bring to bear on analytical methodologies. When we initially create our transformational levels of the melody in figure 7.25, we think that we are judiciously applying Narmour's rules. When the KIRS analysis does not match ours, we are forced to search for reasons. Through this process we realize that we make several assumptions that are not represented in Narmour's rules. We all bring prior knowledge and experience to bear on our analyses and evaluation of theories, but these assumptions are rarely identified or acknowledged. Knowledge-based simulations bring such assumptions to the fore precisely because the program has *only* the knowledge we give it.

Second, knowledge-based simulations provide an environment where hypotheses can be tested quickly and efficiently. When we encounter the discrepancies between our analysis and that of KIRS, we start theorizing and hypothesizing as to why. The first theory concerns the problems caused by repeated pitches in the transformational levels. We quickly reprogram the rules to eliminate repeated pitches and can observe the results (figure 7.52). Next, we generate another hypothesis concerning the surface-level rhythms, adjust the program, and observe the effects as shown in figure 7.53. In Prolog, the process of theorizing, hypothesizing, and testing can be performed expediently, and a large quantity of analyses can be generated quickly to observe the results of changing the theory.

Third, knowledge-based simulations often leave a more complete expression of the theory. After we modified the rule base to generate more plausible hierarchic levels, we have in effect extended the theory. We have created a more complete set of transformation rules as a result of the simulation process. Throughout the examination of Narmour's theory, we have generated many changes and extensions. This discussion of the transformation rules represents the type of information that knowledge-based simulations can generate and where they can be most beneficial.

■ PART 5: CONCLUSION

In this chapter, we introduced the concept of a knowledge-based simulation. We described in considerable detail the process of constructing and implementing such a system. We followed this with a detailed explanation of the knowledge-engineering portion of the KIRS project and demonstrated how this was translated into the operational simulation. We discussed an example of the type of information that such a simulation provides and how that influences our perception and/or criticism of the theory under consideration. We conclude this chapter with a brief discussion of the benefits and limitations of such a process.

Process versus Product

We believe that the most important outcome of simulating music theories is *not* derived from observing the results or output of the simulation. Rather, it is found in the process of constructing, implementing, and modifying the simulation. The *process* is far more beneficial in terms of generating useful information about the theory and its underlying premises than the output generated by the simulation. While constructing a model we must become intimately familiar with the theory and its underlying premises, including the biases, omissions, and aspects of the theory that are not so clearly defined. During the development of KIRS, we frequently encountered formulations and definitions in Narmour's theory that appeared to be completely logical on a first reading, such as creating a three-way system for representing registral direction (same, similar, or different) that parallels that of intervallic motion. When building the model, however, it became apparent that Narmour was imposing a three-way division on a two-possibility system. This observation could have been made without attempting to simulate the theory, but it was through constructing the model for this purpose that such a "discovery" was made.

Constructing a computer simulation forces us to break that theory into two parts: the premises set forth by the theory, which determine the rules incorporated into the knowledge base, and the process of applying those rules to the music, thereby generating an analysis. Narmour sufficiently defines the first of these components but does not adequately define the analytical process. It is entirely possible for someone to read Narmour's book, apply the rules, and generate analyses without the analytical process being explicitly presented. Such analyses draw on the individual analyst's interpretation, past experience, and musicality to create plausible results. For his theory to succeed, Narmour depends on the musical application of his rules when creating analyses because the rules in and of themselves are not sufficient to generate musical segmentations. Narmour requires that the rules be applied by sensitive musicians, but this does not help us understand the process we should use when applying his rules.

This is not to say that the analyses generated by a computer simulation are worthless. Quite to the contrary, the results can give us a tremendous amount of information concerning how well the system imitates the analytical process, how the system appears to operate, and many of the contributing factors not yet present in the system. The simulation should present plausible analytical results; yet, many of the analyses created by KIRS are not musical, and searching for reasons may enhance our understanding of the theory in question. For example, some of the analyses generated by KIRS differed from Narmour's analyses of the same excerpts because he apparently employed metric information in his analyses that was not available to KIRS, and we had not implemented it in the knowledge base. Likewise, the output generated by KIRS helped us refine the inference engine, thereby creating musically plausible analyses. Further, after instructing KIRS to analyze each of Narmour's "basic structures" and observing the output from the program, we noticed that KIRS did not analyze two structures correctly (IP, (IP)). The error was not in our translation of Narmour's rule but rather in Narmour's omission of an additional constraint required to separate the *intervallic process* from *intervallic duplication*. In this case, the output from the simulation pointed to an inconsistency in Narmour's formulation of the rules.

Benefits of Simulations

Building a computer simulation often results in our clarifying theoretical statements. Most theories are verbally expressed and can often best be described as "loose." A loose verbal theory is frequently riddled with gaps in logic, contradictions, unspecified relationships, unknown parameters, and a host of other difficulties. The weaknesses of a theory become apparent when we attempts to build a model on the basis of those weaknesses. Narmour's theory contains a variety of contradictions and ambiguities, many (but not all) of which can be identified, addressed, and resolved through the simulation process. Building a simulation requires that we address and correct these ambiguities for the simulation to operate in a manner sympathetic to the theory.

The resulting knowledge base and inference engine of an operating computer simulation often constitute a more complete expression of the theory than the original statement within the parameters established for the simulation. We feel that the knowledge base and inference engine that make up KIRS do in fact represent a more detailed expression of Narmour's theory because they codify in more complete terms many undefined and ambiguous components of the theory and illuminate some of the complexities prevalent in Narmour's premises. KIRS also requires that the analytical process be explicitly defined, something Narmour does not do. Even though we do not mean for KIRS to replicate exactly all Narmour's analyses, it certainly represents a more complete expression of the theory within the parameters established for the project.

Another important benefit of computer modeling and simulation is through its ability to document—in other words, that the simulation in its final form leaves a permanent record of the theory. The knowledge base and inference engine record the rules and the analytical process as defined in the current project. This is an advantage over humans, who have the tendency to forget portions of a theory or relationships among the individual components. The simulation does not forget in this manner—once the information has been saved, it can always be recalled. The computer does not need to be retaught or refreshed. This permanent record can serve as a source for others to criticize or use as a point of departure for further research. KIRS provides an account of the rules defining the bottom-up component of Narmour's implication-realization theory. It does not represent the entire theory, but it is a beginning. Our project could continue to grow over time by codifying more rules concerning implication-realization and including them in the knowledge base.

A computer simulation is frequently an economical approach to the development of a theoretical position. Through modeling, a new theory or component of a theory can often be developed rather quickly. This was the case with KIRS when we were determining how to define the analytical process. There were places where the decisions we made caused KIRS to generate analyses that contradicted those of Narmour. We formulated a variety of ways to deal with these inconsistencies and tested the results quickly, certainly more quickly than by the traditional "hypothesize-test" cycle that most theorists employ in some form or another. Computer simulations provide us with a vehicle for generating and exploring new hypotheses and implications of a theory. A model is developed from a theory, perhaps giving the theory greater clarity than before. Then the model is implemented as an operating simulation, thus allowing us to observe the consequences of the theory. Less than optimal agreement between simulation and the analyses of others may cause us to modify the programmed model and consequently the theory itself. The net result of this complex interconnection between theory, simulation, and experimentation is an advancement in theoretical understanding. If Narmour had constructed a model of his theory, many of the ambiguities, gaps in logic, and contradictions would undoubtedly already have been identified and adjusted.

A computer simulation represents an operating model of some real process. The activities of a program are designed to parallel the actual processes to a greater extent than is possible with other forms of models, creating a benefit even in simple and well-specified theories because it allows the theory to be more easily understood—it makes it possible for us to watch the process unfold over the course of operating the program. The declarative aspects of AI programs allow us to express relationships among objects and then observe how the system solves related problems—in the case of KIRS, to observe how the system applies the rules to generate an analysis. When observing the relationships among the subparameters of melody, as in KIRS, we just *might* gain insight into the manner in which people mentally process music.

Limitation of Simulations

A major difficulty with any computer simulation is determining the validity of a system: Does the model operating in the simulation really reflect the real-world system it is intended to parallel? This is perhaps the most difficult question for us to answer in terms of music theories because direct measurable evidence of what is happening in the mind when perceiving music is nearly impossible to obtain. When a traditional computer simulation is generated to model some physical environment, we can judge the validity of the simulation by statistically comparing the output from the simulation with empirical evidence from the real-world system under investigation. It is relatively easy for us to examine the operation of an airport and determine if a simulation matches the activity because the air traffic, landing traffic, ground traffic, and all the other components of the system are directly observable and measurable. When the simulation appears to model the current system, we add additional information as a variable (such as a new runway), and airport congestion is predicted on the basis of the new information. The results of this process are not certain—they still represent a prediction of future events based on current information—but they have been deemed accurate enough to provide predictions within an acceptable degree of tolerance. Also note that the validation of real-world systems is based on the results, the product of the simulation, and not on the process involved.

We cannot observe the operation of a music theory in the same manner as that of a physical real-world system. Music theories are largely, if not completely, mental models that serve as guides or filters through which we generate meaningful musical patterns. The operation of these mental models or processes is not measurable or observable in a direct manner. In this sense, a simulation of a music theory cannot be validated because there is no comparable manner in which a simulation of a music theory or any other theory of mental constructs can be codified, as are models of physical systems at this time. Although it is possible that a music theory simulation may generate musically plausible results, this is not a direct validation. Rather, it is an indirect and subjective validation based on our biases. We believe that KIRS represents a valid model and simulation of the specific aspects of Narmour's theory as specified in part 2 of this chapter, but there may be others who challenge this assertion. It is not possible to achieve a totally harmonious resolution to such challenges because of the interpretive nature of analysis, providing yet another reason for emphasizing the process of computer simulations rather than the final product. Such a product is the result of our individual interpretations of the given theory and/or music, whereas the process enlightens the theoretical claims, premises, and logic of that theory.

Another problem concerns the amount of specificity incorporated into the model while developing the simulation. The risk here is twofold. First, there is a danger that the simulation will not be faithful to the theory as a whole if the portion modeled is too specialized. Second, it is entirely possible that the model can be too specific and have no relevance to anything other than the circumscribed situation and perhaps the specific data sets used. One possible criticism of KIRS is that it models a portion of the theory that is too small or specific and that the majority of the theory has been ignored. The theory as presented by Narmour, however, deals primarily with the bottom-up component; thus, it is this dimension that we modeled, criticized, and restructured. An effective integration of the various components of the theory is possible only when all the theory has been completely presented. In one sense perhaps, any project will provide useful insights that may be applied to the theory as a whole. The product of such a simulation, however, may not be particularly useful or carry the importance that the process does. Each project must be evaluated on an individual basis. We hope that as more research of this type is conducted, specific criteria may be developed that will assist us in evaluating the relevance of a project.

Although KIRS models a specific subset of Narmour's theory, the information gained through the process of generating the simulation does not directly correspond to the percentage of the theory modeled. Through generating the computer simulation, many additional aspects of Narmour's theory, including its foundations, are challenged and modified. These modifications extend beyond the bottom-up component of the theory and thus affect the formulation of the theory in general, not only the specific aspect modeled. KIRS represents a moderate position on these two points. Our simulation is specific enough that it may be modeled by computer. The portion of the theory modeled represents a logical point for the division of the theory, and it represents the portion of the theory that is the most well developed and presented at this time. As for the project being so specific as to lose relevance, we believe that the knowledge gained through the construction of the simulation has addressed, modified, and generally illuminated the larger structure of the theory as well as the premises that form the foundation for the theory. It also suggests a variety of modifications to the theory, some of which have been incorporated into the simulation and others that have been presented but not fully implemented.

There is a seductiveness about computer simulation that we could consider to be a major disadvantage. It is dangerously easy to become so involved in programming that the importance of the enterprise from a theoretical point of view becomes secondary. As a consequence, the potential for advancement and understanding inherent in the simulation may be negated. As programmers, most of us have experienced that uncontrollable urge to add one more item to the program before it is finished, the addition of which begets the idea for another. This process has the potential to continue ad infinitum, resulting in a program that loses its initial focus and potentially spirals into an abyss of incompletion. The project is never satisfactorily concluded, and the potential for advancing the theory is lost. The development of KIRS represents a practical solution to this problem by our selecting a rather arbitrary yet logical point as a stopping place (modeling only the bottom-up component of the theory and stopping when the framework for continuation is completed). Although there is still the potential for additional enhancements, such an approach encourages one to remain focused on the project at hand. Our solution adopted in this project may not be the best one, but by selecting a stopping point and sharing the information obtained, other theorist or programmers may continue, modify, and expand on our ideas and the work we present here. It is important to set goals for moments of repose where the efforts expended and the knowledge acquired can be evaluated and the course of the project altered, continued, or concluded.

Although the evils of relying solely on the output of a simulation project have already been explained, it is easy to overlook the necessary assumptions that have been made to generate the program. In KIRS, we assumed that the items described as representing the bottom-up portion of the theory should produce musically plausible results. We also assumed that the components of this portion of the theory could be used to generate such results without the interference of the top-down portion of the theory. Further, we assumed that the process by which the rules are applied would indeed produce such results. These assumptions need to be addressed by the programmer and those interested in the results of such a study. Unfortunately, it is entirely possible for a programmer with a certain level of skill to create a system to generate results that appear to be plausible while the foundations or assumptions guiding the creation of the system are suspect or downright false. The only way to protect against this type of project is to address as completely as possible where the information for the knowledge base was derived, how that information was encoded, and where and how the inference engine was derived and encoded. Armed with this information, the work can be fairly scrutinized and criticized. We hope that, given these precautions, such problems will not become insurmountable. Perhaps the most immediate need is to define explicit procedures for extracting the premises or knowledge from an existing music theory in a form that is amenable to encryption into a computer knowledge base. There is an entire subfield of computer science (*knowledge engineering*) that is dedicated to defining these principles. This task is often the most difficult and time-consuming aspect of a knowledge-based project because it frequently requires codifying knowledge that professional musicians apply intuitively to musical analysis. Music theories presented in logical step-by-step procedures or in terms of rules are frequently the first choices in knowledge-based projects because the time required to codify such a theory is significantly reduced because of its structure and presentation. There is a need for some specific criteria concerning the codification of music theories. Such criteria can ensure the consistency of results among various researchers and assist those involved with identifying all the aspects of the theory that indeed need to be codified for the project to produce useful and plausible results. We believe that we can rely quite heavily on the work already completed and available from our colleagues in computer science. There is a plethora of material available concerning knowledge engineering in a variety of fields, ranging from the hard and soft sciences to business applications. The majority of the principles are general enough to be used across all disciplines, but each discipline has some domain-specific criteria—aspects of knowledge engineering that must be codified for a larger number of knowledge-based projects in music to become viable and useful.

As we stated earlier, if Narmour had constructed a knowledge-based simulation on the basis of his ideas during the development of his theory, many of the inconsistencies and ambiguities would have been eliminated before its presentation to a general audience. These tools may become one of the most influential forces in contemporary theory formation. We believe the theories generated through such a process will be more robust, less contradictory, less ambiguous, and more carefully documented than the theories that have been generated without the application of this technology. Bo Alphonce (1980) projected that the use of computers in theory formation would be an important application of computer technology by the end of the twentieth century. Through the development of knowledge-based models and simulations, one giant step toward this realization is possible.

APPENDIX 1
Tonal Harmonic Model: Middle-Tiered Control Heuristics

(Rule numbers appear in '[..]')

"I" can harmonize a note IF
> the next note is not harmonized AND
> the next note is capable of supporting an acceptable chord
> OR
> it follows the rules for movement within a class [2.1d] AND
> it does not repeat across a bar line [9b] AND
> if relevant, it follows the rules about cadential chords [1a–c]
> OR
> it follows the rules of (T)onic-class movement [2.1a] AND
> it is NOT the same chord AND
> if relevant, it follows the rules about cadential chords [1a–c] AND
> if relevant, it is a proper preparation for a V7 [7.1a–b].

"I6" can harmonize a note IF
> the next note is not harmonized AND
> the next note is capable of supporting an acceptable chord
> OR
> it follows the rules for movement within a class [2.1d] AND
> it does not repeat across a bar line [9b] AND
> if relevant, it follows the rules about cadential chords [1a–c]
> OR
> it follows the rules of (T)onic-class movement [2.1a] AND
> it is NOT the same chord AND
> if a 1st inversion, it is preferred to resolve by step [4c] AND
> if relevant, it follows the rules about cadential chords [1a–c]

OR

it follows the rules of (T)onic-class movement [2.1a] AND
succession_of_inv AND
if relevant, it follows the rules about cadential chords [1a–c]
OR
it follows the rules of (T)onic-class movement [2.1a] AND
it is NOT the same chord AND
if a 1st inversion, it is preferred to resolve by step [4c] AND
if relevant, it follows the rules about cadential chords [1a–c] AND
if relevant, it is a proper preparation for a V7 [7.1a–b].

"I6/4" can harmonize a note IF
the next note is not harmonized AND
the next note is capable of supporting an acceptable chord AND
it must be part of a cadence [5d]
OR
it must resolve to a root-position dominant [5a] AND
the chord preceding it should be acceptable [5b] AND
it should be approached by step [5c] AND
it must resolve to a weaker beat [5.1a] AND
it must be part of a cadence [5d]
OR
it follows the rules for passing six-fours [11a] AND
it must be on a weak beat [11.1]
OR
it follows the rule for neighbor six-fours [11b] AND
it must be on a weak beat [11.1] .

"V" can harmonize a note IF
the next note is not harmonized AND
the next note is capable of supporting an acceptable chord
OR
it resolves to a V7 [6a] AND
it does not repeat across a bar line [9b]
OR
it follows the rules for movement within a class [2.1d] AND
it does not repeat across a bar line [9b]
OR
it follows the rules for movement within a class [2.1d] AND
it is NOT the same chord
OR
it follows the rules for (D)-class movement [2.1c].

"V7" can harmonize a note IF
　　the next note is not harmonized AND
　　the next note is capable of supporting an acceptable chord.
　　OR
　　it progresses to the same chord AND
　　it does not resolve to a triad of the same class [6b] AND
　　if relevant, it is a proper preparation for a V7 [7.1a–b]   AND
　　it progresses to the same chord in inversion [4a] AND
　　it does not repeat across a bar line [9b]
　　OR
　　it must resolve to a (T)-class chord [7a].

"V6" can harmonize a note IF
　　the next note is not harmonized AND
　　the next note is capable of supporting an acceptable chord
　　OR
　　it resolves to a V7 [6a] AND
　　it does not repeat across a bar line [9b]
　　OR
　　it progresses to the same chord AND
　　it shouldn't move to the same chord in root position [4b] AND
　　it does not repeat across a bar line [9b]
　　OR
　　it follows the rules for movement within a class [2.1d] AND
　　it is NOT the same chord
　　OR
　　it is part of a descending succession of inversions [10]
　　OR
　　if a 1st inversion, it is preferred to resolve by step [4c] AND
　　it follows the rules for (D)-class movement [2.1c].

"V6/4" can harmonize a note IF
　　the next note is not harmonized AND
　　the next note is capable of supporting an acceptable chord
　　OR
　　it follows the rules for passing six-fours [11a] AND
　　it must be on a weak beat [11.1].

"V6/5," "V4/3," or "V4/2" can harmonize a note IF
　　the next note is not harmonized AND
　　the next note is capable of supporting an acceptable chord
　　OR

if relevant, it is a proper preparation for a V7 [7.1a–b] AND
it resolves correctly [7.2a–c].

"VII°6" can harmonize a note IF
the next note is not harmonized AND
the next note is capable of supporting an acceptable chord
OR
it follows the rules for movement within a class [2.1d] AND
if relevant, it is a proper preparation for a V7 [7.1a–b]
OR
it is part of a descending succession of inversions [10]
OR
it follows the rules for (D)-class movement [2.1c] AND
if relevant, it is a proper preparation for a V7 [7.1a–b] AND
if a 1st inversion, it is preferred to resolve by step [4c].

"IV" or "II" can harmonize a note IF
the next note is not harmonized AND
the next note is capable of supporting an acceptable chord
OR
it progresses to the same chord AND
it progresses to the same chord in inversion [4a] AND
it does not repeat across a bar line [9b] AND
if relevant, it follows the rules about cadential chords [1a–c]
OR
it follows the rules for movement within a class [2.1d] AND
it is NOT the same chord AND
if relevant, it follows the rules about cadential chords [1a–c]
OR
it follows the rules of (S)ubdominant-class movement AND
if relevant, it follows the rules about cadential chords [1a–c].

"IV6" or "II6" can harmonize a note IF
the next note is not harmonized AND
the next note is capable of supporting an acceptable chord
OR
it progresses to the same chord AND
it shouldn't move to the same chord in root position [4b] AND
it does not repeat across a bar line [9b] AND
if relevant, it follows the rules about cadential chords [1a–c]
OR
it follows the rules for movement within a class [2.1d] AND

it is NOT the same chord AND
if relevant, it follows the rules about cadential chords [1a–c]
OR
if a 1st inversion, it is preferred to resolve by step [4c] AND
it is NOT the same chord
OR
it is part of a descending succession of inversions [10]
OR
it follows the rules of (S)ubdominant-class movement AND
if relevant, it follows the rules about cadential chords [1a–c].

"IV6/4" can harmonize a note IF
it follows the rule for neighbor six-fours [11b] AND
it must be on a weak beat [11.1].

{"II" same as "IV"}

"II7" can harmonize a note IF
it follows the rules for movement within a class [2.1d] AND
it does not repeat across a bar line [9b]
OR
it does not resolve to a triad of the same class [6b] AND
it does not repeat across a bar line [9b]
OR
it resolves to a (D)-class chord [8] .

{"II6" same as "IV6"}

"II6/5" can harmonize a note IF
it follows the rules for movement within a class [2.1d] AND
it does not repeat across a bar line [9b]
OR
it does not resolve to a triad of the same class [6b] AND
it does not repeat across a bar line [9b]
OR
if a 1st inversion, it is preferred to resolve by step [4c] AND
it is NOT the same chord AND
it resolves to a (D)-class chord [8]
OR
it resolves to a (D)-class chord [8]
OR
it is part of a descending succession of inversions [10].

"VI" can harmonize a note IF
>   it follows the rules of (S)ubdominant-class movement AND
>   it cannot be penultimate to a tonic final [1b] AND
>   if the final chord, it must function as a deceptive cadence [1c] AND
>   if relevant, it follows the rules about cadential chords [1a–c]
>   OR
>   it follows the rules of (T)onic-class movement [2.1a] AND
>   it cannot be penultimate to a tonic final [1b] AND
>   if the final chord, it must function as a deceptive cadence [1c] AND
>   if relevant, it follows the rules about cadential chords [1a–c].

"VI6" can harmonize a note IF
>   it is part of a descending succession of inversions [10].

"III" can harmonize a note IF
>   it must progress to a subdominant or submediant [10.1] .

"III6" can harmonize a note IF
>   it is part of a descending succession of inversions [10].

APPENDIX 2

Tonal Harmonic Model: The THM Program Code

```
/************************
 * Data
 ************************/

    class("null","null",null,0,0).          class("I","I",tonic,1,1).
    class("I","I6",tonic,1,3).              class("vi","vi",tonic,6,6).
    class("i","i",tonic,1,1).               class("i","i6",tonic,1,3).
    class("VI","VI",tonic,6,6).             class("V","V",dominant,5,5).
    class("V","V7",dominant,5,5).           class("V","V6",dominant,5,7).
    class("V","V6/5",dominant,5,7).         class("V","V4/3",dominant,5,2).
    class("V","V4/2",dominant,5,4).         class("vii0","vii0",dominant,7,7).
    class("vii0","vii06",dominant,7,2).     class("vii0","vii06/4",dominant,7,4).
    class("vii0","vii07",dominant,7,7).     class("vii0","vii06/5",dominant,7,2).
    class("vii0","vii04/3",dominant,7,4).   class("vii0","vii04/2",dominant,7,6).
    class("IV","IV",subdominant,4,4).       class("IV","IV6",subdominant,4,6).
    class("ii","ii",subdominant,2,2).       class("ii","ii7",subdominant,2,2).
    class("ii","ii6",subdominant,2,4).      class("ii","ii6/5",subdominant,2,4).
    class("iv","iv",subdominant,4,4).       class("iv","iv6",subdominant,4,6).
    class("ii0","ii0",subdominant,2,2).     class("ii0","ii07",subdominant,2,2).
    class("ii0","ii06",subdominant,2,4).    class("ii0","ii06/5",subdominant,2,4).
    class("I","I6/4",linear,1,5).           class("IV","IV6/4",linear,4,1).
    class("V","V6/4",linear,5,2).           class("vi","vi6",linear,6,1).
    class("iii","iii",linear,3,3).          class("iii","iii6",linear,3,5).
    class("i","i6/4",linear,1,5).           class("iv","iv6/4",linear,4,1).
    class("VI","VI6",linear,6,1).           class("III+","III+",linear,3,3).
    class("III+","III+6",linear,3,5).

    has_quad_beat_val(1,4).                 has_quad_beat_val(2,2).
    has_quad_beat_val(3,3).                 has_quad_beat_val(4,1).
```

323

```
has_triple_beat_val(1,3).          has_triple_beat_val(2,2).
has_triple_beat_val(3,1).
has_duple_beat_val(1,2).           has_duple_beat_val(2,1).

do_harmonizes(bass,Chord,Note) :-
  harmonizes(Mode,Chord,[Note|_]).
do_harmonizes(melody,Chord,Note) :-
  harmonizes(Mode,Chord,List),
  member(Note,List).

  harmonizes(major,"I",[1,3,5]).          harmonizes(major,"I6",[3,1,5]).
  harmonizes(major,"I6/4",[5,1,3]).       harmonizes(major,"V",[5,7,2]).
  harmonizes(major,"V7",[5,7,2,4]).       harmonizes(major,"V6",[7,5,2]).
  harmonizes(major,"V6/4",[2,5,7]).
  harmonizes(major,"V6/5",[7,5,2,4]).     harmonizes(major,"V4/3",[2,5,7,4]).
  harmonizes(major,"V4/2",[4,5,7,2]).
  harmonizes(major,"vii0",[7,2,4]).       harmonizes(major,"vii06",[2,7,4]).
  harmonizes(major,"vii06/4",[4,7,2]).    harmonizes(major,"vii07",[7,2,4,6]).
  harmonizes(major,"vii06/5",[2,7,4,6]).
  harmonizes(major,"vii04/3",[4,7,2,6]).
  harmonizes(major,"vii04/2",[6,7,2,4]).
  harmonizes(major,"IV",[4,6,1]).         harmonizes(major,"IV6",[6,4,1]).
  harmonizes(major,"IV6/4",[1,4,6]).
  harmonizes(major,"ii",[2,4,6]).         harmonizes(major,"ii7",[2,4,6,1]).
  harmonizes(major,"ii6",[4,2,6]).        harmonizes(major,"ii6/5",[4,2,6,1]).
  harmonizes(major,"vi",[6,1,3]).         harmonizes(major,"vi6",[1,6,3]).
  harmonizes(major,"iii",[3,5,7]).        harmonizes(major,"iii6",[5,3,7]).
  harmonizes(minor,"i",[1,3,5]).          harmonizes(minor,"i6",[3,1,5]).
  harmonizes(minor,"i6/4",[5,1,3]).       harmonizes(minor,"V",[5,7,2]).
  harmonizes(minor,"V7",[5,7,2,4]).       harmonizes(minor,"V6",[7,5,2]).
  harmonizes(minor,"V6/4",[2,5,7]).
  harmonizes(minor,"V6/5",[7,5,2,4]).     harmonizes(minor,"V4/3",[2,5,7,4]).
  harmonizes(minor,"V4/2",[4,5,7,2]).
  harmonizes(minor,"vii0",[7,2,4]).       harmonizes(minor,"vii06",[2,7,4]).
  harmonizes(minor,"vii06/4",[4,7,2]).    harmonizes(minor,"vii07",[7,2,4,6]).
  harmonizes(minor,"vii06/5",[2,7,4,6]).
  harmonizes(minor,"vii04/3",[4,7,2,6]).
  harmonizes(minor,"vii04/2",[6,7,2,4]).
  harmonizes(minor,"iv",[4,6,1]).         harmonizes(minor,"iv6",[6,4,1]).
  harmonizes(minor,"iv6/4",[1,4,6]).
  harmonizes(minor,"ii06",[4,2,6]).
  harmonizes(minor,"ii07",[2,4,6,1]).     harmonizes(minor,"ii06/5",[4,2,6,1]).
  harmonizes(minor,"VI",[6,1,3]).         harmonizes(minor,"VI6",[1,6,3]).
  harmonizes(minor,"III+",[3,5,7]).       harmonizes(minor,"III+6",[5,3,7]).
```

```
/************************
 * Third-Tier Heuristics
 ************************/

  test(Chord,Pos) :-                        % Last POSition:
    ex_length(Pos),                         %       non-null predecesor
    notes(_,Pos,Note,_,_,Key),
    get_mode(Key,Mode),
    do_harmonizes(Mode,Chord,Note),
    Pos2 is Pos - 1,
    notes(_,Pos2,_,Chord2,_,_),
    not Chord2 = "null",
    test_last_pos(Chord,Pos),
    try_chord2(Chord,Pos,Chord2,Pos2),
    record_chord_choice(Chord,Pos,on),
    record_answer(true),
    clear_variables2(Chord,Pos),!.
  test(Chord,Pos) :-                        % Last POSition:
    ex_length(Pos),                         %       null predecesor
    notes(_,Pos,Note,_,_,Key),
    get_mode(Key,Mode),
    do_harmonizes(Mode,Chord,Note),
    Pos2 is Pos - 1,
    notes(_,Pos2,_,"null",_,_),
    test_last_pos(Chord,Pos),
    record_chord_choice(Chord,Pos,on),
    record_answer(true),
    clear_variables2(Chord,Pos),!.
  test(Chord,Pos) :-                        % First POSition:
    Pos = 1,
    can_harmonize(Chord,Pos),
    record_chord_choice(Chord,Pos,on),
    record_answer(true),
    clear_variables2(Chord,Pos),!.
  test(Chord,Pos) :-                        % Middle POSition(s):
    not ex_length(Pos) ,                    %       non-null predecesor
    Pos > 1,
    Pos2 is Pos - 1,
    notes(_,Pos2,_,Chord2,_,_),
    not Chord2 = "null",
    can_harmonize(Chord,Pos),
    try_chord2(Chord,Pos,Chord2,Pos2),
    record_chord_choice(Chord,Pos,on),
    record_answer(true),
    clear_variables2(Chord,Pos),!.
```

```
  test(Chord,Pos) :-                          % Middle POSition(s):
    not ex_length(Pos),                       %      null predecesor
    Pos > 1,
    Pos2 is Pos - 1,
    notes(_,Pos2,_,"null",_,_),
    can_harmonize(Chord,Pos),
    record_chord_choice(Chord,Pos,on),
    record_answer(true),
    clear_variables2(Chord,Pos),!.
  test(Chord,Pos) :-                          % Any POSition:
    notes(_,Pos,Note,_,_,Key),                %      ERR: can't harmonize
    get_mode(Key,Mode),
    not do_harmonizes(Mode,Chord,Note),
    error_list("cannot support"),
    record_answer(false),
    clear_variables2(Chord,Pos),!.
  test(Chord,Pos) :-                          % Other FAILURE!
    old_chord(OldChrd),
    record_chord_choice(OldChrd,Pos,off),
    record_answer(false),
    clear_variables2(Chord,Pos),!.
  test(_,_).

  try_chord2(Chord,Pos,Chord2,Pos2) :-
    record_chord_choice(Chord,Pos,off),
    goodlist(List1),
    clear_variables2(Chord2,Pos2),!,
    can_harmonize(Chord2,Pos2),
    goodlist(List2),
    retract(goodlist(_)),
    retract(goodlist2(_)),
    assertz(goodlist(List1)),
    assertz(goodlist2(List2)),!.

    test_last_pos(Chord,Pos) :-
      empty_goodlist,!,
      last_chord(Chord,Pos),!.                /* 1a */

/***********************
 * Second-Tier Heuristics
 ***********************/

  can_harmonize(C,Pos) :-                     /* Rule 19.1a */
    member(C,["I","i"]),                      % system predicate
    notes(_,Pos,N,_,_,_),
    lsn_mode(M),
    check_mode(M,N,[1,3,5],1),
```

```prolog
    empty_goodlist,
    Pos2 is Pos+1,
    notes(_,Pos2,_,"null",_,_),
    good_list("19null"),!.
 can_harmonize(C,Pos)  :-
    member(C,["I","i"]),
    notes(_,Pos,N,_,_,_),
    lsn_mode(M),
    check_mode(M,N,[1,3,5],1),
    empty_goodlist,
    same_class_movement(C,Pos),
    not_across_barline(Pos),
    last_chord(C,Pos),!.
can_harmonize(C,Pos)  :-
    member(C,["I","i"]),
    notes(_,Pos,N,_,_,_),
    lsn_mode(M),
    check_mode(M,N,[1,3,5],1),
    empty_goodlist,
    t_class_movement(C,Pos),
    not same_chord(C,Pos),
    last_chord(C,Pos),
    cannot_precede_v7(Pos),!.

 can_harmonize(C,Pos)  :-                    /* Rule 19.3a  */
    member(C,["I6","i6"]),
    notes(_,Pos,N,_,_,_),
    lsn_mode(M),
    check_mode(M,N,[1,3,5],3),
    empty_goodlist,
    Pos2 is Pos+1,
    notes(_,Pos2,_,"null",_,_),
    good_list("19null"),!.
 can_harmonize(C,Pos)  :-
    member(C,["I6","i6"]),
    notes(_,Pos,N,_,_,_),
    lsn_mode(M),
    check_mode(M,N,[1,3,5],3),
    empty_goodlist,
    same_class_movement(C,Pos),
    not_across_barline(Pos),
    last_chord(C,Pos),!.
can_harmonize(C,Pos)  :-
    member(C,["I6","i6"]),
    notes(_,Pos,N,_,_,_),
    lsn_mode(M),
    check_mode(M,N,[1,3,5],3),
```

```
      empty_goodlist,
      t_class_movement(C,Pos),
      not same_chord(C,Pos),
      inversion_step_motion(C,Pos),
      last_chord(C,Pos),!.
  can_harmonize(C,Pos) :-
      member(C,["I6","i6"]),
      notes(_,Pos,N,_,_,_),
      lsn_mode(M),
      check_mode(M,N,[1,3,5],3),
      empty_goodlist,
      t_class_movement(C,Pos),
      succession_of_inv(C,Pos),
      last_chord(C,Pos),!.
  can_harmonize(C,Pos) :-
      member(C,["I6","i6"]),
      notes(_,Pos,N,_,_,_),
      lsn_mode(M),
      check_mode(M,N,[1,3,5],3),
      empty_goodlist,
      t_class_movement(C,Pos),
      not same_chord(C,Pos),
      inversion_step_motion(C,Pos),
      last_chord(C,Pos),
      cannot_precede_v7(Pos),!.


  can_harmonize(C,Pos) :-                    /* Rule 19.5a  */
      member(C,["I6/4","i6/4"]),
      notes(_,Pos,N,_,_,_),
      lsn_mode(M),
      check_mode(M,N,[1,3,5],5),
      empty_goodlist,
      Pos2 is Pos+1,
      notes(_,Pos2,5,"null",_,_),
      must_be_cadence(Pos),!,
      good_list("19null"),!.
  can_harmonize(C,Pos) :-
      member(C,["I6/4","i6/4"]),
      notes(_,Pos,N,_,_,_),
      lsn_mode(M),
      check_mode(M,N,[1,3,5],5),
      empty_goodlist,
      i64_to_dominant(Pos),
      precede_i64_with(Pos),
      step_to_i64(Pos),
      strong_beat(Pos),
      must_be_cadence(Pos),!.
```

```
can_harmonize(C,Pos) :-              % Passing Six-Four Chord
  member(C,["I6/4","i6/4"]),
  not Pos = 1,
  not ex_length(Pos),
  notes(_,Pos,N,_,_,_),
  lsn_mode(M),
  check_mode(M,N,[1,3,5],5),
  empty_goodlist,
  passing_64(Pos),
  weak_beat(Pos),!.
can_harmonize(C,Pos) :-              % Neighbor Six-Four Chord
  member(C,["I6/4","i6/4"]),
  not Pos = 1,
  not ex_length(Pos),
  notes(_,Pos,N,_,_,_),
  lsn_mode(M),
  check_mode(M,N,[1,3,5],5),
  empty_goodlist,
  neighbor_64(Pos),
  weak_beat(Pos),!.

can_harmonize("V",Pos) :-           /* 19.5b */
  notes(_,Pos,N,_,_,_),
  lsn_mode(M),
  check_mode(M,N,[5,7,2],5),
  empty_goodlist,
  Pos2 is Pos+1,
  notes(_,Pos2,_,"null",_,_),
  good_list("19null"),!.
can_harmonize("V",Pos) :-
  notes(_,Pos,N,_,_,_),
  lsn_mode(M),
  check_mode(M,N,[5,7,2],5),
  empty_goodlist,
  triad_to_7th("V",Pos),
  not_across_barline(Pos),!.
can_harmonize("V",Pos) :-
  notes(_,Pos,N,_,_,_),
  lsn_mode(M),
  check_mode(M,N,[5,7,2],5),
  empty_goodlist,
  same_class_movement("V",Pos),
  not_across_barline(Pos),!.
can_harmonize("V",Pos) :-
  notes(_,Pos,N,_,_,_),
  lsn_mode(M),
  check_mode(M,N,[5,7,2],5),
```

```
      empty_goodlist,
      same_class_movement("V",Pos),
      not same_chord("V",Pos),!.
   can_harmonize("V",Pos) :-
      notes(_,Pos,N,_,_,_),
      lsn_mode(M),
      check_mode(M,N,[5,7,2],5),
      empty_goodlist,
      d_class_movement("V",Pos),!.

   can_harmonize("V7",Pos) :-                     /* 19.5.1a */
      notes(_,Pos,N,_,_,_),
      lsn_mode(M),
      check_mode(M,N,[5,7,2,4],5),
      empty_goodlist,
      same_chord("V7",Pos),
      not_7th_to_triad("V7",Pos),
      cannot_precede_v7(Pos),
      root_to_inversion("V7",Pos),
      not_across_barline(Pos),!.
   can_harmonize("V7",Pos) :-
      notes(_,Pos,N,_,_,_),
      lsn_mode(M),
      check_mode(M,N,[5,7,2,4],5),
      empty_goodlist,
      v7_to_tclass(Pos),!.
   can_harmonize("V7",Pos) :-
      notes(_,Pos,N,_,_,_),
      lsn_mode(M),
      check_mode(M,N,[5,7,2,4],5),
      empty_goodlist,
      Pos2 is Pos + 1,
      notes(_,Pos2,_,"null",_,_),
      good_list("19null"),!.

   can_harmonize("V6",Pos) :-                     /* 19.7a */
      notes(_,Pos,N,_,_,_),
      lsn_mode(M),
      check_mode(M,N,[5,7,2],7),
      empty_goodlist,
      Pos2 is Pos+1,
      notes(_,Pos2,_,"null",_,_),
      good_list("19null"),!.
   can_harmonize("V6",Pos) :-
      notes(_,Pos,N,_,_,_),
      lsn_mode(M),
      check_mode(M,N,[5,7,2],7),
```

```
      empty_goodlist,
      triad_to_7th("V6",Pos),
      not_across_barline(Pos),!.
can_harmonize("V6",Pos) :-
      notes(_,Pos,N,_,_,_),
      lsn_mode(M),
      check_mode(M,N,[5,7,2],7),
      empty_goodlist,
      same_chord("V6",Pos),
      inversion_to_root("V6",Pos),
      not_across_barline(Pos),!.
can_harmonize("V6",Pos) :-
      notes(_,Pos,N,_,_,_),
      lsn_mode(M),
      check_mode(M,N,[5,7,2],7),
      empty_goodlist,
      same_class_movement("V6",Pos),
      not same_chord("V6",Pos),!.
can_harmonize("V6",Pos) :-
      notes(_,Pos,N,_,_,_),
      lsn_mode(M),
      check_mode(M,N,[5,7,2],7),
      empty_goodlist,
      succession_of_inv("V6",Pos),!.
can_harmonize("V6",Pos) :-
      notes(_,Pos,N,_,_,_),
      lsn_mode(M),
      check_mode(M,N,[5,7,2],7),
      empty_goodlist,
      inversion_step_motion("V6",Pos),
      d_class_movement("V6",Pos),!.

can_harmonize("V6/4",Pos) :-              % Passing Six-Four Chord
      not Pos = 1,
      not ex_length(Pos),
      notes(_,Pos,N,_,_,_),
      lsn_mode(M),
      check_mode(M,N,[5,7,2],2),
      empty_goodlist,
      passing_64(Pos),
      weak_beat(Pos),!.

can_harmonize("V6/5",Pos) :-              /* 19.7.1a */
      lsn_mode(X), member(X,[4,6]),
      notes(_,Pos,7,_,_,_),
      empty_goodlist,
      Pos2 is Pos+1,
```

```prolog
    notes(_,Pos2,Bass2,Chord2,_,_),
    cannot_precede_v7(Pos),
    invertedV7_goes_to(Chord2,["I","i"],Bass2,[1]),!.
can_harmonize("V6/5",Pos) :-
    lsn_mode(X), member(X,[3,5]),
    notes(_,Pos,N,_,_,_),
    member(N,[5,7,2,4]),
    empty_goodlist,
    Pos2 is Pos+1,
    notes(_,Pos2,_,Chord2,_,_),
    class(_,Chord2,_,_,Bass2),
    cannot_precede_v7(Pos),
    invertedV7_goes_to(Chord2,["I","i"],Bass2,[1]),!.

can_harmonize("V4/3",Pos) :-                        /* 19.4.1a */
    lsn_mode(X), member(X,[4,6]),
    notes(_,Pos,2,_,_,_),
    empty_goodlist,
    Pos2 is Pos+1,
    notes(_,Pos2,Bass2,Chord2,_,_),
    cannot_precede_v7(Pos),
    invertedV7_goes_to(Chord2,["I","i","I6","i6"],Bass2,[1,3]),!.
can_harmonize("V4/3",Pos) :-
    lsn_mode(X), member(X,[3,5]),
    notes(_,Pos,N,_,_,_),
    member(N,[5,7,2,4]),
    empty_goodlist,
    Pos2 is Pos+1,
    notes(_,Pos2,_,Chord2,_,_),
    class(_,Chord2,_,_,Bass2),
    cannot_precede_v7(Pos),
    invertedV7_goes_to(Chord2,["I","i","I6","i6"],Bass2,[1,3]),!.

can_harmonize("V4/2",Pos) :-                        /* 19.2.2a */
    lsn_mode(X), member(X,[4,6]),
    notes(_,Pos,4,_,_,_),
    empty_goodlist,
    Pos2 is Pos+1,
    notes(_,Pos2,Bass2,Chord2,_,_),
    cannot_precede_v7(Pos),
    invertedV7_goes_to(Chord2,["I6","i6"],Bass2,[3]),!.
can_harmonize("V4/2",Pos) :-
    lsn_mode(X), member(X,[3,5]),
    notes(_,Pos,N,_,_,_),
    member(N,[5,7,2,4]),
    empty_goodlist,
    Pos2 is Pos+1,
```

```
      notes(_,Pos2,_,Chord2,_,_),
      class(_,Chord2,_,_,Bass2),
      cannot_precede_v7(Pos),
      invertedV7_goes_to(Chord2,["I6","i6"],Bass2,[3]),!.

  can_harmonize("vii06",Pos) :-              /* 19.2a */
      notes(_,Pos,N,_,_,_),
      lsn_mode(M),
      check_mode(M,N,[7,2,4],2),
      empty_goodlist,
      Pos2 is Pos+1,
      notes(_,Pos2,_,"null",_,_),
      good_list("19null"),!.
  can_harmonize("vii06",Pos) :-
      notes(_,Pos,N,_,_,_),
      lsn_mode(M),
      check_mode(M,N,[7,2,4],2),
      empty_goodlist,
      same_class_movement("vii06",Pos),
      cannot_precede_v7(Pos),!.
  can_harmonize("vii06",Pos) :-
      notes(_,Pos,N,_,_,_),
      lsn_mode(M),
      check_mode(M,N,[7,2,4],2),
      empty_goodlist,
      succession_of_inv("vii06",Pos),!.
  can_harmonize("vii06",Pos) :-
      notes(_,Pos,N,_,_,_),
      lsn_mode(M),
      check_mode(M,N,[7,2,4],2),
      empty_goodlist,
      d_class_movement("V6",Pos),
      cannot_precede_v7(Pos),
      inversion_step_motion("vii06",Pos),!.

  can_harmonize("vii0",Pos) :-               /* 19.7b */
      notes(_,Pos,N,_,_,_),
      lsn_mode(M),
      check_mode(M,N,[7,2,4],7),
      empty_goodlist,
      root_position_diminished,!.

  can_harmonize(C,Pos) :-                     /* Rule 19.4a */
      member(C,["IV","iv"]),
      notes(_,Pos,N,_,_,_),
      lsn_mode(M),
      check_mode(M,N,[4,6,1],4),
```

```
    empty_goodlist,
    Pos2 is Pos+1,
    notes(_,Pos2,_,"null",_,_),
    good_list("19null"),!.
can_harmonize(C,Pos) :-
  member(C,["IV","iv"]),
  notes(_,Pos,N,_,_,_),
  lsn_mode(M),
  check_mode(M,N,[4,6,1],4),
  empty_goodlist,
  same_chord(C,Pos),
  root_to_inversion(C,Pos),
  not_across_barline(Pos),
  last_chord(C,Pos),!.
can_harmonize(C,Pos) :-
  member(C,["IV","iv"]),
  notes(_,Pos,N,_,_,_),
  lsn_mode(M),
  check_mode(M,N,[4,6,1],4),
  empty_goodlist,
  same_class_movement(C,Pos),
  not_same_chord(C,Pos),
  last_chord(C,Pos),!.
can_harmonize(C,Pos) :-
  member(C,["IV","iv"]),
  notes(_,Pos,N,_,_,_),
  lsn_mode(M),
  check_mode(M,N,[4,6,1],4),
  empty_goodlist,
  s_class_movement(C,Pos),
  last_chord(C,Pos),!.

 can_harmonize(C,Pos) :-                    /* Rule 19.6a */
   member(C,["IV6","iv6"]),
   notes(_,Pos,N,_,_,_),
   lsn_mode(M),
   check_mode(M,N,[4,6,1],6),
   empty_goodlist,
   Pos2 is Pos+1,
   notes(_,Pos2,_,"null",_,_),
   good_list("19null"),!.
 can_harmonize(C,Pos) :-
   member(C,["IV6","iv6"]),
   notes(_,Pos,N,_,_,_),
   lsn_mode(M),
   check_mode(M,N,[4,6,1],6),
   empty_goodlist,
```

```
    same_chord(C,Pos),
    inversion_to_root(C,Pos),
    not_across_barline(Pos),
    last_chord(C,Pos),!.
can_harmonize(C,Pos)  :-
    member(C,["IV6","iv6"]),
    notes(_,Pos,N,_,_,_),
    lsn_mode(M),
    check_mode(M,N,[4,6,1],6),
    empty_goodlist,
    same_class_movement(C,Pos),
    not same_chord(C,Pos),
    last_chord(C,Pos),!.
can_harmonize(C,Pos)  :-
    member(C,["IV6","iv6"]),
    notes(_,Pos,N,_,_,_),
    lsn_mode(M),
    check_mode(M,N,[4,6,1],6),
    empty_goodlist,
    inversion_step_motion(C,Pos),
    not same_chord(C,Pos),!.
can_harmonize(C,Pos)  :-
    member(C,["IV6","iv6"]),
    notes(_,Pos,N,_,_,_),
    lsn_mode(M),
    check_mode(M,N,[4,6,1],6),
    empty_goodlist,
    succession_of_inv(C,Pos),!.
can_harmonize(C,Pos)  :-
    member(C,["IV6","iv6"]),
    notes(_,Pos,N,_,_,_),
    lsn_mode(M),
    check_mode(M,N,[4,6,1],6),
    empty_goodlist,
    s_class_movement(C,Pos),
    last_chord(C,Pos),!.

can_harmonize(C,Pos)  :-                    % Neighbor Six-Four Chord
    member(C,["IV6/4","iv6/4"]),
    not Pos = 1,
    not ex_length(Pos),
    notes(_,Pos,N,_,_,_),
    lsn_mode(M),
    check_mode(M,N,[4,6,1],1),
    empty_goodlist,
    neighbor_64(Pos),
    weak_beat(Pos),!.
```

```
can_harmonize(C,Pos) :-                        /* Rule 19.2b; identical to [IV,iv] */
  member(C,["ii","ii0"]),
  notes(_,Pos,N,_,_,_),
  lsn_mode(M),
  check_mode(M,N,[2,4,6],2),
  empty_goodlist,
  Pos2 is Pos+1,
  notes(_,Pos2,_,"null",_,_),
  good_list("19null"),!.
can_harmonize(C,Pos) :-
  member(C,["ii","ii0"]),
  notes(_,Pos,N,_,_,_),
  lsn_mode(M),
  check_mode(M,N,[2,4,6],2),
  empty_goodlist,
  same_chord(C,Pos),
  root_to_inversion(C,Pos),
  not_across_barline(Pos),
  last_chord(C,Pos),!.
can_harmonize(C,Pos) :-
  member(C,["ii","ii0"]),
  notes(_,Pos,N,_,_,_),
  lsn_mode(M),
  check_mode(M,N,[2,4,6],2),
  empty_goodlist,
  same_class_movement(C,Pos),
  not same_chord(C,Pos),
  last_chord(C,Pos),!.
can_harmonize(C,Pos) :-
  member(C,["ii","ii0"]),
  notes(_,Pos,N,_,_,_),
  lsn_mode(M),
  check_mode(M,N,[2,4,6],2),
  empty_goodlist,
  s_class_movement(C,Pos),
  last_chord(C,Pos),!.

can_harmonize(C,Pos) :-                         /* 19.2.1a */
  member(C,["ii7","ii07"]),
  notes(_,Pos,N,_,_,_),
  lsn_mode(M),
  check_mode(M,N,[2,4,6,1],2),
  empty_goodlist,
  same_class_movement(C,Pos),
  not_across_barline(Pos),!.
can_harmonize(C,Pos) :-
```

```
  member(C,["ii7","ii07"]),
  notes(_,Pos,N,_,_,_),
  lsn_mode(M),
  check_mode(M,N,[2,4,6,1],2),
  empty_goodlist,
  not_7th_to_triad(C,Pos),
  not_across_barline(Pos),!.
can_harmonize(C,Pos) :-
  member(C,["ii7","ii07"]),
  notes(_,Pos,N,_,_,_),
  lsn_mode(M),
  check_mode(M,N,[2,4,6,1],2),
  empty_goodlist,
  ii7_must_resolve_to(Pos),!.

can_harmonize(C,Pos) :-                    /* Rule 19.4b; same as [IV6,iv6] */
  member(C,["ii6","ii06"]),
  notes(_,Pos,N,_,_,_),
  lsn_mode(M),
  check_mode(M,N,[2,4,6],4),
  empty_goodlist,
  Pos2 is Pos+1,
  notes(_,Pos2,_,"null",_,_),
  good_list("19null"),!.
can_harmonize(C,Pos) :-                    % except this clause
  member(C,["ii6","ii06"]),
  notes(_,Pos,N,_,_,_),
  lsn_mode(M),
  check_mode(M,N,[2,4,6],4),
  empty_goodlist,
  same_chord(C,Pos),
  triad_to_7th(C,Pos),
  not_across_barline(Pos),
  last_chord(C,Pos),!.
can_harmonize(C,Pos) :-
  member(C,["ii6","ii06"]),
  notes(_,Pos,N,_,_,_),
  lsn_mode(M),
  check_mode(M,N,[2,4,6],4),
  empty_goodlist,
  same_chord(C,Pos),
  inversion_to_root(C,Pos),
  not_across_barline(Pos),
  last_chord(C,Pos),!.
can_harmonize(C,Pos) :-
  member(C,["ii6","ii06"]),
  notes(_,Pos,N,_,_,_),
```

```
    lsn_mode(M),
    check_mode(M,N,[2,4,6],4),
    empty_goodlist,
    same_class_movement(C,Pos),
    not same_chord(C,Pos),
    last_chord(C,Pos),!.
can_harmonize(C,Pos) :-
    member(C,["ii6","ii06"]),
    notes(_,Pos,N,_,_,_),
    lsn_mode(M),
    check_mode(M,N,[2,4,6],4),
    empty_goodlist,
    inversion_step_motion(C,Pos),
    not same_chord(C,Pos),!.
can_harmonize(C,Pos) :-
    member(C,["ii6","ii06"]),
    notes(_,Pos,N,_,_,_),
    lsn_mode(M),
    check_mode(M,N,[2,4,6],4),
    empty_goodlist,
    succession_of_inv(C,Pos),!.
can_harmonize(C,Pos) :-
    member(C,["ii6","ii06"]),
    notes(_,Pos,N,_,_,_),
    lsn_mode(M),
    check_mode(M,N,[2,4,6],4),
    empty_goodlist,
    s_class_movement(C,Pos),
    last_chord(C,Pos),!.

can_harmonize(C,Pos) :-                /* 19.4.1a */
    member(C,["ii6/5","ii06/5"]),
    notes(_,Pos,N,_,_,_),
    lsn_mode(M),
    check_mode(M,N,[2,4,6,1],4),
    empty_goodlist,
    same_class_movement(C,Pos),
    not_across_barline(Pos),!.
can_harmonize(C,Pos) :-
    member(C,["ii6/5","ii06/5"]),
    notes(_,Pos,N,_,_,_),
    lsn_mode(M),
    check_mode(M,N,[2,4,6,1],4),
    empty_goodlist,
    not_7th_to_triad(C,Pos),
    not_across_barline(Pos),!.
```

```
can_harmonize(C,Pos) :-
  member(C,["ii6/5","ii06/5"]),
  notes(_,Pos,N,_,_,_),
  lsn_mode(M),
  check_mode(M,N,[2,4,6,1],4),
  empty_goodlist,
  inversion_step_motion(C,Pos),
  not same_chord(C,Pos),
  ii7_must_resolve_to(Pos),!.
can_harmonize(C,Pos) :-
  member(C,["ii6/5","ii06/5"]),
  notes(_,Pos,N,_,_,_),
  lsn_mode(M),
  check_mode(M,N,[2,4,6,1],4),
  empty_goodlist,
  ii7_must_resolve_to(Pos),!.
can_harmonize(C,Pos) :-
  member(C,["ii6/5","ii06/5"]),
  notes(_,Pos,N,_,_,_),
  lsn_mode(M),
  check_mode(M,N,[2,4,6,1],4),
  empty_goodlist,
  succession_of_inv(C,Pos),!.

can_harmonize(C,Pos) :-                        /* 19.6b */
  member(C,["vi","VI"]),
  notes(_,Pos,N,_,_,_),
  lsn_mode(M),
  check_mode(M,N,[6,1,3],6),
  empty_goodlist,
  s_class_movement(C,Pos),
  penultimate_chord(C,Pos),
  penultimate_deceptive(C,Pos),
  last_chord(C,Pos),!.
can_harmonize(C,Pos) :-
  member(C,["vi","VI"]),
  notes(_,Pos,N,_,_,_),
  lsn_mode(M),
  check_mode(M,N,[6,1,3],6),
  empty_goodlist,
  t_class_movement(C,Pos),
  penultimate_chord(C,Pos),
  penultimate_deceptive(C,Pos),
  last_chord(C,Pos),!.

can_harmonize(C,Pos) :-                        /* 19.1b */
  member(C,["vi6","VI6"]),
  notes(_,Pos,N,_,_,_),
```

```
    lsn_mode(M),
    check_mode(M,N,[6,1,3],1),
    empty_goodlist,
    succession_of_inv(C,Pos).

  can_harmonize(C,Pos) :-                         /* 19.3b */
    member(C,["iii","III+"]),
    notes(_,Pos,N,_,_,_),
    lsn_mode(M),
    check_mode(M,N,[3,5,7],3),
    empty_goodlist,
    progress_to_subXXX(Pos).

  can_harmonize(C,Pos) :-                         /* 19.5c */
    member(C,["iii6","III+6"]),
    notes(_,Pos,N,_,_,_),
    lsn_mode(M),
    check_mode(M,N,[3,5,7],5),
    empty_goodlist,
    succession_of_inv(C,Pos).

can_harmonize(Chord,Pos) :-
    notes(_,Pos,Note,_,_,_),
    mode(Mode),
    not do_harmonizes(Mode,Chord,Note),
    error_list("19null"), fail.


/***********************
 *  Third-Tier Heuristics
 **********************/

last_chord(Chord,Pos) :-                          /* 1a */
  ex_length(Pos),
  notes(_,Pos,_,_,_,Key),
  get_mode(Key,major),
  member(Chord,["I","I6","V","V7","vi"]),
  good_list("1a"),!.
last_chord(Chord,Pos) :-
  ex_length(Pos),
  notes(_,Pos,_,_,_,Key),
  get_mode(Key,minor),
  member(Chord,["i","i6","V","V7"]),
  good_list("1a"),!.
last_chord(_,Pos) :-
  not ex_length(Pos),!.
last_chord(_,_) :-
  error_list("1a"),!,
  fail.
```

```
penultimate_chord(Chord,Pos) :-                        /* 1b */
  ex_length(Lnth),
  Pos = Lnth-1,
  notes(_,Lnth,_,Chord2,_,_),
  member(Chord2,["I","I6","i","i6"]),
  member(Chord,["V","V7","V6","V6/5","V4/3","V4/2","IV","IV6","iv","iv6"]),
  good_list("1b"),!.
penultimate_chord(_,Pos) :-
  ex_length(Lnth),
  Pos = Lnth-1,
  notes(_,Lnth,_,Chord,_,_),
  not member(Chord,["I","I6","i","i6"]),
  good_list("1b"),!.
penultimate_chord(_,Pos) :-
  ex_length(Lnth),
  Pos \= Lnth-1,
  good_list("1b"),!.
penultimate_chord(_,_) :-
  error_list("1b"),!,
  fail.

penultimate_deceptive(Chord,Pos) :-                    /* 1c */
  ex_length(Lnth),
  Pos = Lnth-1,
  notes(_,Lnth,_,Chord2,_,_),
  member(Chord2,["VI","vi"]),
  member(Chord,["V","V7","V6","V6/5"]),
  good_list("1c"),!.
penultimate_deceptive(_,Pos) :-
  ex_length(Lnth),
  Pos = Lnth-1,
  notes(_,Lnth,_,Chord,_,_),
  not member(Chord,["VI","vi"]),
  good_list("1c"),!.
penultimate_deceptive("vi",Pos) :-
  ex_length(Pos),
  Pos2 is Pos-1,
  notes(_,Pos2,_,Chord2,_,_),
  member(Chord2,["V","V7","V6","V6/5","null"]),
  good_list("1c"),!.
penultimate_deceptive(Chord,Pos) :-
  ex_length(Pos),
  not member(Chord,["VI","vi"]),
  good_list("1b"),!.
penultimate_deceptive(_,Pos) :-
  ex_length(Lnth),
  Pos \= Lnth-1,
  good_list("1c"),!.
```

```prolog
penultimate_deceptive(_,_) :-
  error_list("1c"),!,
  fail.

t_class_movement(Chord,_) :-                    /* 2.1a */
  class(_,Chord,tonic,_,_),
  good_list("2.1a").

s_class_movement(Chord,Pos) :-                  /* 2.1b */
  class(_,Chord,subdominant,_,_),
  Pos2 is Pos+1,
  notes(_,Pos2,_,Chord2,_,_),
  member(Chord2,["I6/4","i6/4"]),
  good_list("2.1b"),!.
s_class_movement(Chord,Pos) :-
  member(Chord,["IV","IV6","iv","iv6"]),
  Pos2 is Pos+1,
  notes(_,Pos2,_,Chord2,_,_),
  class(_,Chord2,C2,_,_),
  member(C2,[dominant,tonic]),
  good_list("2.1b"),!.
s_class_movement(Chord,Pos) :-
  member(Chord,["ii","ii6","ii7","ii6/5","ii06","ii07","ii06/5"]),
  Pos2 is Pos+1,
  notes(_,Pos2,_,Chord2,_,_),
  class(_,Chord2,dominant,_,_),
  good_list("2.1b"),!.
s_class_movement(Chord,Pos) :-
  class(_,Chord,subdominant,_,_),
  Pos2 is Pos+1,
  notes(_,Pos2,_,"null",_,_),
  good_list("2.1b"),!.
s_class_movement(_,_) :-
  error_list("2.1b"),!,
  fail.

d_class_movement(Chord,Pos) :-                  /* 2.1c */
  class(_,Chord,dominant,_,_),
  Pos2 is Pos+1,
  notes(_,Pos2,_,Chord2,_,_),
  class(_,Chord2,tonic,_,_),
  good_list("2.1c"),!.
d_class_movement(Chord,Pos) :-
  Pos2 is Pos+1,
  notes(_,Pos2,_,Chord2,_,_),
  class(X1,Chord,dominant,_,_),
  class(X2,Chord2,dominant,_,_),
```

```
  X1 \= X2,
  good_list("2.1c"),!.
d_class_movement(Chord,Pos) :-
  class(_,Chord,dominant,_,_),
  Pos2 is Pos+1,
  notes(_,Pos2,_,Chord2,_,_),
  member(Chord2,["IV6","iv6"]),
  good_list("2.1c"),!.
d_class_movement(Chord,Pos) :-
  class(_,Chord,dominant,_,_),
  Pos2 is Pos+1,
  notes(_,Pos2,_,"null",_,_),
  good_list("2.1c"),!.
d_class_movement(_,_) :-
  error_list("2.1c"),!,
  fail.

same_class_movement(Chord,Pos) :-              /* 2.1d */
  not ex_length(Pos),
  Pos2 is Pos+1,
  notes(_,Pos2,_,Chord2,_,_),
  Chord2 \= "null",
  class(_,Chord,X,_,_),
  class(_,Chord2,X,_,_),
  not member(Chord2,["I6/4","i6/4"]),
  not repeated_chords(Chord,Chord2,Pos,Pos2),
  check_inversion(Chord,Pos),
  good_list("2.1d"),!.
same_class_movement(Chord,Pos) :-
  not ex_length(Pos),
  Pos2 is Pos+1,
  notes(_,Pos2,_,Chord2,_,_),
  Chord2 \= "null",
  class(_,Chord,X,_,_),
  class(_,Chord2,X,_,_),
  same_class_movement2(Chord,Chord2,Pos,Pos2),
  error_list("2.1d"),!,
  fail.

  same_class_movement2(_,Chord2,_,_) :-
    member(Chord2,["I6/4","i6/4"]),!.
  same_class_movement2(Chord,Chord2,Pos,Pos2) :-
    repeated_chords(Chord,Chord2,Pos,Pos2),!.

  check_inversion(Chord,Pos) :-
    same_chord(Chord,Pos),
    not is_inverted(Chord),
    root_to_inversion(Chord,Pos).
```

```
  check_inversion(Chord,Pos) :-
    same_chord(Chord,Pos),
    is_inverted(Chord),
    inversion_to_root(Chord,Pos).
  check_inversion(Chord,Pos) :-
    not same_chord(Chord,Pos).

/*********************
 * RULES 4a-c
 *********************/

root_to_inversion(Chord,Pos) :-                    /* 4a */
  not ex_length(Pos),
  Pos2 is Pos+1,
  notes(_,Pos2,_,Chord2,_,_),
  not Chord2 = "null",
  class(Type,Chord,_,_,_),
  class(Type,Chord2,_,_,_),
  not is_inverted(Chord),
  is_inverted(Chord2),
  check_for_7th(Chord,Chord2),
  good_list("4a"),!.
root_to_inversion(Chord,Pos) :-
  not ex_length(Pos),
  Pos2 is Pos+1,
  notes(_,Pos2,_,Chord2,_,_),
  class(Type,Chord,_,_,_),
  class(Type,Chord2,_,_,_),
  acceptable_list("4a"),
  good_list("4a"),!.

inversion_to_root(Chord,Pos) :-                    /* 4b */
  not ex_length(Pos),
  Pos2 is Pos+1,
  notes(_,Pos2,_,Chord2,_,_),
  class(Type,Chord,_,_,_),
  class(Type,Chord2,_,_,_),
  not is_inverted(Chord2),
  is_inverted(Chord),
  good_list("4b"),!.
inversion_to_root(Chord,Pos) :-
  not ex_length(Pos),
  Pos2 is Pos+1,
  notes(_,Pos2,_,Chord2,_,_),
  class(Type,Chord,_,_,_),
  class(Type,Chord2,_,_,_),
  not is_inverted(Chord2),
```

```
      is_inverted(Chord),
      good_list("4b"),!.
  inversion_to_root(Chord,Pos) :-
    not ex_length(Pos),
    Pos2 is Pos+1,
    notes(_,Pos2,_,Chord2,_,_),
    class(Type,Chord,_,_,_),
    class(Type,Chord2,_,_,_),
    is_inverted(Chord2),
    is_inverted(Chord),
    good_list("4b"),!.
  inversion_to_root(Chord,Pos) :-
    not ex_length(Pos),
    Pos2 is Pos+1,
    notes(_,Pos2,_,Chord2,_,_),
    class(Type,Chord,_,_,_),
    class(Type,Chord2,_,_,_),
    acceptable_list("4b"),
    good_list("4b"),!.

  inversion_step_motion(Chord,Pos) :-              /* 4c */
    lsn_mode(X), member(X,[4,6]),
    not ex_length(Pos),
    Pos2 is Pos+1,
    is_inverted(Chord),
    notes(_,Pos,Bass,_,_,_),
    notes(_,Pos2,Bass2,_,_,_),
    step(Bass,Bass2),
    good_list("4c").
  inversion_step_motion(Chord,Pos) :-
    lsn_mode(X), member(X,[3,5]),
    not ex_length(Pos),
    Pos2 is Pos+1,
    is_inverted(Chord),
    notes(_,Pos2,_,Chord2,_,_),
    class(_,Chord,_,_,Bass),
    class(_,Chord2,_,_,Bass2),
    step(Bass,Bass2),
    good_list("4c").
  inversion_step_motion(_,Pos) :-
    not ex_length(Pos),
    acceptable_list("4c").

  i64_to_dominant(Pos) :-                           /* 5a */
    not ex_length(Pos),
    Pos2 is Pos+1,
    notes(_,Pos2,_,Chord2,_,_),
```

```
    member(Chord2,["V","V7"]),
    good_list("5a"),!.
i64_to_dominant(Pos) :-
    not ex_length(Pos),
    Pos2 is Pos+1,
    notes(_,Pos2,5,"null",_,_),
    good_list("5a"),!.
i64_to_dominant(_) :-
    why_not(on),
    error_list("5a"),!,
    fail.

precede_i64_with(1) :-                          /* 5b */
    good_list("5b"),!.
precede_i64_with(Pos) :-
    Pos > 1,
    Pos2 is Pos-1,
    notes(_,Pos2,_,Chord2,_,_),
    class(_,Chord2,tonic,_,_),
    good_list("5b"),!.
precede_i64_with(Pos) :-
    Pos > 1,
    Pos2 is Pos-1,
    notes(_,Pos2,_,Chord2,_,_),
    class(_,Chord2,subdominant,_,_),
    good_list("5b"),!.
precede_i64_with(Pos) :-
    lsn_mode(X), member(X,[3,5]),
    Pos > 1,
    Pos2 is Pos-1,
    notes(_,Pos2,Bass2,"null",_,_),
    member(Bass2,[1,2,3,4,6]),
    good_list("5b"),!.
precede_i64_with(Pos) :-
    lsn_mode(X), member(X,[4,6]),
    Pos > 1,
    Pos2 is Pos-1,
    notes(_,Pos2,Note2,"null",_,_),
    not Note2 = 7,
    good_list("5b"),!.
precede_i64_with(_) :-
    error_list("5b"),!,
    fail.

step_to_i64(1) :-                               /* 5c */
    good_list("5c"),!.
```

```
step_to_i64(Pos) :-
  lsn_mode(X), member(X,[4,6]),
  Pos > 1,
  Pos2 is Pos-1,
  notes(_,Pos,Bass,_,_,_),
  notes(_,Pos2,Bass2,_,_,_),
  step(Bass,Bass2),
  good_list("5c"),!.
step_to_i64(Pos) :-
  lsn_mode(X), member(X,[3,5]),
  Pos > 1,
  Pos2 is Pos-1,
  notes(_,Pos,_,Chord,_,_),
  notes(_,Pos2,_,Chord2,_,_),
  class(_,Chord,_,_,Bass),
  class(_,Chord2,_,_,Bass2),
  step(Bass,Bass2),
  good_list("5c"),!.
step_to_i64(1) :-
  acceptable_list("5c"),!.

must_be_cadence(Pos) :-                          /* 5d */
  not ex_length(Pos),
  ex_length(Lnth),
  Pos > Lnth-4,
  good_list("5d"),!.
must_be_cadence(_) :-
  error_list("5d"),!.

strong_beat(Pos) :-                              /* 5.1a */
  not ex_length(Pos),
  Pos2 is Pos+1,
  notes(_,Pos,_,_,Beat,_),
  notes(_,Pos2,_,_,Beat2,_),
  stronger_than(Beat,Beat2),
  good_list("5.1a"),!.
strong_beat(_) :-
  error_list("5.1a"),!,
  fail.

stronger_than(Beat,Beat2) :-                     /* 5.2a */
  meter(4),
  has_quad_beat_val(Beat,Value),
  has_quad_beat_val(Beat2,Value2),
  Value > Value2,!.
```

```
stronger_than(Beat,Beat2) :-                    /* 5.2b */
  meter(3),
  has_triple_beat_val(Beat,Value),
  has_triple_beat_val(Beat2,Value2),
  Value > Value2,!.
stronger_than(Beat,Beat2) :-                    /* 5.2c */
  meter(2),
  has_duple_beat_val(Beat,Value),
  has_duple_beat_val(Beat2,Value2),
  Value > Value2,!.

triad_to_7th(Chord,Pos) :-                      /* 6a */
  not ex_length(Pos),
  Pos2 is Pos+1,
  notes(_,Pos2,_,Chord2,_,_),
  class(X,Chord,_,_,_),
  class(X,Chord2,_,_,_),
  is_seventh(Chord2),
  good_list("6a"),!.
triad_to_7th(Chord,Pos) :-
  lsn_mode(X), member(X,[4,6]),
  not ex_length(Pos),
  Pos2 is Pos+1,
  notes(_,Pos,Bass,_,_,_),
  notes(_,Pos2,Bass,Chord2,_,_),
  class(X,Chord,_,_,_),
  class(X,Chord2,_,_,_),
  acceptable_list("6a"),!.
triad_to_7th(Chord,Pos) :-
  lsn_mode(X), member(X,[3,5]),
  not ex_length(Pos),
  Pos2 is Pos+1,
  class(_,Chord,_,_,Bass),
  notes(_,Pos2,_,Chord2,_,_),
  class(_,Chord2,_,_,Bass),
  class(X,Chord,_,_,_),
  class(X,Chord2,_,_,_),
  acceptable_list("6a"),!.

not_7th_to_triad(Chord,Pos) :-                  /* 6b */
  not ex_length(Pos),
  Pos2 is Pos+1,
  notes(_,Pos2,_,Chord2,_,_),
  class(X,Chord,_,_,_),
  class(X,Chord2,_,_,_),
  is_seventh(Chord2),
  good_list("6b"),!.
```

```
not_7th_to_triad(Chord,Pos)  :-
   not ex_length(Pos),
   Pos2 is Pos+1,
   notes(_,Pos2,_,Chord2,_,_),
   class(X,Chord,_,_,_),
   class(X,Chord2,_,_,_),
   error_list("6b"),!,
   fail.

check_for_7th(Chord,Chord2)  :-
   member(Chord,["ii7","ii07","ii6/5","ii06/5","V7","V6/5","V4/3","V4/2"]),
   member(Chord2,["ii7","ii07","ii6/5","ii06/5","V7","V6/5","V4/3","V4/2"]),!.
check_for_7th(Chord,_)  :-
   not
member(Chord,["ii7","ii07","ii6/5","ii06/5","V7","V6/5","V4/3","V4/2"]),!.
check_for_7th(_,_)  :-
   error_list("6b"),!,
   fail.

v7_to_tclass(Pos)  :-                              /* 7a-b */
   not ex_length(Pos),
   Pos2 is Pos+1,
   notes(_,Pos2,_,Chord2,_,_),
   member(Chord2,["I","I6","i","i6"]),
   good_list("7a-b"),!.
v7_to_tclass(Pos)  :-
   lsn_mode(X), member(X,[4,6]),
   not ex_length(Pos),
   Pos2 is Pos+1,
   notes(_,Pos2,Bass2,"null",_,_),
   member(Bass2,[6,1,3]),
   good_list("7a-b"),!.
v7_to_tclass(Pos)  :-
   lsn_mode(X), member(X,[3,5]),
   not ex_length(Pos),
   Pos2 is Pos+1,
   notes(_,Pos2,Note2,"null",_,_),
   member(Note2,[6,1,3,5]),
   good_list("7a-b"),!.
v7_to_tclass(Pos)  :-
   not ex_length(Pos),
   Pos2 is Pos+1,
   notes(_,Pos2,_,Chord2,_,_),
   member(Chord2,["vi","VI"]),
   acceptable_list("7t"),
   good_list("7a-b"),!.
```

```
v7_to_tclass(_) :-
  error_list("7a-b"),!,
  fail.

cannot_precede_v7(1).                              /* 7.1a */
cannot_precede_v7(Pos) :-
  lsn_mode(X), member(X,[4,6]),
  not ex_length(Pos),
  Pos2 is Pos-1,
  notes(_,Pos2,5,Chord2,_,_),
  member(Chord2,["V","V7","I6/4","i6/4","null"]),
  good_list("7.1a"),!.
cannot_precede_v7(Pos) :-
  lsn_mode(X), member(X,[4,6]),
  not ex_length(Pos),
  Pos2 is Pos-1,
  notes(_,Pos2,Bass2,Chord2,_,_),
  Bass2 \= 5,
  not member(Chord2,["iii","III+","iii6","III+6"]),
  good_list("7.1a"),!.
cannot_precede_v7(Pos) :-
  lsn_mode(X), member(X,[4,6]),
  not ex_length(Pos),
  Pos2 is Pos-1,
  notes(_,Pos2,5,_,_,_),
  acceptable_list("7.1a"),
  good_list("7.1a"),!.
cannot_precede_v7(Pos) :-
  lsn_mode(X), member(X,[3,5]),
  not ex_length(Pos),
  Pos2 is Pos-1,
  notes(_,Pos2,_,Chord2,_,_),
  class(_,Chord2,_,_,5),
  member(Chord2,["V","V7","I6/4","i6/4","null"]),
  good_list("7.1a"),!.
cannot_precede_v7(Pos) :-
  lsn_mode(X), member(X,[3,5]),
  not ex_length(Pos),
  Pos2 is Pos-1,
  notes(_,Pos2,_,Chord2,_,_),
  not class(_,Chord2,_,_,5),
  not member(Chord2,["iii","III+","iii6","III+6"]),
  good_list("7.1a"),!.
cannot_precede_v7(Pos) :-
  lsn_mode(X), member(X,[3,5]),
  not ex_length(Pos),
  Pos2 is Pos-1,
```

```
      notes(_,Pos2,_,Chord2,_,_),
      class(_,Chord2,_,_,5),
      acceptable_list("7.1a"),
      good_list("7.1a"),!.

invertedV7_goes_to("null",_,0,_) :-               /* 7.2a-c */
    good_list("7.2a"),!.
invertedV7_goes_to("null",_,Bass,Basses) :-
    member(Bass,Basses),
    good_list("7.2a"),!.
invertedV7_goes_to(Chord2,List2,_,_) :-
    member(Chord2,List2),
    good_list("7.2a"),!.
invertedV7_goes_to(_,_,_,_) :-
    error_list("7.2a"),!,
    fail.
root_position_diminished :-                        /* 7.3 */
    error_list("7.3"),!,
    fail.

ii7_must_resolve_to(Pos) :-                        /* 8 */
    not ex_length(Pos),
    Pos2 is Pos+1,
    notes(_,Pos2,_,Chord2,_,_),
    member(Chord2,["V","V7","V6","V6/5","V4/3","V4/2","I6/4","i6/4","vii06"]),
    good_list("8"),!.
ii7_must_resolve_to(Pos) :-
    lsn_mode(X), member(X,[4,6]),
    not ex_length(Pos),
    Pos2 is Pos+1,
    notes(_,Pos2,Bass2,"null",_,_),
    member(Bass2,[5,7,2]),
    good_list("8"),!.
ii7_must_resolve_to(Pos) :-
    lsn_mode(X), member(X,[3,5]),
    not ex_length(Pos),
    Pos2 is Pos+1,
    notes(_,Pos2,Note2,"null",_,_),
    Note2 \= 6,
    good_list("8"),!.
ii7_must_resolve_to(Pos) :-
    ex_length(Pos),
    good_list("8"),!.
ii7_must_resolve_to(_) :-
    error_list("8"),!,
    fail.
```

```
not_across_barline(Pos) :-                          /* 9 */
  not ex_length(Pos),
  Pos2 is Pos+1,
  notes(_,Pos,_,_,Beat,_),
  notes(_,Pos2,_,_,Beat2,_),
  Beat < Beat2,
  good_list("9"),!.
not_across_barline(_) :-
  acceptable_list("9"),
  good_list("9"),!.

succession_of_inv(_,Pos) :-                         /* 10a */
  lsn_mode(X), member(X,[4,6]),
  not ex_length(Pos),
  Pos > 1,
  Pos2 is Pos+1,
  notes(_,Pos,Bass,_,_,_),
  notes(_,Pos2,Bass2,Chord2,_,_),
  is_inverted(Chord2),
  step_down(Bass,Bass2),
  good_list("10a"),!.
succession_of_inv(_,Pos) :-
  lsn_mode(X), member(X,[4,6]),
  not ex_length(Pos),
  Pos > 1,
  Pos2 is Pos+1,
  notes(_,Pos,Bass,_,_,_),
  notes(_,Pos2,Bass2,"null",_,_),
  step_down(Bass,Bass2),
  good_list("10a"),!.
succession_of_inv(_,Pos) :-
  lsn_mode(X), member(X,[4,6]),
  not ex_length(Pos),
  Pos > 1,
  Pos2 is Pos-1,
  notes(_,Pos,Bass,_,_,_),
  notes(_,Pos2,Bass2,Chord2,_,_),
  is_inverted(Chord2),
  step_down(Bass2,Bass),
  good_list("10a"),!.
succession_of_inv(_,Pos) :-
  lsn_mode(X), member(X,[4,6]),
  not ex_length(Pos),
  Pos > 1,
  Pos2 is Pos-1,
  notes(_,Pos,Bass,_,_,_),
  notes(_,Pos2,Bass2,"null",_,_),
```

```prolog
  step_down(Bass2,Bass),
  good_list("10a"),!.

 succession_of_inv(_,Pos) :-
   lsn_mode(X), member(X,[3,5]),
   not ex_length(Pos),
   Pos > 1,
   Pos2 is Pos+1,
   notes(_,Pos2,_,"null",_,_),
   good_list("10a"),!.
 succession_of_inv(Chord,Pos) :-
   lsn_mode(X), member(X,[3,5]),
   not ex_length(Pos),
   Pos > 1,
   Pos2 is Pos+1,
   class(_,Chord,_,_,Bass),
   notes(_,Pos2,_,Chord2,_,_),
   class(_,Chord2,_,_,Bass2),
   is_inverted(Chord2),
   step_down(Bass,Bass2),
   good_list("10a"),!.
 succession_of_inv(Chord,Pos) :-
   lsn_mode(X), member(X,[3,5]),
   not ex_length(Pos),
   Pos > 1,
   Pos2 is Pos-1,
   class(_,Chord,_,_,Bass),
   notes(_,Pos2,_,Chord2,_,_),
   class(_,Chord2,_,_,Bass2),
   is_inverted(Chord2),
   step_down(Bass2,Bass),
   good_list("10a"),!.
 succession_of_inv(_,Pos) :-
   lsn_mode(X), member(X,[3,5]),
   not ex_length(Pos),
   Pos > 1,
   Pos2 is Pos-1,
   notes(_,Pos2,_,"null",_,_),
   good_list("10a"),!.
 succession_of_inv(Chord,Pos) :-
   not ex_length(Pos),
   member(Chord,["iii6","vi6","III+6","VI6"]),
   error_list("10a"),!,
   fail.

progress_to_subXXX(Pos) :-          /* 10.1a */
  ex_length(Pos),
  good_list("10.1a"),!.
```

```
progress_to_subXXX(Pos) :-
  not ex_length(Pos),
  Pos2 is Pos+1,
  notes(_,Pos2,_,Chord2,_,_),
  member(Chord2,["IV","IV6","iv","iv6","vi","VI"]),
  good_list("10.1a"),!.
progress_to_subXXX(Pos) :-
  lsn_mode(X), member(X,[4,6]),
  not ex_length(Pos),
  Pos2 is Pos+1,
  notes(_,Pos2,Bass2,"null",_,_),
  member(Bass2,[4,6]),
  good_list("10.1a"),!.
progress_to_subXXX(Pos) :-
  lsn_mode(X), member(X,[3,5]),
  not ex_length(Pos),
  Pos2 is Pos+1,
  notes(_,Pos2,Note2,"null",_,_),
  member(Note2,[4,6,1,3]),
  good_list("10.1a"),!.
progress_to_subXXX(Pos) :-
  why_not(on),
  Pos2 is Pos+1,
  notes(_,Pos2,_,"null",_,_),
  error_list("cannot support"),          /* null note can't support that
                                         note *
  error_list("10.1a"),!,
  fail.
progress_to_subXXX(_) :-
  error_list("10.1a"),!,
  fail.

passing_64(Pos2) :-                       /* 11b */
  lsn_mode(X), member(X,[4,6]),
  Pos1 is Pos2-1, Pos3 is Pos2+1,
  notes(_,Pos1,Bass1,Chord1,_,_),
  notes(_,Pos2,Bass2,_,_,_),
  notes(_,Pos3,Bass3,Chord3,_,_),
  step_up(Bass1,Bass2),
  step_up(Bass2,Bass3),
  class(Type,Chord1,_,_,_),
  class(Type,Chord3,_,_,_),
  not is_inverted(Chord1),
  is_inverted(Chord3),
  good_list("11a"),!.
passing_64(Pos2) :-
  lsn_mode(X), member(X,[4,6]),
```

```
        Pos1 is Pos2-1, Pos3 is Pos2+1,
        notes(_,Pos1,Bass1,Chord1,_,_),
        notes(_,Pos2,Bass2,_,_,_),
        notes(_,Pos3,Bass3,Chord3,_,_),
        step_down(Bass1,Bass2),
        step_down(Bass2,Bass3),
        class(Type,Chord1,_,_,_),
        class(Type,Chord3,_,_,_),
        is_inverted(Chord1),
        not is_inverted(Chord3),
        good_list("11a"),!.

passing_64(Pos2) :-                              /* 11a */
    lsn_mode(X), member(X,[3,5]),
    Pos1 is Pos2-1, Pos3 is Pos2+1,
    notes(_,Pos1,_,Chord1,_,_),
    notes(_,Pos2,_,Chord2,_,_),
    notes(_,Pos3,_,Chord3,_,_),
    class(_,Chord1,_,_,Bass1),
    class(_,Chord2,_,_,Bass2),
    class(_,Chord3,_,_,Bass3),
    step_up(Bass1,Bass2),
    step_up(Bass2,Bass3),
    class(Type,Chord1,_,_,_),
    class(Type,Chord3,_,_,_),
    not is_inverted(Chord1),
    is_inverted(Chord3),
    good_list("11a"),!.
passing_64(Pos2) :-
    lsn_mode(X), member(X,[3,5]),
    Pos1 is Pos2-1, Pos3 is Pos2+1,
    notes(_,Pos1,_,"null",_,_),
    notes(_,Pos2,_,Chord2,_,_),
    notes(_,Pos3,_,Chord3,_,_),
    class(_,Chord2,_,_,Bass2),
    class(_,Chord3,_,_,Bass3),
    step_up(Bass2,Bass3),
    is_inverted(Chord3),
    good_list("11a"),!.
passing_64(Pos2) :-
    lsn_mode(X), member(X,[3,5]),
    Pos1 is Pos2-1, Pos3 is Pos2+1,
    notes(_,Pos1,_,Chord1,_,_),
    notes(_,Pos2,_,Chord2,_,_),
    notes(_,Pos3,_,"null",_,_),
    class(_,Chord1,_,_,Bass1),
    class(_,Chord2,_,_,Bass2),
```

```
        step_up(Bass1,Bass2),
        not is_inverted(Chord1),
        good_list("11a"),!.
passing_64(Pos2) :-
        lsn_mode(X), member(X,[3,5]),
        Pos1 is Pos2-1, Pos3 is Pos2+1,
        notes(_,Pos1,_,Chord1,_,_),
        notes(_,Pos2,_,Chord2,_,_),
        notes(_,Pos3,_,Chord3,_,_),
        class(_,Chord1,_,_,Bass1),
        class(_,Chord2,_,_,Bass2),
        class(_,Chord3,_,_,Bass3),
        step_down(Bass1,Bass2),
        step_down(Bass2,Bass3),
        class(Type,Chord1,_,_,_),
        class(Type,Chord3,_,_,_),
        is_inverted(Chord1),
        not is_inverted(Chord3),
        good_list("11a"),!.
passing_64(Pos2) :-
        lsn_mode(X), member(X,[3,5]),
        Pos1 is Pos2-1, Pos3 is Pos2+1,
        notes(_,Pos1,_,"null",_,_),
        notes(_,Pos2,_,Chord2,_,_),
        notes(_,Pos3,_,Chord3,_,_),
        class(_,Chord2,_,_,Bass2),
        class(_,Chord3,_,_,Bass3),
        step_down(Bass2,Bass3),
        not is_inverted(Chord3),
        good_list("11a"),!.
passing_64(Pos2) :-
        lsn_mode(X), member(X,[3,5]),
        Pos1 is Pos2-1, Pos3 is Pos2+1,
        notes(_,Pos1,_,Chord1,_,_),
        notes(_,Pos2,_,Chord2,_,_),
        notes(_,Pos3,_,"null",_,_),
        class(_,Chord1,_,_,Bass1),
        class(_,Chord2,_,_,Bass2),
        step_down(Bass1,Bass2),
        is_inverted(Chord1),
        good_list("11a"),!.
passing_64(Pos2) :-
        lsn_mode(X), member(X,[3,5]),
        Pos1 is Pos2-1, Pos3 is Pos2+1,
        notes(_,Pos1,_,"null",_,_),
        notes(_,Pos3,_,"null",_,_),
        good_list("11a"),!.
```

```
passing_64(_) :-
  error_list("11a"),!,
  fail.

neighbor_64(Pos2) :-                              /* 11b */
  lsn_mode(X), member(X,[4,6]),
  Pos1 is Pos2-1, Pos3 is Pos2+1,
  notes(_,Pos2,Bass2,_,_,_),
  notes(_,Pos1,Bass2,Chord1,_,_),
  notes(_,Pos3,Bass2,Chord3,_,_),
  member(Chord1,["I","i","V","null"]),
  member(Chord3,["I","i","V","null"]),
  good_list("11b"),!.
neighbor_64(Pos2) :-
  lsn_mode(X), member(X,[3,5]),
  Pos1 is Pos2-1, Pos3 is Pos2+1,
  notes(_,Pos1,_,Chord1,_,_),
  notes(_,Pos2,_,Chord2,_,_),
  notes(_,Pos3,_,Chord1,_,_),
  member(Chord1,["I","i","V"]),
  class(_,Chord1,_,_,Bass),
  class(_,Chord2,_,_,Bass),
  good_list("11b"),!.
neighbor_64(Pos2) :-
  lsn_mode(X), member(X,[3,5]),
  Pos1 is Pos2-1, Pos3 is Pos2+1,
  notes(_,Pos1,Note1,"null",_,_),
  notes(_,Pos2,_,Chord2,_,_),
  notes(_,Pos3,_,Chord3,_,_),
  member(Chord3,["I","i","V"]),
  member(Note1,[1,2,3,5,7]),
  class(_,Chord2,_,_,Bass),
  class(_,Chord3,_,_,Bass),
  good_list("11b"),!.
neighbor_64(Pos2) :-
  lsn_mode(X), member(X,[3,5]),
  Pos1 is Pos2-1, Pos3 is Pos2+1,
  notes(_,Pos1,_,Chord1,_,_),
  notes(_,Pos2,_,Chord2,_,_),
  notes(_,Pos3,Note3,"null",_,_),
  member(Chord1,["I","i","V"]),
  class(_,Chord1,_,_,Bass),
  class(_,Chord2,_,_,Bass),
  member(Note3,[1,2,3,5,7]),
  good_list("11b"),!.
neighbor_64(Pos2) :-
  lsn_mode(X), member(X,[3,5]),
```

```
  Pos1 is Pos2-1, Pos3 is Pos2+1,
  notes(_,Pos1,Note1,"null",_,_),
  notes(_,Pos3,Note3,"null",_,_),
  member(Note1,[1,2,3,5,7]),
  member(Note3,[1,2,3,5,7]),
  good_list("11b"),!.
neighbor_64(_) :-
  error_list("11b"),!,
  fail.


weak_beat(Pos) :-                          /* 11.1 */
  not ex_length(Pos),
  Pos2 is Pos+1,
  notes(_,Pos,_,_,Beat,_),
  notes(_,Pos2,_,_,Beat2,_),
  not stronger_than(Beat,Beat2),
  good_list("11.1"),!.
weak_beat(_) :-
  error_list("11.1"),!,
  fail.


/**************************
 * UTILITIES for Rule Base *
 **************************/

  check_mode(1,N,_,N).                     % Bass-line harmonization
  check_mode(2,N,List,_) :-                % Melody harmonization
    member(N,List).

  clear_variables(Chord,Pos) :-
    empty_errlist,
    empty_acceptlist,
    clear_variables2(Chord,Pos),
    retractall(answer(_)),
    assertz(answer(false)).

  clear_variables2(Chord,Pos) :-
    retractall(chord_choice(_)),
    retractall(exercise_pos(_)),
    assertz(chord_choice(Chord)),
    assertz(exercise_pos(Pos)).

  good_list(Rule_no) :-
    goodlist(X),
    append([Rule_no],X,Y),
    retractall(goodlist(X)),
    assertz(goodlist(Y)).
  good_list(_).
```

```
empty_goodlist :-
  retractall(goodlist(_)),
  assertz(goodlist([])),
  retractall(goodlist2(_)),
  assertz(goodlist2([])),!.
empty_goodlist.

acceptable_list(Rule_no) :-
  acceptlist(X),
  not member(Rule_no,X),
  append([Rule_no],X,Y),
  retractall(acceptlist(_)),
  assertz(acceptlist(Y)).
acceptable_list(_).

empty_acceptlist :-
  not acceptlist([]),
  retractall(acceptlist(_)),
  assertz(acceptlist([])),!.
empty_acceptlist.

error_list(Rule_no) :-
  errlist(X),
  not member(Rule_no,X),
  append([Rule_no],X,Y),
  retractall(errlist(X)),
  assertz(errlist(Y)).
error_list(_).

empty_errlist :-
  not errlist([]),
  retractall(errlist(_)),
  assertz(errlist([])),!.
empty_errlist.

erase_old_data :-
  retractall(notes(_,_,_,_,_,_)),
  retractall(ex_length(_)),
  retractall(meter(_)),!.

record_answer(X) :-
  retractall(answer(_)),
  assertz(answer(X)).
record_answer(_).

record_chord_choice(Chord,Pos,D) :-
  notes(Names,Pos,Note,_,Beat,Key),
```

```
    retractall(notes(_,Pos,_,_,_,_)),
    assertz(notes(Names,Pos,Note,Chord,Beat,Key)),!.
record_chord_choice(_,_,_).

repeated_chords(Chord,Chord,Pos,Pos2) :-
    notes([_,_,_,X],Pos,_,_,_,_),
    notes([_,_,_,X],Pos2,_,_,_,_).

get_mode(Key,major) :-
    stringlength(Key,Lnth),
    char(Key,Lnth,X),
    X = `M`,!.
get_mode(_,minor).

get_mode2(Key,Mode) :-
    stringlength(Key,Lnth),
    substring(Key,Mode,Lnth,1).

same_chord(Chord,Pos) :-
    not ex_length(Pos),
    Pos2 is Pos+1,
    notes(_,Pos2,_,Chord2,_,_),
    not chord2 = "null",
    class(X,Chord,_,_,_),
    class(X,Chord2,_,_,_).

is_inverted(Chord) :-
    stringlength(Chord,Lnth),
    char(Chord,Lnth,X),!,
    member(X,['6','4','5','3','2']).

is_seventh(Chord) :-
    stringlength(Chord,Lnth),
    char(Chord,Lnth,X),!,
    member(X,['7','5','3','2']).

step(Note,Note2) :-
    step_up(Note,Note2),!.
step(Note,Note2) :-
    step_down(Note,Note2),!.

    step_up(_,_) :-
        lsn_mode(X),
        member(X,[3,5]).
    step_up(Note,Note2) :-
        Temp2 is Note2-1,
        modulus(Note,7,Temp),
        Temp = Temp2.
```

```
     step_down(_,_) :-
       lsn_mode(X),
       member(X,[3,5]).
     step_down(Note,Note2) :-
       Temp is Note-1,
       modulus(Note2,7,Temp2),
       Temp = Temp2.

modulus(X,Y,Z) :-
   Temp is X mod Y,
   mod_convert(Temp,Z,Y).

   mod_convert(Temp,Z,_) :-
     Temp >= 0,!,
     Z is Temp.
   mod_convert(Temp,Z,Y) :-
     Z1 is Temp+Y,
     mod_convert(Z1,Z,Y).
```

APPENDIX 3
Implication-Realization
English Rule-Base:
After Narmour

Five Properties of Melodic Implication

1. Registral direction
2. Intervallic motion
3. Pitch specificity
4. Time point (metric position)
5. Time span (duration)

General Concepts of Implication-Realization

Register
Ascending registral direction implies ascending continuation.
Descending registral direction implies descending continuation.
Lateral registral direction implies lateral continuation.

Intervals
Unison implies continuation of sameness (unison); weakest implication
m2   implies continuation
M2   implies continuation
m3   implies continuation
M3   implies continuation
P4   implies continuation; also weak reversal; threshold interval
TT   implies continuation of similarity and reversal equally; threshold interval
P5   implies reversal; also weak continuation; threshold interval
m6   implies reversal
M6   implies reversal
m7   implies reversal

M7   implies reversal

P8   implies a closed dyad prospectively, with an inherent potential to function retrospectively as a reversal

Registral Sameness
IF the registral motion of two intervals is in the same direction
(up/up, down/down, or lateral/lateral)
THEN Registral Sameness = true

Intervallic Sameness
IF there are two successive intervals of identical size then
the intervals are the same. (used only in duplicative structures)
IF Interval1 = Interval2 THEN Intervallic Sameness = true

Intervallic Similarity
IF registral sameness = true AND
the difference between the intervals is ≤ m3
THEN intervallic similarity = true
OTHERWISE intervallic similarity = false
IF registral sameness = false AND
the difference between the intervals ≤ M2
THEN intervallic similarity = true
OTHERWISE intervallic similarity = false

Time Span (*duration*)
Two pitches of equal duration implies that the next pitch will be of the same duration;
for example, two quarter notes imply that the next note will be a quarter note.

Time Point (*metric position*)
Given two pitches of equal duration, the third pitch will follow at the time point exactly
the given duration away from the second note; for example, two quarter notes imply that
the next note will occur exactly a quarter note away from the second note.

Principle Archetypes

Process, P
General definition: Similar intervallic motion (small to small; large to large);
same registral direction.
IF Interval1 = m2; M2; m3; M3; or P4 AND
1. registral sameness = true AND
2. intervallic similarity = true
THEN Process = true
Function = nonclosural

Retrospective Process, (P)
    IF Interval1 = P5; m6; m7; or M7 AND
        1. registral sameness = true AND
        2. intervallic similarity = true
        THEN Retrospective Process = true
    Function = retrospectively nonclosural

Duplication, D
    General definition: Same intervallic motion; lateral registral direction.
    IF Interval1 = unison AND
        1. registral direction = lateral AND
        2. registral sameness = true
        THEN Duplication = true
    Function = nonclosural

Retrospective Duplication, (D)
    discussion delayed until Volume 3.
    possible only on low levels in presence of stylistic context
    possible on high level
    involves only unision
    only example is 13.17a and does not discuss (D)
    Function = retrospectively nonclosural

Reversal, R
    General definition: Differentiated intervallic motion (large to relatively small);
        different registral direction.
    IF Interval1 = d5; P5; m6; M6; m7; M7 AND
        1. registral sameness = false AND
        2. intervallic similarity = false AND
        3. Interval2 < Interval1 AND
        THEN Reversal = true
    Function = closural

Retrospective Reversal, (R)
    IF Interval1 = m3; M3; or P4 AND
        1. registral sameness = false AND
        2. intervallic similarity = false AND
        3. Interval2 < Interval1 AND
        THEN Retrospective Reversal = true

Retrospective Reversal, (R)
    IF Interval1 = P8 AND
        1. registral sameness = false AND

2. intervallic similarity = false AND
3. Interval2 < Interval1 AND
THEN Retrospective Reversal = true
Function = retrospectively closural

Intervallic Process, IP
General definition: Similar intervallic motion (small to small; large to large); different registral direction.
IF Interval1 = m2; M2; m3; M3; P4 or A4 AND
  1. registral sameness = false AND
  2. intervallic similarity = true AND
  3. intervallic sameness = false
  THEN Intervallic Process = true
Function = retrospectively partly closural (register) and
      prospectively partly nonclosural (interval)

Retrospective Intervallic Process, (IP)
IF Interval1 = P5; m6; M6; m7; or M7 AND
  1. registral sameness = false AND
  2. intervallic similarity = true AND
  3. intervallic sameness = false
  THEN Retrospective Intervallic Process = true
Function = prospectively partly closural (register) and
      retrospectively partly nonclosural (interval)

Intervallic Duplication, ID
General definition: Same intervallic motion (small to small; large to large); different registral direction.
IF Interval1 = m2; M2; m3; M3; P4 or A4 AND
  1. registral sameness = false AND
  2. intervallic similarity = true
  THEN Intervallic Duplication = true
Function = retrospectively partly closural (register) and
      prospectively partly nonclosural (interval)

Retrospective Intervallic Duplication, (ID)
IF Interval1 = P5; m6; M6; m7; or M7 AND
  1. intervallic sameness = true AND
  2. registral sameness = false
  THEN Retrospective Registral Reversal = true
Function = prospectively partly closural (register) and
      retrospectively partly nonclosural (interval)

Registral Process, VP

General definition: Differentiated intervallic motion (small to relatively large); same registral direction.

IF Interval1 = m2; M2; m3; M3; or P4 AND

1. registral sameness = true AND
2. intervallic similarity = false

THEN Registral Process = true

Function = nonclosural, even though a partial denial of (I); the second interval implies reversal, and its intervallic motion is always mR/AB

Retrospective Registral Process, (VP)

IF Interval = P5; m6; M6; m7; or M7 AND

1. registral sameness = true AND
2. Interval2 > Interval1

THEN Retrospective Registral Process = true

Function = nonclosural and a total denial; implies a reversal because its intervallic motion is always mR/AB

Intervallic Reversal, IR

General definition: Differentiated intervallic motion (large to relatively small); same registral direction.

IF Interval = P5; m6; M6; m7; or M7 AND

1. registral sameness = true AND
2. intervallic similarity = false AND
3. Interval2 > Interval1

THEN Intervallic Reversal = true

Function = prosectively partly closural (interval) and retrospectively partly nonclosural (register)

Retrospective Intervallic Reversal, (IR)   (only P4 large enough)

IF Interval1 = P4 AND

1. registral sameness = true AND
2. intervallic similarity = false

THEN Retrospective Intervallic Reversal = true

Function = prosectively partly closural (interval) and retrospectively partly nonclosural (register)

Registral Reversal, VR

General definition: Differentiated intervallic motion (large to larger); different registral direction.

IF Interval1 = P5; m6; M6; m7; or M7 AND

1. registral sameness = false AND

2. intervallic similarity = false
THEN Registral Reversal = true
Function = retrospectively partly closural (register) and
  prospectively partly nonclosural

Retrospective Registral Reversal, (VP)   (small to large in different direction)
IF Interval1 = m2; M2; m3; M3; or P4 AND
  1. registral sameness = false AND
  2. intervallic similarity = false AND
  3. Interval2 = large interval
  THEN Retrospective Registral Reversal = true
Function = prospectively partly closural (register) and
  retrospectively partly nonclosural

Registral Return, aba
General definition: Exact or nearly exact discontiguous pitch relation
  (falling within ± M2).

Exact Registral Return
IF pitch1 = pitch3 AND
  interval1 = interval2 AND
  registral direction = up/down OR down/up
  THEN Exact Registral Return = true

Near Registral Return
IF (pitch2 − pitch1 ≥ −2 and ≤ 2) AND
  (interval2 − interval1 ≥ −2 and ≤ 2) AND
  registral similarity = false
  THEN Near Registral Return = true

Dyads
General definition: Unrealized implication.
  the first note of a dyad can function implicatively; that is, if dissonant,
  expect resolution
Dyads are permanently suppressed implication intervals indicated by an
  integer (6), (5), etc.

Monads, M
General definition: Single-tone structure

Monads can become a part of processes, etc., because registral and intervallic
  connections of similarity between pitches tend to be stronger within the
  parameter of melody than disjunctions of differentiation between pitches
  caused by silence.

Closure

General Definition: Events whereby termination, blunting, inhibiting, or weakening of melodic implication occurs.

Three Types of Closure:
1. high degree of closure = transformation
2. moderate degree of closure = formation
3. weak closure = articulation

Closure Caused By
1. rests;
2. reversal of melodic direction;
3. reversal of motion to a small interval;
4. durational cumulation;
5. metric emphasis;
6. strong resolution of dissonance;
7. repetition;
8. the interruption of a pattern; or
9. or some combination of the above.

Closure by Rests
IF next event = rest
      THEN closure = true AND type = transformational

Closure by Reversal of Melodic Direction
IF registral sameness = false
      THEN closure = true AND type = transformational

Closure by Motion to a Small Interval
IF Interval1 = large interval AND
      Interval2 = small interval
      THEN closure = true AND type = transformational

Closure by Durational Cumulation
1. Releasable suppression
      IF cumulation < 50 percent
            THEN closure = true AND type = articulative (Releasable)
2. Nonreleasable suppression
      IF a note exceeds implied location or implied duration by 50 percent OR more
            THEN closure = true AND type = transformational
3. Rests contribute to closure in a manner analogous to durational cumulation (the rests are added to the previous note)
4. Rests affect the interpretation of durational class by the amount of their length

Closure by Metric Emphasis

Closure by Resolution of Dissonance
    sequel discusses interactive rules between noncongruent harmonic dissonance
        (NCL) and durational cumulation (CL)
    ** undefined, no examples

Closure by Repetition
    when a repetition interrupts an implied patterning closure occurs
    ** undefined, no examples

Closure by Interruption of a Pattern
    the onset of a new archetypal pattern creates closure
    ** undefined, no examples / seems redundant

Dyads and Monads and Closure
    *may be closed or non-closed (open)
    may be closed by cumulation
    Low-level monads: become closed by:
        1. ensuing silence
        2. high degree of textural change
        3. high degree of dynamic differentiation
        4. OR some combination

Rules of Structure (Transformation)

Initial and terminal notes of three or more note structures:
    function as the structural tones of melodic groupings and make
        dyads on the next level.
    IF a note is the initial note of a structure
        THEN it is transformed to the next level
    IF a note is the terminal note of a structure
        THEN it is transformed to the next level

Structural tone of a dyad:
    If a dyad is countercumulative then initial note is transformed.
    If a dyad is cumulative then terminal note is transformed.
    If a dyad is durationally cumulative and
        1. stress is present
        then stressed tone is transformed
    A dyadic structural tone emerges as a monad on the next transformational level.

Higher-level structures:
    created recursively!

APPENDIX 4

KIRS Program Code

```
%***********************
% KIRS: knowledge-base *
%***********************

% Registral direction and intervallic similarity predicates

%   register_same compares the registral directions articulated by two
%   intervals. If the directions are the same then register_sameness is true;
%   otherwise it is false.

      register_same :-
        register1(X),
        register2(Y),
        retractall(register_sameness(_)),
        compare_reg(X,Y).

        compare_reg(X,X) :-              % registral directions are the same
          asserta(register_sameness(true)).
        compare_reg(_,_) :-             % registral directions are different
          asserta(register_sameness(false)).

%   interval_same compares the sizes of two intervals articulated by three
%   notes. If the intervals are the same size then interval_sameness is true;
%   otherwise it is false.

      interval_same :-
        interval1(X),
        interval2(Y),
        retractall(interval_sameness(_)),
        compare_int(X,Y).
```

```
      compare_int(X,X) :-                % intervals are the same size
        asserta(interval_sameness(true)).
      compare_int(_,_) :-                % intervals are different size
        asserta(interval_sameness(false)).
%   interval_sim compares the sizes of two intervals articulated by three notes.
%   If the intervals are similar in  size then interval_similarity is true;
%   otherwise it is false.
      interval_sim :-                    % tests for intervallic similarity
        register_sameness(true),         % if registral direction is the same
        retractall(interval_similarity(_)),
        interval_diff(Difference),
        compare_int1(fabs(Difference)).

      compare_int1(X) :-
        X =< 3,
        asserta(interval_similarity(true)).
      compare_int1(_) :-
        asserta(interval_similarity(false)).


      interval_sim :-                    % tests for intervallic similarity
        register_sameness(false),        % if registral direction is different
        retractall(interval_similarity(_)),
        interval_diff(Difference),
        compare_int2(fabs(Difference)).

      compare_int2(X) :-
        X =< 2,
        asserta(interval_similarity(true)).
      compare_int2(_) :-
        asserta(interval_similarity(false)).


      interval_diff(Difference) :-     % computer the difference between
        interval1(A),                  % two intervals
        interval2(B),
        Difference is B - A.


%***********************************************************
%   Basic Structures
%***********************************************************

      structure_type("P") :-              % process
        interval1(A),
        member(A,[1,2,3,4,5]),
```

```prolog
    register_sameness(true),
    interval_similarity(true),
    !.

structure_type("(P)") :-              % retro_process
    interval1(A),
    A >= 7,
    register_sameness(true),
    interval_similarity(true),
    !.

structure_type("D") :-                % duplication
    register_sameness(true),
    interval_sameness(true),
    register1(C),
    C = lateral,
    !.

structure_type("VP") :-               % registral_process
    interval1(A),
    member(A,[1,2,3,4,5]),
    register_sameness(true),
    interval_similarity(false),
    interval2(B),
    B > A,
    !.

structure_type("(VP)") :-             % retro_registral_process
    interval1(A),
    A >= 7,
    register_sameness(true),
    interval_similarity(false),
    interval2(B),
    B > A,
    !.

structure_type("IP") :-               % intervallic_process
    interval1(A),
    member(A,[1,2,3,4,5,6]),
    register_sameness(false),
    interval_sameness(false),
    interval_similarity(true),
    !.

structure_type("(IP)") :-             % retro_intervallic_process
    interval1(A),
    A >= 7,
```

```
      register_sameness(false),
      interval_sameness(false),
      interval_similarity(true),
      !.
   structure_type("ID") :-          % intervallic_duplication
      interval1(A),
      member(A,[1,2,3,4,5]),
      register_sameness(false),
      interval_sameness(true),
      !.
   structure_type("(ID)") :-        % retro_intervallic_duplication
      interval1(A),
      A >= 7,
      register_sameness(false),
      interval_sameness(true),
      !.
   structure_type("R") :-           % reversal
      interval1(A),
      A >= 7,
      not member(A,[12,24,36,48,60]),
      register_sameness(false),
      interval_similarity(false),
      interval2(B),
      B < A,
      !.
   structure_type("(R)") :-         % retro_reversal
      interval1(A),
      member(A,[12,24,36,48,60]),   % if interval = P8
      register_sameness(false),
      interval_similarity(false),
      interval2(B),
      B < A,
      !.
   structure_type("(R)") :-         % retro_reversal
      interval1(A),
      member(A,[3,4,5]),            % if interval = m3,M3,P4
      register_sameness(false),
      interval_similarity(false),
      interval2(B),
      B < A,
      !.
```

```prolog
    structure_type("VR") :-          % registral_reversal
      interval1(A),
      A >= 7,
      register_sameness(false),
      interval_similarity(false),
      interval2(B),
      B > A,
      !.

    structure_type("(VR)") :-        % retro_registral_reversal
      interval1(A),
      member(A,[1,2,3,4,5]),
      register_sameness(false),
      interval_similarity(false),
      interval2(B),
      B >= 7,
      !.

    structure_type("IR") :-          % intervallic_reversal
      interval1(A),
      A >= 7,
      register_sameness(true),
      interval_similarity(false),
      interval2(B),
      B < A,
      !.

    structure_type("(IR)") :-        % retro_intervallic_reversal
      interval1(A),
      A = 5,
      register_sameness(true),
      interval_similarity(false),
      interval2(B),
      B < A,
      !.

% Closure Rules

  closure_by_register_change :-      % closure by change in registral
    register_sameness(false).        % direction

  closure_by_motion_to_small_interval :-    % closure by a change
                                            % in interval size
    interval1(X),
    not member(X,[1,2,3,4,5,6,7]),
```

```prolog
    interval2(Y),
    member(Y,[1,2,3,4,5]).

  closure_by_durational_cumulation      % closure by durational
      (En1,En2) :-                      % % cumulation
    event(En1,_,[Start1,End1,_],_,_,_,_,_,_),
    event(En2,_,[Start2,End2,_],_,_,_,_,_,_),
    (End2-Start2) >= ((End1-Start1) * 1.5).


% Transformation Rules

  transform(En1,En2) :-                 % transform two events to the next
    trans(OldList),                     % level
    retractall(trans(_)),
    append(OldList,[En1,En2],TempList),
    asserta(trans(TempList)).

  transform(En1) :-                     % transform one event (one note from a
    trans(OldList),                     % dyad or a monad) to the next level
    retractall(trans(_)),
    append(OldList,[En1],TempList),
    asserta(trans(TempList)).

  transform_dyad(En1,En2,En1) :-        % cumulative + stress
    event(En1,_,[Start1,End1,_],_,_,_,[_,Art,_,_],_,_),
    event(En2,_,[Start2,End2,_],_,_,_,_,_,_),
    (End2-Start2) > (End1 - Start1),
    Art = 2.
  transform_dyad(En1,En2,En1) :-        % cumulative + stress
    event(En1,_,[Start1,End1,_],_,_,_,[_,Art,_,_],_,_),
    event(En2,_,[Start2,End2,_],_,_,_,_,_,_),
    (End2-Start2) > (End1 - Start1),
    Art = 8.
  transform_dyad(En1,En2,En1) :-        % cumulative + stress
    event(En1,_,[Start1,End1,_],_,_,_,[_,Art,_,_],_,_),
    event(En2,_,[Start2,End2,_],_,_,_,_,_,_),
    (End2-Start2) > (End1 - Start1),
    Art = 16.
  transform_dyad(En1,En2,En1) :-        % cumulative + stress
    event(En1,_,[Start1,End1,_],_,_,_,[_,_,_,Dyn],_,_),
    event(En2,_,[Start2,End2,_],_,_,_,_,_,_),
    (End2-Start2) > (End1 - Start1),
    Dyn = 999.
```

```
   transform_dyad(En1,En2,En2)  :-        % cumulative
      event(En1,_,[Start1,End1,_],_,_,_,_,_,_),
      event(En2,_,[Start2,End2,_],_,_,_,_,_,_),
      (End2-Start2) > (End1 - Start1).
   transform_dyad(En1,En2,En1)  :-        % countercumulative
      event(En1,_,[Start1,End1,_],_,_,_,_,_,_),
      event(En2,_,[Start2,End2,_],_,_,_,_,_,_),
      (End2-Start2) > (End1 - Start1).
   transform_dyad(En1,En2,En1)  :-        % additive
      event(En1,_,[Start1,End1,_],_,_,_,_,_,_),
      event(En2,_,[Start2,End2,_],_,_,_,_,_,_),
      (End2-Start2) =:= (End1 - Start1).


%**************
% Inference Engine **
%**************
%   The inference engine controls emulates the analytical process deduced for
%   Narmour's theory in Chapter 2. This portion of the program is considerably
%   more complex than the rules in the knowledge base. I hope the annotations
%   will facilitate (or at least ease) reading the code.

%   The following three Prolog facts, initial empty lists for use by the
%   inference engine

main_list([]).
analysis([]).
trans([]).


%   begin is the top-level control predicate for the inference engine. A
%   pseudo-code explanation of this predicate is given in Chapter 6.

begin :-
   time_spine(L1,_),
   extract_event_num(L1),
   main_list(Event_List),
   start_search(Event_List),
   analysis(X),
   write(X), nl,
   trans(Y),
   write(Y), nl,
   transform1(Y).
```

```
%   extract_event_num and extract_num combine to make a copy of only the
%   starting event numbers of notes and rests from the time_spine. These
%   predicates store that list in the predicate main_list.
    extract_event_num([]).
    extract_event_num([Head|Tail]) :-
       extract_num(Head),
       extract_event_num(Tail).

       extract_num([]).
       extract_num([Head|Tail]) :-
          check_num(Head,_,Chk),
          check_head(Head,Chk,Tail).

          check_head(X,X,Tail) :-
             main_list(OldList),
             retractall(main_list(_)),
             append(OldList,[X],TempList),
             asserta(main_list(TempList)),
             extract_num(Tail).
          check_head(_,_,Tail) :-
             extract_num(Tail).
```

```
%   check_num examines each event in the time_spine throwing out objects other
%   than notes, number representing time points, and event numbers indicating
%   the conclusion of an event.
          check_num(ENum,_,Return) :-
             ENum < 1,
             Return = noway,
             !.
          check_num(ENum,_,Return) :-
             ENum > 100,
             Return = noway,
             !.
          check_num(ENum,_,Return) :-
             event(ENum,_,_,_,"object",_,_,_,_),
             Return = noway,
             !.
          check_num(ENum,_,Return) :-
             event(ENum,_,_,_,"barline",_,_,_,_),
             Return = noway,
             !.
          check_num(ENum,_,Return) :-
             Return = ENum,
             !.
          check_num(_,_,_).
```

```
%   start_search is the second level of control for the inference engine. A
%   pseudo-code explanation of this predicate was given in Chapter 6.

    start_search([]).
    start_search(Event_List) :-
       build_sublist(Event_List,SubList,Tail1),
       analyze(SubList,Tail1,Tail2),
       start_search(Tail2).


%   build_sublist removes three (or less if there fewer than three) events from
%   the Event_List.  These events are sent to the analyze predicate, which
%   checks the knowledge base for an analysis.

       build_sublist([],_,_).
       build_sublist([En1,En2,En3|Tail],SubList,Tail) :-
          SubList = [En1,En2,En3],
          !.
       build_sublist([En1,En2|Tail],SubList,Tail) :-
          SubList = [En1,En2],
          !.
       build_sublist([En1|Tail],SubList,Tail) :-
          SubList = [En1],
          !.


%   the analyze predicate checks the current sublist against the rules defining
%   the "basic structures" in the knowledge base.

       analyze([Head|Tail],Tail1,          % initial rest
             Tail2) :-
          event(Head,_,_,_,"rest",_,_,_,_),
             append(Tail,Tail1,Tail2),
             !.

       analyze([En1|Tail],Tail1,Tail2) :-   % monad1
          Tail = [],
          Archetype = monad,
          record_analysis([En1,[],Archetype]),
          transform(En1),
          append(Tail,Tail1,Tail2),
          !.
       analyze([En1,En2|Tail],Tail1,        % monad2
             Tail2) :-
          event(En2,_,_,_,"rest",_,_,_,_),
          Archetype = monad,
          record_analysis([En1,[],Archetype]),
```

```
        transform(En1),
        append(Tail,Tail1,Tail2),
        !.

    analyze([En1,En2|Tail],Tail1,         % dyad1
            Tail1) :-
        Tail = [],
        event(En1,_,_,CBR1,_,_,_,_,_),
        event(En2,_,_,CBR2,_,_,_,_,_),
        Archetype = dyad,
        compute_dyad_interval(CBR1,CBR2,Interval),
        transform_dyad(En1,En2,Return),
        record_analysis([En1,En2,Archetype,Interval]),
        transform(Return),
        !.

    analyze([En1,En2,En3|_],Tail1,      % dyad2
            Tail1) :-
        event(En3,_,_,_,"rest",_,_,_,_),
        event(En1,_,_,CBR1,_,_,_,_,_),
        event(En2,_,_,CBR2,_,_,_,_,_),
        Archetype = dyad,
        compute_dyad_interval(CBR1,CBR2,Interval),
        transform_dyad(En1,En2,Return),
        record_analysis([En1,En2,Archetype,Interval]),
        transform(Return),
        !.

    analyze([En1,En2,En3|_],              % all but p,(p),d
            [Head|Tail],Tail2) :-
        event(En1,_,_,CBR1,_,_,_,_,_),
        event(En2,_,_,CBR2,_,_,_,_,_),
        event(En3,_,_,CBR3,_,_,_,_,_),
        check_rule_base(CBR1,CBR2,CBR3,Archetype),
        not member(Archetype,["P","(P)","D"]),
        check_closure(En1,En2,En3,Return),
        compare_dur(Return,CBR1,CBR2,En1,En2,En3,Archetype,Head,
            Tail,Tail1,Tail2),
        !.
```

```
%   if a "basic structure" is closed as a result of durational cumulation, but
%   the closure occurs on the second note rather than the third note in the
%   melodic pattern, this clause computes the dyad and adjusts the event for the
%   next pass through the analyze predicate.
```

```prolog
    compare_dur(duration1,CBR1,CBR2,En1,En2,En3,Archetype,Head,Tail,Tail1,
        Tail2) :-
      Archetype2 = dyad,
      compute_dyad_interval(CBR1,CBR2,Interval),
      record_analysis([En1,En2,Archetype2,Interval]),
      transform_dyad(En1,En2,Return2),
      transform(Return2),
      append([En3,Head],Tail,Tail1),
      Tail2 = Tail1.

    compare_dur(_,_,_,En1,_,En3,Archetype,Head,Tail,Tail1,Tail2) :-
      record_analysis([En1,En3,Archetype]),
      transform(En1,En3),
      append([Head],Tail,Tail1),
      check_duration(En3,Tail1,Tail1,Tail2) .

  analyze([En1,En2,En3|_],Tail1,Tail3) :-  % p,(p),d
     event(En1,_,_,CBR1,_,_,_,_,_),
     event(En2,_,_,CBR2,_,_,_,_,_),
     event(En3,_,_,CBR3,_,_,_,_,_),
     check_rule_base(CBR1,CBR2,CBR3,Archetype),
     check_closure(En1,En2,En3,ReturnedInfo),
     check_returned(ReturnedInfo,En1,En2,En3,CBR1,CBR2,Tail1,Tail3,
         Archetype).
```

%   The check_returned predicate test for closure in open-ended structures like
%   "processes" and "duplications." If a melodic pattern is not closed, this
%   predicate will record the starting event number and adjust the second and
%   third notes into the first and second positions in the sublist. The it will
%   continue on to extract a "new" third event, continuing the analysis.

```prolog
    check_returned(duration1,En1,En2,En3,CBR1,CBR2,Tail1,Tail3,_) :-
      Archetype2 = dyad,
      compute_dyad_interval(CBR1,CBR2,Interval),
      transform_dyad(En1,En2,Return2),
      record_analysis([En1,En2,Archetype2,Interval]),
      transform(Return2),
      append([En3],Tail1,Tail3),
      !.
    check_returned(nonclosed,En1,En2,En3,_,_,Tail1,Tail3,Archetype) :-
      check_extra(En2,En3,EndPoint,Tail1,Archetype,Tail2),
      record_analysis([En1,EndPoint,Archetype]),
      transform(En1,EndPoint),
```

```
      check_duration(EndPoint,Tail2,Tail2,Tail3),
      !.
check_returned(_,En1,_,En3,_,_,Tail1,Tail3,Archetype) :-
   record_analysis([En1,En3,Archetype]),
   transform(En1,En3),
   check_duration(En3,Tail1,Tail1,Tail3),
   !.

   check_extra(_,En2,EndPoint,Tail1,_,Tail2) :-
     extract_one_event(Tail1,En3,Tail2),
     event(En3,_,_,_,"rest",_,_,_,_),
     EndPoint = En2,
      !.
   check_extra(En1,En2,EndPoint,Tail1,OArchetype,Tail2) :-
     extract_one_event(Tail1,En3,Tail),
     not En3 = null,
     event(En1,_,_,CBR1,_,_,_,_,_),
     event(En2,_,_,CBR2,_,_,_,_,_),
     event(En3,_,_,CBR3,_,_,_,_,_),
     check_rule_base(CBR1,CBR2,CBR3,Archetype),
     check_archetype(OArchetype,Archetype,En1,En2,En3,EndPoint,Tail,
         Archetype,Tail2).
   check_extra(_,En3,EndPoint,_,_,_) :-
     EndPoint = En3.

   check_archetype(OArchetype,Archetype,En1,En2,En3,EndPoint,Tail,
       Archetype,Tail2) :-
     OArchetype = Archetype,
     check_closure(En1,En2,En3,ReturnedInfo),
     check_ret(ReturnedInfo,En1,En2,En3,EndPoint,Tail,Archetype,
         Tail2).
   check_archetype(_,_,_,En2,En3,EndPoint,Tail,_,Tail2) :-
     EndPoint = En2,
     append([En3],Tail,Tail2).

   check_ret(duration2,_,En2,En3,EndPoint,Tail,_,Tail2) :-
     EndPoint = En3,
     Tail2 = Tail.
   check_ret(_,_,En2,En3,EndPoint,Tail,Archetype,Tail2) :-
     check_extra(En2,En3,EndPoint,Tail,Archetype,Tail2).

   extract_one_event([],En3,_) :-
     En3 = null.
   extract_one_event([Event_Num|Tail],En3,Tail) :-
     En3 = Event_Num.
```

```prolog
%   check_rule_base is the predicate that calls the rules in the
%   knowledge base for an analysis.
     check_rule_base(CBR1,CBR2,CBR3,Archetype) :-
       compute_int1(CBR1,CBR2),
       compute_int2(CBR2,CBR3),
       compute_reg1(CBR1,CBR2),
       compute_reg2(CBR2,CBR3),
       register_same,
       interval_same,
       interval_sim,
       structure_type(Archetype).

     compute_int1(CBR1,CBR2) :-        % computes the first interval
       C11 is CBR1 // 10,
       C12 is (C11 mod 100),
       C13 is CBR1 // 1000,
       C21 is CBR2 // 10,
       C22 is (C21 mod 100),
       C23 is CBR2 // 1000,
       C31 is ((C13 - C23) * 12),
       compare_oct(C12,C22,X,C22,C12,C31,C23,C13),
       retractall(interval1(_)),
       asserta(interval1(X)).

     compute_int2(CBR1,CBR2) :-        % computes the second interval
       C11 is CBR1 // 10,
       C12 is (C11 mod 100),
       C13 is CBR1 // 1000,
       C21 is CBR2 // 10,
       C22 is (C21 mod 100),
       C23 is CBR2 // 1000,
       C31 is ((C13 - C23) * 12),
       compare_oct(C12,C22,X,C22,C12,C31,C23,C13),
       retractall(interval2(_)),
       asserta(interval2(X)).

     compare_oct(C1,C2,X,C22,        % tests the octave to guarantee an
         C12,C31,_,_) :-             % absolute interval size is returned.
       C1 =\= C2,
       X is integer(fabs(C22 - (C12 + C31))).
     compare_oct(_,_,X,_,_,_,C23,C13) :-
       X is 12 * (integer(fabs(C23 - C13))).

     compute_reg1(CBR1,CBR2) :-       % computes the registral direction of
       C11 is CBR1 // 10,            % the first interval.
       P1 is C11 mod 100,
```

```prolog
    O1 is CBR1 // 1000,
    C21 is CBR2 // 10,
    P2 is C21 mod 100,
    O2 is CBR2 // 1000,
    check_octave(O1,O2,P1,P2,X),
    retractall(register1(_)),
    assert(register1(X)).
compute_reg2(CBR1,CBR2) :-          % computes the registral direction of
    C11 is CBR1 // 10,              % the second interval.
    P1 is C11 mod 100,
    O1 is CBR1 // 1000,
    C21 is CBR2 // 10,
    P2 is C21 mod 100,
    O2 is CBR2 // 1000,
    check_octave(O1,O2,P1,P2,X),
    retractall(register2(_)),
    assert(register2(X)).

    check_pitch(P1,P2,X) :-
      P1 > P2,
      X = 'descending',
      !.
    check_pitch(P1,P2,X) :-
      P1 < P2,
      X = 'ascending',
      !.

    check_pitch(P1,P2,X) :-
      P1 =:= P2,
      X = 'lateral'.
    check_octave(O1,O2,_,_,X) :-
      O1 > O2,
      X = 'descending',
      !.
    check_octave(O1,O2,_,_,X) :-
      O1 < O2,
      X = 'ascending',
      !.
    check_octave(O1,O2,P1,P2,X) :-
      O1 =:= O2,
      check_pitch(P1,P2,X).
```

```prolog
    compute_dyad_interval                    % computes the interval of a dyad
        (CBR1,CBR2,Interval) :-
      compute_int1(CBR1,CBR2),
      interval1(Interval).

    check_closure(En1,En2,_,duration1) :-
      closure_by_durational_cumulation(En1,En2),
      !.
    check_closure(_,En2,En3,duration2) :-
      closure_by_durational_cumulation(En2,En3),
      !.
    check_closure(_,_,_,reg_change):-
      closure_by_register_change,
      !.
    check_closure(_,_,_,int_motion) :-
      closure_by_motion_to_small_interval,
      !.
    check_closure(_,_,_,nonclosed).

    record_analysis(NewList) :-             % record the analysis of a "basic
      analysis(OldList),                    % structure"
      retractall(analysis(_)),
      append(OldList,[NewList],TempList),
      asserta(analysis(TempList)).

    check_duration(_,[Head|_],Tail1,Tail1) :-
      Head = [].
    check_duration(_,[Head|_],Tail1,Tail1) :-
      event(Head,_,_,_,"rest",_,_,_,_).
    check_duration(En3,[Head|_],Tail1,Tail2) :-
      event(En3,_,[Start1,End1,_],_,_,_,_,_,_),
      event(Head,_,[Start2,End2,_],_,_,_,_,_,_),
      (End1 - Start1) =:= (End2 - Start2),
      append([En3],Tail1,Tail2).
    check_duration(_,_,Tail1,Tail1).

%   transform1 is the recursive predicate that analyzes all of the higher-levels.
    transform1([]).
    transform1([One_Element]) :-
      retractall(trans(_)),
      asserta(trans([])),
      retractall(analysis(_)),
      asserta(analysis([[One_Element,monad]])),
```

```
          analysis(A),
          write(A), nl,
          trans(X),
          write(X), nl.
     transform1(Z) :-
          retractall(trans(_)),
          asserta(trans([])),
          retractall(analysis(_)),
          asserta(analysis([])),
          start_search(Z),
          analysis(A),
          write(A), nl,
          trans(X),
          write(X), nl,
          transform1(X).
```

%   clean_up removes all lists, events, time spines, etc. from the Prolog database.

```
     clean_up :-
          retractall(event(_,_,_,_,_,_,_,_,_)),
          retractall(time_spine(_,_)),
          retractall(composition(_,_)),
          retractall(main_list(_)),
          asserta(main_list([])),
          retractall(analysis(_)),
          asserta(analysis([])),
          retractall(trans(_)),
          asserta(trans([])).
```

Bibliography

Addis, T. R. 1985. *Designing Knowledge-Based Systems.* Englewood Cliffs, N.J.: Prentice-Hall.

Aldwell, Edward, and Schacter, Carl. 1989. *Harmony and Voice Leading.* 2d ed. New York: Harcourt, Brace, Jovanovich.

Aleksander, Igor. 1984. *Designing Intelligent Systems: An Introduction.* New York: UNIPUB.

Alphonce, Bo. 1980. "Music Analysis by Computer—a Field for Theory Formation." *Computer Music Journal* 4:26–35.

———. 1989. "Computer Applications in Music Research: A Retrospective." *Computers in Music Research* 1:1–74.

Anderson, David P., and Ron Kuivila. 1989. "Continuous Abstractions for Discrete Event Languages." *Computer Music Journal* 13:11–23.

Arenson, Michael. 1981. "A Model for Systematic Revision of Computer-Based Instruction Materials in Music Theory." *Journal of Computer-Based Instruction* 7:78–84.

"Artificial Intelligence and Music: Selected Proceedings of the European Workshop on Artificial Intelligence and Music." 1990. Entire issue of *Interface* 19.

Ashley, Richard D. 1985. "KSM: An Essay in Knowledge Representation in Music." In *Proceedings of the International Computer Music Conference, 1985,* edited by Barray Truax. San Francisco: Computer Music Association.

Baird, B. 1990. "The Artificially Intelligent Computer Performer: The Second Generation." *Interface* 19:197–203.

Balaban, Mira. 1985. "Foundations for Artificial Intelligence Research of Western Tonal Music." In *Proceedings of the International Computer Music*

Conference, 1985, edited by Barray Truax, San Fransisco: Computer Music Association.

————. 1989. "The Cross Fertilization Relationship between Music and AI." *Interface* 18:89–97.

Bales, W. Kenton. 1986. "Computer-Assisted Instruction and Music Technology in Education." *Journal of Computer-Based Instruction* 13:2–5.

Baroni, Mario, and L. Callegari, eds. 1984. *Musical Grammars and Computer Analysis.* Florence: L.S. Olschki.

Bartle, Barton L. 1987. *Computer Software in Music and Music Education: A Guide.* Metuchen, N.J.: Scarecrow Press.

Bauer-Mengelberg, Stefan. 1970. "The Ford-Columbia Input Language." In *Musicology and the Computer,* edited by D.S. Brook. New York: New York City University Press.

Bel, B. 1990. "Time and Musical Structures." *Interface* 19:107–36.

Benward, Bruce. 1993. *Music: In Theory and Practice.* 5th edition. Dubuque, Iowa: Brown and Benchmark.

Berliner, Hans J. 1984. "Search vs. Knowledge: An Analysis from the Domain of Games." In *Artificial Intelligence,* edited by Alick Elithorn and Ranan Banerji. New York: Elsevier Science.

Bharucha, J. J., and Peter M. Todd. 1990. "Modeling the Perception of Tonal Structure with Neural Nets." *Computer Music Journal* 13:44–53.

Bratley, Paul, Bennett Fox, and Linus Schrage. 1983. *A Guide to Simulation.* New York: Springer-Verlag.

Bratko, Ivan. 1986. *Prolog Programming for Artificial Intelligence.* Reading, Mass.: Addison-Wesley.

Bregman, Albert S. 1990. *Auditory Scene Analysis: The Perceptual Organization of Sound.* Cambridge: MIT Press.

Brinkman, Alexander. 1986a. "Representing Musical Scores for Computer Analysis." *Journal of Music Theory* 30:225–75.

————. 1986b. "A Binomial Representation of Pitch for Computer Processing of Music Data." *Music Theory Spectrum* 8:58–74.

————. 1990. *Pascal Programming for Music Research.* Chicago: University of Chicago Press.

Buchanan, Bruce G., and Edward H. Shortliffe, eds. 1984. *Rule-Based Expert Systems: The MYCIN Experiments of the Stanford Heuristic Programming Project.* Reading, Mass.: Addison-Wesley.

Bulgren, W. G. 1982. *Discrete Event Simulation.* Englewood Cliffs, N.J.: Prentice-Hall.

Camurri, Antonio. 1990. "The Role of Artificial Intelligence in Music." *Interface* 19:219–48.

Camilleri, Lelio, Francesco Carreras, and Chiara Duranti. 1990. "An Expert System Prototype for the Study of Musical Segmentation." *Interface* 19:147–54.

Camilleri, Lelio, Francesco Carreras, Pietro Grossi, and Giovanni Nencini. 1987. "A Software Tool for Music Analysis." *Interface* 16:23–38.

Campbell, J.A., ed. 1984. *Implementations of Prolog.* New York: Halsted Press.

Cantor, Don. 1990. "A Knowledge Acquisition System for Segmentation in Music." Ph. D. diss., Boston University.

Clancey, William J. 1987. *Knowledge-Based Tutoring: The Guidon Program.* Cambridge: MIT Press.

Clark, Keith L., and Frank G. McCabe. 1984. *Micro-PROLOG: Programming in Logic.* Englewood Cliffs, N.J.: Prentice-Hall.

Clocksin, William F., and Christopher S. Mellish. 1987. *Programming in Prolog.* 3d ed. New York: Springer-Verlag.

Collins, Harry M. 1990. *Artificial Experts: Social Knowledge and Intelligent Machines.* Cambridge: MIT Press.

Cooper, Grosvenor, and Leonard Meyer. 1960. *The Rhythmic Structure of Music.* Chicago: University of Chicago Press.

Cope, David. 1987. "An Expert System for Computer-Assisted Composition." *Computer Music Journal* 11:30–46.

———. 1991. *Computers and Musical Style.* The Computer Music and Digital Audio Series, vol. 6. Madison, Wis: A-R Editions.

Dannenberg, Roger B., et al. 1990. "A Computer-Based Multi-Media Tutor for Beginning Piano Students." *Interface* 19:155–73.

Davis, Deta S., ed. 1988. *Computer Applications in Music: A Bibliography.* The Computer Music and Digital Audio Series, vol. 4. Madison, Wis: A-R Editions.

———. 1992. *Computer Applications in Music: A Supplement.* The Computer Music and Digital Audio Series, vol. 10. Madison, Wis: A-R Editions.

Davis, Randall, and Douglas Lenat. 1982. *Knowledge-Based Systems in Artificial Intelligence.* New York: McGraw-Hill.

De Poli, Giovanni, Luca Irone, and Alvise Vidolin. 1990. "Music Score Interpretation Using a Multilevel Knowledge Base." *Interface* 19:137–146.

Desain, Peter. 1990. "Parsing the Parser: A Case Study in Programming Style." *Computers in Music Research* 2:39–90.

Desain, Peter, and Henkjan Honing. 1989. "The Quantization of Musical Time: A Connectionist Approach." *Computer Music Journal* 13:56–66.

Di Nola, Antonio, et al. 1989. *Fuzzy Relation Equations and Their Applications to Knowledge Engineering.* Foreword by Lotfi A. Zadeh. Boston: Kluwer Academic.

Dodd, Anthony. 1990. *Prolog: A Logical Approach.* New York: Oxford University Press.

Dolson, Mark. 1989. "Machine Tongues XII: Neural Networks." *Computer Music Journal* 13:28–40.

Duisberg, Robert. 1984. "On the Role of Affect in Artificial Intelligence and Music." *Perspectives of New Music* 23:6–35.

Ebcioglu, Kemal. 1988. "An Expert System for Harmonizing Four-Part Chorales." *Computer Music Journal* 12:43–51.

Erickson, Raymond F. 1975. "The DARMS Project: A Status Report." *Computers and the Humanities* 9:219–98.

———. 1976. *DARMS: A Reference Manual.* New York: DARMS Project, Department of Music, Queens College, CUNY.

Forte, Allen. 1973. *The Structure of Atonal Music.* New Haven, Conn.: Yale University Press.

———. 1979. *Tonal Harmony in Theory and Practice.* 3rd ed. New York: Holt, Reinhart, & Winston.

Forte, Allen, and Steven Gilbert. 1982. *Introduction to Schenkerian Analysis.* New York: W. W. Norton.

Frankel, Robert E., Stanley J. Rosenschein, and Stephen W. Smoliar. 1976. "A LISP-Based System for the Study of Schenkerian Analysis." *Computers and the Humanities* 10:21–32.

Franta, W. R. 1977. *The Process View of Simulation.* New York: Elsevier North-Holland.

Frost, Richard A. 1986. *Introduction to Knowledge Based Systems.* New York: Macmillan.

Garton, Bradford. 1989. "The Elthar Program." *Perspectives of New Music* 27:6–41.

Gevarter, William B. 1984. *Artificial Intelligence, Expert Systems, Computer Vision and Natural Language Processing.* Park Ridge, N.J.: Noyes Publications.

Gjerdigen, Robert O. 1989. "Using Connectionist Models to Explore Complex Musical Patterns." *Computer Music Journal* 13:67–75.

Glass, Arnold L., and Keith J. Holyoak. 1985. *Cognition.* 2d ed. New York: Random House.

Goodman, Irwin R., and Hung T. Nguyen. 1985. *Uncertainty Models for Knowledge-Based Systems: A Unified Approach to the Measurement of Uncertainty.* New York: Elsevier Science Publishing.

Graham, Ian, and Peter L. Jones. 1988. *Expert Systems: Knowledge, Uncertainty, and Decision.* New York: Chapman and Hall.

Gross, Dorothy. 1984. "Computer Applications to Music Theory: A Retrospective." *Computer Music Journal* 8:35–42.

————. 1985. "An Intelligent Ear-Training Lesson." In *Proceedings of the International Computer Music Conference, 1984,* edited by William Buxton. San Francisco: Computer Music Association.

Haugeland, John. 1985. *Artificial Intelligence: The Very Idea.* Cambridge: MIT Press.

Hayes-Roth, Frederick, Donald A. Waterman, and Douglas B Lenat. 1983. *Building Expert Systems.* Reading, Mass.: Addison-Wesley.

Hewlitt, Walter B., and Eleanor Selfridge-Field. 1985. *Directory of Computer Assisted Research in Musicology.* Annual publication. Menlo Park, Calif.: Center for Computer Assisted Research in the Humanities.

Hiller, Lejaren A., and Burt Levy. 1984. "General System Theory as Applied to Music Analysis, Part 1." In *Musical Grammars and Computer Analysis,* edited by M. Baroni and L. Callegari. Florence: L.S. Olschki.

Hopkins, Robert G. 1990. *Closure in Mahler.* Philadelphia: University of Pennsylvania Press.

International Journal of Expert Systems. Greenwich, Conn.: JAI Press.

Jackson, Peter. 1986. *Introduction to Expert Systems.* Reading, Mass.: Addison-Wesley.

Jackson, Peter, Han Reichgelt, and Frank van Harmelen. 1989. *Logic-Based Knowledge Representation.* Cambridge: MIT Press.

Kassler, Michael, and Hubert S. Howe. 1980. "Computers and Music." In *The New Grove Dictionary of Music and Musicians,* vol. 4, edited by Stanley Sadie, London: Macmillan.

Klahr, Philip and Donald A. Waterman. 1986. *Expert Systems: Techniques, Tools, and Applications.* Reading, Mass.: Addison-Wesley.

Kluzniak, Feliks. 1985. *Prolog for Programmers.* London: Academic Press.

Kolosick, Timothy J. 1986. "A Machine-Independent Data Structure for the Representation of Musical Pitch Relationships: Computer-Generated Musical Examples for CBI." *Journal of Computer-Based Instruction* 13:9–13.

Kostka, Stefan and Dorothy Payne. 1995. *Tonal Harmony.* 3rd ed. New York: McGraw-Hill.

Kuipers, Pieter. 1986. "CANON: A System for the Description of Musical Patterns." *Interface* 15:257–69.

Laden, Bernice, and Douglas H. Keefe. 1990. "The Representation of Pitch in a Neural Net Model of Chord Classification." *Computer Music Journal* 13:12–26.

Laske, Otto. 1978. "Considering Human Memory in Designing User Interfaces for Computer Music." *Computer Music Journal* 2:39–45.

————. 1980. "Toward an Explicit Cognitive Theory of Musical Listening." *Computer Music Journal* 4:73–83.

————. 1981. *Music and Mind: An Artificial Intelligence Perspective.* Boston: Otto Laske.

————. 1984. "KEITH: A Rule-System for Making Music-Analytical Discoveries." In *Musical Grammars and Computer Analysis,* edited by M. Baroni and L. Callegari. Florence: L.S. Olschki.

Leman, Marc. 1985. "Dynamical-Hierarchical Networks as Perceptual Memory Representations of Music." *Interface* 14:125–64.

Lenzerini, Maurizio, Daniele Nardi, and Maria Simi, eds. 1991. *Inheritance Hierarchies in Knowledge Representation and Programming Languages.* New York: Wiley.

Lerdahl, Fred, and Ray Jackendoff. 1983. *A Generative Theory of Tonal Music.* Cambridge: MIT Press.

Lewin, David. 1983. "An Interesting Global Rule for Species Counterpoint." *In Theory Only* 6:19–44.

Logrippo, Luigi, and Bernard Stepien. 1986. "Cluster Analysis for the Computer-Assisted Statistical Analysis of Melodies." *Computers and the Humanities* 20:19–33.

Longuet-Higgins, H. Christopher. 1987. *Mental Processes: Studies in Cognitive Sciences.* Cambridge: MIT Press.

Loy, D. Gareth. 1989. "Preface to the Special Issue on Parallel Distributed Processing and Neural Networks." *Computer Music Journal* 13:24–27.

————. 1989. "Preface to the Second Special Issue on Parallel Distributed Processing and Neural Networks." *Computer Music Journal* 13:10–11.

Luger, George F., and William A. Stubblefield. 1989. *Artificial Intelligence and the Design of Expert Systems.* Redwood City, Calif. : Benjamin/Cummings Publishing.

Marcus, Sandra, ed. 1988. *Automating Knowledge Acquisition for Expert Systems.* Boston: Kluwer Academic Publishers.

Mason, Robert M. 1985. *Modern Methods of Music Analysis Using Computers.* Peterborough, N.H.: Schoolhouse Press.

Maxwell, Harry John. 1984. "An Artificial Intelligence Approach to Computer-Implemented Analysis of Harmony in Tonal Music." Ph.D. diss. Indiana University.

McDerrmitt, John. 1981. "R1's Formative Years." *AI Magazine* 2(2) (quoted in Donald A. Waterman, *A Guide to Expert Systems* [Reading, Mass.: Addison-Wesley, 1986], 29–30).

McGee, Deron L. 1993. "Musical Rules: A Knowledge-Based Simulation of an Implication-Realization Model." Ph.D. diss. University of Wisconsin-Madison.

McLean, Bruce. 1982. "The Design of a Portable Translator for DARMS." In *Proceedings of the 1980 International Computer Music Conference,* compiled by H.S. Howe. San Francisco: Computer Music Association.

————. 1983. "Current Problems in Score Input Methods." Abstract in *Proceedings, 1981 International Computer Music Conference, November 5–8,* compiled by Larry Austin and Thomas Clark. Denton: North Texas State University.

Meehan, James. 1980. "An Artificial Intelligence Approach to Tonal Music Theory." *Computer Music Journal* 4:60–65.

Meyer, Leonard B. 1956. E*motion and Meaning in Music.* Chicago: University of Chicago Press.

————. 1973. *Explaining Music.* Berkeley: University of California Press.

Minsky, Marvin. 1981. "Music, Mind, and Meaning." *Computer Music Journal* 5:28–44.

Mitchell, Tom M. 1984. "Toward Combining Empirical and Analytical Methods for Inferring Heuristics." In *Artificial Intelligence,* edited by Alick Elithorn and Ranan Banerji. New York: Elsevier Science.

Morris, Robert D. 1987. *Composition with Pitch Class Sets.* New Haven, Conn.: Yale University Press.

Murray, Linda A., and John I. E. Richardson, eds. 1989. *Intelligent Systems in a Human Context: Development Implications, and Applications.* New York: Oxford University Press.

Naish, Lee. 1986. *Negation and control in PROLOG.* New York: Springer-Verlag.

Narmour, Eugene. 1977. Beyond Schenkerism: *The Need for Alternatives in Music Analysis.* Chicago: University of Chicago Press.

————. 1984. "Toward an Analytical Symbology: The Melodic, Harmonic and Durational Functions of Implication and Realization." In *Musical Grammars and Computer Analysis,* edited by M. Maroni and L. Callegari. Florence: L.S. Olschki.

————. 1990. *The Analysis and Cognition of Basic Melodic Structures: The Implication-Realization Model.* Chicago: University of Chicago Press.

————. 1992. *The Analysis and Cognition of Melodic Complexity: The Implication-Realization Model.* Chicago: University of Chicago Press.

Neelamkavil, F. 1987. *Computer Simulation and Modelling.* New York: Wiley.

Neumeyer, David, and Susan Tepping. 1992. *A Guide to Schenkerian Analysis.* Englewood Cliffs, N.J.: Prentice Hall.

Newell, Allen, and Herbert A. Simon. 1976. "Computer Science as Empirical Inquiry: Symbols and Search." *Communications of the ACM* 19 (quoted in Elaine Rich and Kevin Knight, *Artificial Intelligence,* 2d ed. [New York: McGraw-Hill, 1991]).

Newcomb, Steven R. 1985. "LASSO: An Intelligent Computer-Based Tutorial in Sixteenth-Century Counterpoint." *Computer Music Journal* 9:49–61.

Newcomb, Steven R., Bradly Weage, and Peter Spencer. 1981. "MEDICI: Tutorial in Melodic Dictation." *Journal of Computer-Based Instruction* 7:63–69.

Nilsson, Nils. 1980. *Principles of Artificial Intelligence.* Palo Alto, Calif.: Tioga Publishing.

Nord, Timothy A. 1992. "Toward Theoretical Verification: Developing a Computer Model of Lerdahl and Jackendoff's *Generative Theory of Tonal Music.*" Ph.D. diss. University of Wisconsin-Madison.

O'Keefe, Richard A. 1990. *The Craft of Prolog.* Cambridge: MIT Press.

Ottman, Robert. 1983. *Elementary Harmony.* 3d ed. Englewood-Cliffs, N.J.: Prentice-Hall.

Palmer, Marlene A. 1990. *Expert Systems and Related Topics: Selected Bibliography and Guide to Information Scources.* Harrisburg, Pa.: Idea Group Publishers.

Papert, Seymour. 1980. *Mindstorms: Children, Compters, and Powerful Ideas.* New York: Basic Books.

Parsaye, Kamran, and Mark Chignell. 1988. *Expert Systems for Experts.* New York: Wiley.

Penneycook, Bruce. 1985. "Computer-Music Interfaces: A Survey." *ACM Computing Surveys* 17:267–89.

Pope, Stephen Travis. 1986. "Music Notations and the Representation of Musical Structure and Knowledge." *Perspectives of New Music* 24:156–89.

Popovic, Igor. 1989. "The Analytical Object: Computer-Based Representation of Musical Scores and Analyses." *Computers in Music Research* 1:103–16.

Prevel, Martin, and Fred Sallis. 1986. "Real-Time Generation of Harmonic Progression in the Context of Microcomputer-Based Ear Training." *Journal of Computer-Based Instruction* 13:6–8.

Rahn, John. 1980. "On Some Computational Models of Music Theory." *Computer Music Journal* 4:66–72.

———. 1990. "Processing Musical Abstraction: Remarks on LISP, the NeXT, and the Future of Musical Computing." *Perspectives of New Music* 28:180–91.

Rich, Elaine, and Kevin Knight. 1991. *Artificial Intelligence.* 2d ed. New York: McGraw-Hill.

Roads, Curtis. 1980. "Artificial Intelligence and Music." *Computer Music Journal* 4:13–25.

———. 1980. "Interview with Marvin Minsky" *Computer Music Journal* 4:25–39.

———. 1984. "An Overview of Music Representations." In *Musical Grammars and Computer Analysis,* edited by M. Baroni and L. Callegari. Florence: L.S. Olschki.

———. 1985. "Research in Music and Artificial Intelligence." *ACM Computing Surveys* 17:163–90.

Roeder, John. 1988. "A Declarative Model of Atonal Analysis." *Music Perception* 6:21–34.

Rolston, David W. 1988. *Principles of Artificial Intelligence and Expert Systems Development.* New York: McGraw-Hill.

Rothgeb, John. 1980. "Simulating Musical Skills by Digital Computer." *Computer Music Journal* 4:36–40.

Rowe, Neil C. 1988. *Artificial Intelligence through Prolog.* Englewood Cliffs, N.J.: Prentice-Hall.

Sano, Hajime, and B. Keith Jenkins. 1989. "A Neural Network Model for Pitch Perception." *Computer Music Journal* 13:41–48.

Scarborough, Don, et. al. 1989. "Connectionist Models for Tonal Analysis." *Computer Music Journal* 13:49–55.

Schaffer, John W. 1988. "Developing an Intelligent Music Tutorial." Ph.D. diss., Indiana University.

Schaffer, John W. 1990. "Intelligent Tutoring Systems: New Realms in CAI?" *Music Theory Spectrum* 12.

———. 1991. "Harmony Coach: An Exploration of Microcomputer-Based Intelligent Tutoring Systems in Music." *Journal of Computer-Based Instruction* 18.

———. 1991. "A Harmony-Based Heuristic Model for Use in an Intelligent Tutoring System." *Journal of Music Theory Pedagogy* 5.

———. 1991. "A Prolog-Based Program for the Interactive Analysis of Atonal Scores." *Musikometrica* 4.

———. 1994. "*Threader:* A Computer Interface for the Graphic Entry, Encoding, and Analysis of Musical Scores." *Computer Music Journal* 18.

Schenker, Heinrich. 1979. *Free Composition: Volume III of New Musical Theories and Fantasies.* translated and edited by Ernst Oster. New York: Longman.

Sell, Peter S. 1985. *Expert Systems: A Practical Introduction.* New York: Wiley.

Shiri, Yoshaki, and Jun-ichi Tsujii. 1984. *Artificial Intelligence: Concepts, Techniques, and Applications,* translated by F. R. D. Apps. New York: Wiley.

Sleeman, D., and J.S. Brown, eds. 1982. *Intelligent Tutoring Systems.* New York: Academic Press.

Smoliar, Stephen W. 1980. "A Computer Aid for Sckenkerian Analysis." *Computer Music Journal* 4:41–59.

———. 1990. "Lewin's Model of Musical Perception Reflected by Artificial Intelligence." *Computers in Music Research* 2:1–38.

Spriet, J.A., and G.C. Vansteenkiste. 1982. *Computer-Aided Modelling and Simulation.* New York: Academic Press.

Sterling, Leon, and Ehud Shapiro. 1986. *The Art of Prolog: Advanced Programming Techniques.* Cambridge: MIT Press.

Taha, Handy A. 1988. *Simulation Modelling and Simnet.* Englewood Cliffs, N.J.: Prentice-Hall.

Todd, Peter M. 1989. "A Connectionist Approach to Algorithmic Composition." *Computer Music Journal* 13:27–43.

Turban, Efraim, and Paul R. Watkins, eds. 1988. *Applied Expert Systems.* New York: Elsevier Science Publishing.

Walker, Adrian, ed. 1987. *Knowledge Systems and Prolog: A Logical Approach to Expert Systems and Natural Language Processing.* Reading, Mass.: Addison-Wesley.

Waterman, Donald A. 1986. *A Guide to Expert Systems.* Reading, Mass.: Addison-Wesley.

Weichselberger, Kurt, and Sigrid Pohlmann. 1990. *A Methodology for Uncertainty in Knowledge-Based Systems.* New York: Springer-Verlag.

Weiss, Sholom M., and Casimir A. Kulikowski. 1984. *A Practical Guide to Designing Expert Systems.* Totowa, N.J.: Rowman & Allanheld.

Widman, Lawrence, Kenneth Loparo, and Norman Nielson, eds. 1989. *Artificial Intelligence, Simulation, and Modelling.* New York: Wiley.

Williams, David, and Denis Bower. 1986. *Designing Computer-Based Instruction for Music and the Arts.* Bellvue, Wash.: Temporal Acuity Products.

Winold, Allen. 1986. *Harmony: Patterns and Principles.* Englewood-Cliffs, N.J.: Prentice Hall.

Winold, Allen, and Jonathan Bein. 1983. "BANALYZE: An Artificial Intelligence System for Harmonic Analysis of Bach Chorales." Unpublished manuscript, School of Music, Indiana University.

Winograd, Terry. 1968. "Linguistics Computer Analysis of Tonal Harmony." *Journal of Music Theory* 12:2–49.

Wittlich, Gary E., John W. Schaffer, and Larry Babb. 1986. *Microcomputers and Music.* Englewood Cliffs, N.J.: Prentice-Hall.

Wittlich, Gary E. 1989. "The State of Research in Music Theory—Computer Applications: Pedagogy." *Music Theory Spectrum* 11:60–65.

Zeigler, B. P. 1977. *Theory of Modelling and Simulation.* New York: Wiley.

Zimmermann, Hans-Jurgen. 1987. *Fuzzy Sets, Decision Making, and Expert Systems.* Boston: Kluwer Academic Publishers.

Index